KU-762-674

THE PLANETS

DK

THE PLANETS

CONTENTS

Senior Editor Ben Morgan
Senior Designer Smiljka Surla
Project Editor Lizzie Davey
Editors Ann Baggaley, Ruth O'Rourke-Jones, Steve Setford
Designers Kathy Gammon, Spencer Holbrook, Fiona Macdonald, Simon Murrell, Steve Woosnam-Savage
Editorial Assistant Olivia Stanford
Illustrators Peter Bull, Infomen, Maltings Partnership, Kees Veenenbos
Managing Editor Paula Regan
Managing Art Editor Owen Peyton Jones
Producer, Pre-Production Nikoleta Parasaki
Senior Producer Mary Slater
DK Picture Library Rob Nunn
Jacket Editor Maud Whatley
Jacket Designer Mark Cavanagh
Jacket Design Development Manager Sophia MTT
Publisher Sarah Larter
Art Director Phil Ormerod
Associate Publishing Director Liz Wheeler
Publishing Director Jonathan Metcalf
Special and Custom Publishing Manager Michelle Baxter

This paperback edition published in 2017

First published in Great Britain in 2014 by
Dorling Kindersley Limited,
80 Strand, London WC2R 0RL

A Penguin Random House Company

4 6 8 10 9 7 5 3
002 – 192970 – Apr/2017

A CIP catalogue record for this book is available from the British Library.

ISBN: 978-0-2413-1664-1

Printed and bound in China

A WORLD OF IDEAS:
SEE ALL THERE IS TO KNOW
www.dk.com

Consultants

Maggie Aderin-Pocock, MBE, is a space scientist, an honorary research associate at University College London, and co-host of the BBC TV series *The Sky at Night*.

Ben Bussey is a planetary scientist and physicist at Johns Hopkins University in Baltimore, Maryland. A specialist in remote sensing, he participated in the Near-Earth Asteroid Rendezvous-Shoemaker (NEAR) mission and is co-author of *The Clementine Atlas of the Moon*.

Andrew K. Johnston is a geographer at the Center for Earth and Planetary Studies at the Smithsonian National Air and Space Museum in Washington, DC. He is author of *Earth from Space* and co-author of the *Smithsonian Atlas of Space Exploration*.

Authors

Heather Couper, CBE, is a former head of the Greenwich Planetarium in London, and past president of the British Astronomical Association. She has presented three TV series and written more than 35 books on astronomy. Asteroid 3922 Heather is named after her.

Robert Dinwiddie specializes in writing educational and illustrated reference books on scientific topics. His particular areas of interest include Earth and ocean science, astronomy, cosmology, and history of science.

John Farndon is the author of many books on science, nature, and ideas. He has been shortlisted four times for the children's Science Book Prize and also for the Society of Authors Education Award.

Nigel Henbest is an astronomer, former editor of the *Journal of the British Astronomical Association*, and author. He has written more than 38 books and more than 1,000 articles on space and astronomy and is a future astronaut with Virgin Galactic.

David W. Hughes is Emeritus Professor of Astronomy at the University of Sheffield. He has published over 200 research papers on asteroids, comets, meteorites, and meteors, and has worked for the European, British, and Swedish space agencies.

Giles Sparrow is an author and editor specializing in astronomy and space science. He is a Fellow of the Royal Astronomical Society.

Carole Stott is an astronomer and author who has written more than 30 books about astronomy and space. She is a former head of astronomy at the Royal Observatory at Greenwich, London.

Colin Stuart is a writer specializing in physics and space. He is a Fellow of the Royal Astronomical Society.

Martian crater
Spacecraft such as NASA's Mars Reconnaissance Orbiter give us an intimate view of worlds we can only dream of visiting in person. This image of a meteorite crater in the Arabia Terra region of Mars reveals incredible details, including "painted" stripes formed where dust has cascaded down the slope towards the centre.

FOREWORD

Whenever I get a chance to look up at the night sky, I seize it. As a space scientist, I am very much aware of the wonderful things that exist out there. My favourites by far are the planets of our Solar System. Many of them can be seen with the naked eye, which gives real delight and the feeling that direct contact has been established. Like many people, I dream of taking that feeling further and making a real tour of our Solar System. This book is the perfect guide to the places I might visit.

In recent years I've developed an interest in archeoastronomy – the study of how our ancestors understood the skies above them. Virtually every culture has had some awareness of the Solar System, weaving mythology with observation and naming planets after their gods. Over the centuries, with the development of better astronomical instruments, people learned more about the planets and began speculating about what they might find if they ventured off-world. Such imaginings inspired science fiction novels and films.

The birth of the space era introduced reality. Since the launch in 1960 of Pioneer 5 – the first spacecraft designed to look beyond our Earth–Moon system – we've discovered worlds more barren and inhospitable than anything we'd imagined. But this hasn't dampened our enthusiasm or discouraged us from launching spacecraft to explore the planets in intimate detail and search for possible signs of life. From flybys and landings, we've assembled a vast wealth of data, much of which is used in this book to reconstruct photorealistic 3D models of the planets.

Working on this book has been a real joy. If I ever do journey to other worlds in the Solar System, I shall take a copy of it with me as an indispensable guide.

Maggie Aderin-Pocock

Maggie Aderin-Pocock, MBE, space scientist

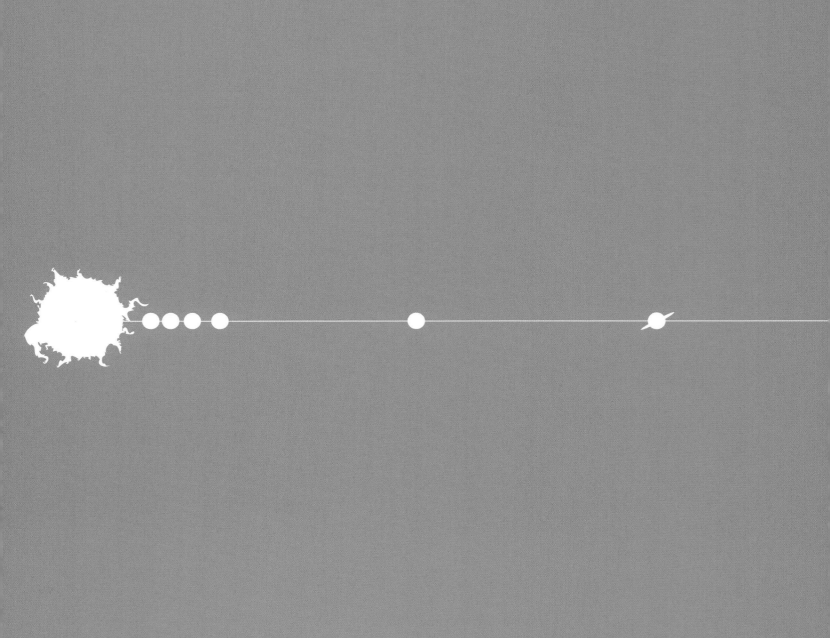

FAMILY OF THE **SUN**

Our Sun is just one of around 200 billion stars that make up the Milky Way – the vast, spiral galaxy we call home. The Sun lies about halfway out from the galactic heart in a minor spiral arm, orbiting the centre once every 200 million years at the brisk pace of 200km (120 miles) a second. Like thousands of other stars, it is surrounded by a family of smaller objects trapped in its vicinity by

OUR PLACE IN **SPACE**

gravity, just as the Sun is caught by the pull of the Milky Way. The largest of these objects are known to us as planets, and their wandering journeys through the night sky have earned them ancient names. Most of the planets detected near other stars are vast, boiling worlds with wayward orbits – habitats impossible for life. Not so in our Solar System. Its eight planets follow stable, almost circular paths around the Sun. The innermost planets – Mercury, Venus, Earth, and Mars – are small, solid globes of rock and iron. In contrast, the outer worlds – Jupiter, Saturn, Uranus, and Neptune – are bloated giants formed of gas and liquid, each accompanied by a large retinue of moons, like a solar system in miniature. Less easily observed, but far more numerous, are the many smaller objects that populate the dark recesses of the Solar System, from dwarf planets like Pluto to comets and asteroids – leftover rubble from the primordial cloud of debris from which the planets formed.

◁ **Milky Way**
Our galaxy is believed to be spiral in shape, but because we view it from within, we see it edge-on. Best seen on the darkest, clearest nights – far from cities and other forms of light pollution – it appears as a milky band across the sky. The bright patches are huge, luminous nebulae – glowing clouds of gas and dust in which new stars and planets are taking shape. The rift that appears to divide the Milky Way in two is a darker cloud, about 300 light years from Earth, that blocks the light from more distant stars behind it.

AROUND **THE SUN**

THE SUN'S GRAVITY HOLDS IN THRALL A DIVERSE ASSORTMENT OF CELESTIAL OBJECTS. AS WELL AS THE EIGHT PLANETS, WITH THEIR OWN FAMILIES OF RINGS AND MOONS, THE SOLAR SYSTEM COMPRISES BILLIONS OF PIECES OF ROCKY AND ICY DEBRIS.

The planets all orbit the Sun in the same direction, and in almost the same flat plane. Closest to the Sun's heat are four small, rocky worlds: Mercury, Venus, Earth, and Mars. In the chilly further reaches of the Solar System lie the giant planets: Jupiter, Saturn, Uranus, and Neptune. They are composed mostly of substances more volatile than rock, such as hydrogen, helium, methane, and water.

The asteroids, most of which reside between Mars and Jupiter, are lumps of rocky debris left over from the birth of the planets. The edge of the planetary system is marked by icy chunks – comets and the Kuiper Belt objects – that have survived from the earliest days of the Solar System.

▽ **Orbits**
The planets journey along paths around the Sun that are not perfectly circular but are slightly elliptical (oval). Smaller bodies typically follow much more elliptical orbits, tipped up from the plane in which the planets move. Most extreme are the comets, which trace very long, thin elliptical orbits from the outer limits of the Solar System, some of them tipped up at a right angle. Certain comets, including Halley, travel around the Sun in the opposite direction to the planets.

Saturn

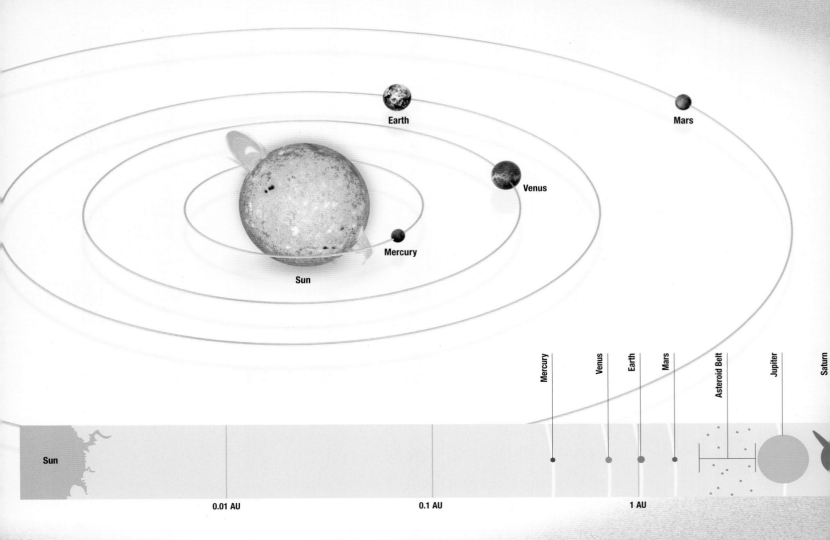

Earth
Mars
Venus
Mercury
Sun
Mercury
Venus
Earth
Mars
Asteroid Belt
Jupiter
Saturn
Sun
0.01 AU
0.1 AU
1 AU

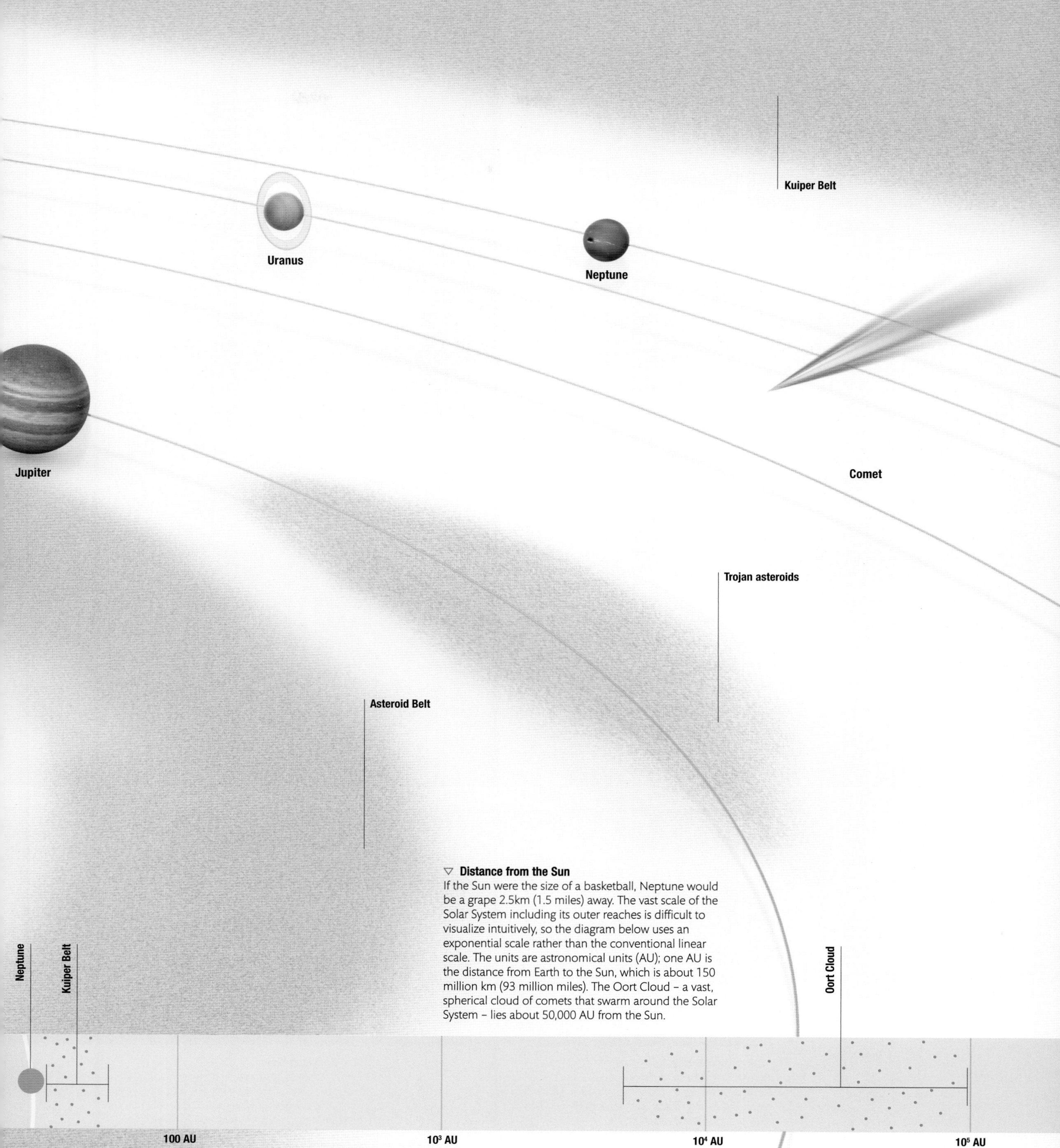
Kuiper Belt
Uranus
Neptune
Jupiter
Comet
Trojan asteroids
Asteroid Belt
Neptune
Kuiper Belt
Oort Cloud
100 AU
10^3 AU
10^4 AU
10^5 AU

▽ **Distance from the Sun**
If the Sun were the size of a basketball, Neptune would be a grape 2.5km (1.5 miles) away. The vast scale of the Solar System including its outer reaches is difficult to visualize intuitively, so the diagram below uses an exponential scale rather than the conventional linear scale. The units are astronomical units (AU); one AU is the distance from Earth to the Sun, which is about 150 million km (93 million miles). The Oort Cloud – a vast, spherical cloud of comets that swarm around the Solar System – lies about 50,000 AU from the Sun.

BIRTH OF THE **SOLAR SYSTEM**

CREATED OUT OF GAS AND DUST, THE SUN FIRST SHONE AS A STAR WITHIN A RING OF DEBRIS – THE LEFTOVERS FROM ITS FORMATION. THESE MATERIALS SLOWLY GREW FROM TINY PARTICLES INTO ASTEROIDS, MOONS, AND PLANETS.

Five billion years ago, the Solar System did not exist. Our galaxy, the Milky Way, was already 8 billion years old, and within it generations of stars had lived and died, seeding space with gas and dust that assembled into huge, dark clouds. Then, on the outskirts of the galaxy, something started to stir. An exploding star – a supernova – squeezed a neighbouring dark cloud, which then began to collapse under its own gravity. Deep within, denser clumps of gas began to coagulate into thousands of protostars. As each one of these shrank, they heated up until nuclear reactions began in their cores and stars were born.

Many of these newly hatched stars were surrounded by whirling discs of gas and icy dust. In one case in particular – the newborn Sun – we know that this material, over millions of years, created the planets of our Solar System.

Solar System nursery

Sheltered from the dangerous radiation of space, the new Solar System developed in the depths of a giant bank of interstellar smog. This cloud was composed mainly of hydrogen and helium gas left over from the Big Bang, polluted with specks of soot and cosmic dust ejected from dying stars. It was so cold that gases such as methane, ammonia, and water vapour froze onto the tiny dust particles. These microscopic hailstones, whirling around the young Sun, were the seeds from which the planets would eventually grow.

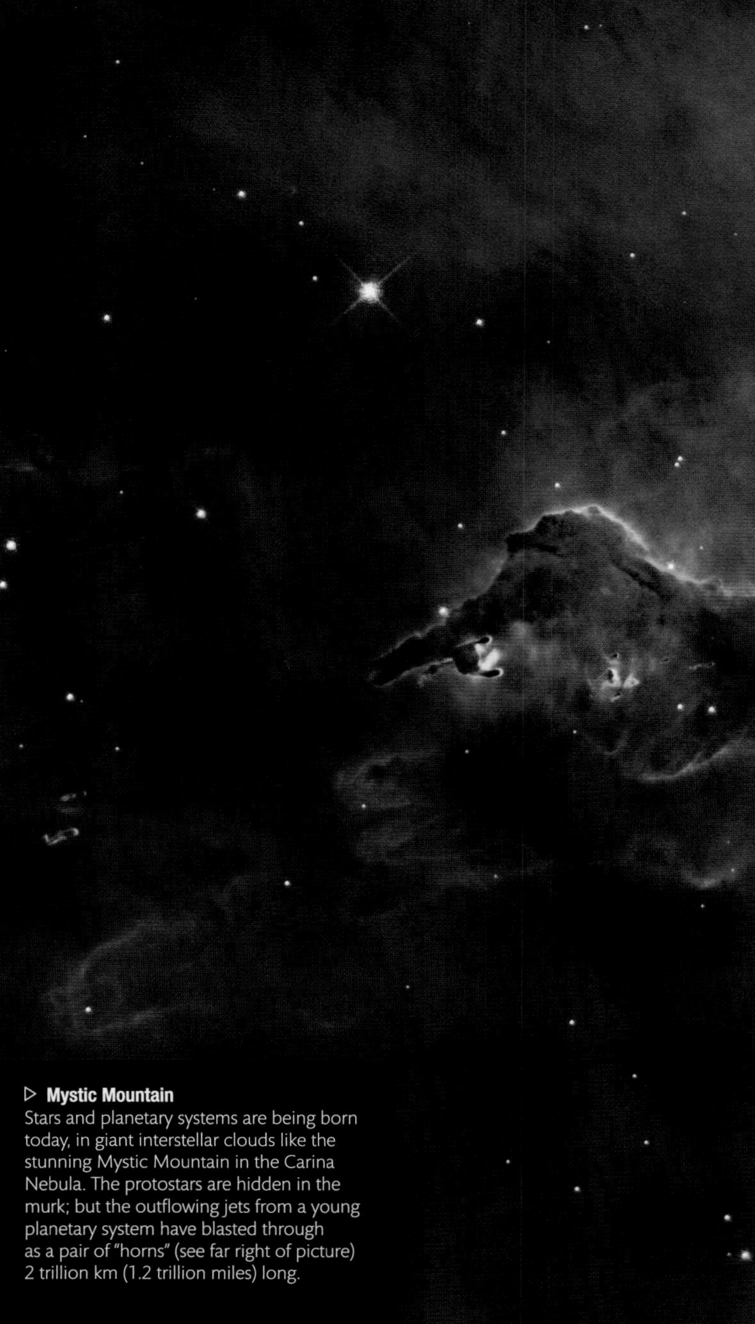

▷ **Mystic Mountain**
Stars and planetary systems are being born today, in giant interstellar clouds like the stunning Mystic Mountain in the Carina Nebula. The protostars are hidden in the murk; but the outflowing jets from a young planetary system have blasted through as a pair of "horns" (see far right of picture) 2 trillion km (1.2 trillion miles) long.

99.8 per cent of **the Solar System's mass** is found in the Sun.

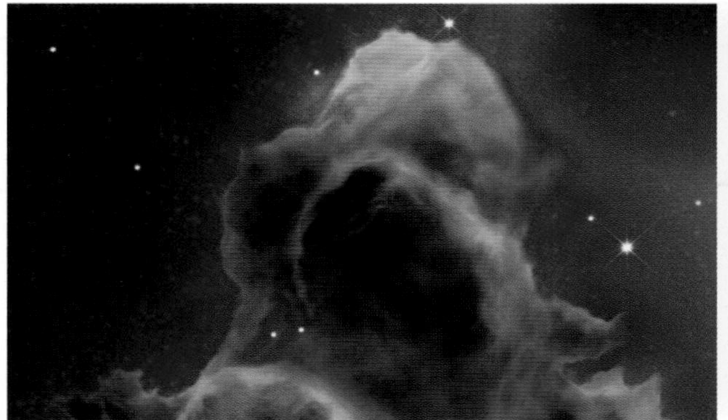

△ **Sun's secret birth**
Hidden in a molecular cloud – a nebula rich with chemical compounds – the embryonic Sun was no more than a collapsing clump of gas. As it contracted, this clump heated up to become a protostar.

△ **Bipolar outflow**
The protostar began to rotate, generating a strong magnetic field that forced streamers of gas away in opposite directions. The gas collapsing around the protostar turned ever faster and flattened out.

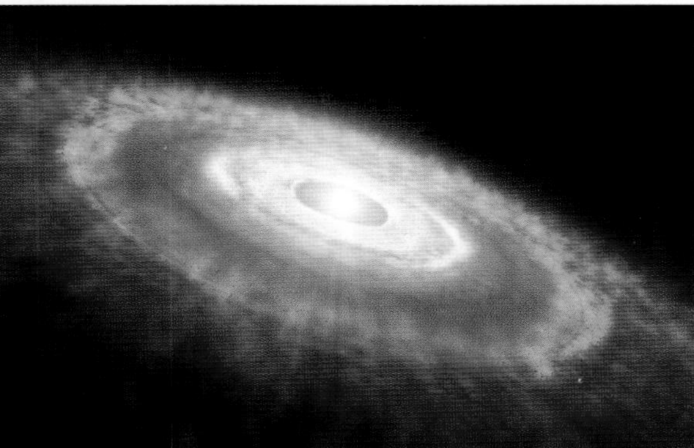

△ **Lighting-up time**
The protostar grew hot enough to ignite nuclear reactions, and the Sun began to shine. Its heat boiled away the ice nearby, leaving only rocky dust in the inner disc. But icy grains still survived on the outer edges.

▷ **Space rubble**
The rubble left over from the building of the Solar System still falls to Earth as meteorites. The rare stony meteorites known as carbonaceous chondrites have remained unchanged since the birth of the planets. By analysing the radioactive atoms in them, scientists can pinpoint the exact age of the Solar System: 4.5682 billion years old. The oldest meteorites contain chondrules – glassy drops of melted rock formed in the heat generated by the development of the Solar System.

FORMATION OF THE **PLANETS**

THE EIGHT PLANETS OF OUR SOLAR SYSTEM, NOW ORBITING SERENELY, WERE BORN IN A MAELSTROM OF COLLIDING DEBRIS LEFT OVER FROM THE SUN'S FORMATION.

The interstellar cloud that gave birth to the Sun was not used up entirely when our star formed. A disc of residual debris was left in orbit around the Sun like rings around Saturn, forming a "solar nebula". This material would eventually form the planets.

In the cold outer regions of the solar nebula, the debris consisted largely of tiny grains of frozen water, methane, and ammonia – hydrogen compounds too volatile to condense into ice in the inner Solar System. Closer in, however, the Sun's heat boiled away volatile compounds, leaving only particles of rock and metal. As a result, the planets that formed in different parts of the solar nebula grew from very different materials. Inside the "frost line" – the point beyond which volatile compounds can survive the Sun's heat – the rocky debris gave rise to four small terrestrial planets with cores of metal. Beyond the frost line, icy debris coalesced into hot globes of spinning fluid, swollen to gigantic proportions by hydrogen and helium gas from the solar nebula.

Debris from the era of planet formation still litters the Solar System in the form of asteroids, comets, and Kuiper Belt objects (icy bodies beyond Neptune). Disturbed by the wanderings of Jupiter and Saturn, some of this icy rubble may even have delivered water to the once-dry Earth, kick-starting the chemical process that gave rise to life.

The **gas giant planets** account for nearly **99 per cent** of the mass orbiting the Sun.

▷ **When worlds collide**
In the first 100 million years after the Sun formed, protoplanets frequently collided as they whirled around the Sun. Mercury may owe its huge core to a catastrophic impact that stripped the nascent planet of its rocky mantle. Venus's anomalous clockwise spin – opposite to most planets – may be the result of another collision. A protoplanet also seems to have hit Earth, almost splitting our world apart; the incandescent spray from this impact formed the Moon.

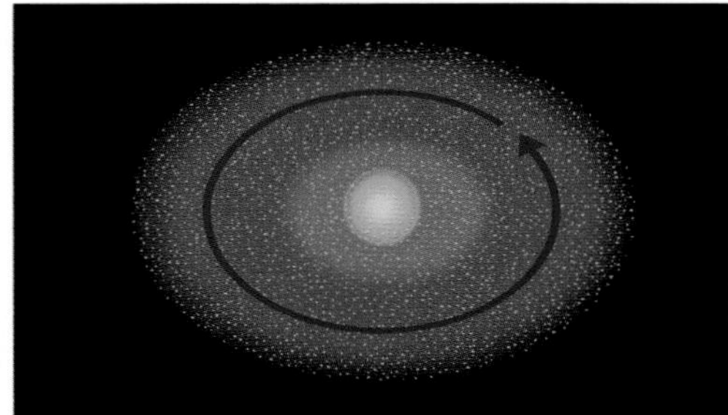

△ **Solar nebula**
The solar nebula started out as a homogeneous disc of gas and dust. As the dust particles jostled together in space, they became electrostatically charged and so began to stick to one another. Closer to the Sun, they built up from grains of rock and metal to form rocky boulders similar in composition to asteroids. Beyond the frost line, they gradually enlarged into masses of ice.

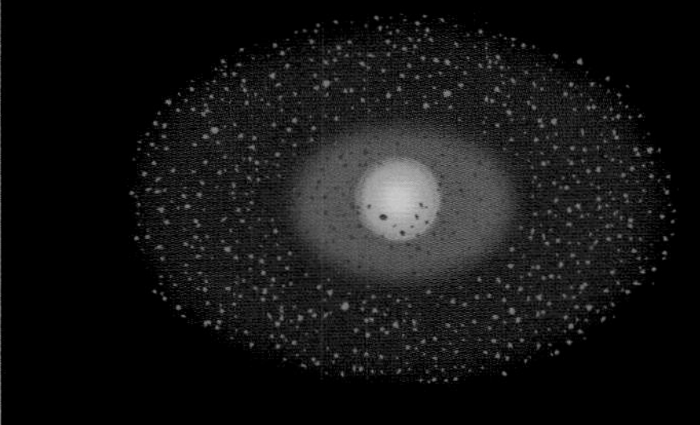

△ **Planetesimals form**
When two solid lumps orbiting the Sun collided at speed, they smashed into each other. However, if the encounter was slow, gravity pulled them together. Overall, the process of construction was more frequent than destruction, so these chunks slowly grew by a few centimetres a year. Eventually, they developed into bodies several kilometres in diameter – planetesimals.

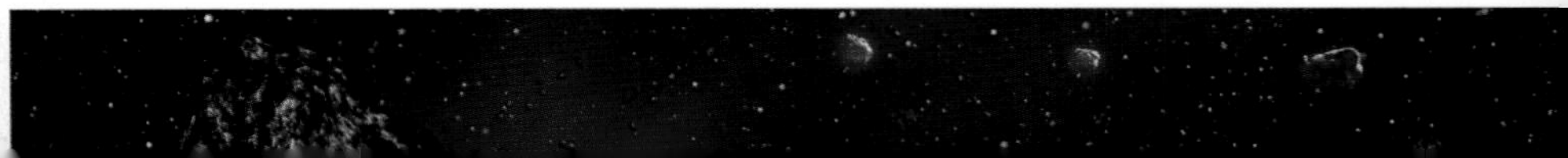

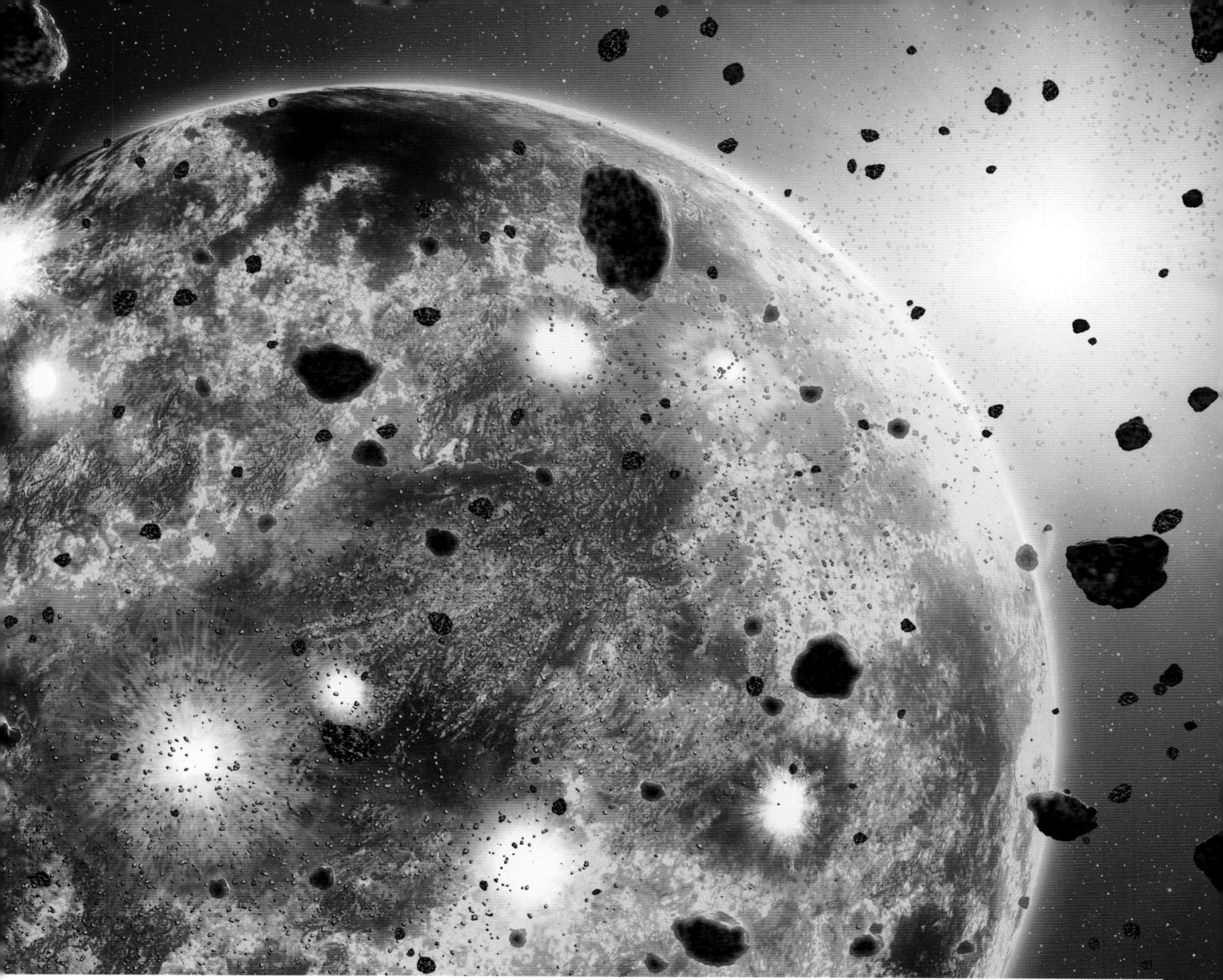

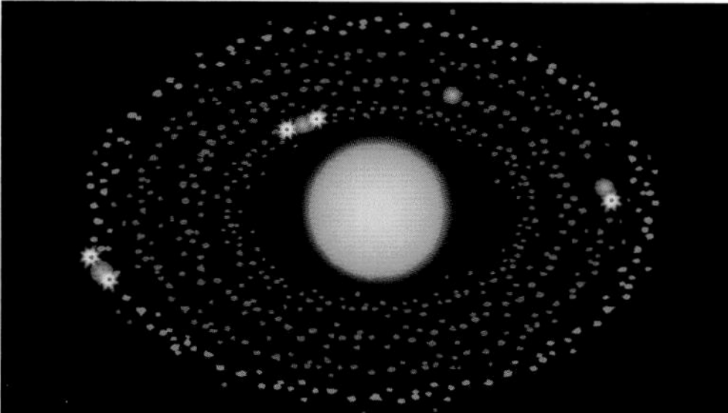

△ **Rocky planets evolve**
A million years after the birth of the Solar System, the region near the Sun swarmed with 50–100 rocky bodies similar in size to Earth's Moon. As these protoplanets hurtled around the Sun, crashing into one another like stock cars, collisions became ever more violent. The bigger protoplanets came off best, scooping up their smaller competitors. Only four would eventually survive, forming today's rocky planets.

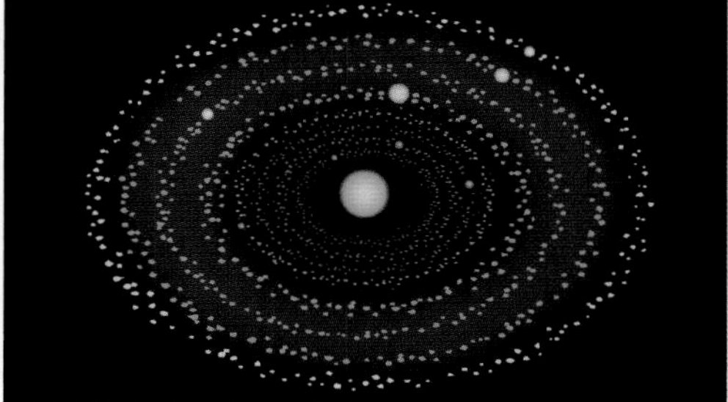

△ **Gas giants expand**
Beyond the frost line, the abundance of icy material created larger bodies. Fast-growing Jupiter developed sufficient gravity to pull in gas from the solar nebula and build up into a massive hydrogen-helium world. Saturn followed suit. However, in the outer reaches of the Solar System, where material was sparse, Uranus and Neptune grew more slowly. Residual debris around the gas giants condensed, creating moons.

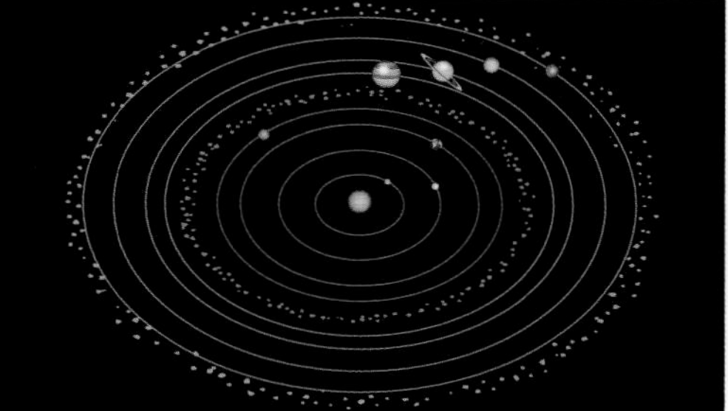

△ **Planets migrate to modern positions**
Originally, Uranus may have been the outermost planet, but the orbits of Jupiter and Saturn gradually changed, and when Saturn's "year" became exactly twice that of Jupiter, the resulting gravitational resonance threw Neptune farther out, followed by Uranus. These outer planets, in turn, threw icy planetesimals all over the Solar System, bombarding the inner planets and forming today's Kuiper Belt.

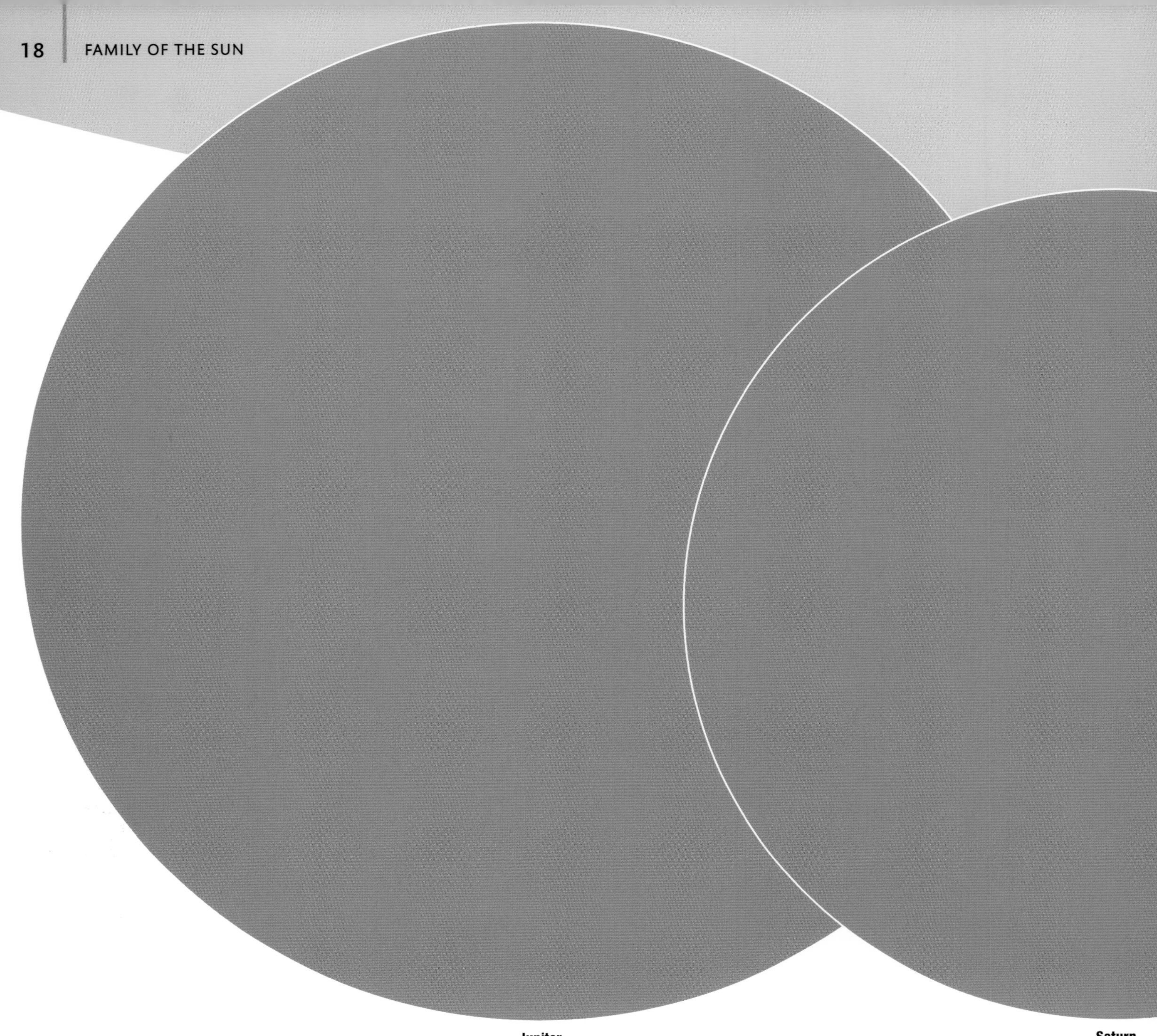

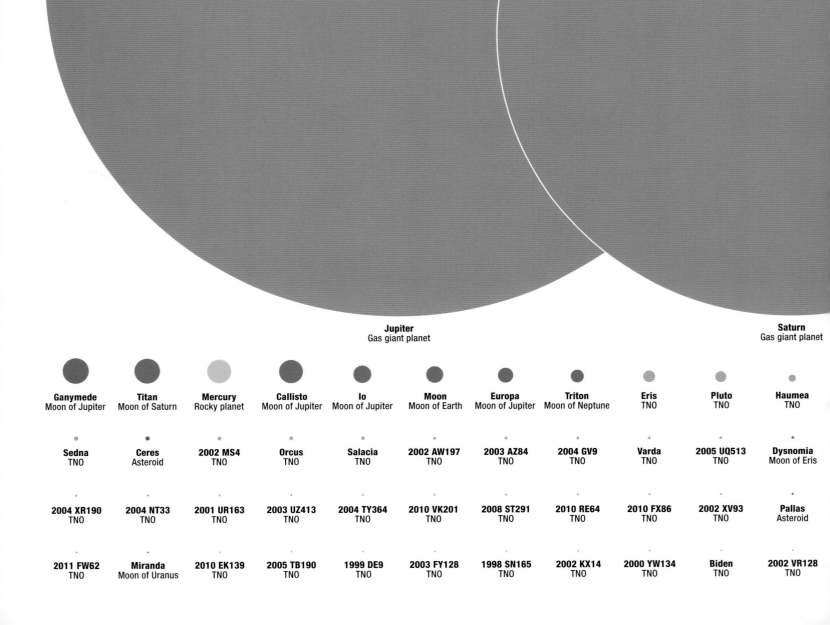

Jupiter
Gas giant planet

Saturn
Gas giant planet

Ganymede Moon of Jupiter	**Titan** Moon of Saturn	**Mercury** Rocky planet	**Callisto** Moon of Jupiter	**Io** Moon of Jupiter	**Moon** Moon of Earth	**Europa** Moon of Jupiter	**Triton** Moon of Neptune	**Eris** TNO	**Pluto** TNO	**Haumea** TNO
Sedna TNO	**Ceres** Asteroid	**2002 MS4** TNO	**Orcus** TNO	**Salacia** TNO	**2002 AW197** TNO	**2003 AZ84** TNO	**2004 GV9** TNO	**Varda** TNO	**2005 UQ513** TNO	**Dysnomia** Moon of Eris
2004 XR190 TNO	**2004 NT33** TNO	**2001 UR163** TNO	**2003 UZ413** TNO	**2004 TY364** TNO	**2010 VK201** TNO	**2008 ST291** TNO	**2010 RE64** TNO	**2010 FX86** TNO	**2002 XV93** TNO	**Pallas** Asteroid
2011 FW62 TNO	**Miranda** Moon of Uranus	**2010 EK139** TNO	**2005 TB190** TNO	**1999 DE9** TNO	**2003 FY128** TNO	**1998 SN165** TNO	**2002 KX14** TNO	**2000 YW134** TNO	**Biden** TNO	**2002 VR128** TNO

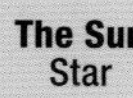
The Sun
Star

SIZE AND **SCALE**

THIS GRAPHIC SHOWS THE RELATIVE SIZES OF THE 100 LARGEST BODIES IN THE SOLAR SYSTEM, FROM THE SUN AND PLANETS TO THE NUMEROUS OTHER OBJECTS THAT ARE PART OF OUR STAR'S FAMILY.

On a cosmic scale, the Sun is the only substantial body in the Solar System, so much larger than anything else that our own planet is a mere dot beside it. The largest of the planets by far are the gas giants, the biggest of which, Jupiter, could swallow Earth 1,300 times over. Farther down the scale come the rocky, inner planets and then a miscellany of other bodies: moons, asteroids, and icy objects that populate the region beyond Neptune (trans-Neptunian objects). Diminution in size does not proceed neatly by class; Pluto, for example, is outsized by seven moons, and even Mercury is smaller than the two largest moons. Some of the largest asteroids and trans-Neptunian objects have sufficient mass to form a spherical shape and are therefore also classified as dwarf planets.

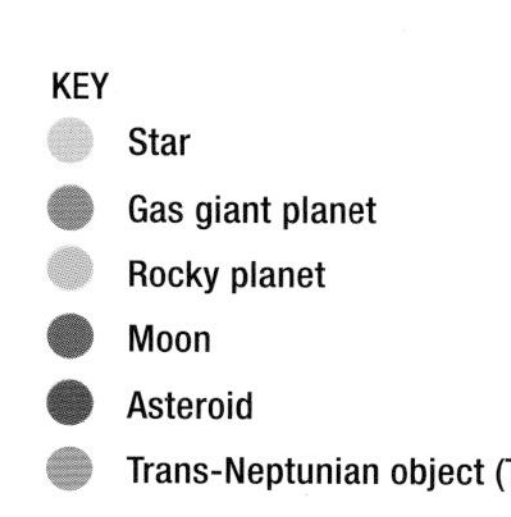
KEY
Star
Gas giant planet
Rocky planet
Moon
Asteroid
Trans-Neptunian object (TNO)

0 10,000 20,000 30,000 km
0 10,000 20,000 miles

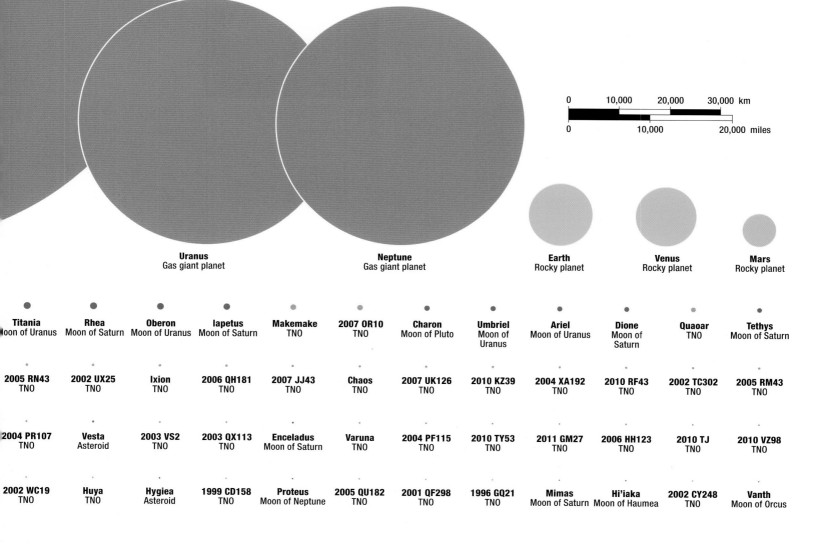

Uranus
Gas giant planet

Neptune
Gas giant planet

Earth
Rocky planet

Venus
Rocky planet

Mars
Rocky planet

Titania Moon of Uranus
Rhea Moon of Saturn
Oberon Moon of Uranus
Iapetus Moon of Saturn
Makemake TNO
2007 OR10 TNO
Charon Moon of Pluto
Umbriel Moon of Uranus
Ariel Moon of Uranus
Dione Moon of Saturn
Quaoar TNO
Tethys Moon of Saturn

2005 RN43 TNO
2002 UX25 TNO
Ixion TNO
2006 QH181 TNO
2007 JJ43 TNO
Chaos TNO
2007 UK126 TNO
2010 KZ39 TNO
2004 XA192 TNO
2010 RF43 TNO
2002 TC302 TNO
2005 RM43 TNO

2004 PR107 TNO
Vesta Asteroid
2003 VS2 TNO
2003 QX113 TNO
Enceladus Moon of Saturn
Varuna TNO
2004 PF115 TNO
2010 TY53 TNO
2011 GM27 TNO
2006 HH123 TNO
2010 TJ TNO
2010 VZ98 TNO

2002 WC19 TNO
Huya TNO
Hygiea Asteroid
1999 CD158 TNO
Proteus Moon of Neptune
2005 QU182 TNO
2001 QF298 TNO
1996 GQ21 TNO
Mimas Moon of Saturn
Hi'iaka Moon of Haumea
2002 CY248 TNO
Vanth Moon of Orcus

OUR **SOLAR SYSTEM**

FOR CENTURIES PEOPLE BELIEVED EARTH WAS AT THE CENTRE OF THE COSMOS, WITH HEAVENLY BODIES IN ORBIT AROUND US. WHEN THIS MODEL WAS FINALLY OVERTURNED, IT LED TO A REVOLUTION IN SCIENCE.

The greatest conceptual breakthrough in our understanding of the Solar System was the idea that Earth orbits the Sun, rather than vice versa. The heliocentric (sun-centred) model of the Solar System was difficult to accept for several reasons. Common sense suggests the Sun moves across the sky; a stationary Sun implies that the apparently fixed and solid Earth must be moving and rotating. Moreover, the ancient Greek model of an Earth-centred Solar System generated good predictions of planetary movements, supporting the faulty theory. And when the heliocentric model was shown to be more accurate, it faced resistance from the prevailing religious notion that Earth was the centre of creation.

Medieval re-creation of ancient Greek world map

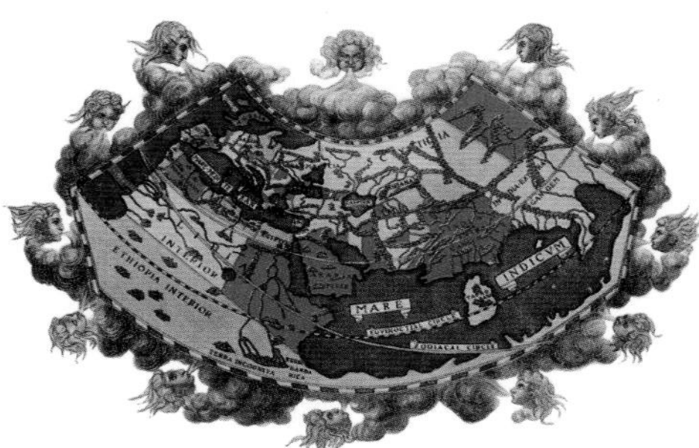

c.3000–500 BCE

Flat Earth
Early philosophers in Egypt and Mesopotamia believe Earth is flat and surrounded by sea, an idea later adopted by the Greeks. The Greek philosopher Thales claims that land floats on the ocean and that earthquakes are caused by giant waves.

c.500 BCE

Spherical Earth
Pythagoras is the first of the Greek philosophers to suggest Earth is a sphere. Around 330 BCE, Aristotle offers further evidence: Earth's shadow during a lunar eclipse is round, and new stars appear as a person travels over Earth's curved surface.

Newton's *Principia*

1781

Discoveries beyond Saturn
German-born British astronomer William Herschel discovers Uranus, a planet beyond Saturn, doubling the size of the known Solar System. A variation in the new-found planet's orbit will eventually lead astronomers to discover Neptune, in 1846.

Ceres, first known asteroid

1801

Asteroids identified
While making routine observations, Italian astronomer Guiseppe Piazzi comes across a rocky body orbiting between Mars and Jupiter. Named Ceres, this is the first, and largest, asteroid to be discovered. In 2006, Ceres is also classified as a dwarf planet.

Sputnik 1

1957

First satellite
The Space Age begins when the Soviet Union sends the first artificial satellite, Sputnik 1, into orbit around Earth. Two years later, the Soviet spacecraft Luna 3 sends back the first photographs of the far side of the Moon.

1962

Voyage to Venus
NASA's Mariner 2 passes Venus, becoming the first spacecraft to fly past another planet. It records Venus's scorching temperature, which is too high to sustain life. In 1964, Mariner 4 flies past Mars and reveals a cold, barren, cratered world.

Apollo 11 Moon landing

1969

First on the Moon
US astronaut Neil Armstrong becomes the first person to set foot on another world. Analysis of rocks brought back to Earth by Apollo astronauts suggests the Moon formed as a result of a massive impact between Earth and another planet.

Viking 1 image of Mars

1976

Landing on Mars
Viking 1 and Viking 2, the first spacecraft to land successfully on Mars, send back breathtaking images. They monitor the weather over two Martian years, analyse the composition of the atmosphere, and test the soil, inconclusively, for signs of life.

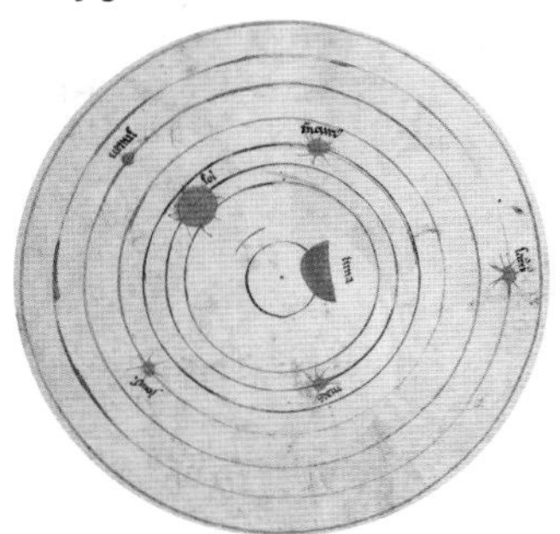

Early geocentric model of the cosmos

Copernicus's model of the Solar System

c.400 BCE

Central fire

Greek philosopher Philolaus proposes that Earth and the Sun orbit a hidden "central fire". Aristarchus later claims the Sun is the centre, and that the stars do not move relative to each other because they are so far away. His ideas are subsequently ignored.

c.150 BCE

The Ptolemaic system

Greek astronomer and geographer Claudius Ptolemy puts forward his geocentric theory, which places Earth at the centre of the cosmos. Belief in the Ptolemaic system dominates astronomy for the next 1,400 years.

1543 CE

Copernican revolution

Just before his death, the Polish astronomer and mathematician Nicolaus Copernicus publishes his revolutionary heliocentric model of the Solar System, putting the stationary Sun at the centre.

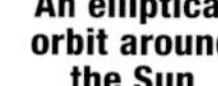

An elliptical orbit around the Sun

1609

Kepler's laws

German mathematician Johannes Kepler calculates that the planets follow non-circular, elliptical orbits and alter speed according to their distance from the Sun. Kepler's laws resolve flaws in the Copernican model and later inspire Isaac Newton's discoveries.

Galileo Galilei

1633

Astronomer on trial

The Catholic Church puts Italian astronomer Galileo Galilei on trial for teaching Copernicus's theory. His pioneering telescopic observations support the Sun-centred model. Galileo is forced to recant and is put under house arrest.

1687

Planetary orbits explained

English scientist Isaac Newton publishes his supremely important *Principia*, laying the foundations of modern physics. He shows how gravity keeps planets in elliptical orbits around the Sun and derives three laws of motion, explaining how forces work.

Voyager 1 image of Jupiter

1979

Flyby of Jupiter

In a trail-blazing mission, Voyager 1 flies by Jupiter and its moons. The US craft reveals erupting volcanoes on the moon Io and an icy crust on Europa. Sister-craft Voyager 2, launched two years earlier, will go on to pass Uranus (1986) and Neptune (1989).

Nucleus of Halley's Comet

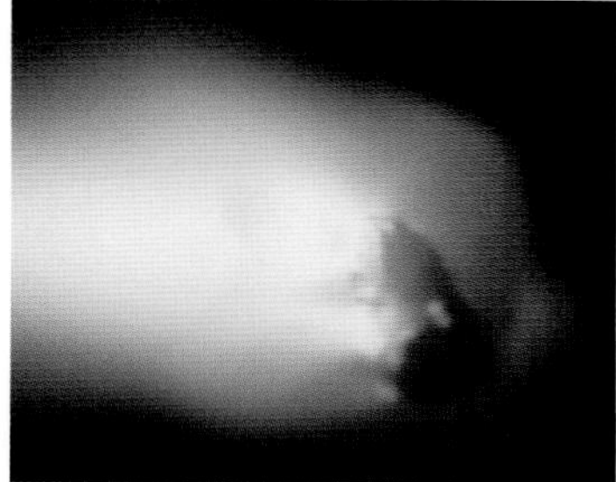

1986

Close encounter with a comet

Intercepting Halley's Comet at 240,000kph (150,000mph), the European spacecraft Giotto takes the first close-up pictures of a comet's nucleus. They reveal a dark-coated lump of ice 15km (9 miles) wide. Giotto then visits a second comet, Grigg-Skjellerup.

Saturn, as viewed by Cassini

2004

Orbit of Saturn

NASA's Cassini-Huygens spacecraft, launched in 1997, enters orbit around Saturn and later lands a probe onto the moon Titan. Cassini witnesses a huge storm in Saturn's clouds and discovers icy geysers erupting from the moon Enceladus.

OUR **STAR**

THE **SUN**

THE SUN IS THE HOTTEST, BIGGEST, AND MOST MASSIVE OBJECT IN THE SOLAR SYSTEM. ITS INCANDESCENT SURFACE BATHES ITS FAMILY OF PLANETS IN LIGHT, AND ITS IMMENSE GRAVITATIONAL FORCE CHOREOGRAPHS THEIR ORBITS.

The Sun is a typical star, little different from billions of others in our galaxy, the Milky Way. It dominates everything around it, accounting for 99.8 per cent of the Solar System's mass. Compared with any of its planets, the Sun is immense. Earth would fit inside the Sun over one million times; even the biggest planet, Jupiter, is a thousandth of the Sun's volume. Yet the Sun is by no means the biggest star; VY Canis Majoris, known as a hypergiant, could hold almost 3 billion Suns.

Our star will not be around forever. Now approximately halfway through its life, in about 5 billion years it will turn into a red giant, swelling and surging out towards the planets. Mercury and Venus will be vaporized. The Earth may experience a similar fate, but even if our planet is not engulfed, it will become a sweltering furnace under the intense glare of a closer Sun. Eventually, the Sun will shake itself apart and puff its outer layers into space, leaving behind a ghostly cloud called a planetary nebula.

Energy travelling from the Sun's core takes **100,000 years** to reach the surface and appear as light.

THE SUN DATA

Diameter	1,393,684km (865,374 miles)
Mass (Earth = 1)	333,000
Energy output	385 million billion gigawatts
Surface temperature	5,500°C (10,000°F)
Core temperature	15 million°C (27 million°F)
Distance from Earth	150 million km (93 million miles)
Polar rotation period	34 Earth days
Age	about 4.6 billion years
Life expectancy	about 10 billion years

▷ **Photosphere**
Photographed in wavelengths of light visible to the human eye, the Sun appears to have a smooth, spherical surface, speckled by cooler areas called sunspots. This apparent surface, called the photosphere, is illusory. It is merely the point in the Sun's vast atmosphere at which hot gas becomes transparent, letting light flood through.

▷ **Chromosphere**
The photosphere merges into an upper, hotter layer called the chromosphere. This ultraviolet image from NASA's Solar Dynamics Observatory reveals structures in both layers. The granular pattern is caused by convection cells – pockets of hot gas rising and sinking within the Sun.

▷ **Corona**
Extending far beyond the chromosphere is the Sun's tenuous outer atmosphere, the corona, revealed here by ultraviolet imagery. Invisible to the naked eye except during a solar eclipse, the corona is even hotter than the chromosphere and seethes with activity as eruptions of plasma burst through it.

Energy from the Sun's surface, or photosphere, escapes as visible light.

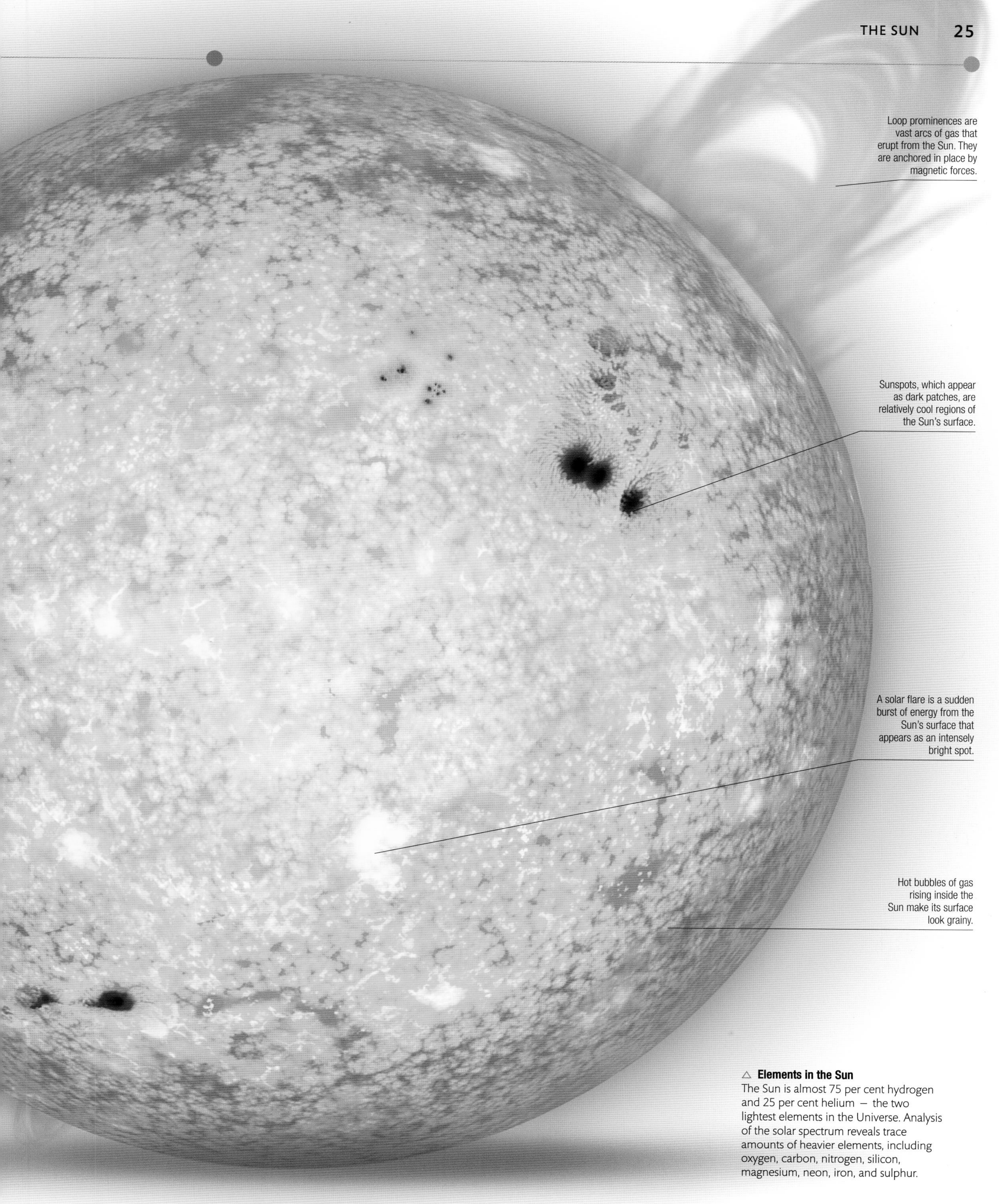
Loop prominences are vast arcs of gas that erupt from the Sun. They are anchored in place by magnetic forces.
Sunspots, which appear as dark patches, are relatively cool regions of the Sun's surface.
A solar flare is a sudden burst of energy from the Sun's surface that appears as an intensely bright spot.
Hot bubbles of gas rising inside the Sun make its surface look grainy.

△ **Elements in the Sun**
The Sun is almost 75 per cent hydrogen and 25 per cent helium – the two lightest elements in the Universe. Analysis of the solar spectrum reveals trace amounts of heavier elements, including oxygen, carbon, nitrogen, silicon, magnesium, neon, iron, and sulphur.

SUN STRUCTURE

IT MAY SEEM AN UNCHANGING YELLOW BALL IN THE SKY, BUT THE SUN IS INCREDIBLY DYNAMIC. A GIANT NUCLEAR FUSION REACTOR, IT FLOODS THE REST OF THE SOLAR SYSTEM WITH ITS BRILLIANT ENERGY.

The Sun has no solid surface – it is made of gas, mostly hydrogen. Intense heat and pressure split the gas atoms into charged particles, forming an electrified state of matter known as plasma. Inside the Sun, density and temperature rise steadily towards the core, where the pressure is more than 100 billion times greater than atmospheric pressure on Earth's surface. In this extreme environment, unique in the Solar System, nuclear fusion occurs. Hydrogen nuclei are fused together to form helium nuclei, and a fraction of their mass is lost as energy, which percolates slowly to the Sun's outer layers and then floods out into the blackness of space, eventually reaching Earth as light and warmth.

Prominences – loops of gas emanating from the photosphere – stretch hundreds of thousands of kilometres into space.

Core
Making up the inner fifth of the Sun, the core is where nuclear fusion creates 99 per cent of the Sun's energy. The centre of the core, where hydrogen has been fused, is mostly helium. The temperature in the core is 15 million °C (27 million °F).

Radiative zone
Light energy works its way slowly up through the radiative zone, colliding with atomic nuclei and being re-radiated billions of times. The radiative zone is so densely packed with matter that energy from the core can take as long as 100,000 years to reach the surface. The radiative zone accounts for 70 per cent of the Sun's radius, and temperatures range from 1.5 to 15 million °C (3.5 to 27 million °F).

Convective zone
In the convective zone, pockets of hot gas expand and rise towards the solar surface. The process, known as convection, carries the energy upwards much faster than in the radiative zone. Temperatures here vary from 5,500 to 1.5 million °C (10,000 to 3.5 million °F).

Photosphere
The photosphere – a region only 100km (60 miles) thick – is the apparent surface of the Sun. This is where energy reaches the top of the convective zone and escapes into space. The temperature here is 5,500°C (10,000°F).

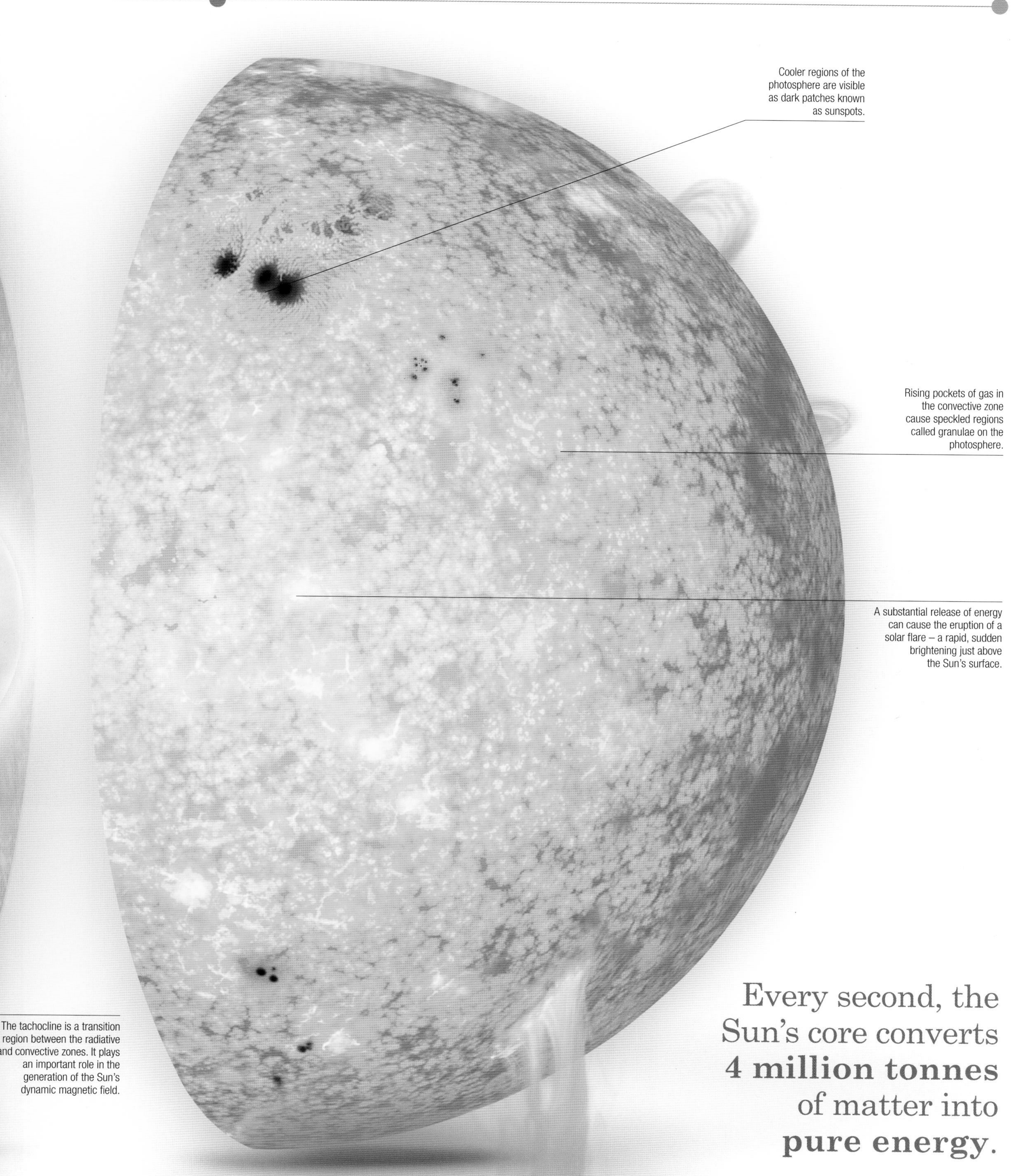
Cooler regions of the photosphere are visible as dark patches known as sunspots.
Rising pockets of gas in the convective zone cause speckled regions called granulae on the photosphere.
A substantial release of energy can cause the eruption of a solar flare – a rapid, sudden brightening just above the Sun's surface.
The tachocline is a transition region between the radiative and convective zones. It plays an important role in the generation of the Sun's dynamic magnetic field.

Every second, the Sun's core converts **4 million tonnes** of matter into **pure energy**.

STORMS ON **THE SUN**

A SEETHING BALL OF PLASMA, THE SUN IS NEVER THE SAME FROM ONE DAY TO THE NEXT. THE SOLAR SURFACE IS IN CONSTANT MAGNETIC TURMOIL, RESULTING IN THE BIGGEST EXPLOSIVE EVENTS IN THE SOLAR SYSTEM.

Heat and light are not all that the Sun gives to its family of orbiting worlds. Our star regularly hurls vast swarms of electrically charged particles out into the Solar System in violent solar storms. For 150 years, astronomers have been able to observe these events from Earth; but it is only in the last 20 years that they have been Sun-watching at closer quarters, using a suite of telescopes launched into space. These instruments are capable of seeing the Sun even when our spinning planet turns ground-based instruments away from it. A thorough understanding of this space weather is crucial as our world becomes ever more reliant on technology – an intense burst of solar activity aimed directly at Earth can disable power grids and wreck satellite circuitry.

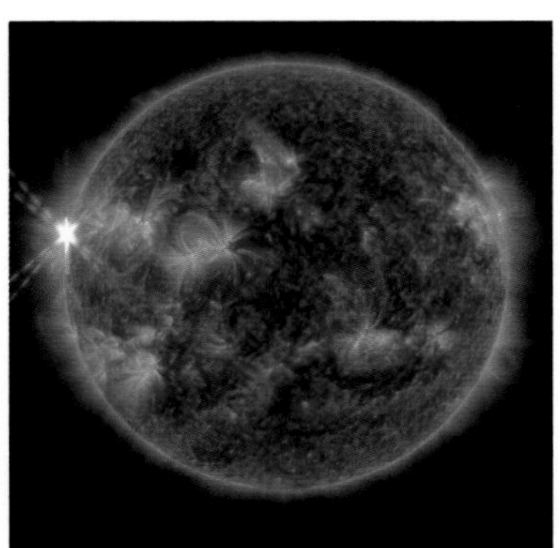

◁ **Solar flares**
Like light bouncing off a gleaming surface, areas of the Sun suddenly and rapidly brighten from time to time. Such events, known as solar flares, often signal the coming onslaught of a coronal mass ejection. The ultraviolet image shown on the left, taken by NASA's Solar Dynamics Observatory, captures a solar flare erupting from the left limb of the Sun.

▷ **Prominences**
The Sun's magnetic field lines sometimes tangle so much that they "snap", releasing their pent-up energy. When this happens, sprawling loops of hot plasma known as prominences erupt from the solar surface, following the magnetic field lines and tracing out vast and beautiful loops. These flame-like plumes can extend 500,000km (300,000 miles) into space, and last from several days to months. Prominences often take a distinctive arch shape, but can emerge in other forms too, including pillars and pyramids. If they erupt Earthwards, so that we see them in front of the Sun rather than against the darkness of space, they are referred to as filaments. This sequence of five photographs shows the eruption of a solar prominence as it gradually bulges out from the surface of the Sun before flaring into full splendour.

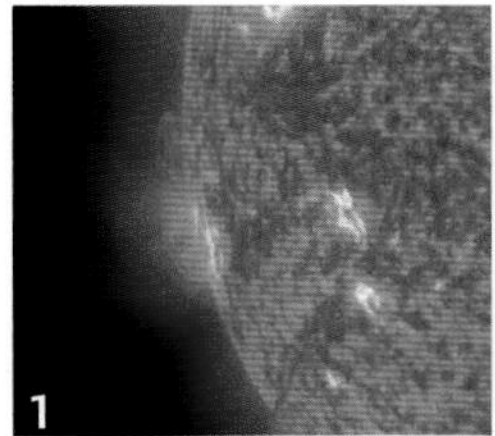
1

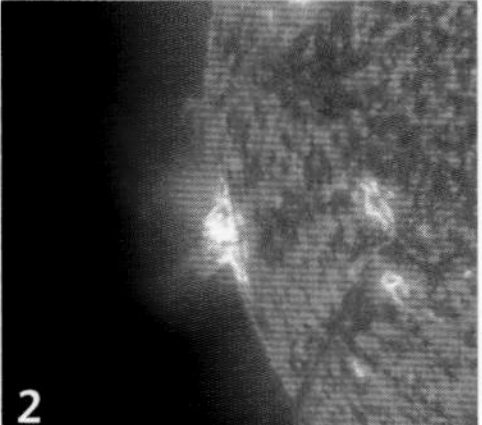
2

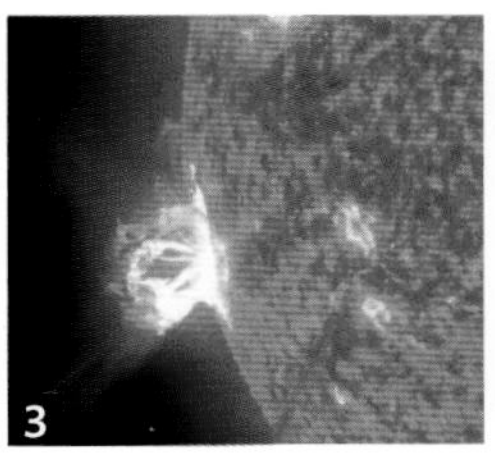
3

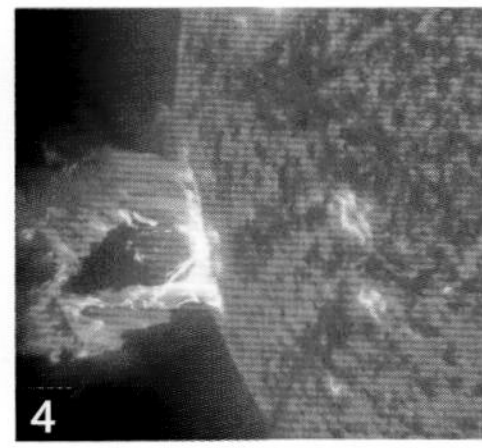
4

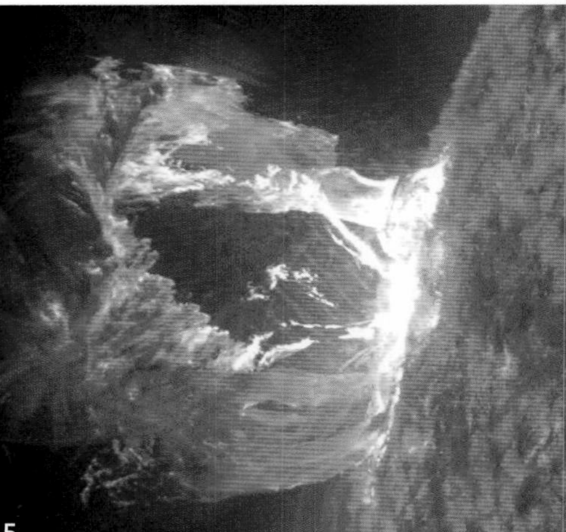
5

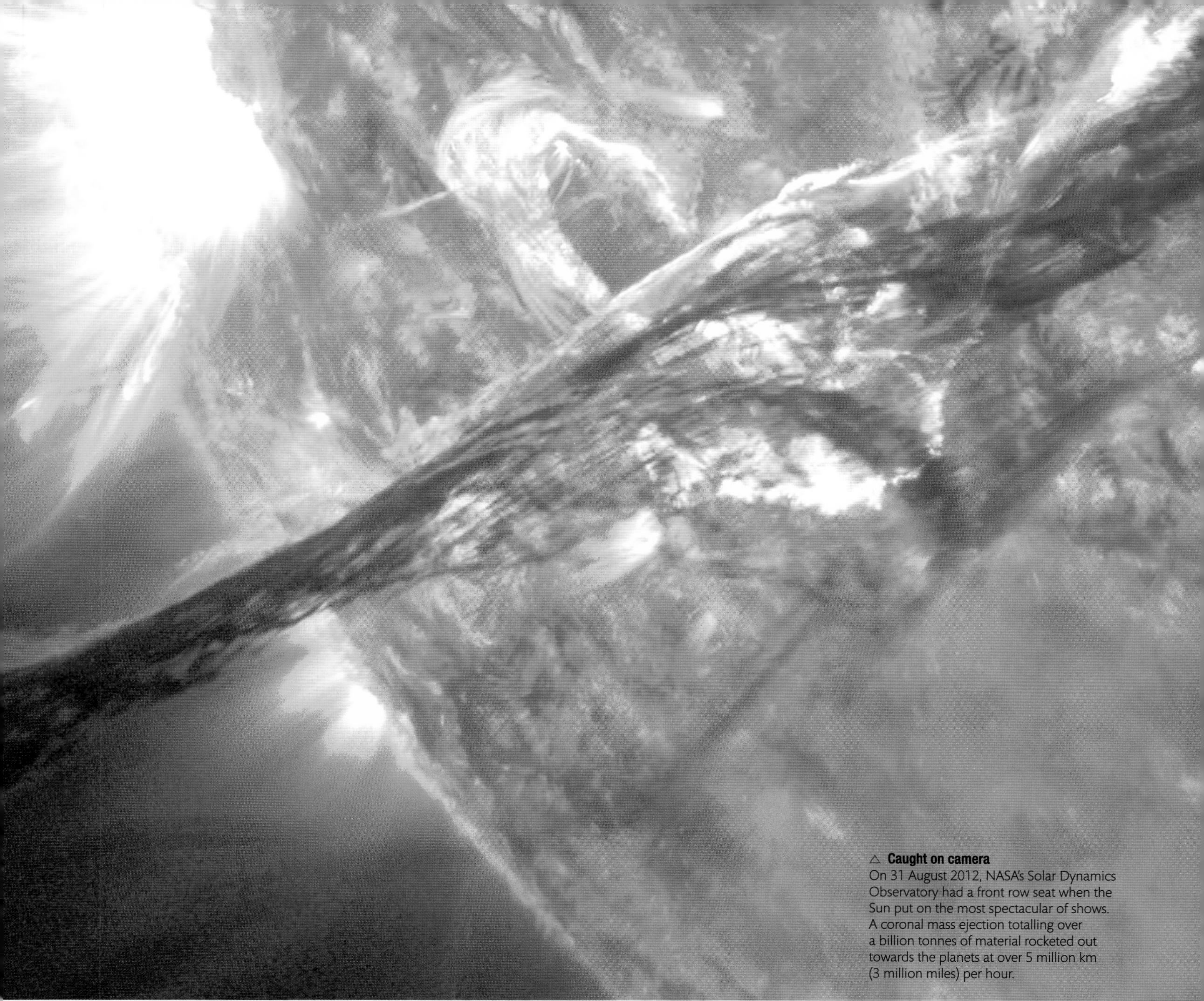

△ **Caught on camera**
On 31 August 2012, NASA's Solar Dynamics Observatory had a front row seat when the Sun put on the most spectacular of shows. A coronal mass ejection totalling over a billion tonnes of material rocketed out towards the planets at over 5 million km (3 million miles) per hour.

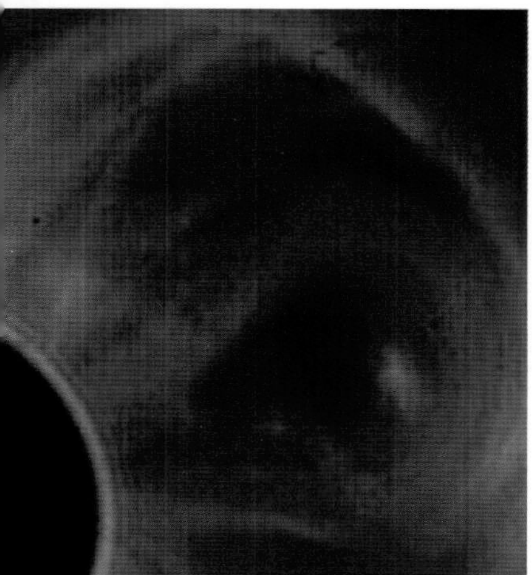

◁ **Coronal mass ejection**
The most sizeable and impressive explosive events anywhere in the Solar System occur when the Sun dispatches a mighty eruption of plasma known as a coronal mass ejection (CME). As the name suggests, the plasma is spat out from the Sun's atmosphere (corona). The sheer violence of the explosion can accelerate solar particles towards the speed of light. The arrival of CME material at Earth can trigger a geomagnetic storm. In the ultraviolet photograph on the left, a CME can be seen swelling out from the Sun's corona like a giant bubble.

△ **Northern lights**
A geomagnetic storm caused by a CME can overwhelm the Earth's magnetic field, channelling energy polewards and producing spectacular aurorae like the one above, photographed over Thingvellir National Park in Iceland. The shimmering curtains of light are the result of oxygen atoms glowing from energy injected into the atmosphere. Normally seen in polar latitudes, aurorae can extend all the way to the tropics after a major CME.

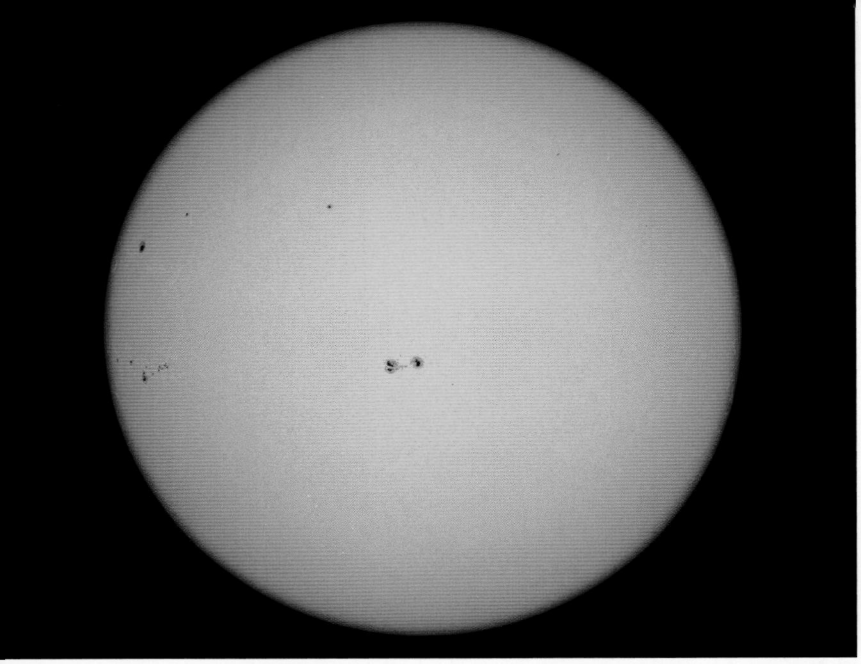

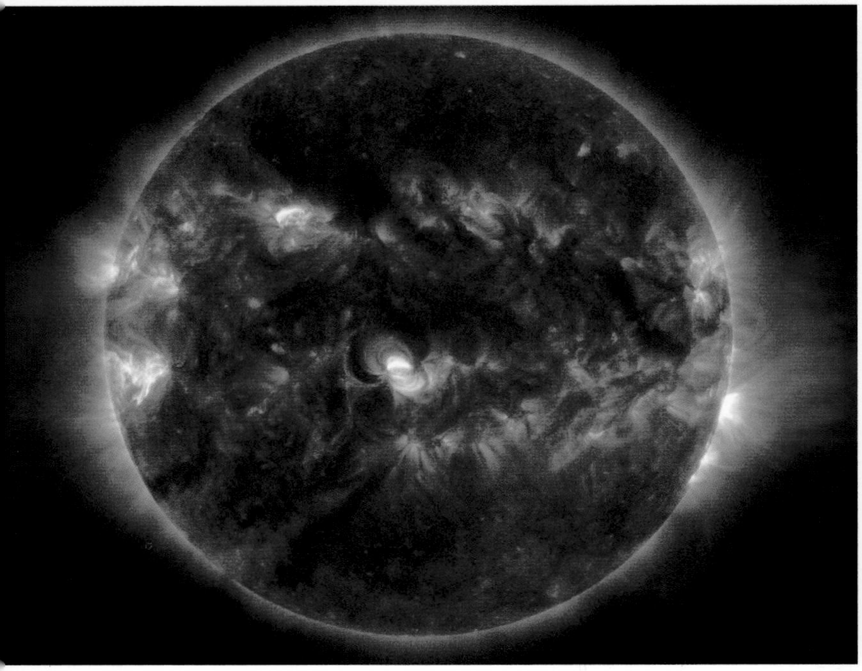

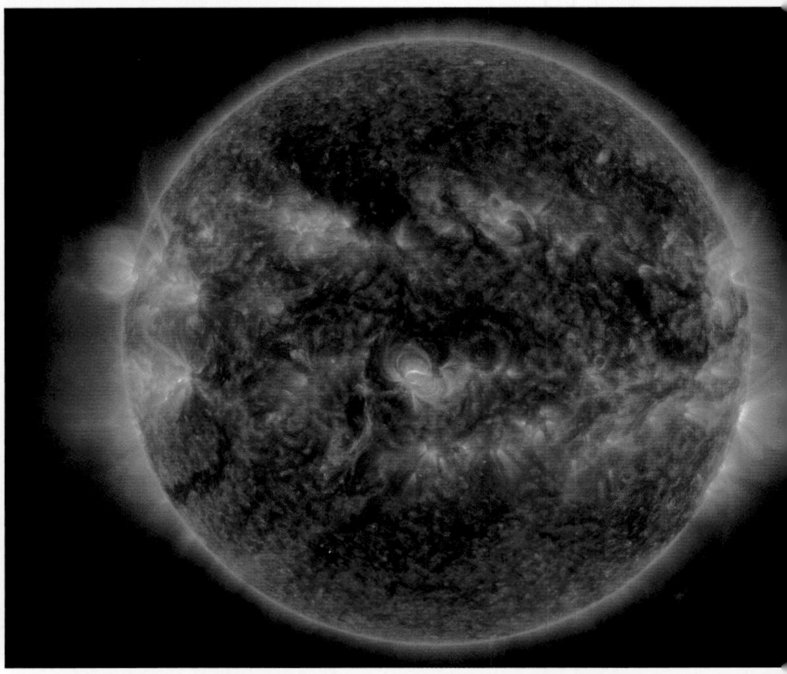

SUN RAYS

As well as producing light in the visible part of the spectrum, the Sun emits wavelengths our eyes cannot see, from radio waves and infrared to ultraviolet radiation. By capturing these rays, solar observatories can image parts of the Sun that are normally invisible. NASA's space-based Solar Dynamics Observatory (SDO) produces new images of the Sun every second; those shown here were all taken in a single hour in April 2014. The first one shows what the human eye would see if a direct glance were possible – the Sun's brilliant photosphere is reduced to a smooth yellow disc, with dark sunspots where magnetic disturbances have cooled the surface. For most of the images that follow, SDO used filters to select various wavelengths of ultraviolet light, revealing solar flares high in the Sun's outer atmosphere above sunspot regions. The final two photographs are composites that combine several wavelengths.

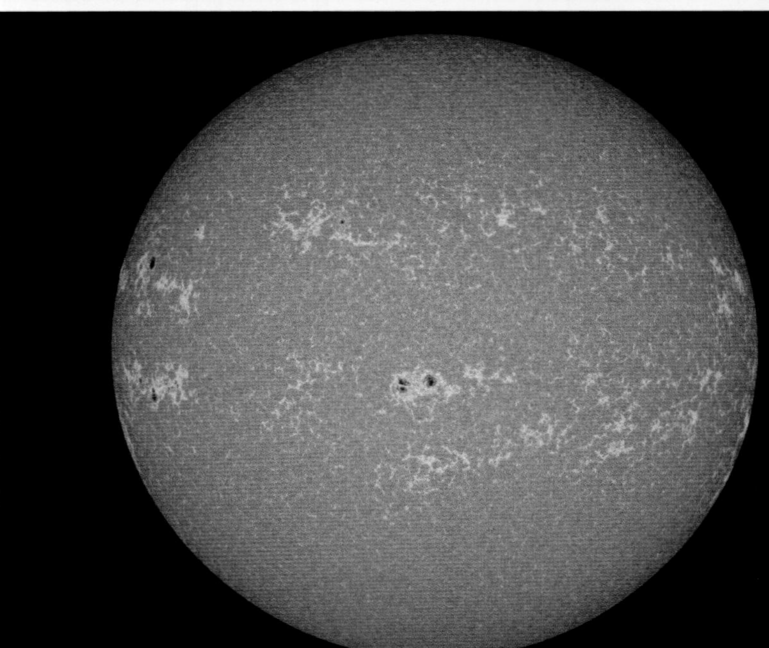

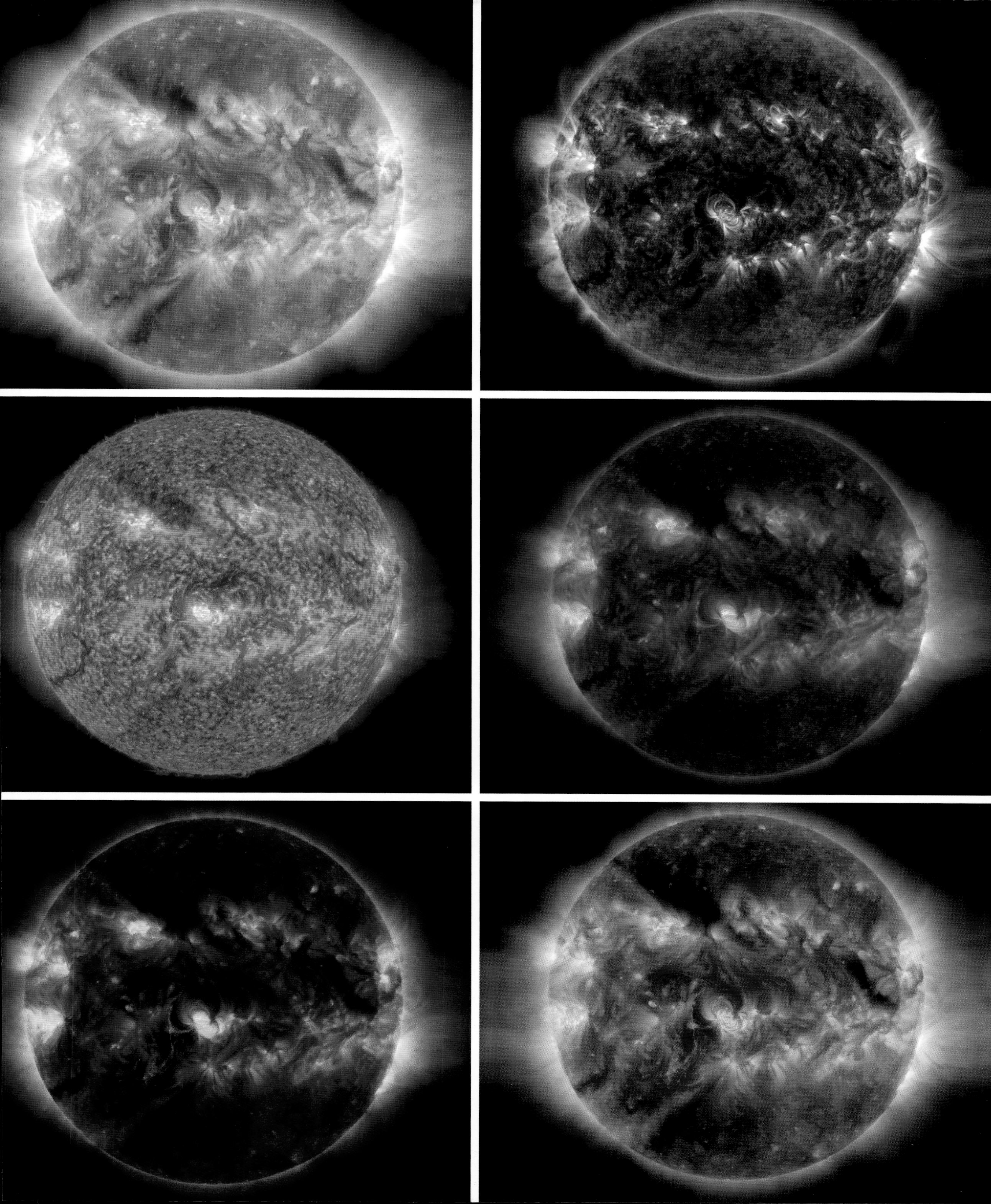

THE **SOLAR** CYCLE

THE SUN IS A CHANGEABLE STAR, SOMETIMES CALM AND PEACEFUL, SOMETIMES ERUPTING WITH GREAT VIOLENCE. THESE CHANGES FOLLOW A CLEAR PATTERN, WITH A CYCLICAL RISE AND FALL OF SOLAR ACTIVITY EVERY 11 YEARS OR SO.

For the last four centuries, scientists have kept records of the Sun's activity. During the early 19th century, German apothecary-turned-astronomer Samuel Heinrich Schwabe spent 17 years trying to spot a planet that he believed existed closer to the Sun than Mercury. He failed to see the silhouette of a new planet against the Sun, but he did keep accurate records of sunspots. Looking back over his observations, he noticed that the number of sunspots varied in a regular way, and the idea of the solar cycle was born. Today's orbiting and ground-based solar telescopes constantly scrutinize the Sun, revealing further details of this recurring pattern.

Sunspots

Once thought to be storms in the atmosphere of the Sun, we now know that sunspots are merely cooler regions of the solar surface. Typically lasting a few weeks, they are caused by intense, local magnetic activity and often appear in pairs. Records of sunspot observations date from the early 17th century, though sunspots were probably seen earlier. Scientists can trace sunspot activity further back by studying tree rings: carbon-14 levels in tree rings are lower during times of sunspot abundance, and greater when there are few sunspots.

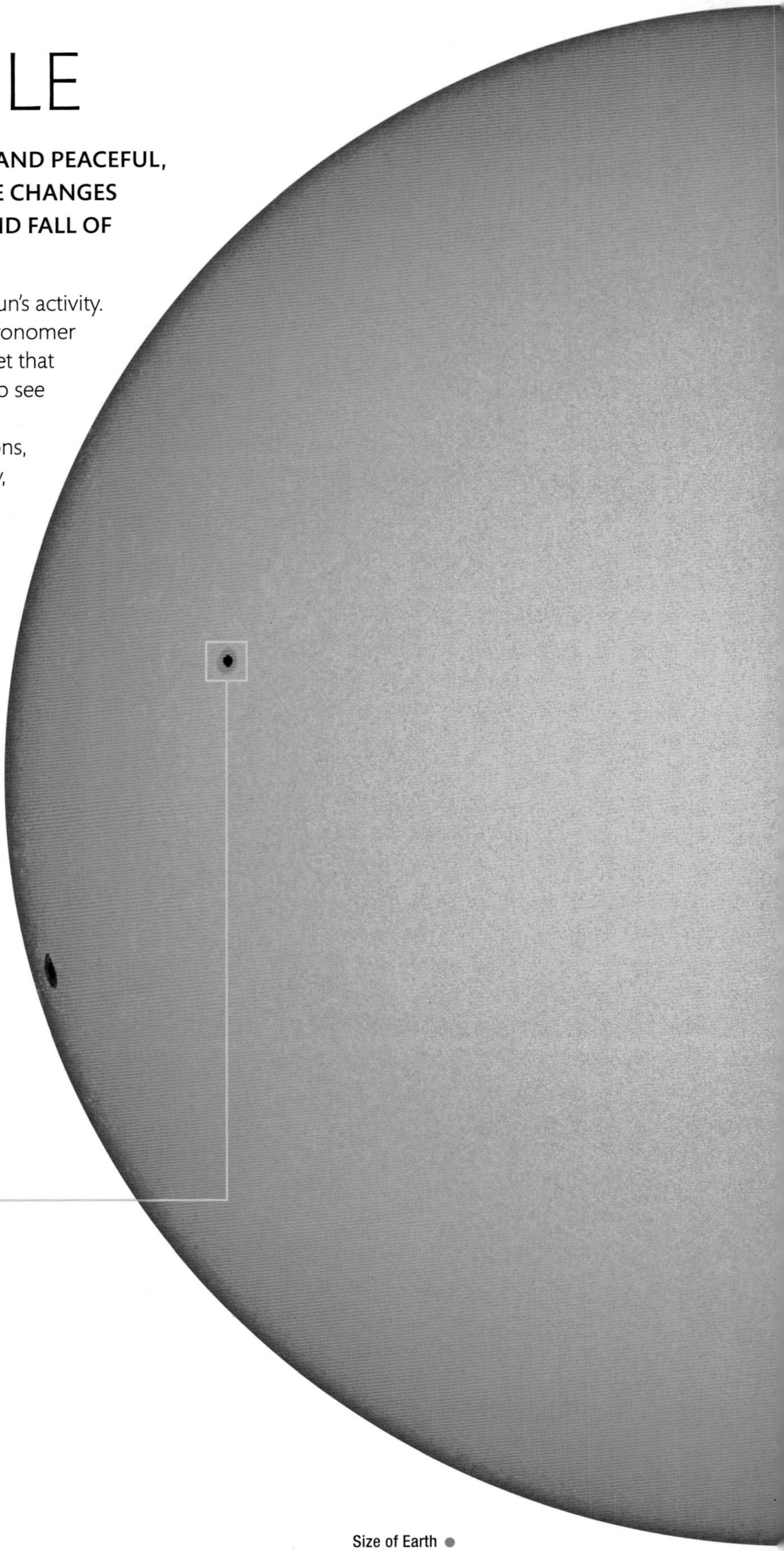

▷ **Sunspot structure**
A sunspot is usually split into two parts: an inner umbra and an outer penumbra. The dark umbra is the cooler part, with temperatures of around 2,500°C (4,500°F). By contrast, the penumbra can reach 3,500°C (6,300°F) and often exhibits streaky filaments called fibrils. The sunspots in a pair tend to have opposite magnetic polarity, akin to the poles of a magnet.

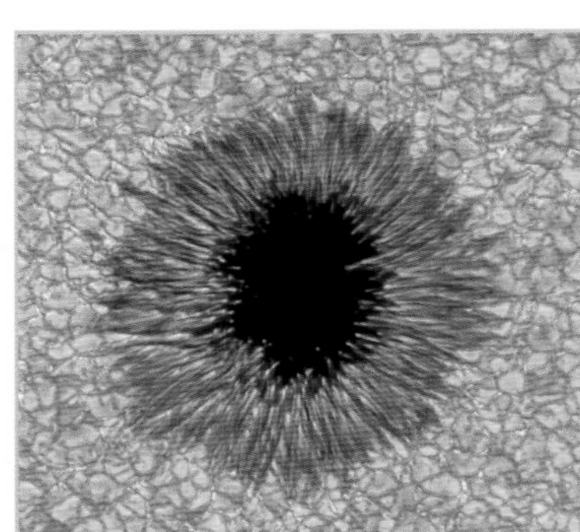

The **Great Sunspot** of 1947 was easily visible to the naked eye at sunset.

Size of Earth ●

Solar cycle

The 11-year solar cycle progresses from solar minimum (fewest sunspots) to solar maximum (most sunspots) and back again. It is linked to changes in the Sun's magnetic field, which becomes twisted during the cycle, before breaking down and renewing itself; every 22 years, the Sun's magnetic poles reverse. Solar maximum is associated not only with greater sunspot activity but also with solar flares, coronal mass ejections, and brighter aurorae on Earth.

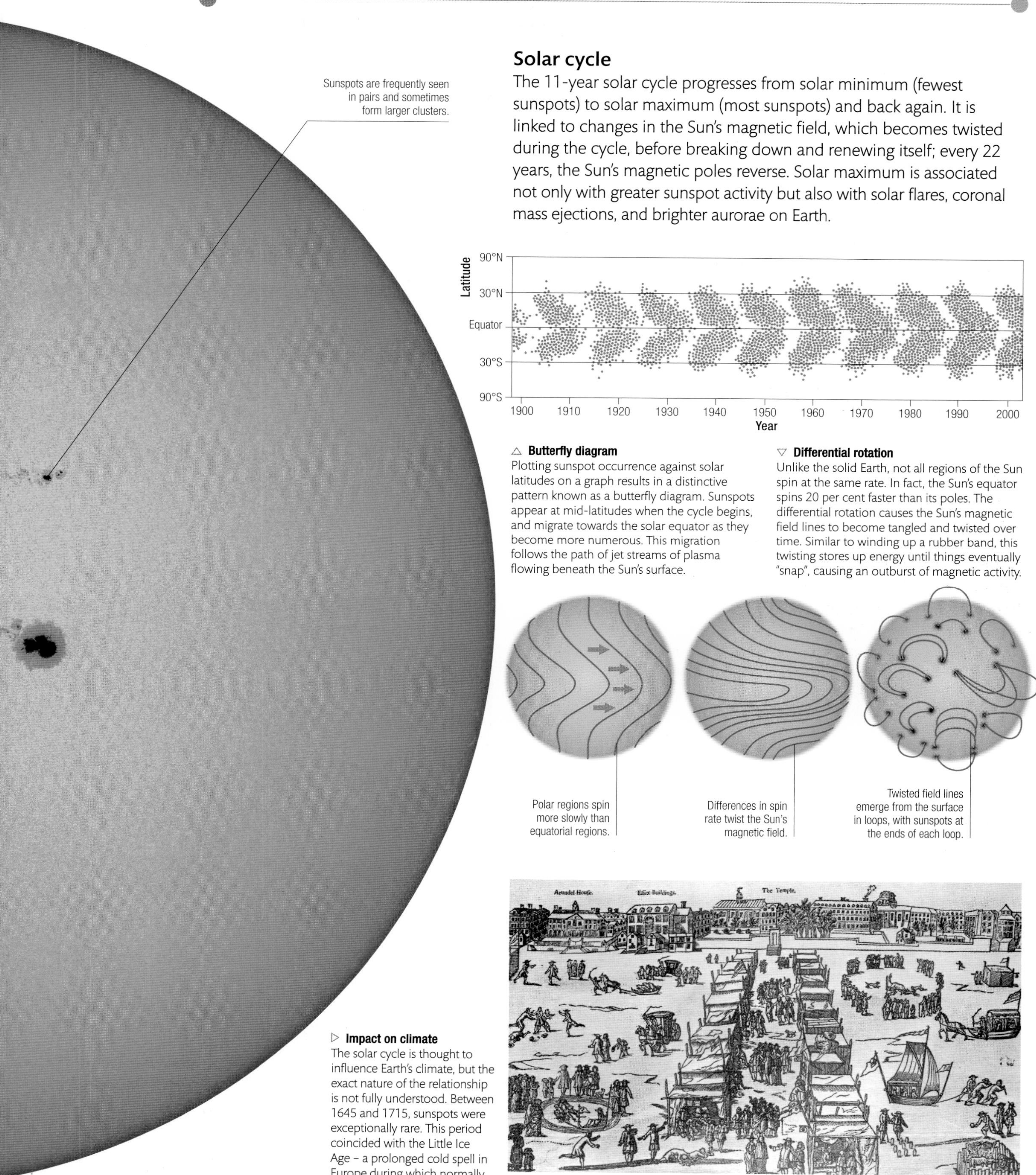

Sunspots are frequently seen in pairs and sometimes form larger clusters.
Latitude
90°N
30°N
Equator
30°S
90°S
1900
1910
1920
1930
1940
1950
1960
1970
1980
1990
2000
Year
Polar regions spin more slowly than equatorial regions.
Differences in spin rate twist the Sun's magnetic field.
Twisted field lines emerge from the surface in loops, with sunspots at the ends of each loop.
Arundel House.
Essex Buildings.
The Temple.

△ **Butterfly diagram**
Plotting sunspot occurrence against solar latitudes on a graph results in a distinctive pattern known as a butterfly diagram. Sunspots appear at mid-latitudes when the cycle begins, and migrate towards the solar equator as they become more numerous. This migration follows the path of jet streams of plasma flowing beneath the Sun's surface.

▽ **Differential rotation**
Unlike the solid Earth, not all regions of the Sun spin at the same rate. In fact, the Sun's equator spins 20 per cent faster than its poles. The differential rotation causes the Sun's magnetic field lines to become tangled and twisted over time. Similar to winding up a rubber band, this twisting stores up energy until things eventually "snap", causing an outburst of magnetic activity.

▷ **Impact on climate**
The solar cycle is thought to influence Earth's climate, but the exact nature of the relationship is not fully understood. Between 1645 and 1715, sunspots were exceptionally rare. This period coincided with the Little Ice Age – a prolonged cold spell in Europe during which normally ice-free rivers froze over.

Frost fair on the River Thames during the Little Ice Age

SOLAR ECLIPSES

WHEN SOMETHING AS CONSTANT AND UNERRING AS THE SUN'S LIGHT IS SUDDENLY INTERRUPTED DURING THE DAY, WE CANNOT FAIL TO NOTICE. FOR A FEW MINUTES, IT SEEMS AS IF THE WORLD STANDS STILL.

History books are littered with tales of the Sun disappearing; today we call these events solar eclipses. Every so often, during its steady crawl around Earth, the Moon occupies the exact same part of daytime sky as the Sun. Since the Moon is closer, its presence obscures our view of the Sun, causing an eclipse.

Total solar eclipses

During a total solar eclipse, the Sun is completely hidden by the Moon's disc for a few minutes. A total solar eclipse is perhaps nature's ultimate spectacle: the sky darkens, the temperature drops, and birds stop singing.

If the Moon orbited exactly on the line between the Sun and Earth, we would get an eclipse every month. However, because the Moon's orbit is tilted by five degrees, eclipses happen only every 18 months or so. Each is visible from only a small part of Earth's surface, where the Moon's shadow falls.

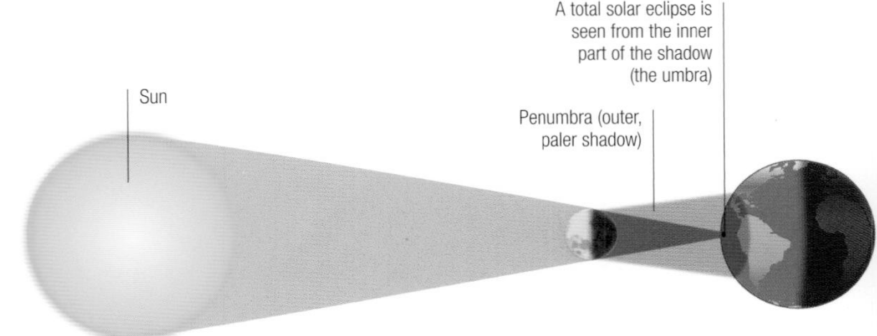
A total solar eclipse is seen from the inner part of the shadow (the umbra)
Sun
Penumbra (outer, paler shadow)

Totality

△ **How total eclipses work**
Despite being 400 times smaller than the Sun, the Moon is able to block our view of the Sun because it is 400 times closer. Where the darker part of the Moon's shadow – the umbra – falls on Earth, a total eclipse is seen; from the penumbra, a partial eclipse is visible. The umbra's path across Earth is typically 16,000km (10,000 miles) long but only 160km (100 miles) wide.

▽ **Totality**
Eclipse watchers view the Sun and Moon from Ellis Beach in Australia in November 2012. Totality – the stage during which the Sun is completely hidden – is a fleeting event, lasting a maximum of 7.5 minutes. During the eclipse of 2012 it lasted only two minutes.

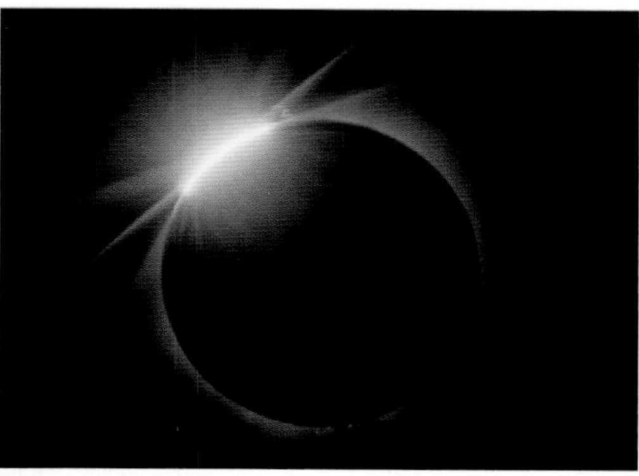

△ **Diamond ring**
The Moon's surface is not perfectly smooth. Mountains and valleys allow sunlight to break through, creating an effect known as Baily's beads. A solitary bead appears as a spectacular "diamond ring", marking the beginning or end of totality.

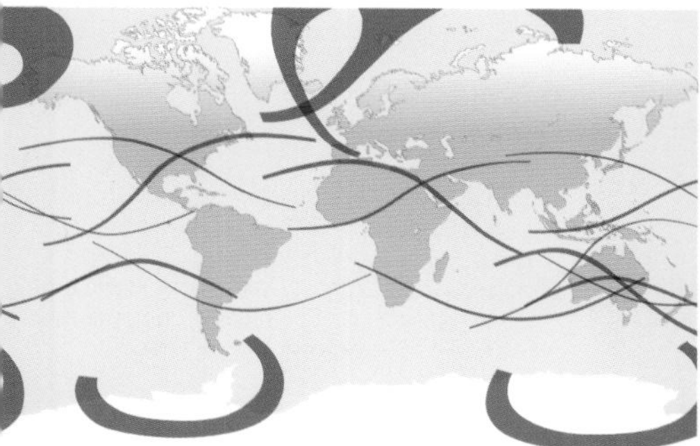

Map of total solar eclipses 2014–2040

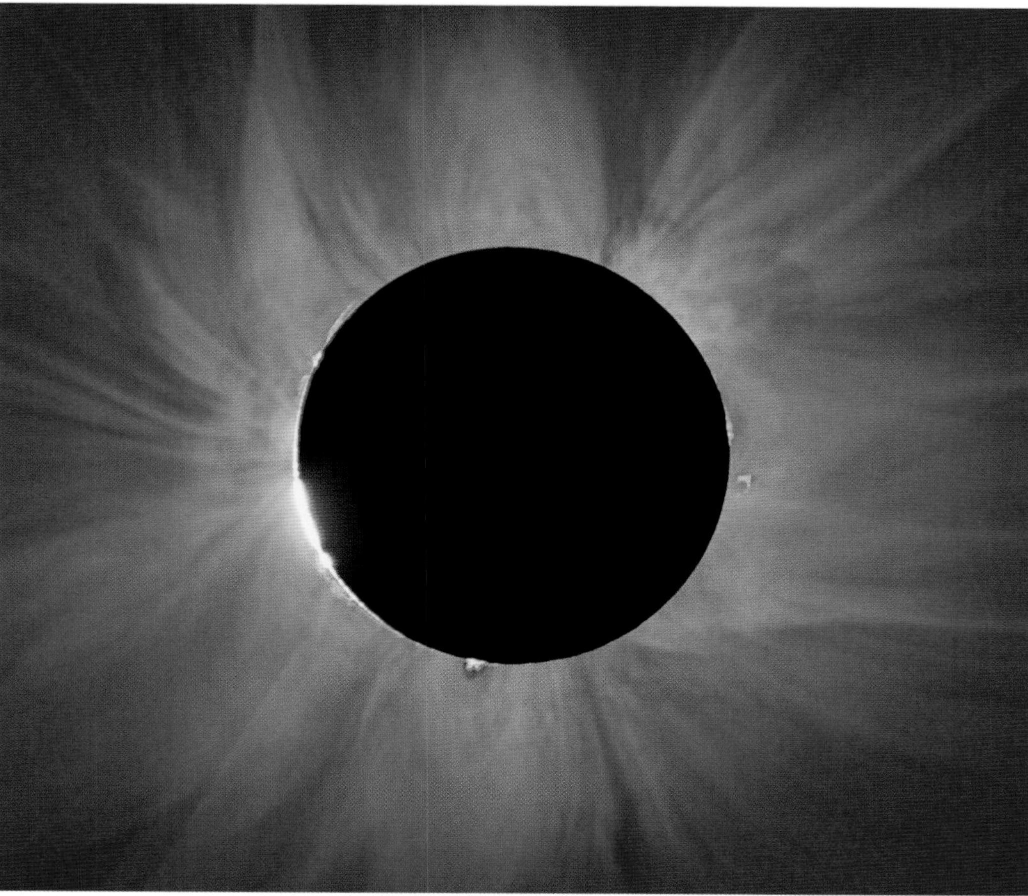

△ **Solar corona**
The Sun's vast and tenuous outer atmosphere – the corona – is normally outshone by its brilliant photosphere, rendering the corona all but invisible. But when the Moon covers the Sun's face, the corona is spectacularly revealed. To study the corona through solar telescopes, astronomers use a coronagraph – an opaque disc that obscures the Sun.

Annular solar eclipses

Sometimes the Moon fails to cover the entire solar disc, allowing us to see the edge of the Sun as a ring around the Moon's silhouette. This is called an annular solar eclipse, from the Latin *annulus*, meaning "little ring". A hybrid solar eclipse – a very unusual event – appears as total from some locations on Earth and as annular from others.

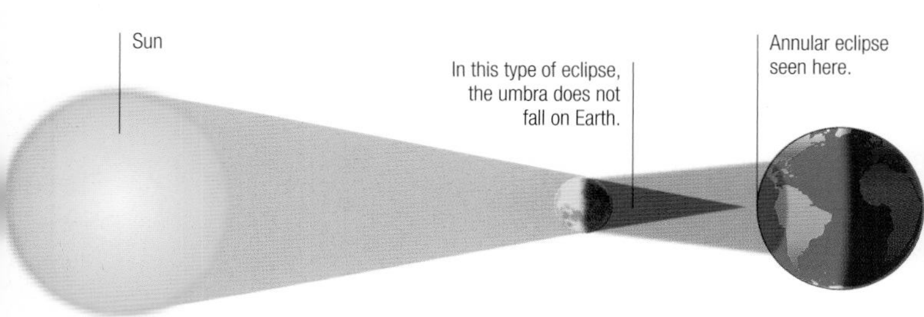
Sun
In this type of eclipse, the umbra does not fall on Earth.
Annular eclipse seen here.

△ **How annular eclipses work**
The Moon's orbit is elliptical rather than circular, so its distance from Earth varies. If a solar eclipse occurs when the Moon is at its furthest from Earth, it is too small in the sky to block out the Sun and causes an annular eclipse.

▷ **Ring of fire**
An annular eclipse is visible where the antumbra – the extension of the umbra – passes over Earth's surface. During the eclipse, the Moon leaves a spectacular "ring of fire" around it. The ring is so bright that the corona cannot be seen.

STORY OF **THE SUN**

OVER THE CENTURIES, THE SUN'S PLACE IN OUR CULTURE HAS CHANGED DRAMATICALLY – SCIENCE AND EXPERIMENTATION HAVE OVERSEEN ITS TRANSITION FROM ALL-POWERFUL GOD TO HOT, GAS-FILLED STAR.

The Sun's movements have been tracked for thousands of years, and were used by many ancient civilizations as the basis for their calendars. However, the same people believed the Sun circled Earth; it was not until 1543 that Copernicus suggested the Sun was at the centre of the Solar System. Later, Newton's theory of gravity allowed the Sun's enormous mass to be calculated, and Einstein's work in the early 20th century explained how the Sun can shine for billions of years without running out of fuel. Modern spacecraft allow us to study the Sun in intimate detail and predict the storms that rage on its surface.

Stonehenge

3000–2000 BCE

Astronomical calendar

Stonehenge monument is built in southwest England. Although its function remains unclear, the alignment of its stones with the sunrise and sunset in midsummer and midwinter suggests it was used as an astronomical calendar.

Sun god worship in ancient Egypt

1350 BCE

Sun god Apollo

The Sun is worshipped as a god by the ancient Egyptians, Greeks, and later Romans. The Romans celebrate the death and rebirth of the Sun god Apollo in midwinter. When Rome converts to Christianity, this festival becomes known as Christmas.

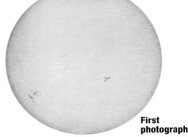

First photograph

1845

First photograph of the Sun

The new technology of photography allows the first image of the Sun to be taken by French astronomers Louis Fizeau and Lion Foucault. The pair use the daguerreotype technique to capture the image, which includes clearly visible sunspots.

Coronal mass ejection

1859

Solar storm recorded

English astronomer Richard Carrington observes the first solar flare. It is followed by the biggest Earth-bound coronal mass ejection ever recorded. The solar storm hits Earth within days, causing aurorae as far south as Hawaii and the Caribbean.

J. Norman Lockyer

1868

Discovery of helium

J. Norman Lockyer, English astronomer, discovers an unknown element in the spectrum of the Sun. He names it helium after Helios, the Greek Sun god. The element is not discovered on Earth until 1895. We now know the Sun is 25 per cent helium.

Butterfly diagram

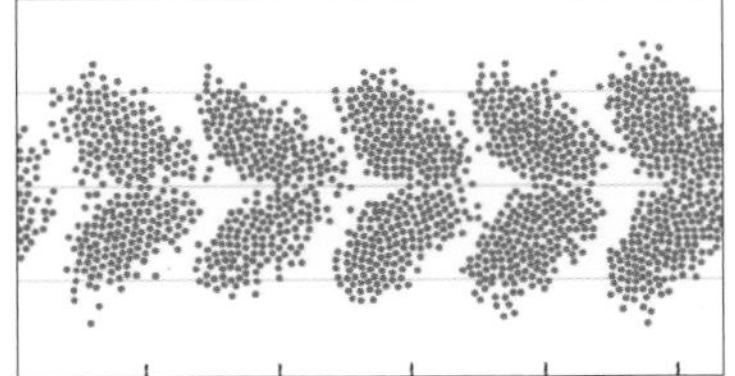

1904

Sunspots plotted

English astronomer Edward Maunder plots sunspot locations during the solar cycle, creating his famous "butterfly diagram". It shows that sunspots increase in number and move towards the solar equator as the solar cycle approaches its peak.

Einstein and Eddington

1919

Theory of relativity

British physicist Arthur Eddington photographs a solar eclipse from Principe in west Africa. His shots capture the positions of stars near the Sun and confirm Albert Einstein's general theory of relativity by showing that the Sun bends light.

Nuclear fusion

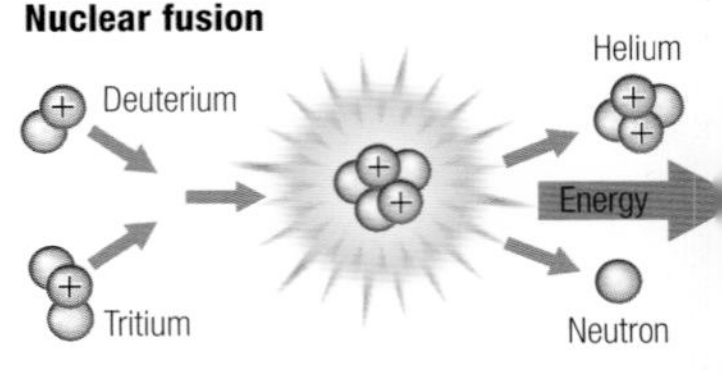
Deuterium
Tritium
Helium
Energy
Neutron

1920

Nuclear fusion in the Sun's core

In his presidential address to the British Association for the Advancement of Science, Arthur Eddington correctly proposes that the Sun's energy is created by nuclear processes at its core. He goes on to publish a detailed account of his ideas in 1926.

Solar eclipse

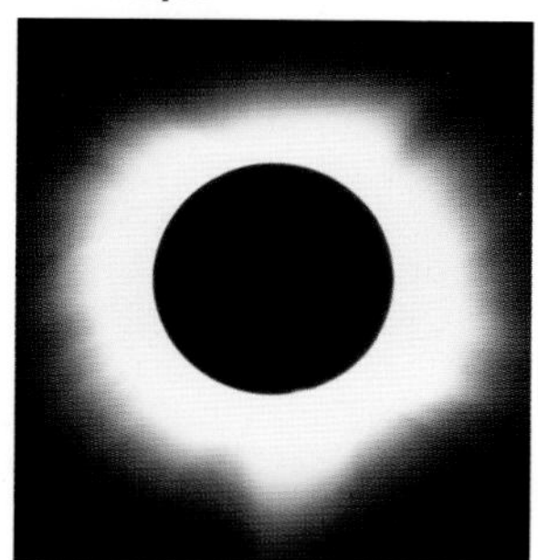

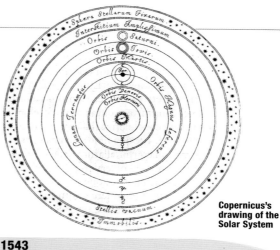

Copernicus's drawing of the Solar System

364 BCE

Earliest record of sunspots
Chinese astronomer Shi Shen makes the earliest record of sunspot observation. He believes the phenomenon is due to a form of eclipse. Today we know that sunspots are cooler regions of the Sun's photosphere.

968

Sun's corona
Byzantine historian Leo Diaconus gives the first reliable description of the Sun's corona, as seen from Constantinople (now Istanbul) during a solar eclipse. He describes a "dim and feeble glow like a narrow band shining in a circle around the edge of the disc".

1543

Centre of the Solar System
Copernicus's *On the Revolutions of the Heavenly Spheres* is printed in Nuremburg in modern-day Germany. Previously, Ptolemy's view that Earth was at the centre of the Solar System prevailed. Copernicus's work places the Sun at the heart of the Solar System.

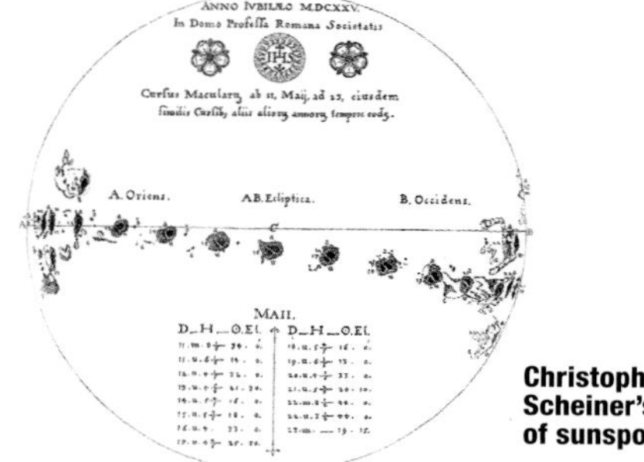
A. Oriens.
AB. Ecliptica.
B. Occidens.
MAII.

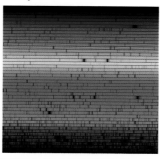

Christoph Scheiner's drawing of sunspots

1609

First telescope view of sunspots
The invention of the telescope leads to the first clear observations of sunspots by Italian scientist Galileo, German physicist Christoph Scheiner, and other astronomers. Galileo's observations of Jupiter and Venus support Copernicus's ideas about the Solar System.

Absorption lines

1802

Discovery of absorption lines
English chemist William Wollaston discovers absorption lines in the spectrum of light from the Sun. These are later found to be caused by chemical elements in the Sun and are used to determine its composition.

1843

Sunspot cycle
German astronomer Heinrich Schwabe publishes his work on sunspots after 17 years studying them in an attempt to find a hypothetical planet, Vulcan. He notes that sunspot numbers rise and fall over a decade or so. We now know this as the solar cycle.

Comet Hale–Bopp

1951

Discovery of the solar wind
German astronomer Ludwig F. Biermann discovers the solar wind by observing comets. He notices the tail of a comet always points away from the Sun no matter which way it is travelling, and concludes that something must be blowing it in that direction.

1995

SOHO mission
NASA and ESA's Solar and Heliospheric Observatory (SOHO) launches. It provides spectacular images and unprecedented scientific analysis of the Sun. By 2012, it would discover over 2,000 sun-grazing comets.

SDO image of Sun

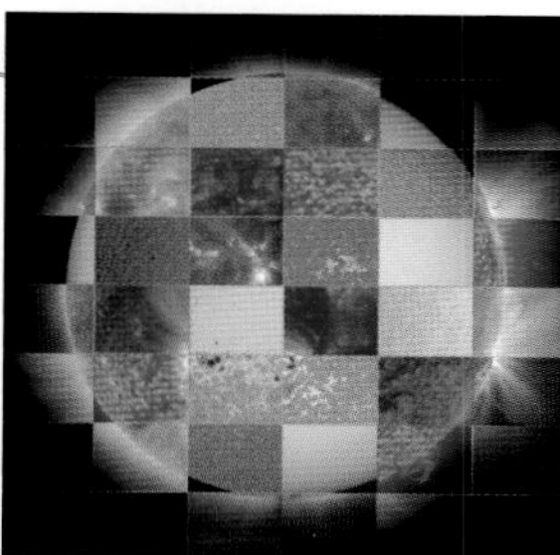

2010

Solar Dynamics Observatory
NASA's Solar Dynamics Observatory (SDO) launches, using high-definition technology to observe the Sun. Taking multiple wavelength images every ten seconds, it sends back data equivalent to half a million music tracks every day.

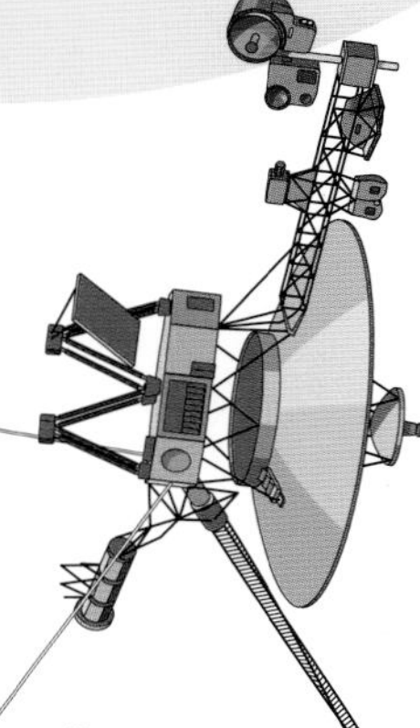

Voyager 1

2012

Voyager 1 leaves heliosphere
The Voyager 1 spacecraft becomes the first man-made object to leave the heliosphere – the vast region of space around the Sun in which the solar wind flows.

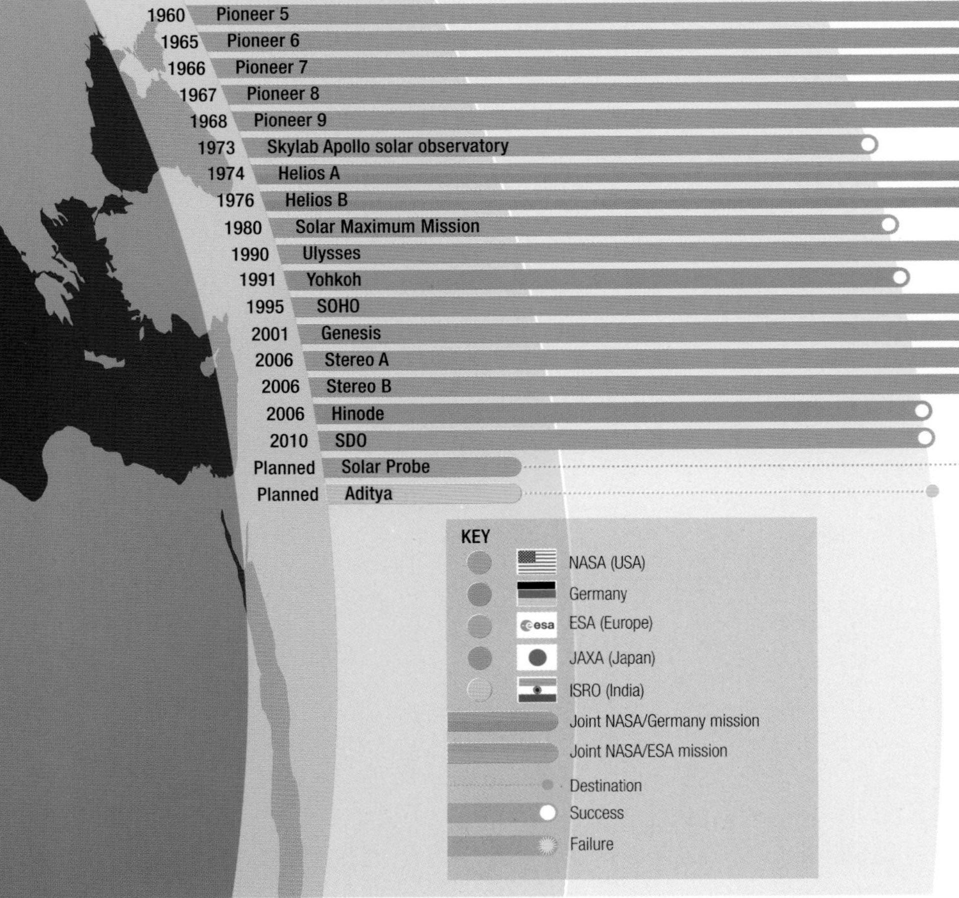
EARTH ORBIT
LAGRANGIAN POINT ORBIT
1960 Pioneer 5
1965 Pioneer 6
1966 Pioneer 7
1967 Pioneer 8
1968 Pioneer 9
1973 Skylab Apollo solar observatory
1974 Helios A
1976 Helios B
1980 Solar Maximum Mission
1990 Ulysses
1991 Yohkoh
1995 SOHO
2001 Genesis
2006 Stereo A
2006 Stereo B
2006 Hinode
2010 SDO
Planned Solar Probe
Planned Aditya
KEY
NASA (USA)
Germany
ESA (Europe)
JAXA (Japan)
ISRO (India)
Joint NASA/Germany mission
Joint NASA/ESA mission
Destination
Success
Failure

△ **Mission destinations**
With a few exceptions, spacecraft launched to observe the Sun are not designed to fly close to it. Some stay in orbit around Earth and take advantage of a view of the Sun unobstructed by Earth's atmosphere. Others orbit the Sun slightly closer than Earth or even from farther away, sometimes en route to other destinations. The SOHO and Genesis spacecraft orbited the Sun at the Lagrangian point – a point in space about 1.5 million km (930,000 miles) from Earth at which the gravity of Earth and the Sun balance, allowing the craft to maintain an orbit synchronous with Earth's.

▷ **Pioneer 5**
This early mission lacked a camera and so could not return images. It was, however, the first true interplanetary spacecraft. Launched on a path that took it between Earth and Venus, Pioneer 5 confirmed the existence of an interplanetary magnetic field for the first time and studied how this field is affected by solar flares.

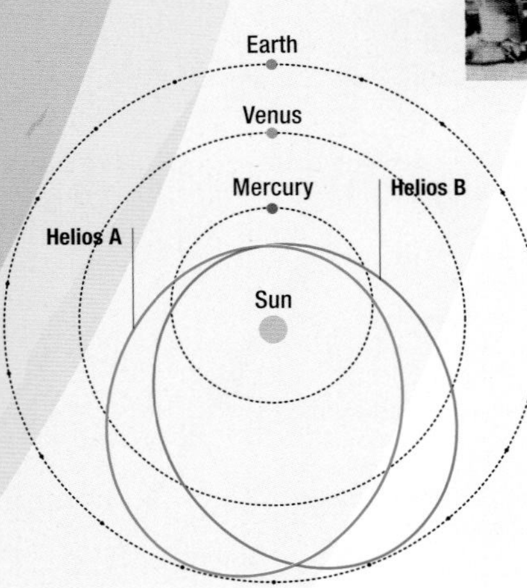
Earth
Venus
Mercury
Helios B
Helios A
Sun

◁ **Helios A and B**
The two Helios spacecraft studied the solar wind and magnetism. They hold the records for making the closest approach to the Sun (slightly nearer than Mercury) and being the fastest man-made objects in history: they reached a top speed of 70km (44 miles) per second. No longer functional but still in orbit, they follow elliptical paths, swooping close to the Sun at top speed and then flying back out towards Earth's orbit.

▷ **Ulysses**
Designed to observe the Sun at high latitudes, Ulysses flew to Jupiter and used the planet's gravity to fling it into an orbit that would take it over the poles of the Sun. On its travels, it discovered that 30 times more dust enters our Solar System than had previously been thought. Contact with Ulysses was terminated in 2009.

▽ **SOHO**
Launched in 1995, the Solar and Heliospheric Observatory (SOHO) was the first of the modern generation of solar observatories. Still at work today, SOHO has returned many spectacular images of the Sun's violent weather, the chromosphere, and the corona, all of which it monitors from a solar orbit. While studying the Sun, SOHO has discovered 2,000 sun-grazing comets.

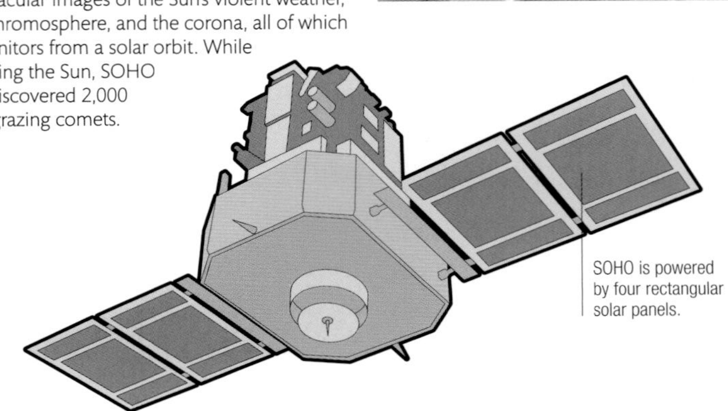
SOHO is powered by four rectangular solar panels.

ORBITER

MISSIONS TO THE **SUN**

TO LEARN MORE ABOUT THE SUN, WE NEED TO OBSERVE IT FROM ABOVE EARTH'S ATMOSPHERE. OVER THE YEARS, A NUMBER OF COUNTRIES HAVE LAUNCHED MISSIONS TO PEER AT OUR NEAREST STAR FROM SPACE.

A suite of spacecraft has revolutionized our understanding of all things solar, from the Sun's dynamic magnetic field to the way its solar wind interacts with the planets. Today, the Sun is under constant surveillance from space, 24 hours a day. Such close scrutiny is important – the more we understand about the Sun, the better we are able to predict when a potentially dangerous solar storm will be unleashed in our direction.

▽ **Genesis**
This was a mission to capture material from the solar wind. It did so in 2005, making it the first NASA mission to return a space sample to Earth since Apollo 17 astronauts returned with lunar rocks in 1972. The mission wasn't without incident, however; Genesis crash-landed, but the sample was successfully salvaged.

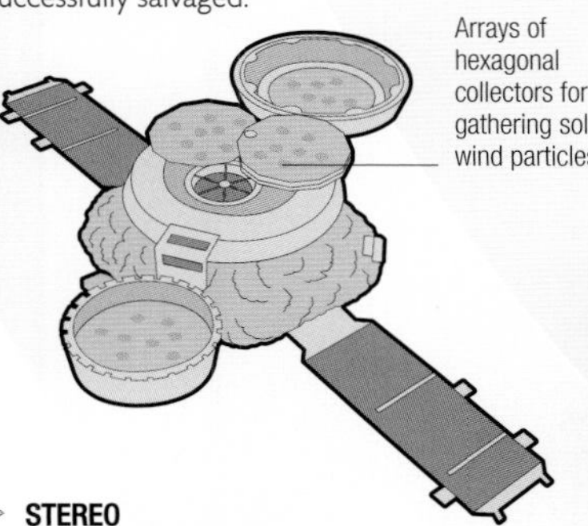
Arrays of hexagonal collectors for gathering solar wind particles

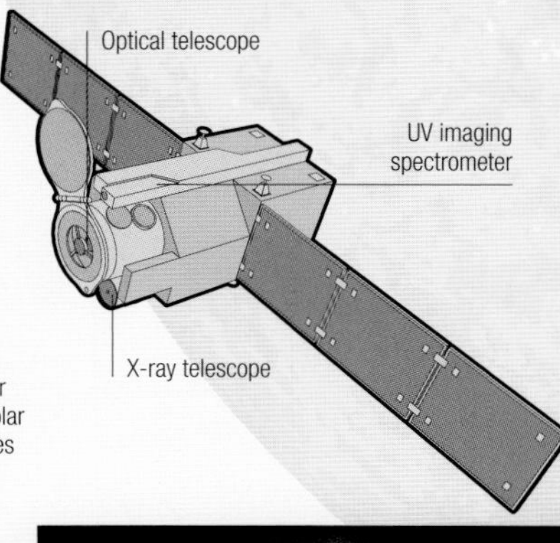
Optical telescope
UV imaging spectrometer
X-ray telescope

◁ **Hinode**
Armed with instruments that can see visible light, ultraviolet, and X-rays, Hinode monitors the Sun's magnetic activity, providing valuable insights into sunspots and solar flares. It is also investigating how magnetic energy moves from the photosphere to the corona.

▷ **SDO**
The Solar Dynamics Observatory (SDO) beams back high-definition images of the Sun every ten seconds. SDO was designed to study space weather. This SDO image shows loops of hot gas following the Sun's twisted magnetic field.

▷ **STEREO**
The Solar Terrestrial Relations Observatory (STEREO) consists of two identical craft orbiting the Sun in tandem. They take stereo (3D) images of the Sun and study events such as coronal mass ejections. In 2007, STEREO photographed the Moon passing in front of the Sun (right) – a lunar transit not visible from Earth.

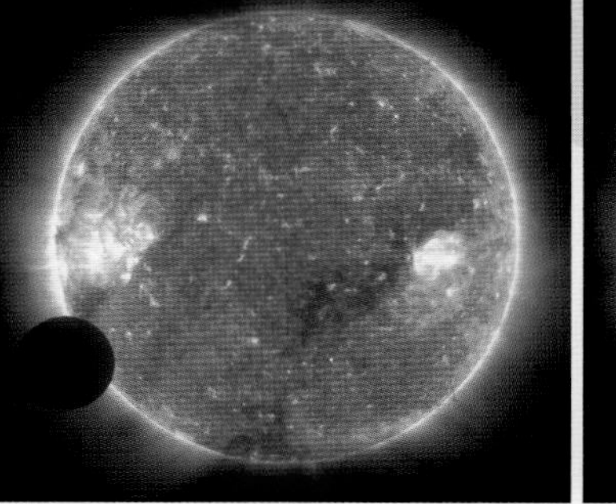

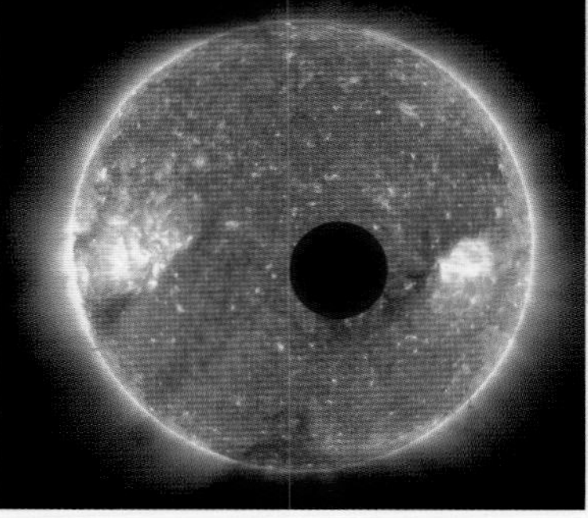

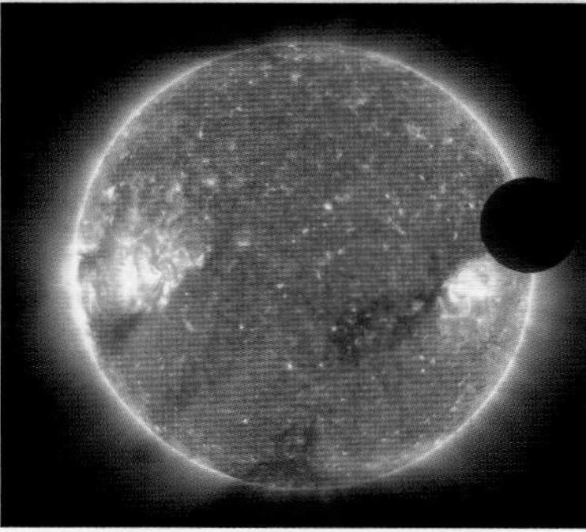

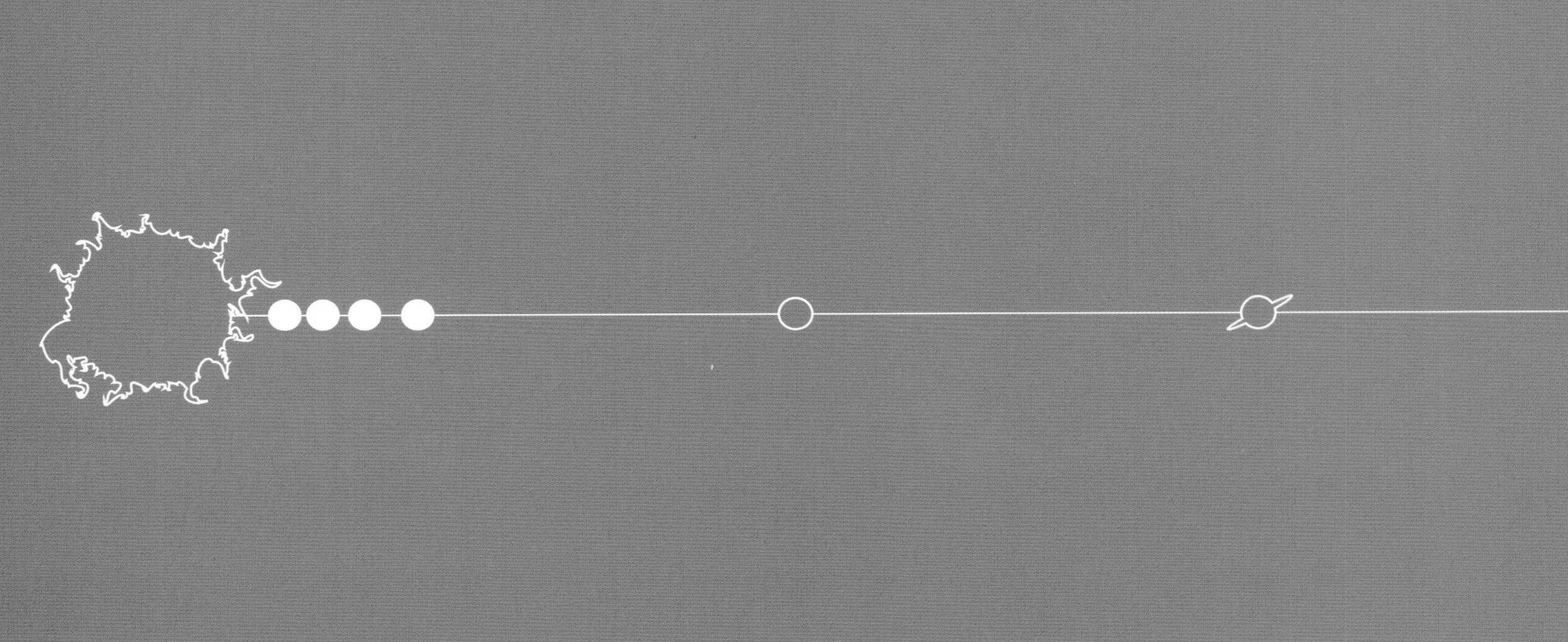

ROCKY **WORLDS**

NEIGHBOURING **WORLDS**

The four planets closest to the Sun – Mercury, Venus, Earth, and Mars – are a diverse group. Our own planet is the biggest of the foursome, with Venus a near twin in size. Formed in a cloud of solar dust and gas, battered by collisions, and reduced to rocky balls by heat and gravity, they all began life in the same way. But, over time, they became very different. Mercury, the smallest of the inner planets, is nearest to the Sun and has little atmosphere to protect it from our star's searing heat. The craters on Mercury's hot, dark surface – scars of long bombardment with cosmic material – resemble the craters on our Moon. While all the inner planets are thought to have an iron core, Mercury's is unusually large, perhaps because the young planet was stripped of its outer layers in a catastrophic collision. Venus, though beautiful in the twilight sky, is obscured by choking clouds of sulphuric acid and may be actively volcanic. The hottest planet in the Solar System, it is the victim of a runaway greenhouse effect. Mars is the coldest rocky planet. Once it may have been warm, with rivers flowing on its surface, but now the planet is an arid wasteland, its remaining water locked in frost and ice. Earth is a world between extremes. The right distance from the Sun for water to exist in liquid form on the surface, our planet has vast oceans, an oxygen-rich atmosphere, and a huge diversity of life forms.

◁ **Traces of the past**
More has been discovered about Mars than any other of our close planetary neighbours. NASA's Mars Reconnaissance Orbiter opened a window into the red planet's past when it captured this image. The layers of rock within a crater in the Arabia Terra region, caused by fluctuations in the amount of sediment deposited, reveal that the Martian climate has changed repeatedly over millions of years.

MERCURY

THE NEAREST PLANET TO THE SUN, MERCURY CAN BE SEEN CLEARLY FROM EARTH ONLY FOR SHORT PERIODS EACH YEAR. IT IS USUALLY VISIBLE IN SPRING AND AUTUMN AS A BRIGHT GLIMMER JUST ABOVE THE HORIZON AT DUSK AND DAWN.

Mercury is a tiny, dense, deeply cratered world, so close to the Sun that it is continually scorched and blasted by solar emissions. Temperatures during its long daytime period reach a roasting 430°C (800°F) – hot enough to melt lead. Yet because there is only a thin atmosphere, heat escapes quickly enough for night-time temperatures to drop to −180°C (−290°F). No other planet experiences such extremes.

Mercury spins on its axis very slowly, with one rotation taking almost 59 Earth days. Yet it is also the fastest orbiting of all the planets, completing its circuit of the Sun in just 88 days. By the time the sunny side begins to turn away, the whole planet has been swept round to face the Sun from the opposite side. So once the Sun comes up, it takes a long time to set again – there are 176 days from one sunrise to the next, during which time the planet orbits the Sun more than twice. Despite the long Mercurial days, Mercury's sky always looks black due to the incredibly thin atmosphere, which is not thick enough to reflect light.

Mercury has a **maximum orbital speed** of 50km (30 miles) per second.

MERCURY DATA

Average diameter	4,879km (3,032 miles)
Mass (Earth = 1)	0.055
Gravity at equator (Earth = 1)	0.38
Mean distance from Sun (Earth = 1)	0.38
Axial tilt	0.01°
Rotation period (day)	58.6 Earth days
Orbital period (year)	87.97 Earth days
Minimum temperature	−180°C (−290°F)
Maximum temperature	430°C (800°F)
Moons	0

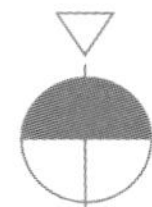
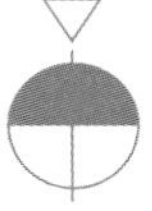

▷ **Northern hemisphere**
At the north pole are huge expanses of smooth plains some 4 million square km (1.5 million square miles) in area – half the size of the USA. A feature known as Goethe Basin contains ghost craters that have been flooded and buried by lava flows.

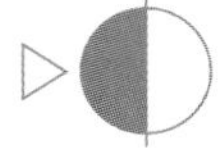

▷ **Western hemisphere**
Until NASA's MESSENGER made its first flyby in 2008, this half of Mercury was unknown. The flyby revealed that 40 per cent of the planet's surface is covered by smooth, volcanic plains. Its crust is more like that of Mars than the Moon's, despite the similar appearance.

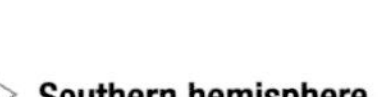

▷ **Southern hemisphere**
Around Mercury's poles, in shadowy places that are permanently shielded from the Sun's heat, such as in Chao Meng-Fu crater, NASA's MESSENGER spacecraft found radar-bright patches that could be a mix of frozen water and organic materials.

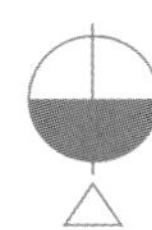

Brahms Crater is a large, old, complex crater with a prominent central peak over 3km (1.9 miles) high.

Tyagaraja Crater

Named after the Hungarian composer, Bartok Crater is about 73km (45 miles) across with a central peak.

Michelangelo Crater

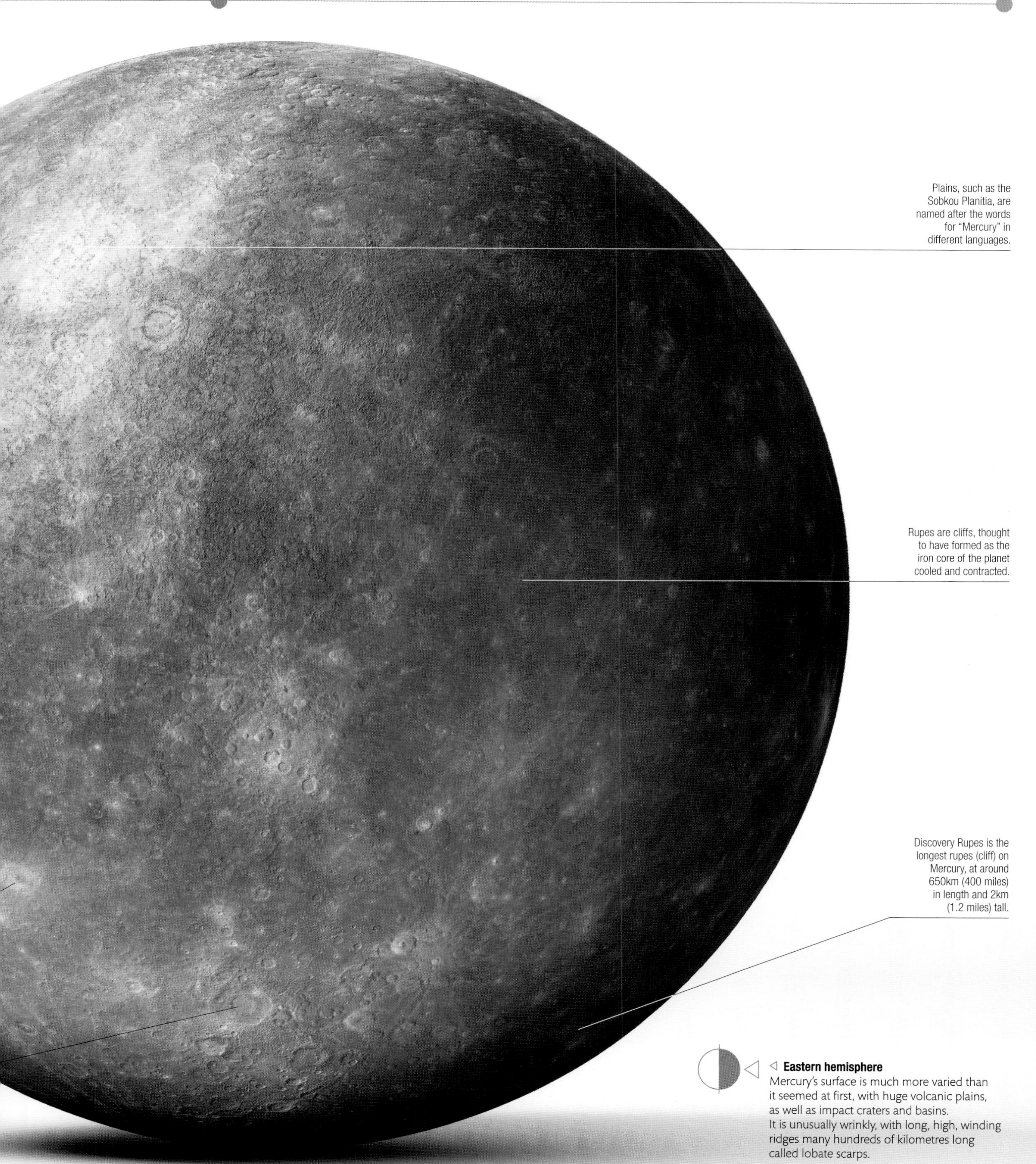
Plains, such as the Sobkou Planitia, are named after the words for "Mercury" in different languages.
Rupes are cliffs, thought to have formed as the iron core of the planet cooled and contracted.
Discovery Rupes is the longest rupes (cliff) on Mercury, at around 650km (400 miles) in length and 2km (1.2 miles) tall.

◁ **Eastern hemisphere**
Mercury's surface is much more varied than it seemed at first, with huge volcanic plains, as well as impact craters and basins.
It is unusually wrinkly, with long, high, winding ridges many hundreds of kilometres long called lobate scarps.

MERCURY STRUCTURE

MERCURY IS ONE OF THE FOUR SOLID, TERRESTRIAL PLANETS MADE OF ROCK AND METAL. IT IS SMALLER THAN SOME MOONS, YET MORE DENSE THAN ANY OTHER PLANET APART FROM EARTH.

For such a small planet to be so dense, Mercury must have a very large iron core. This suggests that it has lost rock from its outer layers. If so, one explanation might be that early in its history Mercury was struck by a planetesimal, one of the many protoplanets that whirled through the Solar System as it formed. The devastating impact caused by this planetesimal – which was probably about one-sixth the size of the planet itself – blasted away much of Mercury's rocky exterior.

Liquid core
The iron core is 3,600km (2,237 miles) wide. Researchers discovered its liquid state by bouncing radio waves off the planet to measu how much it wobbles as it rotates. A solid core would have rigid rotation, but Mercury's wobbl spin indicates liquid sloshing around inside.

In places, Mercury's surface is tinged yellow by sulphur. There is more of this element in Mercury than any other planet.

Mercury's **iron core** takes up 61% of its volume – Earth's takes up only 17%.

▷ **Layer by layer**
Data from MESSENGER and the forthcoming BepiColombo missions may support the theory that Mercury's unusual structure – having a vast core and narrow outer layers – is due to the loss of rock when it was struck by a planetesimal. Another explanation is that rock vaporized in the hot conditions of the early Solar System, before the Sun stabilized. A third idea is that rock was stripped away by the drag of the solar nebula early on.

Mantle
The semi-molten rock of the mantle layer is around 600km (400 miles) thick. Like Earth's mantle, Mercury's consists of silicate rocks and is far less dense than the planet's core. It is a relatively thin layer, accounting for approximately 20 per cent of the planet's radius.

Crust
Mercury's crust is likely to be made of magnesium-rich basalt and other silicate rocks. It is 100–300km (70–190 miles) thick. The surface is stable, with no moving plates, meaning that features such as impact craters remain undisturbed on the planet for billions of years.

▽ **Atmosphere**
Mercury has an atmosphere, but it is very thin, which is why it is called an exosphere. Some astronomers believe Mercury once had a thick atmosphere like Earth, but because the planet is small its gravity could not stop the atmosphere being blown away by the solar wind. The gases that remain include hydrogen, oxygen, helium, water vapour, sodium, and potassium.

MERCURY UP CLOSE

AS BLEAK AND BARE AS EARTH'S MOON, MERCURY IS COVERED BY GREYISH-BROWN DUST AND BEARS THE SCARS OF COUNTLESS METEORITE IMPACTS, FROM TINY POCKMARKS TO VAST, MULTI-RINGED BASINS.

With almost no atmosphere for protection, Mercury is exposed to the battering of even small meteorites. Impact craters of all sizes pit the planet's surface. The largest meteorites have created multi-ring basins such as the Caloris Basin. The heaviest meteorite bombardment came early in the planet's history, punching out most of the largest craters before quietening down some 3.8 billion years ago. Soon afterwards, lava flows spread across the surface to create smooth plains that obliterated some craters. Later, the planet's interior cooled and shrank, breaking the crust into cracks and ridges. Eventually, about 750 million years ago, Mercury's mantle shrank so much that lava ceased to flow out. Since then, the planet's surface has hardly changed, though it continues to be scarred by minor impacts.

The naming of Mercury's surface features follows a system: craters are named after artists, composers, and authors – for example, the Tolstoy and Beethoven basins; valleys (valles) are named after observatories; cliffs (rupes) after ships; ridges (dorsa) after scientists; and plains (planitia) take international names for Mercury.

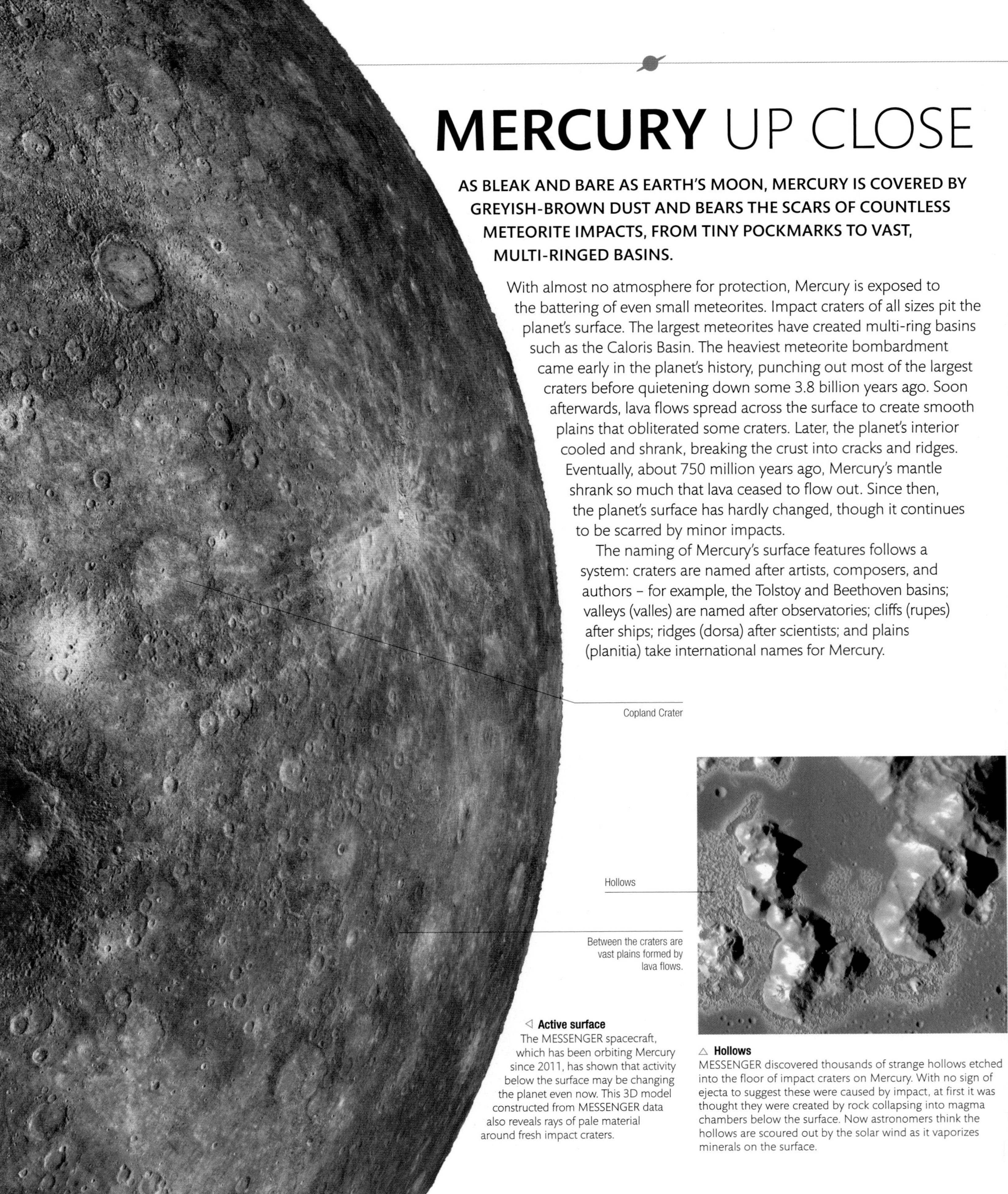

Copland Crater
Hollows
Between the craters are vast plains formed by lava flows.

◁ **Active surface**
The MESSENGER spacecraft, which has been orbiting Mercury since 2011, has shown that activity below the surface may be changing the planet even now. This 3D model constructed from MESSENGER data also reveals rays of pale material around fresh impact craters.

△ **Hollows**
MESSENGER discovered thousands of strange hollows etched into the floor of impact craters on Mercury. With no sign of ejecta to suggest these were caused by impact, at first it was thought they were created by rock collapsing into magma chambers below the surface. Now astronomers think the hollows are scoured out by the solar wind as it vaporizes minerals on the surface.

▷ **Rachmaninoff Crater**
Rachmaninoff Crater is named after the Russian composer Sergei Rachmaninoff (1873–1943). It was photographed by MESSENGER on its third flyby in 2009. The crater has a distinctive double-ring structure; the central ring formed from uplifted material after impact. This false-colour image highlights the range of different materials in Mercury's surface.

A circle of mountains some 130km (80 miles) wide makes up the central ring.

The central plain contains concentric troughs perhaps formed when lava cooled and solidified.

Outer ring (crater rim)

The colour of the central plain differs markedly from the material outside it.

Debris and shock waves from the Caloris impact shot to the opposite side of Mercury, **buckling the crust.**

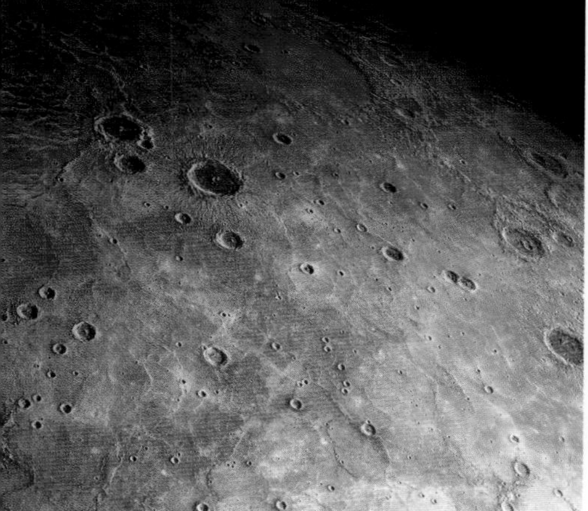

△ **Plains**
Much of Mercury's surface comprises vast, empty plains, or planitiae. Most are ancient, and heavily scarred with craters. Other, gently rolling plains called intercrater plains are pitted with only small craters; these plains probably formed when lava buried older terrain. There are even younger smooth lava plains, like those around Caloris Basin, laid down too recently to show many craters.

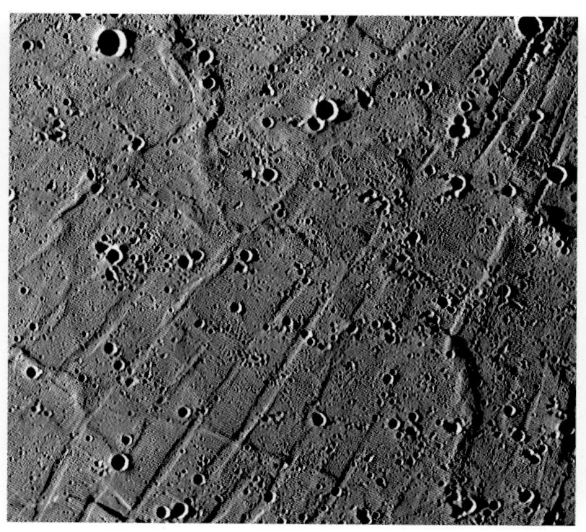

△ **Spider troughs**
One of the most striking discoveries of MESSENGER's first Mercury flyby in 2008 was this extraordinary series of troughs, or fossae. They radiate around the centre of Caloris Basin like the threads of a spider's web, which is why the feature was originally called the Spider. Now it is officially named Pantheon Fossae, after its resemblance to the sunken panels that radiate around the dome of the Pantheon in Rome.

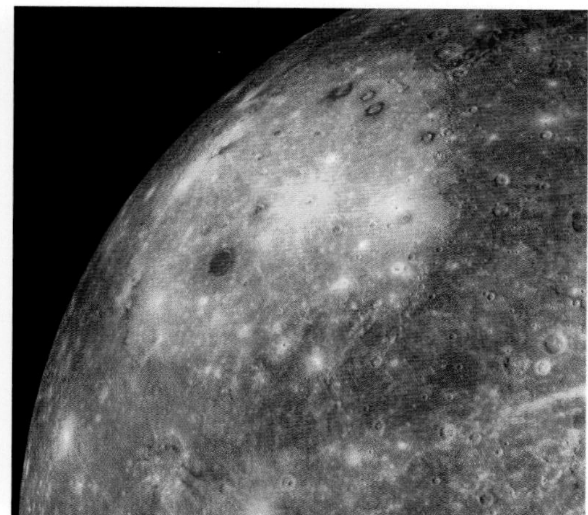

△ **Basins**
The large yellow patch in this false-colour image is Caloris Basin, one of the largest impact craters in the Solar System, some 1,300km (800 miles) across and now partially filled by a lava flow. It probably formed when a huge asteroid crashed into Mercury early in its history, creating a vast basin, sending ejecta 1000km (600 miles) from the crater's rim, and fracturing rocks around it into troughs.

MERCURY MAPPED

NASA's MESSENGER spacecraft, which has been orbiting Mercury since 2011, has built up a global map of the planet. The probe's imaging systems continue to seek details of regions in permanent shadow.

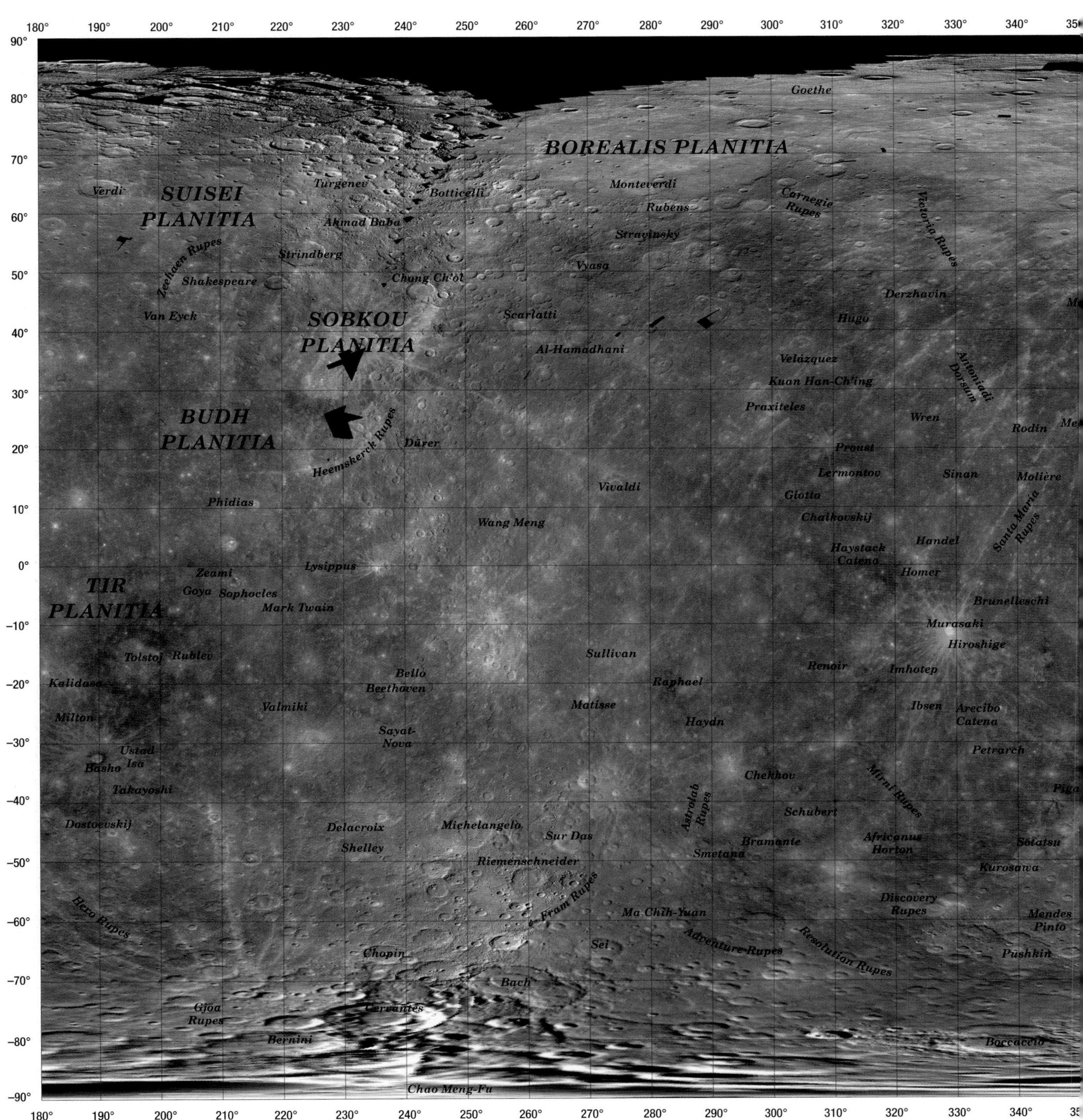
BOREALIS PLANITIA
SUISEI PLANITIA
SOBKOU PLANITIA
BUDH PLANITIA
TIR PLANITIA
Goethe
Verdi
Turgenev
Botticelli
Monteverdi
Rubens
Carnegie Rupes
Victoria Rupes
Ahmad Baba
Stravinsky
Zeehaen Rupes
Strindberg
Vyasa
Shakespeare
Chung Ch'ol
Derzhavin
Van Eyck
Scarlatti
Hugo
Al-Hamadhani
Velázquez
Antoniadi Dorsum
Kuan Han-Ch'ing
Praxiteles
Wren
Rodin
Heemskerck Rupes
Dürer
Proust
Lermontov
Sinan
Molière
Vivaldi
Giotto
Phidias
Wang Meng
Chaikovskij
Santa Maria Rupes
Handel
Haystack Catena
Lysippus
Homer
Zeami
Goya
Sophocles
Mark Twain
Brunelleschi
Murasaki
Hiroshige
Tolstoj
Rublev
Sullivan
Renoir
Imhotep
Bello
Beethoven
Raphael
Kalidasa
Valmiki
Matisse
Ibsen
Arecibo Catena
Milton
Haydn
Sayat-Nova
Ustad Isa
Basho
Petrarch
Chekhov
Mirni Rupes
Takayoshi
Astrolab Rupes
Schubert
Dostoevskij
Delacroix
Michelangelo
Sur Das
Bramante
Africanus Horton
Sōtatsu
Shelley
Smetana
Riemenschneider
Kurosawa
Hero Rupes
Fram Rupes
Discovery Rupes
Ma Chih-Yuan
Mendes Pinto
Adventure Rupes
Resolution Rupes
Sei
Chopin
Pushkin
Bach
Gjöa Rupes
Cervantes
Bernini
Boccaccio
Chao Meng-Fu

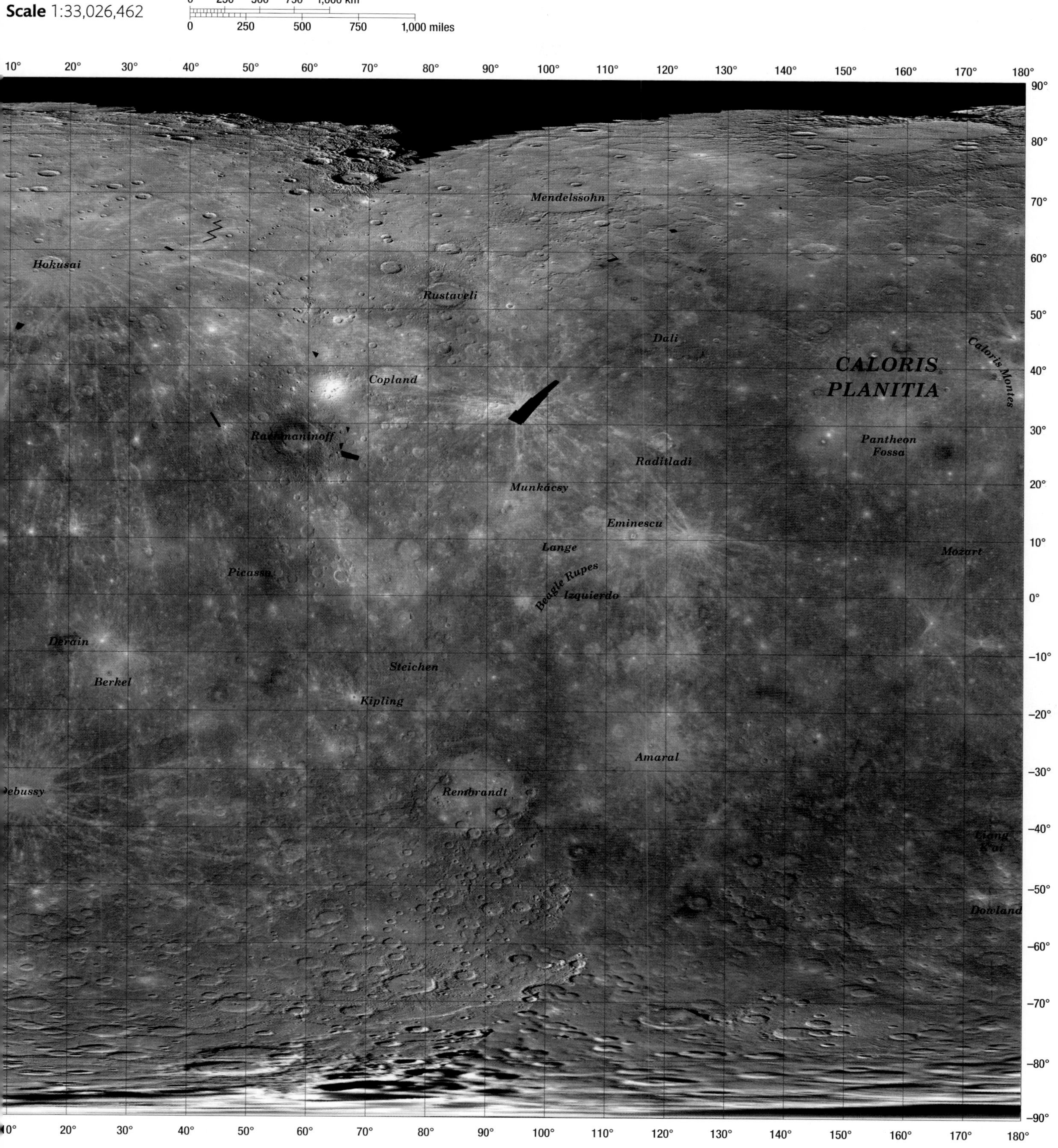
Scale 1:33,026,462
0 250 500 750 1,000 km
0 250 500 750 1,000 miles
Mendelssohn
Hokusai
Rustaveli
Dali
CALORIS PLANITIA
Caloris Montes
Copland
Rachmaninoff
Pantheon Fossa
Raditladi
Munkácsy
Eminescu
Lange
Mozart
Picasso
Beagle Rupes
Izquierdo
Derain
Berkel
Steichen
Kipling
Amaral
Rembrandt
Dowland

DESTINATION CARNEGIE RUPES

AMONG MERCURY'S MOST DISTINCTIVE FEATURES ARE STRANGE CLIFFS THAT WIND FOR MILES ACROSS THE LANDSCAPE, CUTTING THROUGH ANCIENT CRATERS. KNOWN AS RUPES, THESE FORMED WHEN THE YOUNG PLANET'S CRUST SHRANK, CAUSING VAST BLOCKS OF CRUST TO HEAVE UPWARDS.

Carnegie Rupes is located in Mercury's northern hemisphere. Like all the planet's rupes, it is the steep face of a long ridge that slopes gently away on the opposite side. Geologists describe such cliffs as lobate scarps, because of their curved shapes. Rupes are thought to have formed at least 3 billion years ago as the planet contracted, cracking the surface. The shrinkage was slight, but enough to thrust up blocks of crust along the cracks, or faults. Some scientists believe the planet's contraction was the result of cooling. Others think the drag of the Sun's gravity slowed Mercury's rotation, a phenomenon known as tidal despinning, reducing the equatorial bulge. Following an established theme, rupes are named after ships of discovery – in the case of Carnegie, a research vessel that mapped the Earth's magnetic field in the early 20th century.

Artist's impression based on images from MESSENGER spacecraft

Unnamed crater
Impact crater
Carnegie Rupes

LOCATION

Latitude 59°N; **longitude** 53°E

TOPOGRAPHY

This image taken by NASA's MESSENGER spacecraft looks northwest across Carnegie Rupes, as it slices across an unnamed crater about 100km (62 miles) in diameter. The colours indicate elevation, with low areas in blue and high areas in red. The line of the cliff shows a sharp change in elevation – over 2km (1.4 miles) in places.

THE **WINGED MESSENGER**

VISIBLE TO THE NAKED EYE AROUND SUNRISE AND SUNSET, MERCURY WAS WELL KNOWN IN ANCIENT TIMES. IT IS THE FASTEST MOVING OF ALL THE PLANETS AND WAS NAMED AFTER THE WINGED MESSENGER OF ROMAN MYTHOLOGY.

Mercury is so small and distant – and it circles so close to the Sun – that it is difficult to see from Earth. Consequently, very little was known about the planet until comparatively recently. Although Mercury was first observed through a telescope by Italian scientist Galileo Galilei in the early 17th century, it was not until the late 20th century that telescopes with sufficient power to resolve surface details were developed.

The big breakthrough in understanding the Sun's closest neighbour came when spacecraft began to beam back close-ups from the planet. The first was Mariner 10, which made flybys in 1974 and 1975. This was followed, after a gap of more than 30 years, by the MESSENGER spacecraft, which remains in orbit today.

Hermes, Greek messenger god

1000 BCE

Babylon tablets
The earliest known record of the observation of Mercury is on the Mul.Apin tablets – catalogues of celestial bodies from ancient Babylon. The Babylonians call the planet Nabu, after their messenger god.

c.350 BCE

Apollo and Hermes
At first, the ancient Greeks believe that Mercury is two planets: they call it Apollo when it appears in the morning sky, and Hermes when they see it after sunset. In the 4th century BCE, they realize it is actually a single planet and name it Hermes.

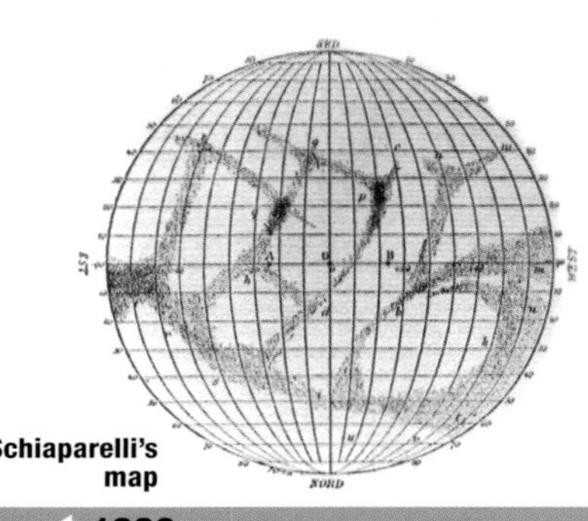

Schiaparelli's map

1800–1808

Clouds on Mercury
German astronomer Johann Schröter claims, wrongly, to have seen features such as clouds and mountains on Mercury. Using Schröter's drawings, the astronomer Friedrich Bessel estimates (wrongly) that Mercury spins at the same speed as Earth and tilts strongly.

1880s

Schiaparelli's map
Italian astronomer Giovanni Schiaparelli observes Mercury and creates the most accurate map yet. He believes, wrongly, that Mercury is locked in its orbit – the same side always faces the Sun, and the planet takes 88 days to orbit the Sun and make one rotation.

1962

Mercury by radar
Soviet scientists led by Vladimir Kotelnikov at Moscow's Institute of Radio-engineering and Electronics become the first to bounce a radar signal off Mercury and receive its echo, enabling them to make the first radar observations of the planet.

Arecibo radio telescope

Mariner 10 mosaic of Mercury

1965

Rotation speed
American astronomers Gordon Pettengill and Rolf Dyce use the radio telescope dish at Arecibo, Puerto Rico, to measure Mercury's spin rate. From radar pulses reflected by the planet's surface, they calculate that Mercury's rotation is not tidally locked, as Schiaparelli had thought, but takes just 59 days – about two-thirds of its orbital period of 88 days. Most of Mercury has now been mapped by the Arecibo dish.

1975

Mariner 10
NASA's Mariner 10 is the first spacecraft to visit Mercury and photograph it up close. In three separate flybys, starting 29 March 1975, Mariner 10 images almost half of the planet's surface, revealing a landscape similar to that of the Moon.

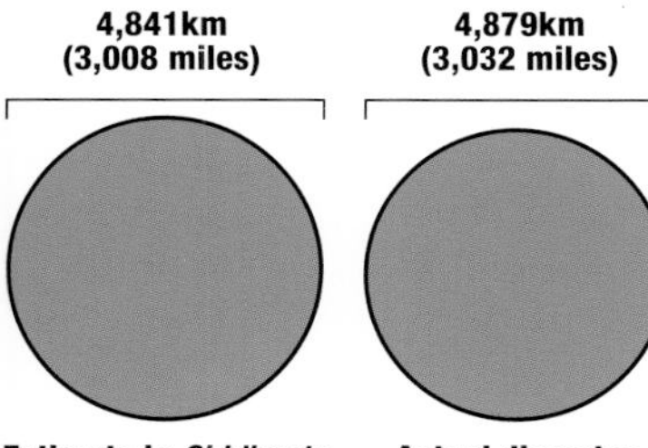
4,841km
(3,008 miles)
4,879km
(3,032 miles)
Estimate in *Siddhanta* Actual diameter

Galileo Galilei

5th century CE

Mercury's diameter

By unknown means and without a telescope, an Indian astronomer estimates Mercury's diameter with 99 per cent accuracy – an astonishing achievement or a lucky guess. The result is recorded in the book *Surya Siddhanta*.

1611

Galileo's observations

Galileo makes the first observations of Mercury through a telescope. He guesses it is a planet, but his telescope is not powerful enough to reveal that Mercury has phases, just like Venus and the Moon, and that these phases depend on how much we see of Mercury's sunlit half.

Transit of Mercury

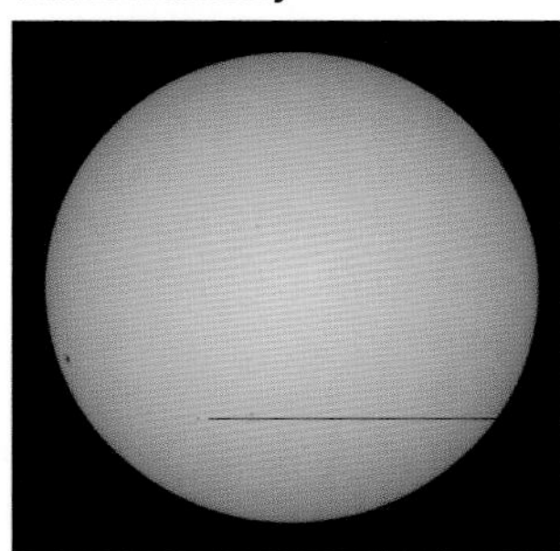
Mercury passes in front of the Sun

Phases of Mercury

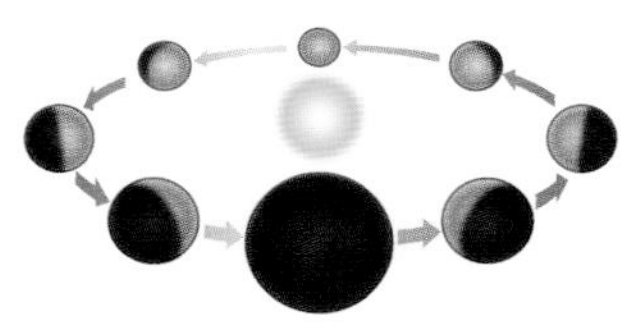

1631

Gassendi observes transit

French astronomer Pierre Gassendi sees Mercury pass in front of the Sun. This is the first time the transit of a planet has been observed through a telescope. It enables Gassendi to make the first reliable measurement of a planet's diameter.

1639

Phases

Italian astronomer Giovanni Zupi observes through a powerful telescope that Mercury has phases similar to those of Earth's Moon. This proves that Mercury orbits the Sun, revealing varying amounts of its surface as it catches the Sun at different angles.

1737

Occultation by Venus

Occultations – when one planet passes in front of another, as seen from Earth – are rare events. English astronomer John Bevis sees the occultation of Mercury by Venus on 28 May – the only time in history that this has been witnessed.

MESSENGER launch

MESSENGER image of Mercury

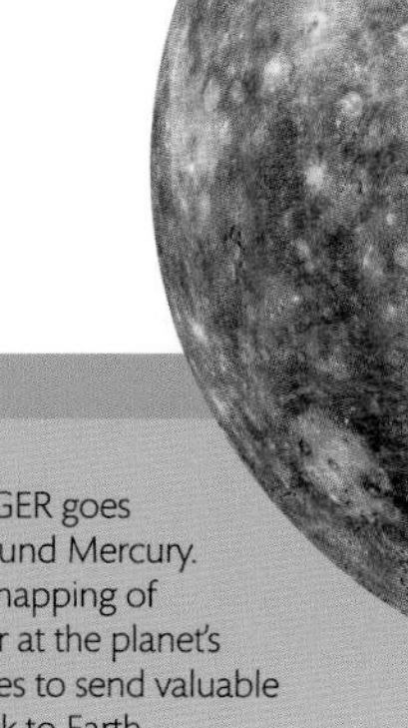

2002

nakas Basin

ronomers at the Skinakas Astrophysical servatory in Crete believe that they have nd a giant crater missed by Mariner 10. sequently, the MESSENGER spacecraft ws that the crater, dubbed the Skinakas in, is in fact an illusion.

2008

MESSENGER flyby

Launched on 3 August 2004, NASA's MESSENGER makes the first of its three flybys of Mercury in January 2008. During the flybys, MESSENGER maps most of the planet's surface in colour and studies the atmosphere and magnetosphere.

2011

MESSENGER in orbit

On 18 March, MESSENGER goes into long-term orbit around Mercury. The craft completes its mapping of Mercury, discovers water at the planet's north pole, and continues to send valuable data about Mercury back to Earth.

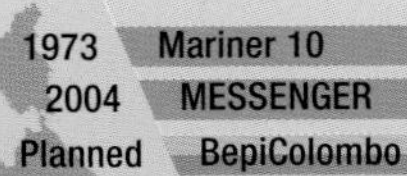

LAUNCH
EARTH ORBIT
JOURNEY TO MERCURY
1973 Mariner 10
2004 MESSENGER
Planned BepiColombo

MISSIONS TO **MERCURY**

MERCURY IS THE LEAST EXPLORED OF THE ROCKY PLANETS, VISITED BY JUST TWO MISSIONS TO DATE: MARINER 10 IN THE MID-1970S AND THE MORE RECENT MESSENGER SPACECRAFT, WHICH STUDIED MERCURY FROM ORBIT.

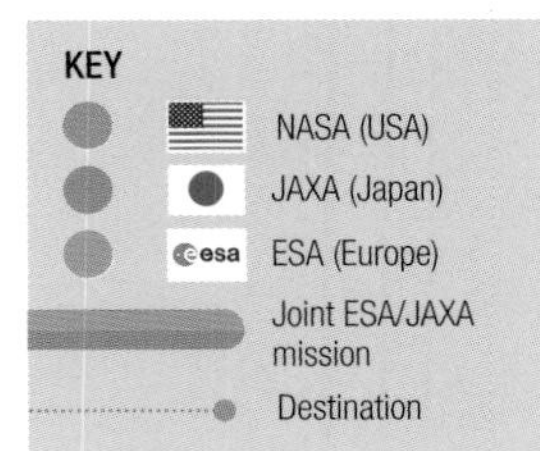

KEY
NASA (USA)
JAXA (Japan)
esa
ESA (Europe)
Joint ESA/JAXA mission
Destination

One reason for the lack of missions to Mercury is the sheer technical difficulty. Spacecraft have to travel extremely fast to get to Mercury, and when they reach the planet they must suddenly slow down enough to get into orbit just as the Sun's gravity is trying to accelerate them even more. In addition, the Sun's pull is so strong near Mercury that orbits around the planet are unstable, and proximity to the Sun makes it hard for spacecraft to maintain a stable temperature. Nonetheless, Mariner and MESSENGER have reached the planet successfully and studied its features and properties. A third major mission, the joint European-Japanese BepiColombo, may reveal more about this intriguing planet.

▽ **Mariner 10**
Mariner 10's first Mercury flyby took place on 29 March 1974. Because getting a craft into orbit around the planet was so difficult, Mariner 10 was designed to orbit the Sun instead, enabling it to fly past Mercury three times. These flybys revealed a highly cratered surface and, to the great surprise of astronomers, a magnetic field around the planet.

Mariner 10 image of Mercury's cratered surface

▷ **MESSENGER**
MESSENGER (Mercury surface, space environment, geochemistry, and ranging) left Earth in 2004 but took over six years to achieve orbit around Mercury – the first spacecraft ever to do so. On 29 March 2011, it sent the first photo from Mercury orbit. Since then, MESSENGER's cameras and other instruments have sent back a flood of data about the planet. Its investigations have discovered water ice and organic compounds in shadowed craters near Mercury's north pole.

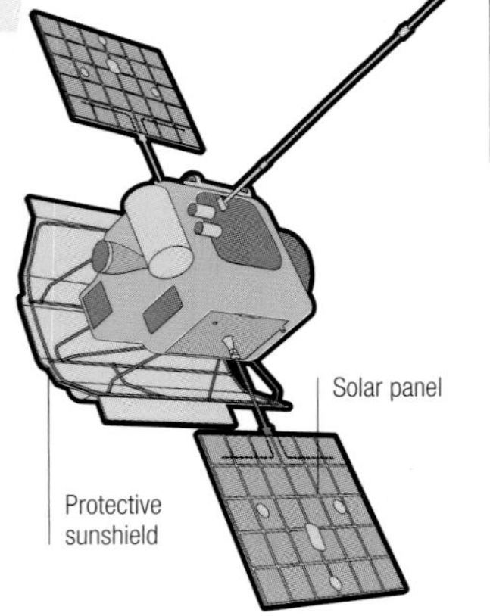

Magnetometer for studying Mercury's magnetic field
Solar panel
Protective sunshield

▽ **MESSENGER's journey**
MESSENGER had to circle the Sun seven times to get into its orbit around Mercury. It passed Earth a year after launch and then Venus twice, using both planets' gravity to slingshot itself onwards. It then made three flybys of Mercury to slow down before entering orbit. Its orbit is very eccentric: its lowest point is just 200km (124 miles) above the surface, while the highest is at an altitude of over 15,000km (9,300 miles).

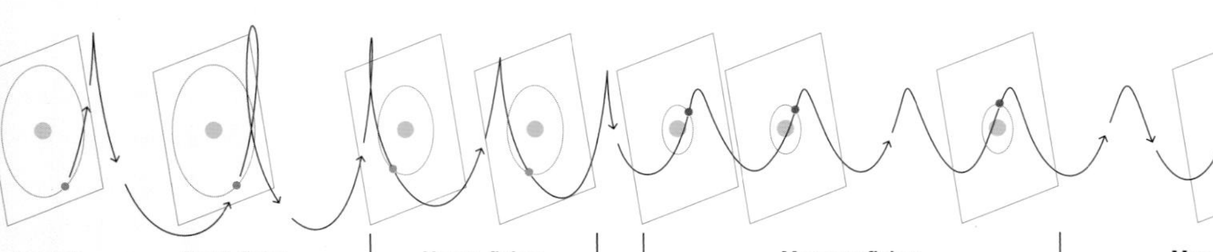

Launch (August 2004)
Earth flyby (2005)
Venus flybys (2006, 2007)
Mercury flybys (2008, 2008, 2009)
Mercury orbit (March 2011)

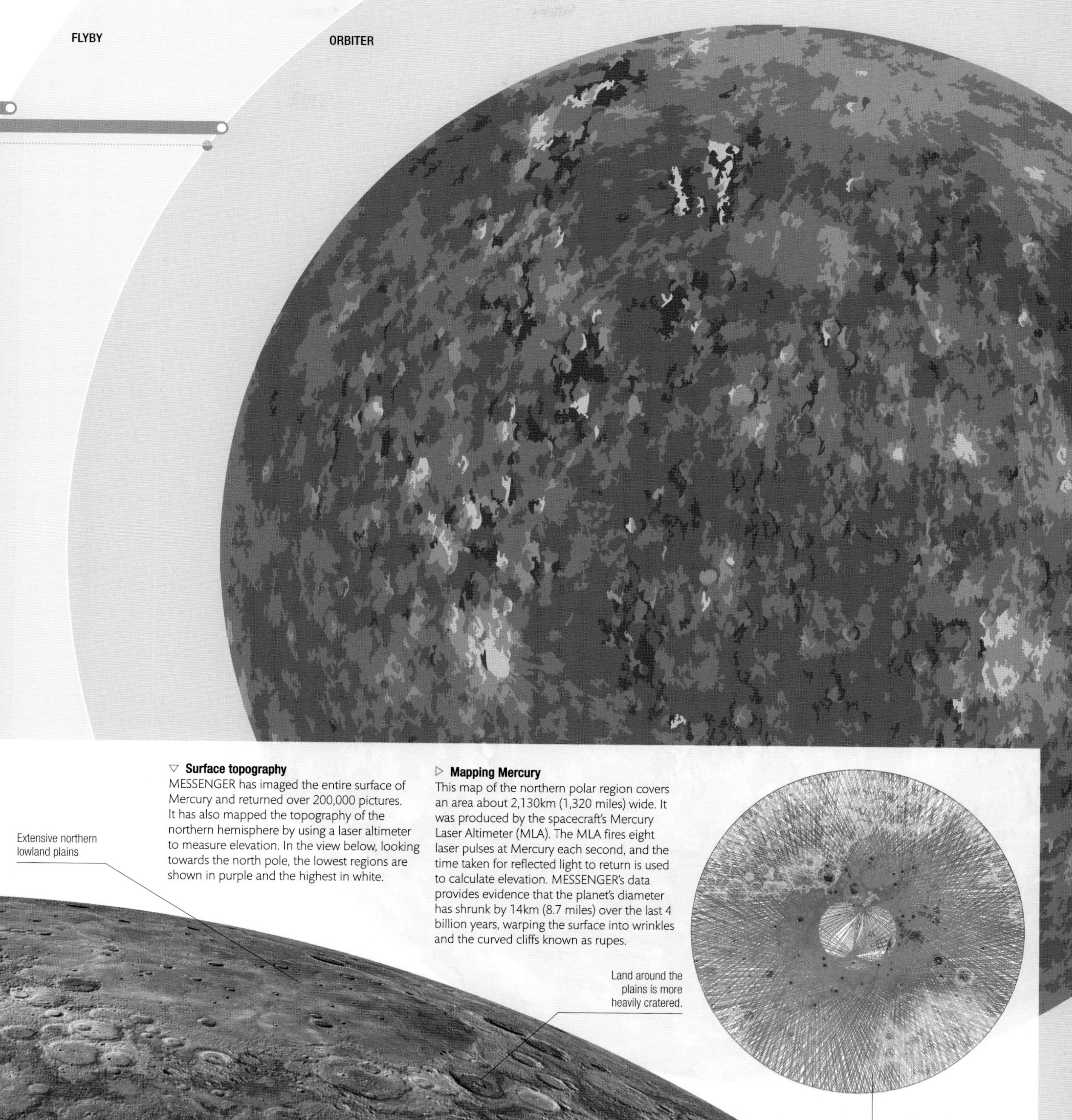
FLYBY
ORBITER
Extensive northern lowland plains
Land around the plains is more heavily cratered.
Each line represents one orbit; white regions are gaps.

▽ Surface topography
MESSENGER has imaged the entire surface of Mercury and returned over 200,000 pictures. It has also mapped the topography of the northern hemisphere by using a laser altimeter to measure elevation. In the view below, looking towards the north pole, the lowest regions are shown in purple and the highest in white.

▷ Mapping Mercury
This map of the northern polar region covers an area about 2,130km (1,320 miles) wide. It was produced by the spacecraft's Mercury Laser Altimeter (MLA). The MLA fires eight laser pulses at Mercury each second, and the time taken for reflected light to return is used to calculate elevation. MESSENGER's data provides evidence that the planet's diameter has shrunk by 14km (8.7 miles) over the last 4 billion years, warping the surface into wrinkles and the curved cliffs known as rupes.

VENUS

VENUS IS THE SECOND PLANET FROM THE SUN AND OUR NEAREST NEIGHBOUR. IT IS A ROCKY WORLD, SIMILAR IN SIZE TO EARTH, BUT THE TWO PLANETS COULD HARDLY BE MORE DIFFERENT IN CHARACTER.

From Earth, Venus is visible at dusk or dawn, just above the horizon, shining brighter than anything in the sky but the Sun and Moon. Through a telescope, the planet can be seen passing through phases, like our Moon's, from crescent to nearly full as it orbits the Sun, revealing different amounts of its sunlit side. Seen from space, Venus is swathed in pale yellow clouds that hide its surface, but radars and probes carried by spacecraft have looked beneath to discover a hellish world.

Venusian clouds are flooded with droplets of sulphuric acid, and the planet's thick atmosphere weighs down so heavily that the pressure on the surface is 90 times that on Earth. The surface comprises either flat, barren rock, or volcanoes both dormant and possibly active. Beneath a deep orange sky, a runaway greenhouse effect traps the Sun's heat, sending temperatures soaring to a blistering 470°C (880°F) and making Venus the hottest planet in the Solar System.

Venus rotates in the **opposite direction** to most of the planets. It turns so **slowly** on its axis that its **day lasts longer** than its year.

VENUS DATA

Average diameter	12,104km (7,520 miles)
Mass (Earth = 1)	0.82
Gravity at equator (Earth = 1)	0.9
Mean distance from Sun (Earth = 1)	0.72
Axial tilt	2.6°
Rotation period (day)	243 Earth days
Orbital period (year)	224.7 Earth days
Average surface temperature	470°C (880°F)
Moons	0

Northern hemisphere The north pole is a scorched landscape of bare rock and rubble. Nearby are the rugged ridges of Atalanta Planitia and Ishtar Terra, Venus's highest mountain range. Blank areas in this 3D model represent gaps in radar mapping data from the Magellan spacecraft.

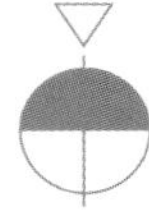

Uplands Besides the three main highland regions, or terrae, Venus has 20 or so smaller upland areas called regio. These include Alpha Regio, the bright patch seen bottom centre, which is highly deformed and probably of ancient origin.

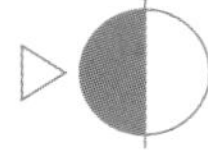

Southern hemisphere Venus's southern regions are as hot and bare as the north. Lada Terra, the second biggest of Venus's three raised land masses, or terrae, is near the south pole. It has more volcanic upwellings, or coronae, than the other terrae.

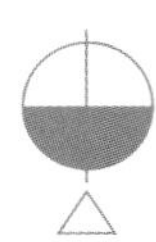

The 92km (57 mile) wide double-ring crater Greenaway has a rough, radar-bright base, suggesting volcanic activity after the impact that formed it.

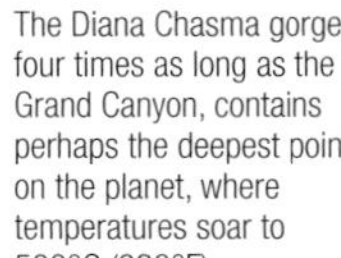

The Diana Chasma gorge, four times as long as the Grand Canyon, contains perhaps the deepest point on the planet, where temperatures soar to 500°C (930°F).

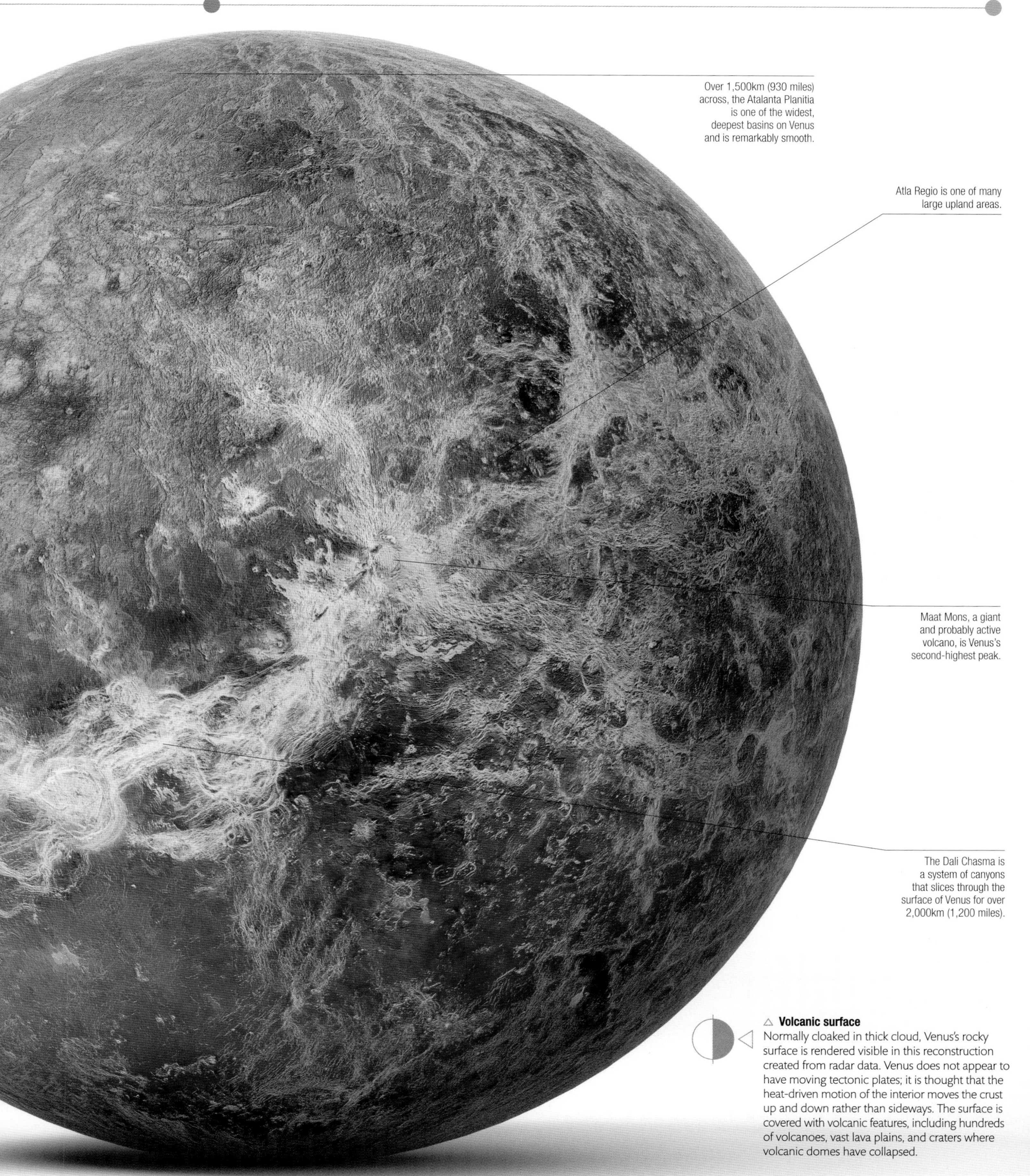
Over 1,500km (930 miles) across, the Atalanta Planitia is one of the widest, deepest basins on Venus and is remarkably smooth.
Atla Regio is one of many large upland areas.
Maat Mons, a giant and probably active volcano, is Venus's second-highest peak.
The Dali Chasma is a system of canyons that slices through the surface of Venus for over 2,000km (1,200 miles).

△ **Volcanic surface**
Normally cloaked in thick cloud, Venus's rocky surface is rendered visible in this reconstruction created from radar data. Venus does not appear to have moving tectonic plates; it is thought that the heat-driven motion of the interior moves the crust up and down rather than sideways. The surface is covered with volcanic features, including hundreds of volcanoes, vast lava plains, and craters where volcanic domes have collapsed.

VENUS STRUCTURE

ALTHOUGH FORMED FROM THE SAME SOLAR DEBRIS AS EARTH, VENUS IS UNDENIABLY DIFFERENT FROM OUR PLANET ON THE OUTSIDE. HOWEVER, SCIENTISTS BELIEVE THAT THE INTERIORS OF THE TWO WORLDS MAY BE SIMILAR.

Almost equal in size and density to Earth, Venus probably has much the same internal structure and chemistry. At the heart of the planet there is thought to be a metal core with a solid centre and a molten outer layer. Surrounding this is a deep mantle of hot rock and a thin, brittle crust that shows abundant evidence of volcanic activity.

Although Venus has a metal core like Earth's, it has no detectable magnetic field. This may be because it rotates too slowly – taking eight months to turn once – to produce the circulations within the outer core that would generate a dynamo effect.

Venus has the thickest, densest atmosphere of all the rocky planets. Its air is 96.5 per cent carbon dioxide and contains small amounts of other chemicals, including sulphuric acid; a thick blanket of sulphuric acid cloud covers the entire planet.

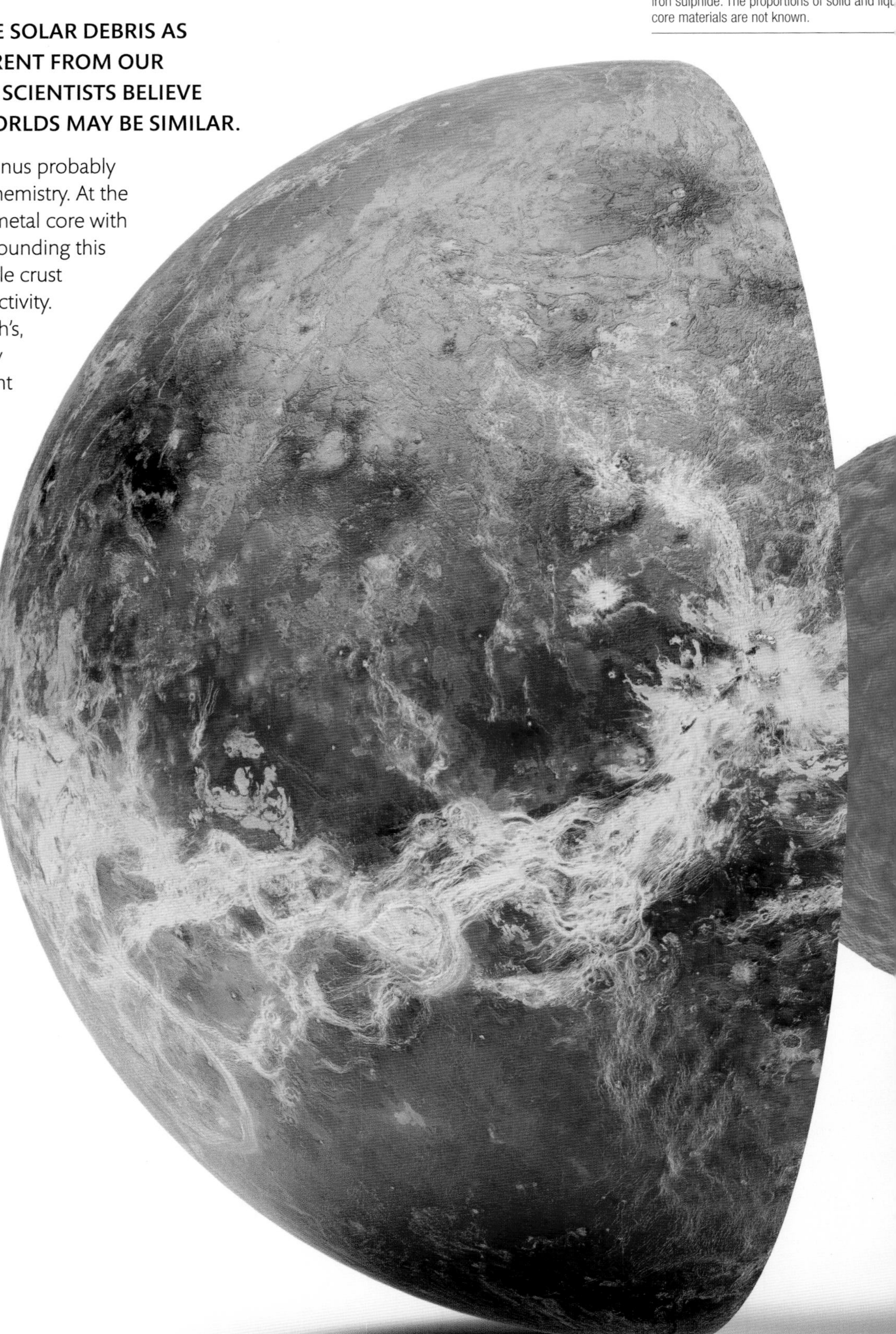

Core
The centre of Venus is a core of mostly solid iron with perhaps a trace of sulphur. There is probably also a semi-liquid outer core of molte iron sulphide. The proportions of solid and liqu core materials are not known.

▷ **Venus on the inside**
While Venus's core is likely to be mostly iron and nickel – the same as Earth's – its slightly lower density suggests there may be a lighter element, such as sulphur, in there too. Again, like Earth, Venus has a mantle of rock that is made fluid enough by interior heat to creep slowly up and down in convection currents. These currents push molten rock through the crust to create volcanoes on the surface.

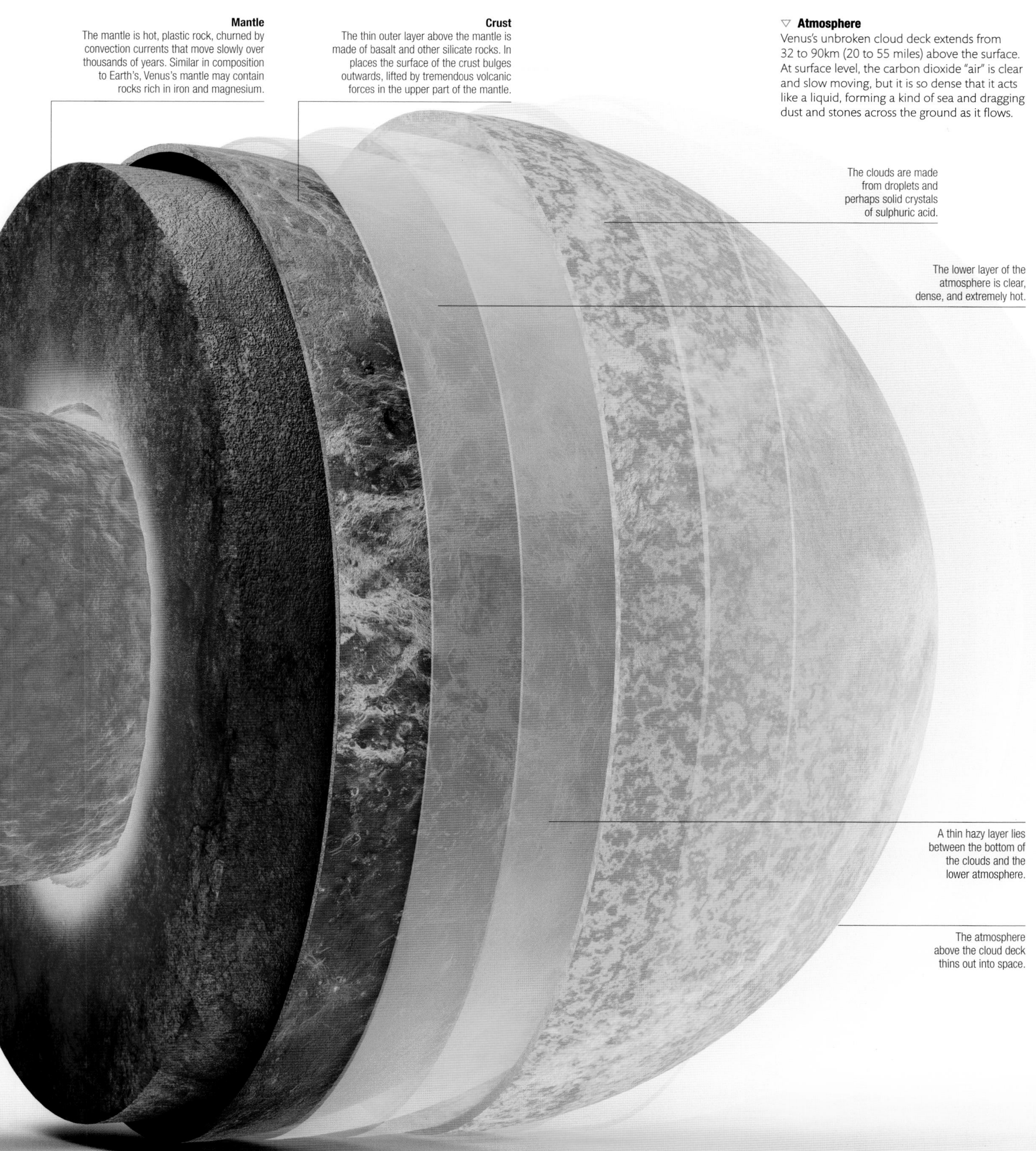

Mantle
The mantle is hot, plastic rock, churned by convection currents that move slowly over thousands of years. Similar in composition to Earth's, Venus's mantle may contain rocks rich in iron and magnesium.
Crust
The thin outer layer above the mantle is made of basalt and other silicate rocks. In places the surface of the crust bulges outwards, lifted by tremendous volcanic forces in the upper part of the mantle.
The clouds are made from droplets and perhaps solid crystals of sulphuric acid.
The lower layer of the atmosphere is clear, dense, and extremely hot.
A thin hazy layer lies between the bottom of the clouds and the lower atmosphere.
The atmosphere above the cloud deck thins out into space.

▽ **Atmosphere**
Venus's unbroken cloud deck extends from 32 to 90km (20 to 55 miles) above the surface. At surface level, the carbon dioxide "air" is clear and slow moving, but it is so dense that it acts like a liquid, forming a kind of sea and dragging dust and stones across the ground as it flows.

VENUS UP CLOSE

THE SURFACE OF THIS INHOSPITABLE WORLD IS ALMOST ENTIRELY VOLCANIC. MORE THAN 1,600 VOLCANOES HAVE BEEN IDENTIFIED ON VENUS, A GREATER NUMBER THAN ON ANY OTHER PLANET IN THE SOLAR SYSTEM.

The first detailed maps of Venus were made in the early 1990s, when the Magellan spacecraft used radar to penetrate the thick cloud hiding the planet. What Magellan's images revealed was a world covered in volcanoes.

The Venusian landscape is characterized by vast plains covered by lava flows, and mountain or highland regions deformed by geological activity. No ongoing eruptions have yet been confirmed, but there are many signs of recent volcanic activity, including ash flows, impact craters partially covered by lava flows, and fluctuating levels of sulphur dioxide in the atmosphere that could be caused by eruptions.

The surface of the planet is young. It is thought that Venus was entirely resurfaced by a cataclysmic volcanic event that created a single gigantic tectonic plate that now wraps around the entire planet – very different from Earth's surface, which is broken into nearly 50 plates. From the estimated rate of asteroid strikes on the planet and slow weathering of the craters, it is thought that this happened some 300–500 million years ago.

Weather on Venus

Venus is cloaked in clouds of sulphuric acid that block out 80 per cent of all sunlight. The atmosphere glides rapidly around the planet on winds of up to 360kph (220mph) – cloud systems can sail completely around the planet in under four days. Venus's clouds rain sulphuric acid, but the lower atmosphere is so hot that the raindrops evaporate before reaching the ground. The heavy cloud layer in Venus's atmosphere appears to shield it from most meteorite bombardments.

▽ **The greenhouse effect**
Most sunlight is reflected back into space from the tops of Venus's thick clouds. However, some penetrates the clouds to reach the surface, and is then reemitted as heat (infrared radiation). This heat cannot escape back into space, and is trapped by carbon dioxide in the atmosphere. Carbon dioxide and other gases give Earth a similar "greenhouse effect", but on Venus the huge quantities of carbon dioxide in the air mean that this effect is extreme – so much heat is trapped that the planet's surface is hot enough to melt lead.

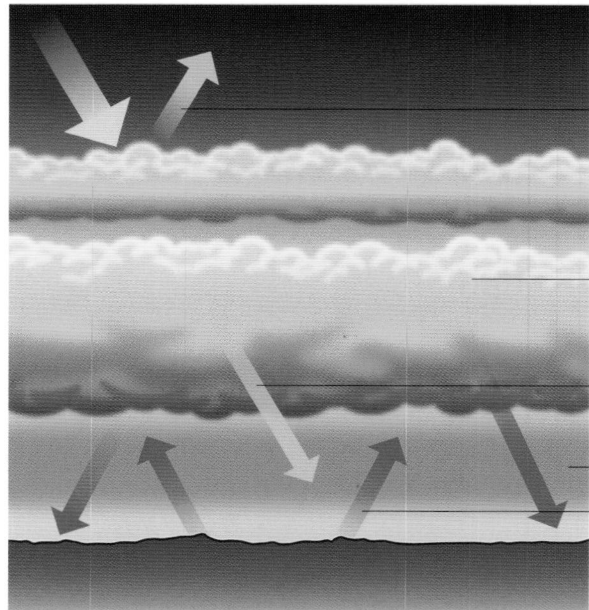
Roughly 80 per cent o
sunlight is reflected of
the cloud deck
Thick layers of gas
and cloud preven
heat from escaping
About 20 per cen
of sunlight reaches
Venus's surface
Carbon dioxide in the
atmosphere holds in heat
Infrared radiation from
the Sun-warmed ground
is absorbed by carbon
dioxide and canno
escape into space

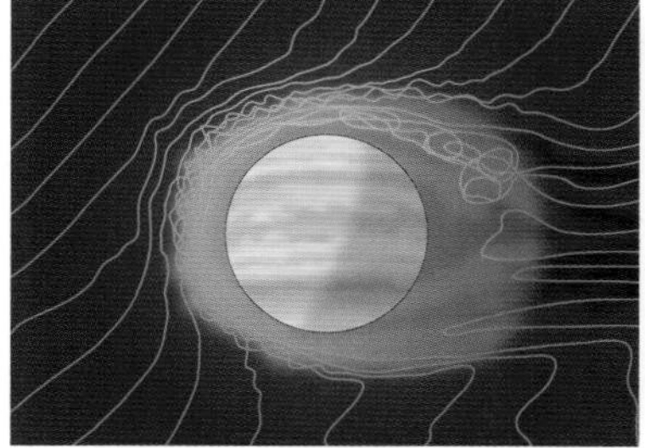
Stable ionosphere

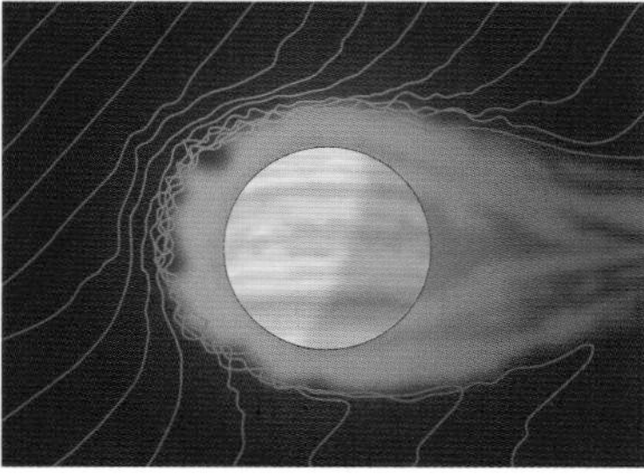
Drifting ionosphere

◁ **The ionosphere**
Like Earth, Venus is enveloped in a cloud of charged particles (ions) called the ionosphere. While Earth's ionosphere is shaped and stabilized by its magnetic field, Venus has almost no magnetic field and its ionosphere is shaped instead by the solar wind – a stream of charged particles flowing from the Sun. When a lull in the solar wind occurs, Venus's ionosphere balloons outward on the downwind side, forming a teardrop shape like the tail of a comet.

Artemis Corona is Venus's largest corona, measuring 2,600km (1,600 miles) in diameter.
Dali Chasma is a system of deep troughs.
Pancake dome – formed when thick lava erupts very slowly.
Shield volcanoes are built from a succession of eruptions of runny lava.
Arachnoid volcanoes look like a series of oval shapes, surrounded by a complex network of fractures.

Venusian volcanoes

△ **Coronae**
Venus's surface features enormous, crown-shaped depressions called coronae. They are thought to be the result of hot magma in the mantle moving upwards. This pushes the surface up, only for it to then collapse when the magma cools.

Venusian volcanoes

Venus does not have steep-sided, explosive volcanoes like typical volcanoes on Earth. Instead, most are shield volcanoes (shallow, gently sloping structures made from multiple layers of lava flows). On the lowland plains are types of volcano called pancake domes, formed by very thick lava, and tick volcanoes, with a central body and radiating leg-like valleys. Other volcanic features include circular depressions called coronae and spider-like arachnoids.

▽ **Volcanic hot spots**
Unlike Earth, Venus's surface is not broken into tectonic plates that create volcanoes as they move. Instead, Venusian volcanoes form above hot spots where plumes of hot magma well up from the interior. The result is runny lava that forms volcanoes of various sizes and shapes.

▽ **Maat Mons**
The second-highest mountain and the highest volcano on Venus, Maat Mons – named after the Egyptian goddess of truth and justice – rises nearly 5km (3 miles) above the surrounding plains. It is a huge shield volcano with a caldera (crater) about 30km (20 miles) across at the summit, and may be active.

△ **Mead Crater**
Most features on Venus are named after historical or mythological women. Mead Crater, for example, is named after cultural anthropologist Margaret Mead (1901–78). At over 280km (174 miles) wide, it is the largest impact crater on Venus. It has two distinct, concentric rings. The bright inner ring is a cliff formed by the initial impact. The darker outer ring is crossed by streaks of ejecta and probably formed when the whole structure later collapsed.

VENUS MAPPED

While most of Venus's surface comprises undulating plains, there are two significant highland areas: Ishtar Terra, where the planet's highest mountains are to be found; and Aphrodite Terra near the equator.

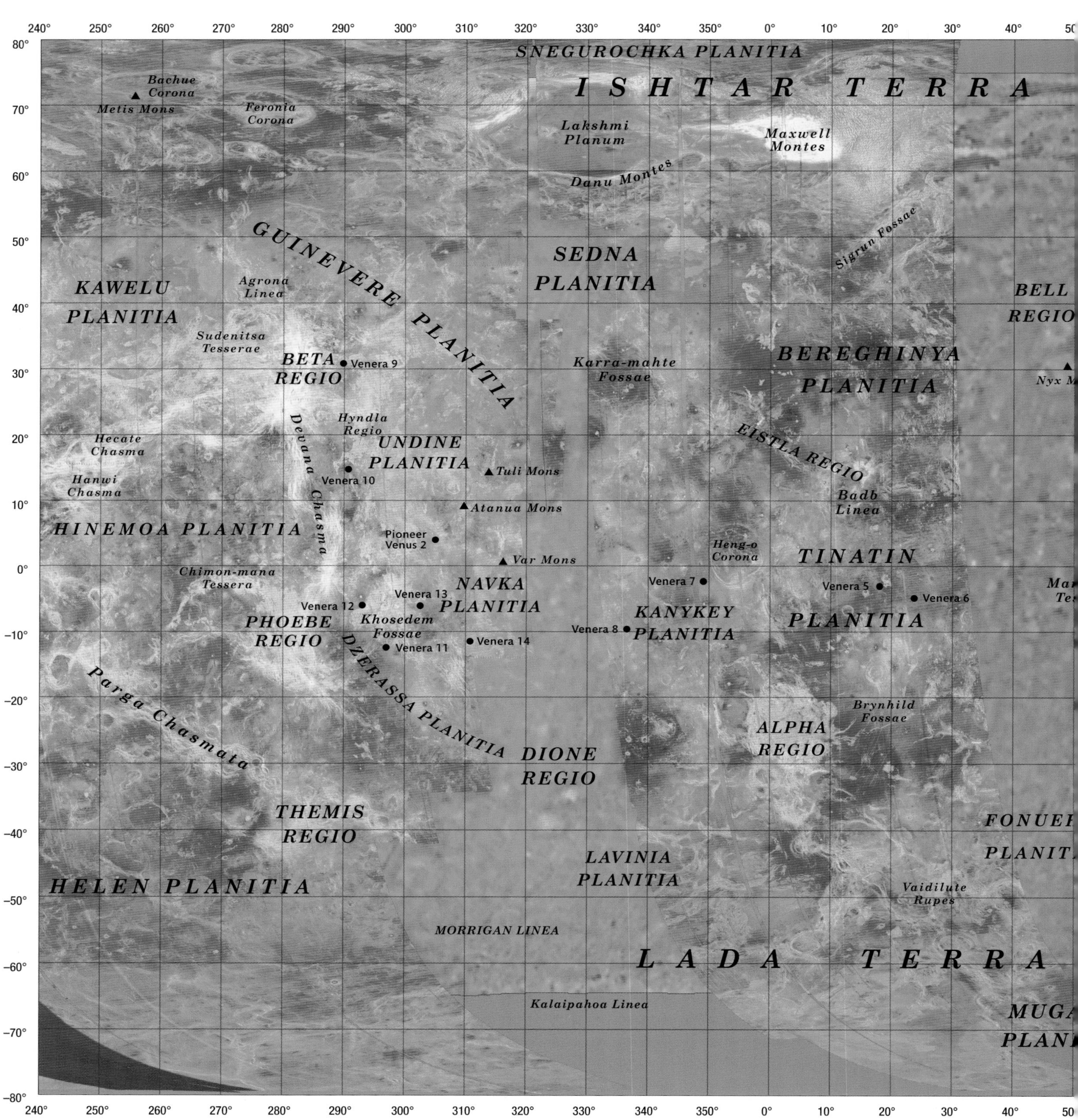

SNEGUROCHKA PLANITIA
ISHTAR TERRA
Bachue Corona
Metis Mons
Feronia Corona
Lakshmi Planum
Maxwell Montes
Danu Montes
Sigrun Fossae
GUINEVERE PLANITIA
SEDNA PLANITIA
KAWELU PLANITIA
Agrona Linea
BELL REGIO
Sudenitsa Tesserae
BETA REGIO
Venera 9
Karra-mahte Fossae
BEREGHINYA PLANITIA
Nyx M
Devana Chasma
Hyndla Regio
UNDINE PLANITIA
Hecate Chasma
EISTLA REGIO
Tuli Mons
Venera 10
Hanwi Chasma
Badb Linea
Atanua Mons
HINEMOA PLANITIA
Pioneer Venus 2
Heng-o Corona
TINATIN PLANITIA
Var Mons
Chimon-mana Tessera
Venera 7
Venera 5
NAVKA PLANITIA
Venera 13
Venera 6
Venera 12
KANYKEY PLANITIA
Khosedem Fossae
PHOEBE REGIO
Venera 8
Venera 11
Venera 14
DZERASSA PLANITIA
Parga Chasmata
Brynhild Fossae
ALPHA REGIO
DIONE REGIO
THEMIS REGIO
FONUEI PLANIT
LAVINIA PLANITIA
HELEN PLANITIA
Vaidilute Rupes
MORRIGAN LINEA
LADA TERRA
Kalaipahoa Linea
MUGA PLAN
240° 250° 260° 270° 280° 290° 300° 310° 320° 330° 340° 350° 0° 10° 20° 30° 40° 50
80° 70° 60° 50° 40° 30° 20° 10° 0° -10° -20° -30° -40° -50° -60° -70° -80°

Scale 1:81,956,988

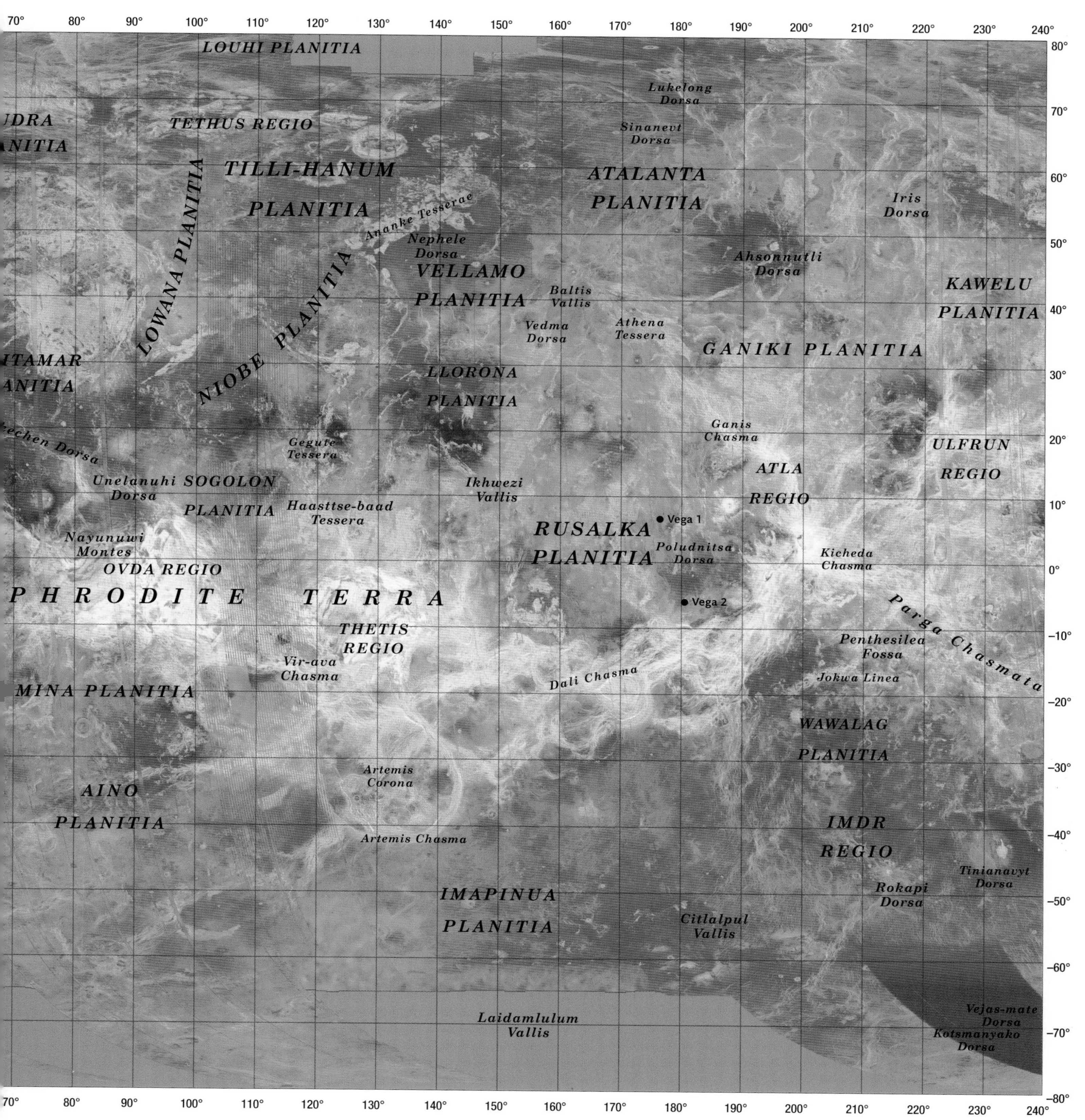
0 500 1000 1500 2000 Km
0 500 1000 1500 2000 Miles
LOUHI PLANITIA
Lukelong Dorsa
JDRA
NITIA
TETHUS REGIO
Sinanevt Dorsa
TILLI-HANUM PLANITIA
LOWANA PLANITIA
ATALANTA PLANITIA
Iris Dorsa
Ananke Tesserae
Nephele Dorsa
Ahsonnutli Dorsa
NIOBE PLANITIA
VELLAMO PLANITIA
Baltis Vallis
KAWELU PLANITIA
Vedma Dorsa
Athena Tessera
GANIKI PLANITIA
ITAMAR
ANITIA
LLORONA PLANITIA
Ganis Chasma
Gegute Tessera
ULFRUN REGIO
Unelanuhi Dorsa
SOGOLON PLANITIA
Ikhwezi Vallis
ATLA REGIO
Haasttse-baad Tessera
Vega 1
Nayunuwi Montes
RUSALKA PLANITIA
Poludnitsa Dorsa
Kicheda Chasma
OVDA REGIO
PHRODITE TERRA
Vega 2
Parga Chasmata
THETIS REGIO
Penthesilea Fossa
Vir-ava Chasma
Dali Chasma
Jokwa Linea
MINA PLANITIA
WAWALAG PLANITIA
Artemis Corona
AINO PLANITIA
IMDR REGIO
Artemis Chasma
Tinianavyt Dorsa
IMAPINUA PLANITIA
Rokapi Dorsa
Citlalpul Vallis
Laidamlulum Vallis
Vejas-mate Dorsa
Kotsmanyako Dorsa
70° 80° 90° 100° 110° 120° 130° 140° 150° 160° 170° 180° 190° 200° 210° 220° 230° 240°
80° 70° 60° 50° 40° 30° 20° 10° 0° –10° –20° –30° –40° –50° –60° –70° –80°

DESTINATION **MAXWELL MONTES**

THE HIGHEST MOUNTAIN RANGE ON VENUS, MAXWELL MONTES RISES TO A PEAK ELEVATION 11KM (7 MILES) ABOVE THE PLANET'S MEAN RADIUS. ALTHOUGH THE TEMPERATURE HERE IS LOWER THAN IN THE LOWLANDS, AND REFLECTIVE MINERALS GIVE THE ILLUSION OF SNOW-CAPPED PEAKS, THE GROUND IS HOT ENOUGH TO MELT LEAD.

The sharp ridges of Maxwell Montes rise above the vast Lakshmi Planum, the volcanic plain that forms the western edge of Ishtar Terra, a continent-sized plateau near Venus's north pole. Just how the mountains formed is uncertain. Compression may have produced folding and faulting in the same process that created large mountains on Earth. Another theory suggests that volcanic action above a hot spot of molten magma in the planet's interior uplifted the range. At certain elevations, radar instruments have detected bright surfaces on Maxwell, shining not with snow but frosted metal. In Venus's fierce heat, minerals vaporize, forming a mist that condenses and freezes, and may even fall as metal snowflakes.

Artist's impression based on Magellan radar data

LOCATION

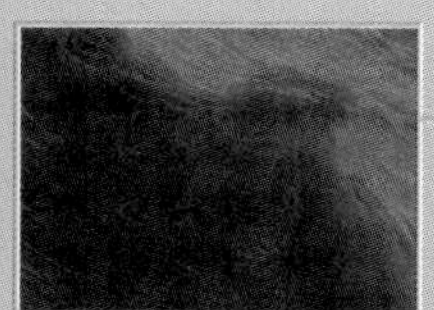

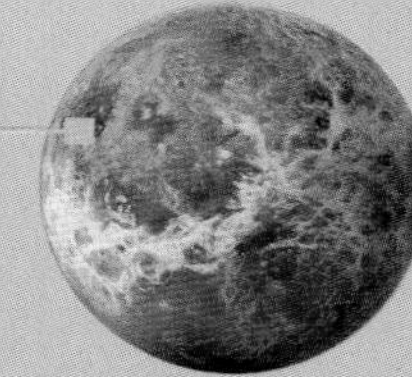

Latitude 65°N; **longitude** 3°E

LAND PROFILE

Maxwell Montes is the highest volcanic range on Venus. It is slightly taller than Mauna Kea in Hawaii, the tallest volcano on Earth, but is dwarfed by Mars's Olympus Mons.

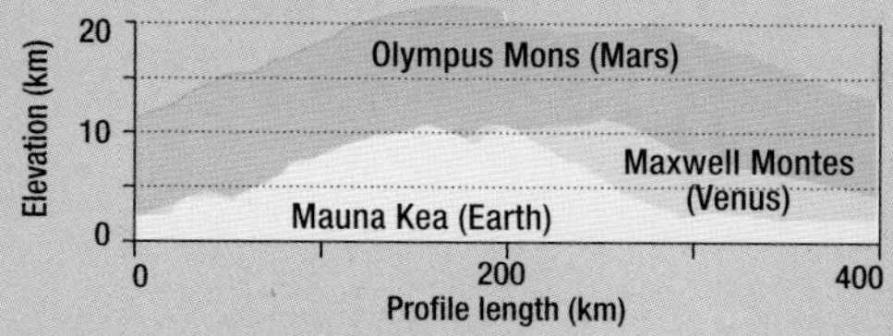
20
10
0
Elevation (km)
Olympus Mons (Mars)
Maxwell Montes (Venus)
Mauna Kea (Earth)
0
200
400
Profile length (km)

797 **KM (495 MILES) – THE LENGTH OF THE MAXWELL MONTES RANGE.**

MINERAL SNOW

The shining metal snow on Maxwell's peaks comprises tiny crystals of minerals, including lead sulphide (galena) and bismuth sulphide (bismuthinite). The rock samples shown below are from Earth.

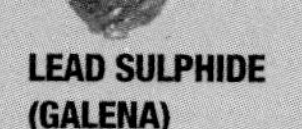

LEAD SULPHIDE (GALENA)

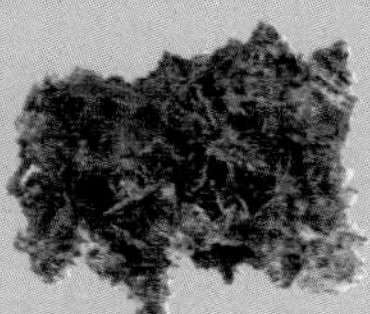

BISMUTH SULPHIDE (BISMUTHINITE)

THE **PLANET OF LOVE**

NAMED BY THE ROMANS AFTER THEIR GODDESS OF LOVE, VENUS HAS A BRIGHT, JEWEL-LIKE APPEARANCE THAT HAS MADE IT AN OBJECT OF CURIOSITY FOR ASTRONOMERS SINCE ANCIENT TIMES.

Venus was the first planet scrutinized through a telescope, when Italian scientist Galileo Galilei observed in 1610 that it had phases like the Moon. However, its thick cloud cover meant that nothing was known of the surface until recently. Venus's proximity to Earth and similar size led to speculation that its clouds hid dense jungles and even civilizations. In the 1970s, the clouds were finally penetrated: Earth-based radar and a succession of spacecraft revealed a surface that is entirely barren and ferociously hot. Since then, the stark Venusian landscape has been mapped in detail.

Venus at twilight

Venus Tablet

c.10,000 BCE

Venus in the night sky
Venus has been familiar since prehistoric times. Its proximity to the Sun and the high reflectivity of its thick cloud cover make it the brightest object in the night sky after the Moon – so bright it can even cast shadows on Earth when the Moon is hidden.

c.1600 BCE

Venus Tablet of King Ammisaduqa
The clay Venus Tablet of Babylonian King Ammisaduqa is one of the most ancient of all astronomical records. It dates from about 1600 BCE and records in cuneiform writing the time that Venus appears on the horizon in the evening and morning over 21 years.

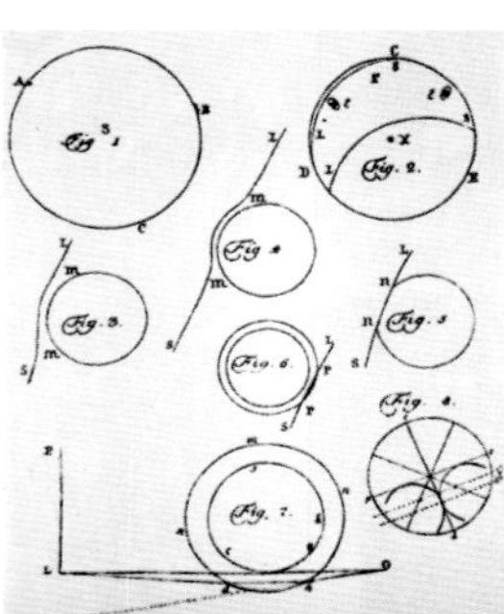
Lomonosov's drawings of atmospheric refraction

1667

Cassini's spot
Italian-French astronomer Giovanni Cassini tracks the movement of a spot on the face of Venus, leading him to estimate, wrongly, that the planet rotates every 24 hours. In 1877, Italian astronomer Giovanni Schiaparelli, correctly calculates the rotation period as 225 days.

1761

Venus's atmosphere
Russian astronomer Mikhail Lomonosov observes a transit of Venus and notices that the Sun's light creates a bulge around Venus. He believes that this bulging is evidence that Venus has an atmosphere, and that the atmosphere is refracting light from the Sun.

Emperor Napoleon I of France

1812

Napoleon and Venus
When advancing with his armies on Moscow, the French Emperor Napoleon sees Venus in the daytime sky – said to be a lucky sign. He views it as an omen of victory. But what follows is his worst military setback as his armies retreat from Russia in disarray.

1813

Polar spots
German physician and astronomer Franz von Gruithuisen – a keen observer of Venus – observes bright spots at Venus's poles. He believes these spots might be polar ice caps, but in fact they turn out to be shifting vortexes of bright cloud in Venus's atmosphere.

Richard Proctor

1875

Life on Venus
English astronomer Richard Proctor believes it is highly likely that life exists elsewhere in the Universe. He suggests that Venus, so similar to Earth in size, could be inhabited, and that its thick clouds may hide an advanced Venusian civilization.

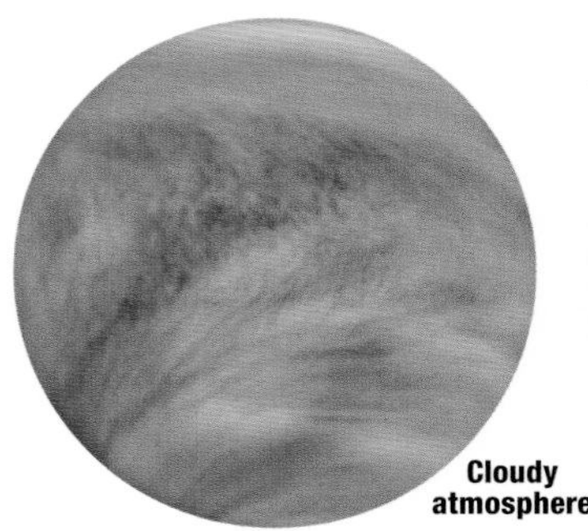
Cloudy atmosphere

1920s

Carbon dioxide identified
Spectroscopy – analysis of the spectrum of light emitted by objects – allows astronomers to identify the chemical elements in celestial bodies. In the 1920s they discover that Venus's cloudy atmosphere consists of unbreathable carbon dioxide.

El Caracol, Chichen Itza

Venus attacks an ocelot warrior in the Dresden Codex

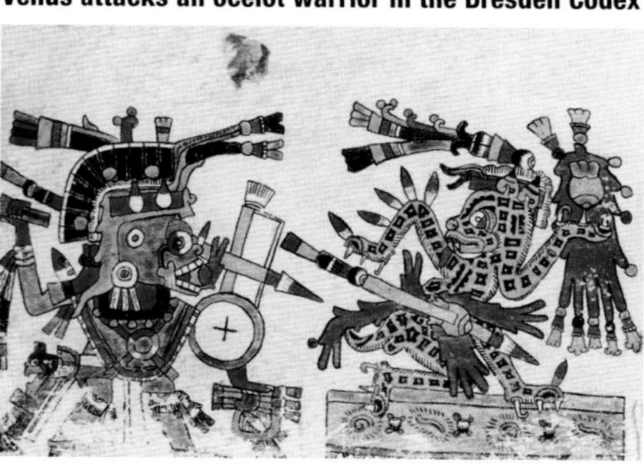

c.6th century BCE

Phosphorus and Hesperus

Originally the ancient Greeks believe the morning and evening star are two planets: Phosphorus and Hesperus. They later agree with the Babylonians that it is actually a single planet, which the Babylonians called Ishtar, after their goddess of love.

906 CE

Mayan observatory

The remarkable structure of El Caracol in the ancient Mayan city of Chichen Itza, Mexico, is an astronomical observatory for Mayan priests. It is designed, in particular, for the observation of Venus. To the Mayans, Venus is Kulkulkán – Earth's twin and a god of war.

12th century

The Dresden Codex

The Codex, possibly found by Spanish conquistador Hernán Cortéz in 1519, is the oldest book written in the Americas. It is believed to be a copy of an 8th century Mayan text, and contains accurate tables charting the arrival of Venus in the sky.

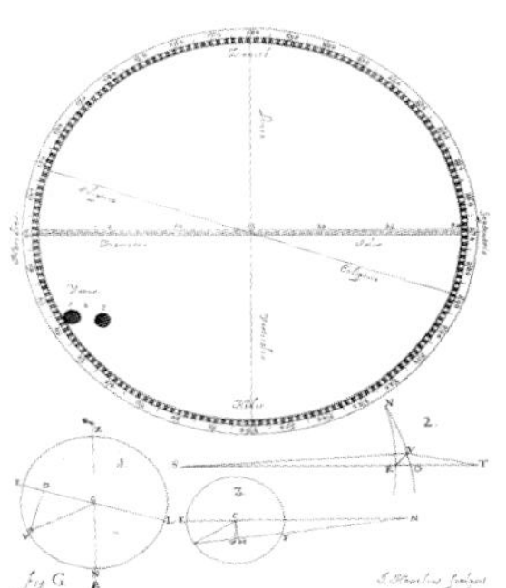

Horrocks's diagram of the 1639 transit of Venus

Venusian phases, sketched by Galileo

1643

Ashen light

The mysterious glow on Venus's night side – the ashen light – is first observed by Italian astronomer-priest Giovanni Battista Riccioli. In 1812, German astronomer Franz von Gruithuisen asserts that ashen light is smoke from the fires of the Venusian emperor.

1639

Transit of Venus

English astronomers Jeremiah Horrocks and William Crabtree are the first to observe a transit of Venus (when the planet passes between Earth and the Sun). It enables astronomers to make the first accurate calculations of the Earth–Sun distance.

1610

Galileo and Venus's phases

While studying Venus through a telescope, Galileo discovers that the planet has phases, as our changing point of view reveals varying amounts of its sunlit face. This supports the idea of Polish astronomer Copernicus that Venus travels around the Sun, not Earth.

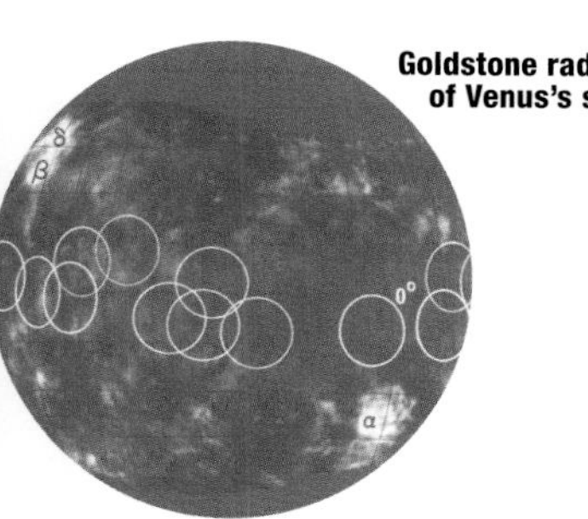

Goldstone radar image of Venus's surface

Surface of Venus from Venera 3

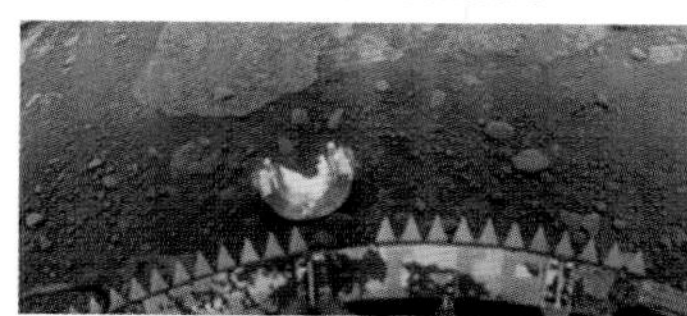

Magellan radar map of Venus

1961

Radar exploration

Venus's thick clouds prevent conventional telescopes from observing its surface. But from 1961, radar images – supplied first by radio telescopes at Goldstone, California, then by the Arecibo dish in Puerto Rico – reveal the Venusian surface for the first time.

1962

First visit: Mariner 2

NASA's Mariner 2 becomes the first spacecraft to fly past another planet when it swings within 35,000km (22,000 miles) of Venus on 14 December. Mariner 2's investigations confirm that Venus has cool clouds and a scorching surface.

1966

First landing: Venera 3

The Soviet Venera 3 is the first spacecraft to reach another planet, crashing onto Venus on 1 March. The first successful landings are made by the Venera 7 and 8 probes of 1970 and 1972, which reveal extreme surface temperatures of 455–475°C (851–887°F).

1990

Magellan mission

NASA's Magellan goes into orbit around Venus, aerobraking to reduce speed. Using radar, it maps 98 per cent of the surface. After completing its mission in 1994, it plunges into Venus's atmosphere.

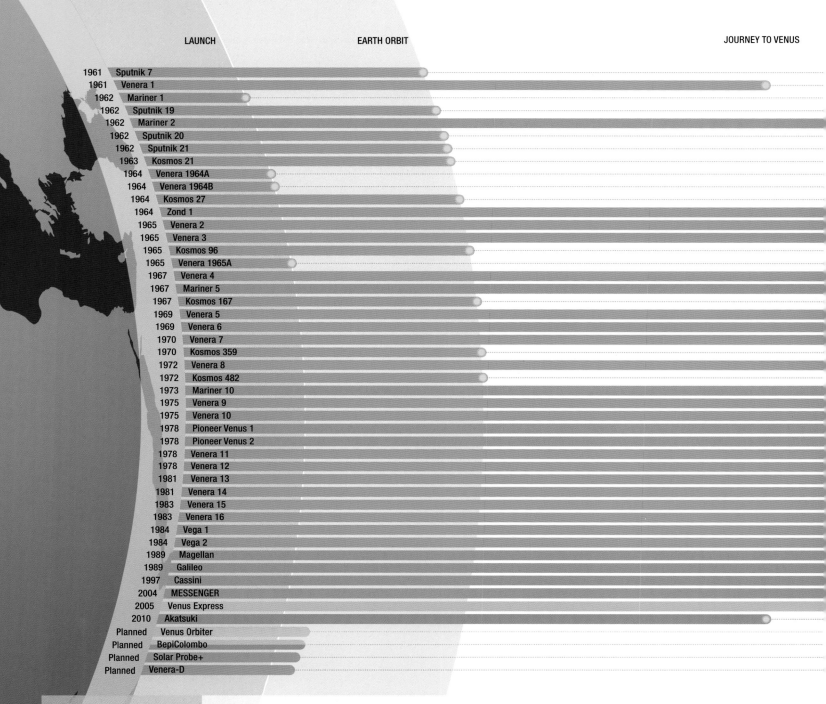

Year	Mission	LAUNCH	EARTH ORBIT	JOURNEY TO VENUS
1961	Sputnik 7			
1961	Venera 1			
1962	Mariner 1			
1962	Sputnik 19			
1962	Mariner 2			
1962	Sputnik 20			
1962	Sputnik 21			
1963	Kosmos 21			
1964	Venera 1964A			
1964	Venera 1964B			
1964	Kosmos 27			
1964	Zond 1			
1965	Venera 2			
1965	Venera 3			
1965	Kosmos 96			
1965	Venera 1965A			
1967	Venera 4			
1967	Mariner 5			
1967	Kosmos 167			
1969	Venera 5			
1969	Venera 6			
1970	Venera 7			
1970	Kosmos 359			
1972	Venera 8			
1972	Kosmos 482			
1973	Mariner 10			
1975	Venera 9			
1975	Venera 10			
1978	Pioneer Venus 1			
1978	Pioneer Venus 2			
1978	Venera 11			
1978	Venera 12			
1981	Venera 13			
1981	Venera 14			
1983	Venera 15			
1983	Venera 16			
1984	Vega 1			
1984	Vega 2			
1989	Magellan			
1989	Galileo			
1997	Cassini			
2004	MESSENGER			
2005	Venus Express			
2010	Akatsuki			
Planned	Venus Orbiter			
Planned	BepiColombo			
Planned	Solar Probe+			
Planned	Venera-D			

KEY
RFSA (USSR/Russia)
NASA (USA)
esa
ESA (Europe)
JAXA (Japan)
ISRO (India)
Joint ESA/JAXA mission
Destination
Success
Failure

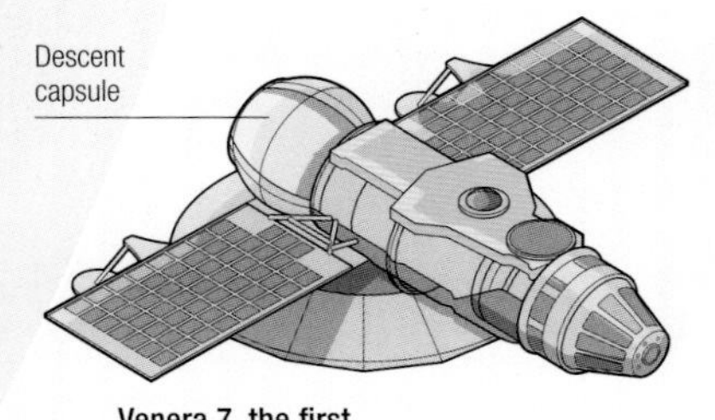
Descent capsule

Venera 7, the first craft to survive a landing on Venus

◁ ▽ **Venera**

In 1966, the Soviet probe Venera 3 crashed into Venus's surface and became the first spacecraft to reach another planet. Over the next 17 years, the Soviet Union sent another 13 craft to Venus, revealing a huge amount about the planet. On 22 October 1975, Venera 9 landed and beamed back the first pictures from the surface, showing a landscape littered with broken rock. Visibility was surprisingly good considering the thickness of Venus's atmosphere; a Soviet scientist described it as like "a cloudy day in Moscow".

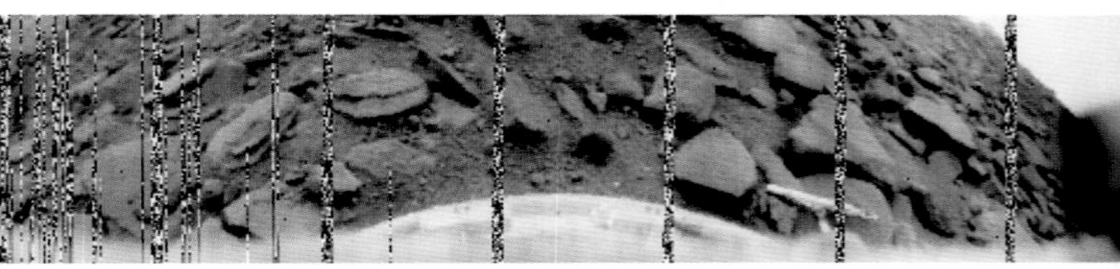

First surface image, from Venera 9

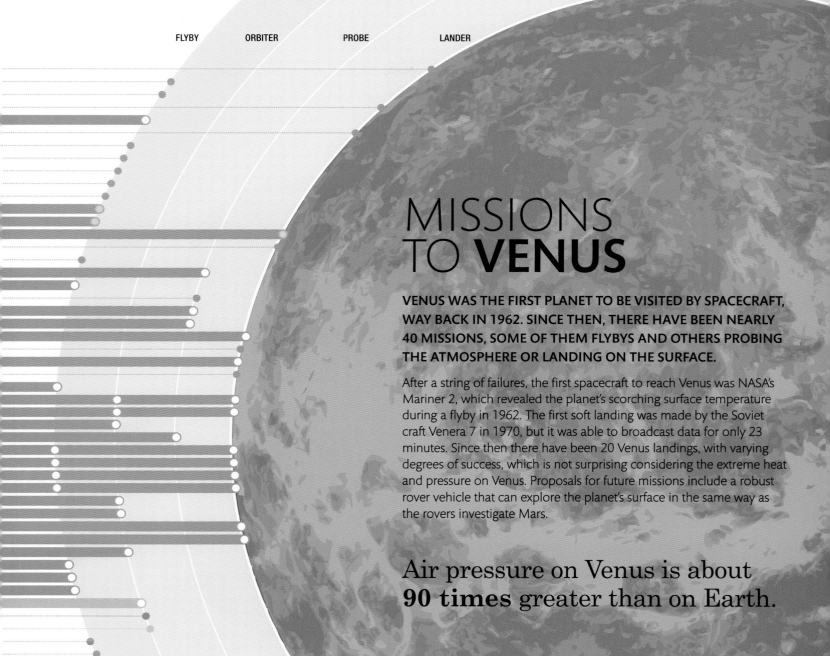

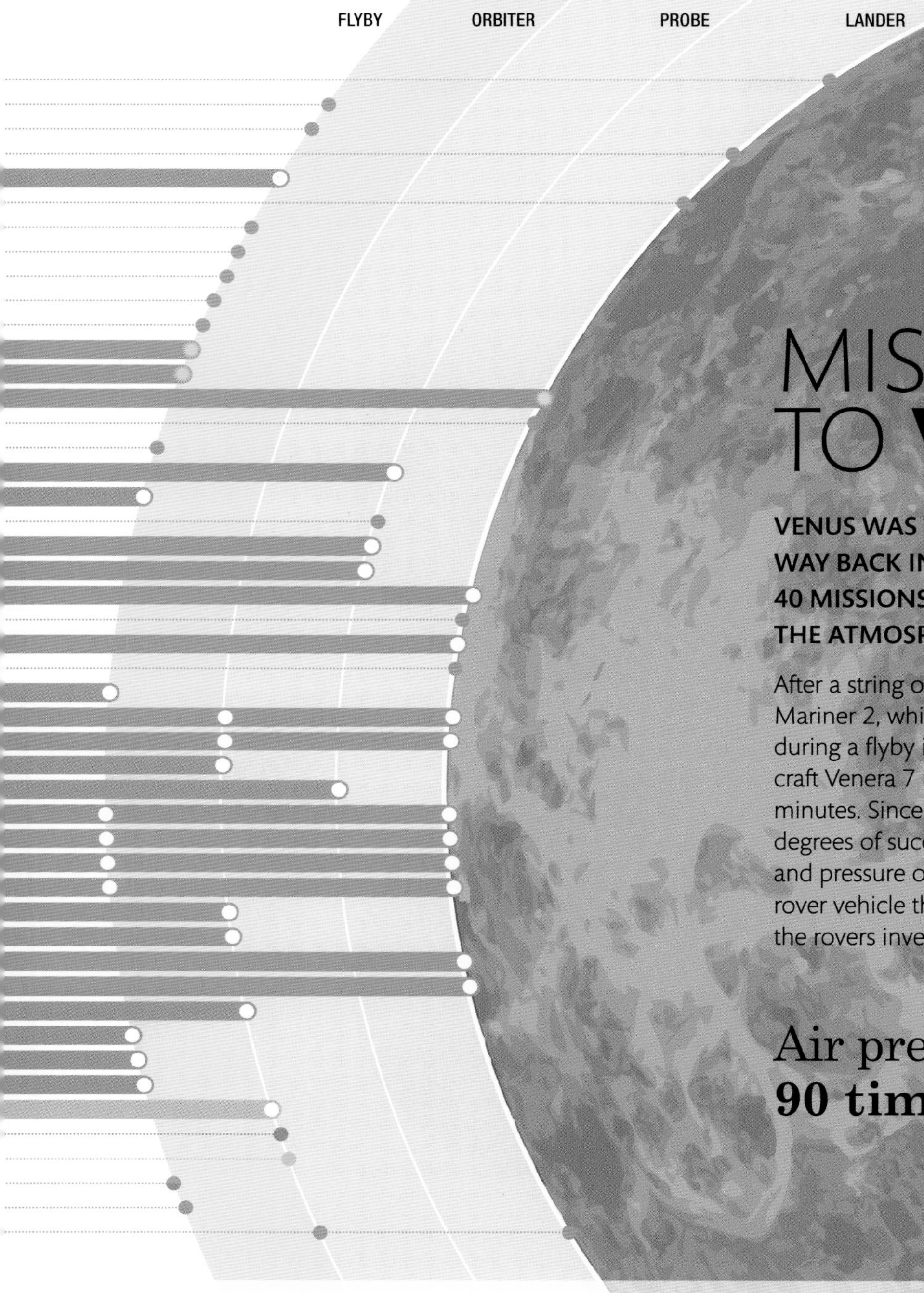

FLYBY ORBITER PROBE LANDER

MISSIONS TO **VENUS**

VENUS WAS THE FIRST PLANET TO BE VISITED BY SPACECRAFT, WAY BACK IN 1962. SINCE THEN, THERE HAVE BEEN NEARLY 40 MISSIONS, SOME OF THEM FLYBYS AND OTHERS PROBING THE ATMOSPHERE OR LANDING ON THE SURFACE.

After a string of failures, the first spacecraft to reach Venus was NASA's Mariner 2, which revealed the planet's scorching surface temperature during a flyby in 1962. The first soft landing was made by the Soviet craft Venera 7 in 1970, but it was able to broadcast data for only 23 minutes. Since then there have been 20 Venus landings, with varying degrees of success, which is not surprising considering the extreme heat and pressure on Venus. Proposals for future missions include a robust rover vehicle that can explore the planet's surface in the same way as the rovers investigate Mars.

Air pressure on Venus is about **90 times** greater than on Earth.

▷ Mapping the surface
Much of our knowledge of Venus comes from the NASA spacecraft Magellan (named after the Portuguese explorer Ferdinand Magellan), which reached the planet on 10 August 1990. It spent four years in orbit and mapped 98 per cent of the surface, peering through the thick Venusian cloud by firing a radar beam at the ground and capturing the echo. It imaged craters, hills, ridges, and a wide range of volcanic formations with incredible detail. Its mission complete, Magellan was lowered into Venus's atmosphere and vaporized, though some wreckage may have reached the surface.

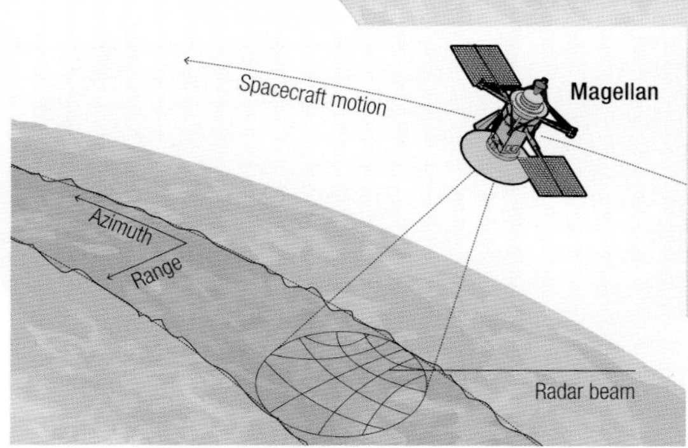
Spacecraft motion
Magellan
Azimuth
Range
Radar beam

▷ Venus Express
Launched in 2005, Europe's Venus Express spacecraft was sent to the planet to study its atmosphere and climate in detail. It arrived in April 2006 and has since beamed back a vast amount of data. It has found evidence of oceans in Venus's past, captured flashes of lightning, and revealed a huge double atmospheric vortex at the south pole.

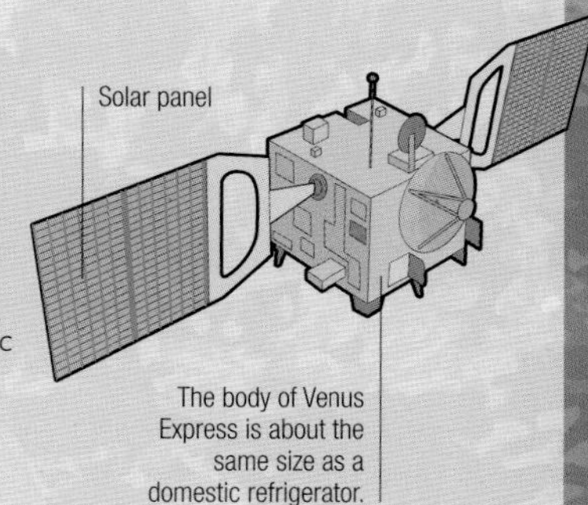
Solar panel
The body of Venus Express is about the same size as a domestic refrigerator.

EARTH

SITUATED AROUND 150 MILLION KM (93 MILLION MILES) FROM THE SUN, EARTH IS ALONE AMONG THE PLANETS IN HAVING VAST OCEANS OF LIQUID WATER ON ITS SURFACE AND THE UNDISPUTED PRESENCE OF LIFE.

When the Solar System formed, Earth was the largest rocky planet to take shape and consequently acquired the most internal heat. The flow of heat from its core towards the surface – a process that continues today – generated convection cycles in the mantle and made the crust fragment into mobile plates that slowly grind past each other, moving only a few centimetres a year.

Through a combination of plate movements, volcanic activity, and comet impacts, large amounts of water accumulated on Earth's surface. The planet's distance from the Sun, its gravity, and an insulating atmosphere combined to create conditions for this water to exist in each of its three physical states, including liquid water, which was essential to the development of life. As a result, Earth today appears unique, with its swirling water clouds, vast oceans, and continents coloured green in parts by the presence of plants.

Earth is the only planet known to have large amounts of **water** in all three states: **solid, liquid, and gas.**

EARTH DATA

Average diameter	12,742km (7,918 miles)
Axial tilt	23.5°
Rotation period (day)	24 hours
Orbital period (year)	365.26 Earth days
Minimum surface temperature	–89°C (–128°F)
Maximum surface temperature	58°C (136°F)
Moons	1

▷ **Northern hemisphere**
This view of Earth is dominated by the continents of North America and Eurasia, which until about 70 million years ago were joined. They are separated by the North Atlantic Ocean and, to its north, the smaller, partly iced-over Arctic Ocean.

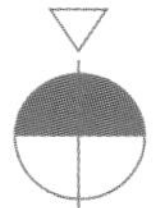

▷ **Eastern hemisphere**
Eurasia is Earth's largest landmass. It sits above the planet's third largest body of water, the Indian Ocean. Australia is the smallest of Earth's seven continents.

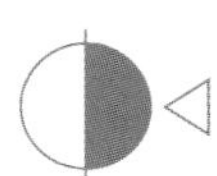

▷ **Southern hemisphere**
Earth's southern hemisphere is centred on a single landmass, Antarctica. The ring-shaped Southern Ocean surrounds the ice-covered continent, with Australia and parts of South America and Africa making major incursions.

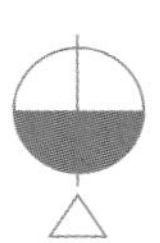

The Rocky Mountains run down the west of the North American Plate for a distance of 4,800km (3,000 miles).

Earth's equator is encircled by a persistent band of cloud, making tropical regions humid and rainy.

The Pacific Ocean has the largest surface area of any body of water on Earth at 169.5 million square km (65.4 million square miles), making up almost half the total area covered by oceans.

Clouds in the southern hemisphere spiral in a clockwise motion, while those in the northern hemisphere spiral anticlockwise.

The Atlantic Ocean is the second largest body of water on Earth at 106.5 million square km (41.1 million square miles). It is bounded by Africa and Europe to the East and the Americas to the West.
The west coast of Africa echoes the shape of the east coast of South America. The two continents were once joined but started separating around 130 million years ago.
The Amazon Basin is a densely forested region covering around 7 million square km (2.7 million square miles).
The longest mountain range on Earth at 7,000km (4,300 miles), the Andes form the western edge of the South American Plate.
The southernmost tip of South America is known as Cape Horn. The winds below this latitude circle the Earth uninterrupted by land, causing formidable waves in the Southern Ocean.

◁ **Western hemisphere**
In this view of the globe, the amount of water that covers the planet is striking. Two vast oceans – the Pacific, covering about one-third of Earth's whole surface, and the Atlantic – are separated by the landmasses of North and South America. The continents are joined by the narrow bridge of Central America.

EARTH STRUCTURE

EARTH'S LAYERED INTERNAL STRUCTURE IS MIRRORED IN A MULTILAYERED ATMOSPHERE THAT EXTENDS FOR HUNDREDS OF KILOMETRES ABOVE THE PLANET'S SURFACE, GRADUALLY MERGING WITH SPACE.

What we know of Earth's internal structure has been learned largely through the study of earthquake waves, particularly the routes they take as they travel inside the planet. Each layer beneath the surface is progressively denser, hotter, and under increased pressure. A unique aspect of Earth is that its outer, rigid shell, the lithosphere (made up of the crust and topmost layer of the mantle), is split into chunks called tectonic plates, which move relative to each other, driven by internal heat flows. Surrounding the planet's surface, Earth's atmosphere provides important protection to the life that flourishes on the planet.

Inner core
The innermost layer of Earth consists of a solid iron-nickel alloy and has an average temperature of about 5,500°C (9,900°F). Despite the high temperature, the metals in the inner core cannot melt because of the intense pressure exerted on them.

Over a quarter of Earth's surface is covered by land. Continental crust is thicker than the oceanic crust that occurs under Earth's oceans.

▷ **Earth layer by layer**
Earth has three primary layers – the core, mantle, and crust – each with a unique chemical composition. The core has two distinct parts, inner and outer. There are also two types of crust – oceanic and thicker continental crust. The layers of the mantle increase in density with depth, and the topmost layer is fused to the crust, forming the lithosphere.

In Earth's early history, the **planet was hot** and **liquid** – heavy **iron sank**, forming the **core.**

Outer core
The outer core is liquid iron with some nickel and has an average temperature of about 5,000°C (9,000°F). Currents in the outer core are thought to generate Earth's magnetic field and cause the magnetic poles to wander.

Mantle
The largest of Earth's internal layers is basically solid, consisting of rocks such as peridotite. However, it can slowly deform, allowing heat to enter from the core and cause convection currents over geological timescales. These currents drive crustal movements.

Crust
Oceanic crust consists of dark volcanic rocks such as basalt and is 7–8km (4–5 miles) thick. Continental crust consists of many types of relatively light rock and is 25–70km (16–45 miles) thick.

Ocean
Saltwater oceans cover almost three-quarters of Earth's surface and vary in depth up to 11,000m (36,000ft).

◁ **Atmosphere**
Earth's atmosphere consists mainly of nitrogen, oxygen, and argon, with small amounts of many other gases, including carbon dioxide. It has five layers, each defined by the way the temperature varies within its boundaries. In the troposphere and mesosphere, temperature falls with increasing height, while in the stratosphere and thermosphere, the temperature rises. The exosphere is so thin that the gas temperature there is of little significance.

The troposphere is the layer in which clouds form and weather occurs; it varies in thickness from about 16km (10 miles) at the equator to 8km (5 miles) at the poles.

The stratosphere is a relatively calm layer above the troposphere, about 30–40km (19–25 miles) thick. Passenger aircraft fly in the bottom of the stratosphere, above the clouds.

The mesosphere is about 30–50km (19–31 miles) thick; its upper boundary is the coldest part of the atmosphere at about –100°C (–146°F).

The thermosphere is a rarefied, ionized layer extending from about 85km (53 miles) to 700km (430 miles) above Earth's surface.

The exosphere is the outermost, highly rarefied zone of Earth's atmosphere. Its outer edge forms a blue halo (corona) around Earth when viewed from space.

TECTONIC **EARTH**

EARTH'S OUTER ROCKY SHELL IS SPLIT INTO HUGE FRAGMENTS CALLED TECTONIC PLATES. THESE SLOW-MOVING STRUCTURES INTERACT WITH EACH OTHER, CAUSING VIOLENT GEOLOGICAL EVENTS THAT CONTINUALLY CHANGE THE PLANET'S SURFACE.

Earth's tectonic plates are irregularly shaped and fit together like a jigsaw puzzle. Their movements relative to each other, caused by convective heat flows deep within the planet, are imperceptibly slow, but over millions of years, continents slide across Earth's face, collide, and change shape. Powerful forces are unleashed at the boundaries between plates, where a variety of distinctive geological features develop. These include mountain ranges, deep-sea trenches, and volcanoes where plates move towards each other; and mid-ocean ridges where they move apart. Earthquakes are more common at all types of plate boundary.

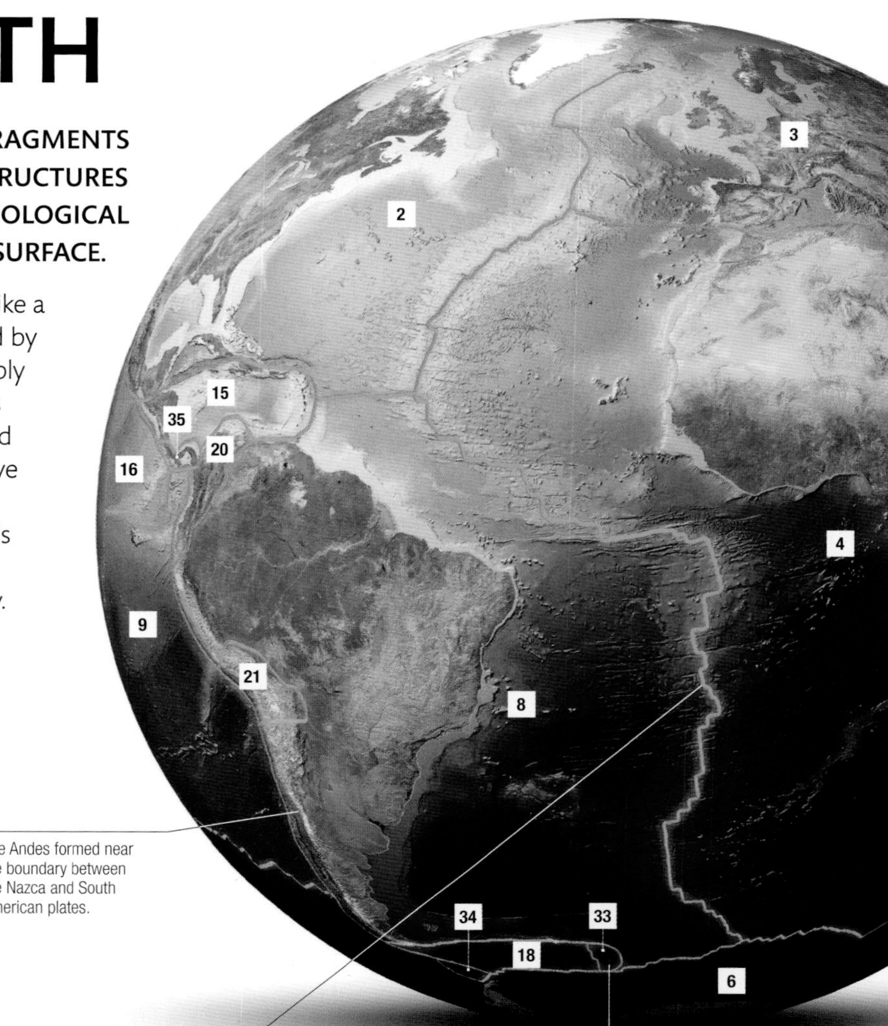
3
2
15
35
20
16
4
9
21
8
34
33
18
6

The Andes formed near the boundary between the Nazca and South American plates.

The Mid-Atlantic Ridge is a divergent plate boundary running down the Atlantic.

The South Sandwich Plate is an example of a microplate.

KEY

1 Pacific
2 North American
3 Eurasian
4 African (Nubian)
5 African (Somalian)
6 Antarctic
7 Australian
8 South American
9 Nazca
10 Indian
11 Sunda
12 Philippine Sea
13 Arabian
14 Okhotsk
15 Caribbean
16 Cocos
17 Yangtze
18 Scotia
19 Caroline
20 North Andes
21 Altiplano
22 Anatolian
23 Banda Sea
24 Burma
25 Okinawa
26 Woodlark
27 Mariana
28 New Hebrides
29 Aegean Sea
30 Timor
31 Bird's Head
32 North Bismarck
33 South Sandwich
34 South Shetland
35 Panama
36 South Bismarck
37 Maoke
38 Solomon Sea

▷ **Earth's plates**
There are seven major plates – for example, the Pacific and Eurasian plates – as well as a dozen or so medium-sized plates, such as the Arabian Plate, and numerous much smaller microplates. Listed here are most of the recognized plates, in approximate order of decreasing size. The plates are also numbered on the globes shown on the right. A few of the microplates are sometimes considered just parts of larger plates.

△ **North American**
The North American Plate (2) makes up just under one-sixth of Earth's surface. It contains parts of the Arctic and Atlantic oceans and a section of Siberia. A notable volcanic hot spot has existed for millions of years under this plate and is currently the cause of vigorous geyser activity in Yellowstone Park, USA.

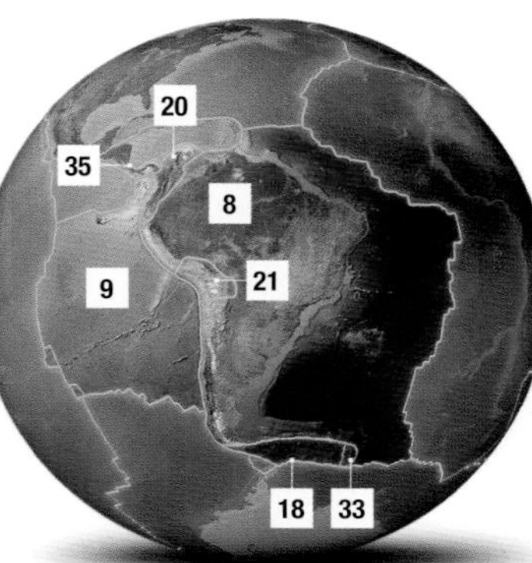
20
35
8
9
21
18
33

△ **South American**
With the neighbouring Nazca (9), Scotia (18), and other smaller plates, the South American Plate (8) accounts for about one-eighth of Earth's surface. The Andes mountain range in South America rises where the easterly moving Nazca Plate is pushed under the edge of the South American Plate.

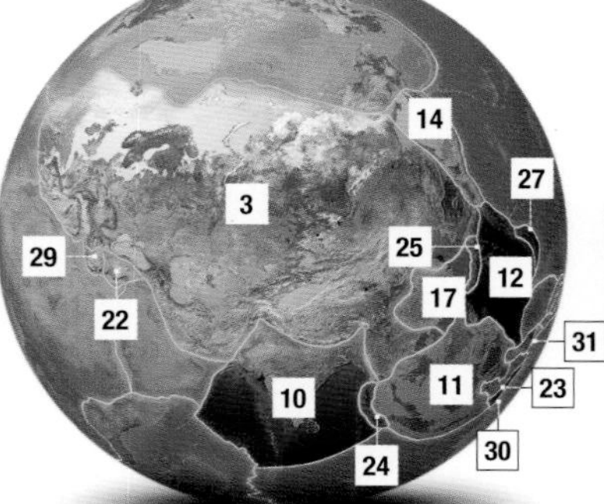
14
27
3
25
29
12
17
22
31
10
11
23
24
30

△ **Eurasian**
This plate (3) includes Europe and most of the landmass of Asia. A number of medium-sized plates to the east and southeast, such as the Sunda Plate (11), were formerly considered part of the Eurasian Plate. Millions of years ago, the Indian Plate (10) crashed into the Eurasian Plate, creating the Himalayas.

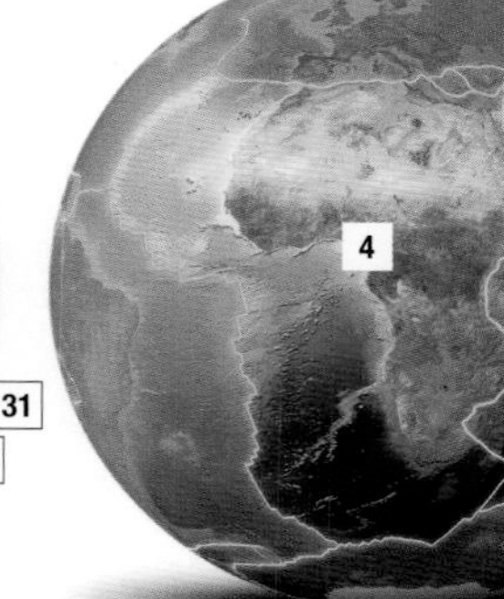
13
4
5

△ **African**
The two African plates (4 and 5) include the African continent and large parts of the Atlantic and Indian oceans. Africa is believed to be in the process of splitting into two parts along the East African Rift – a gigantic split in Earth's crust that runs for about 4,000km (2,500 miles) through East Africa.

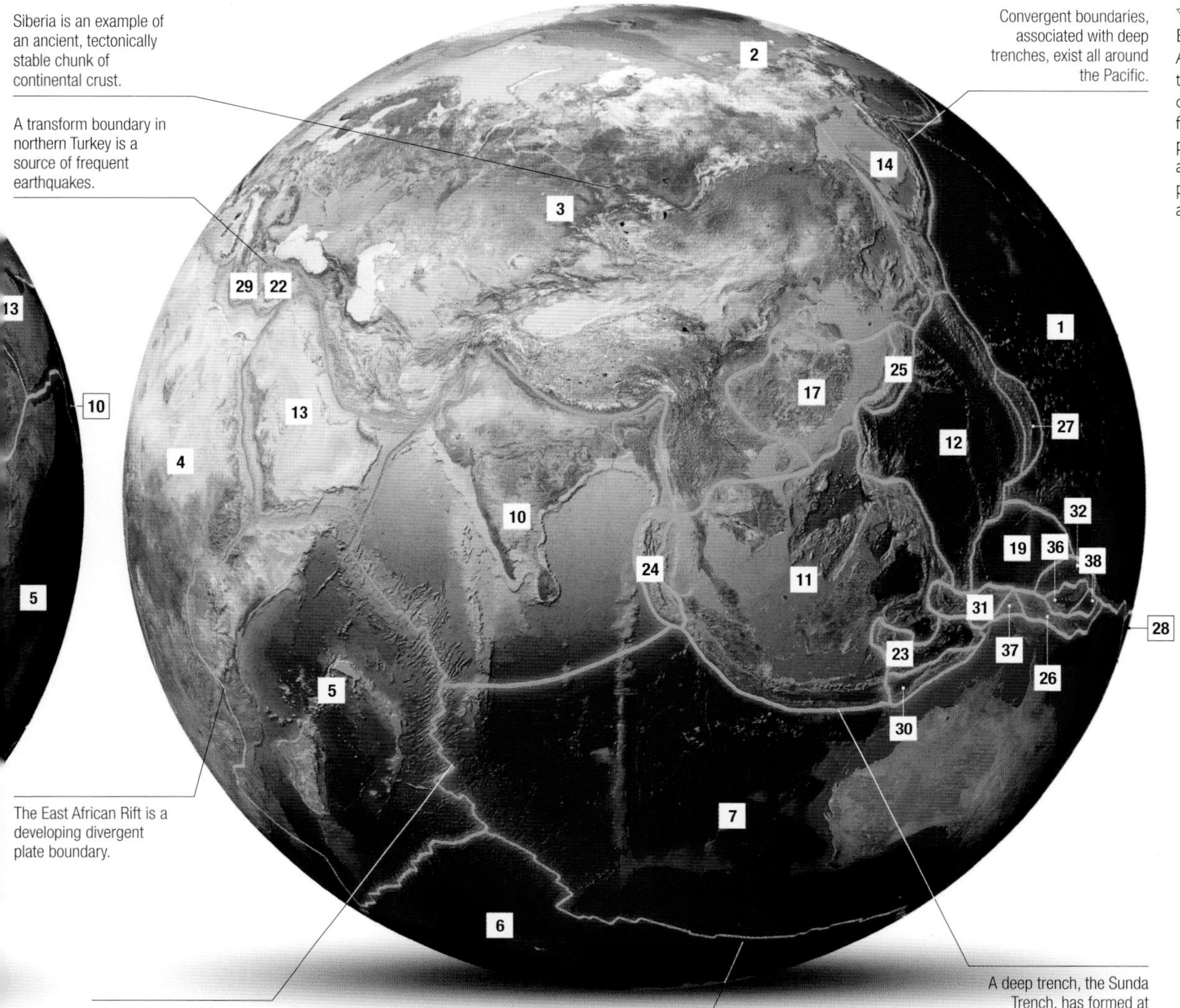

Siberia is an example of an ancient, tectonically stable chunk of continental crust.

A transform boundary in northern Turkey is a source of frequent earthquakes.

Convergent boundaries, associated with deep trenches, exist all around the Pacific.

The East African Rift is a developing divergent plate boundary.

The Mid-Indian Ridge separates the African and Australian plates.

The Southeast Indian Ridge separates the Australian and Antarctic plates.

A deep trench, the Sunda Trench, has formed at this boundary.

▽ Plate boundaries

Boundaries between plates are of three types. At convergent boundaries, two plates move towards one another; one may dip beneath the other, often causing volcanoes or mountains to form. At transform boundaries, plates grind past each other. At divergent boundaries, which are either mid-ocean ridges or continental rifts, plates move apart and new plate is created along the boundary.

Convergent

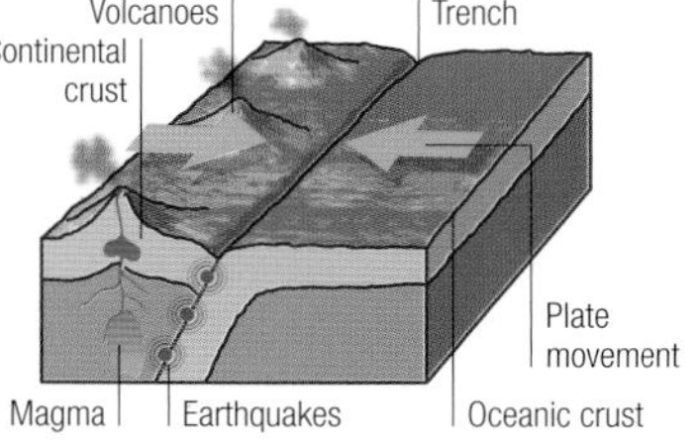
Volcanoes
Trench
Continental crust
Plate movement
Magma
Earthquakes
Oceanic crust

Transform

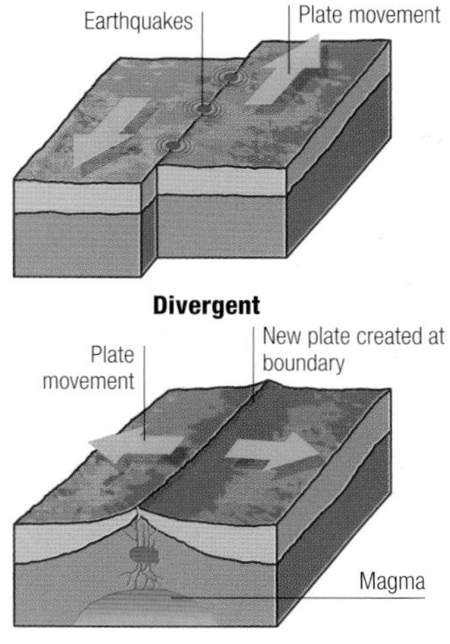
Earthquakes
Plate movement

Divergent

Plate movement
New plate created at boundary
Magma

▽ Swimming between plates

Divers and snorkellers visiting Thingvallavatn Lake in southwestern Iceland can swim in a gap between the North American and Eurasian plates. At the lake floor, the plate boundary is visible in the clear water at a deep rift, known as Silfra. In one section, the fissure is 63m (200ft) deep at the bottom, too narrow and steep-sided for most divers to risk exploring.

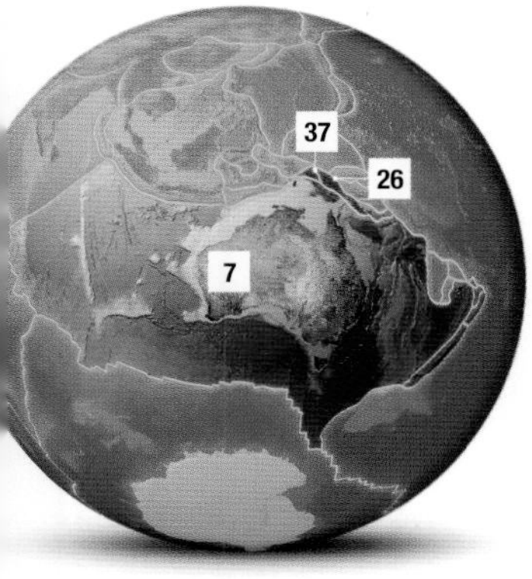

△ Australian

This plate (7) comprises Australia, parts of New Zealand and New Guinea, and parts of the Indian and Southern oceans. Major features include Australia's deserts, the Great Dividing Range, and the Great Barrier Reef. The whole plate is moving in a northeastern direction at a rate of about 6.5cm (2.5in) a year.

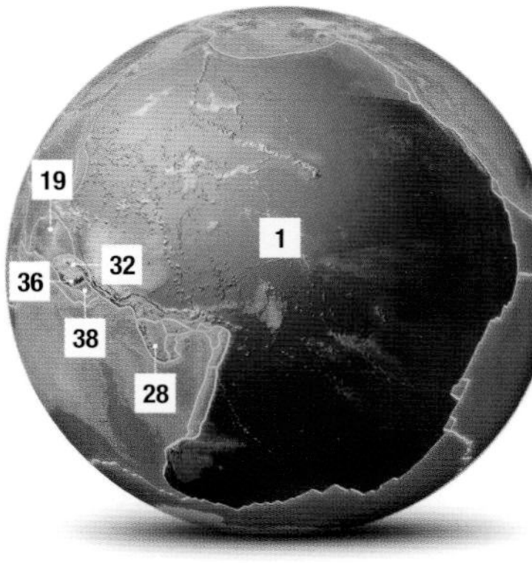

△ Pacific

The largest tectonic plate, the Pacific Plate (1) covers about one-fifth of Earth. It contains no large landmasses, but many volcanic islands and subsea volcanoes occur where plumes of magma burst through the surface. The Pacific Plate is moving northwest at a rate of about 10cm (4in) a year.

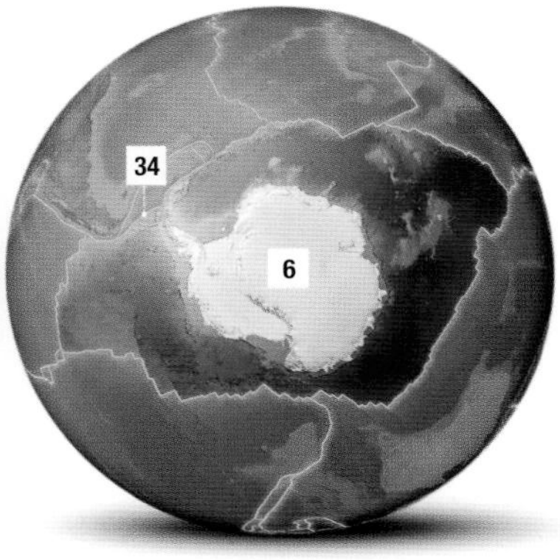

△ Antarctic

Making up about one-eighth of Earth's surface, the Antarctic Plate (6) includes the Antarctic continent at its centre, together with most of the encircling Southern Ocean. Over millions of years, this plate has become larger, as all around its edges new plate is continually created at divergent plate boundaries.

EARTH'S CHANGING SURFACE

UNLIKE THE FACE OF OUR MOON, WHICH HAS CHANGED LITTLE IN MILLIONS OF YEARS, EARTH'S SURFACE IS DYNAMIC. OUR PLANET IS SHAPED BY MANY PROCESSES, FROM RESTLESS TECTONIC PLATES TO CORROSIVE WATER IN THE ATMOSPHERE.

Some of the main drivers of change are internal, such as convection within Earth's mantle, which drives the movement of tectonic plates and builds new landscapes. On the surface, rock is subjected to continual weathering and erosion, processes driven ultimately by the Sun's energy. Over millions of years, these processes wear down entire mountain ranges, reducing rock to rubble, sand, and silt. Some of these processes are unique to Earth, helping to explain why the planet's surface changes so rapidly compared to other rocky worlds.

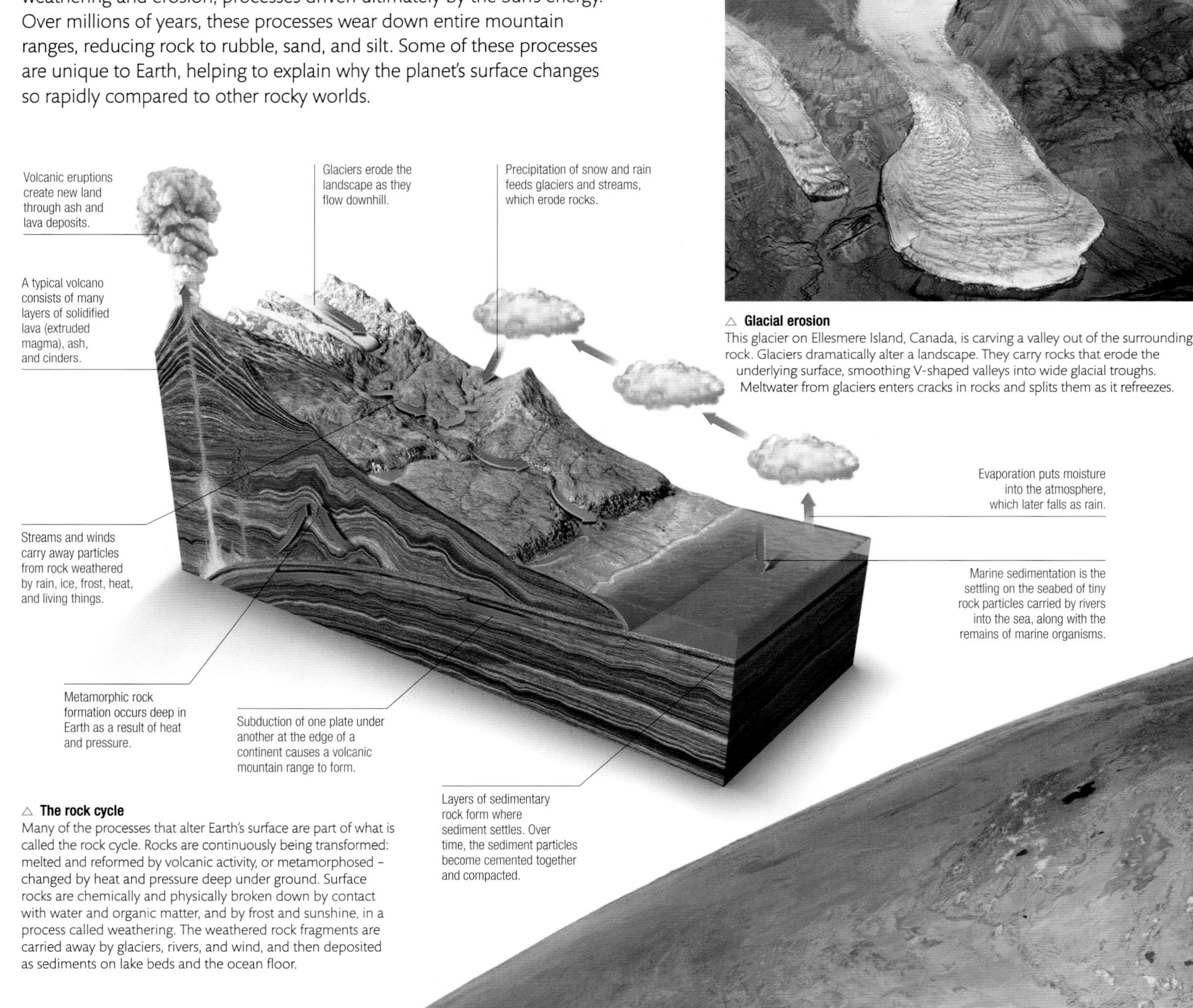
Volcanic eruptions create new land through ash and lava deposits.
Glaciers erode the landscape as they flow downhill.
Precipitation of snow and rain feeds glaciers and streams, which erode rocks.
A typical volcano consists of many layers of solidified lava (extruded magma), ash, and cinders.
Evaporation puts moisture into the atmosphere, which later falls as rain.
Streams and winds carry away particles from rock weathered by rain, ice, frost, heat, and living things.
Marine sedimentation is the settling on the seabed of tiny rock particles carried by rivers into the sea, along with the remains of marine organisms.
Metamorphic rock formation occurs deep in Earth as a result of heat and pressure.
Subduction of one plate under another at the edge of a continent causes a volcanic mountain range to form.
Layers of sedimentary rock form where sediment settles. Over time, the sediment particles become cemented together and compacted.

△ **Glacial erosion**
This glacier on Ellesmere Island, Canada, is carving a valley out of the surrounding rock. Glaciers dramatically alter a landscape. They carry rocks that erode the underlying surface, smoothing V-shaped valleys into wide glacial troughs. Meltwater from glaciers enters cracks in rocks and splits them as it refreezes.

△ **The rock cycle**
Many of the processes that alter Earth's surface are part of what is called the rock cycle. Rocks are continuously being transformed: melted and reformed by volcanic activity, or metamorphosed – changed by heat and pressure deep under ground. Surface rocks are chemically and physically broken down by contact with water and organic matter, and by frost and sunshine, in a process called weathering. The weathered rock fragments are carried away by glaciers, rivers, and wind, and then deposited as sediments on lake beds and the ocean floor.

△ **Eroded landscape**
These stunning rock formations, called hoodoos, in Bryce Canyon, USA, were formed primarily by a process called frost wedging. The canyon area experiences numerous freeze-thaw cycles a year. In the winter, water produced by melting snow seeps into cracks in the layers of limestone and other sedimentary rocks and then freezes at night. Water expands as it freezes, prising open the cracks, and causing the rocks to fracture.

A mountain range as high as the **Himalayas** could be worn flat in less than **20 million years.**

▷ **Mountain building**
A major surface-changing process affecting Earth's land areas is mountain-building. This typically occurs where tectonic plates are pushed together. A lateral squeezing of multi-layered sedimentary rock causes thrust faulting, in which the rock layers break along gently inclined planes called faults. Mountains gradually rise as the rock layers stack on top of each other. This is how most of Earth's major mountain ranges have been built at different times in the past.

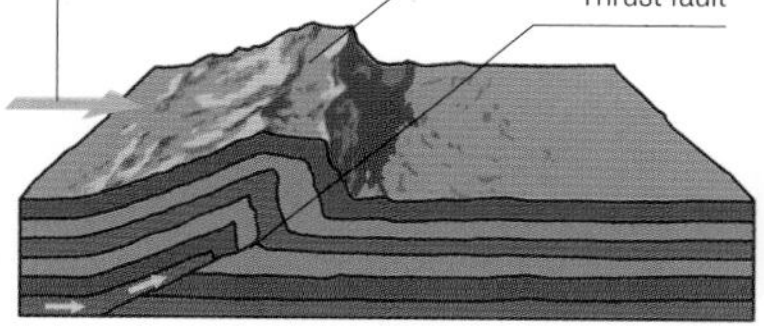

Rock layers are pushed horizontally.
The layers buckle above the fault.
Thrust fault

Initial break along thrust fault

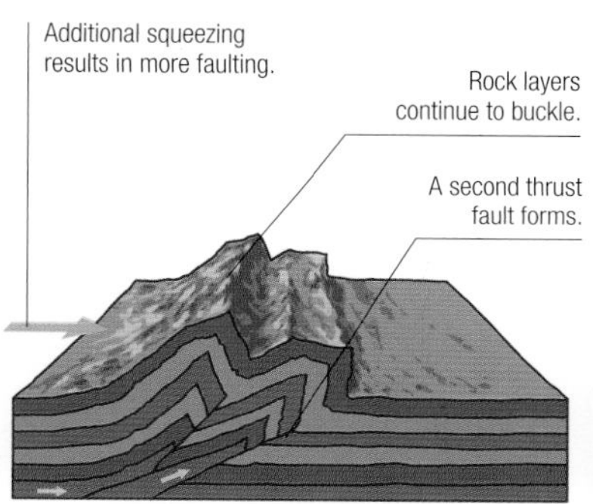
Additional squeezing results in more faulting.
Rock layers continue to buckle.
A second thrust fault forms.

Further faulting and buckling

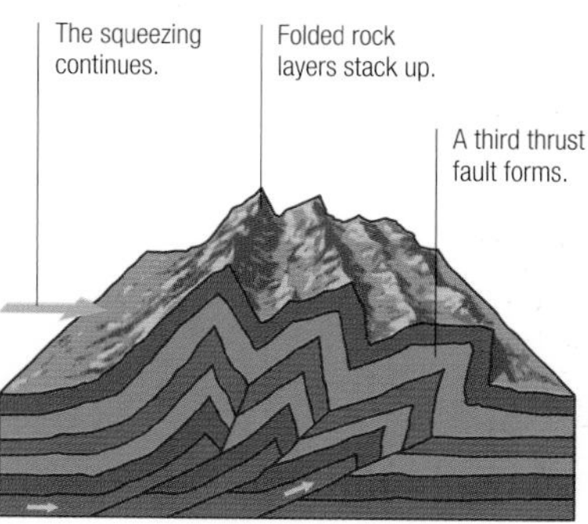
The squeezing continues.
Folded rock layers stack up.
A third thrust fault forms.

Complex of fractured and buckled rock layers

▽ **Himalayas**
Earth's highest mountain range, the Himalayas, began forming about 50–70 million years ago, when the Indian Plate crashed into the Eurasian Plate. If the neighbouring Karakoram Range is included, this mountain belt includes Earth's 14 highest peaks, each over 8km (5 miles) high.

1

WATER AND **ICE**

1 Coral atoll
Sculpted by water, many of Earth's features are unique in the Solar System. The Great Blue Hole off the coast of Belize is a submerged sinkhole surrounded by a coral atoll. Stretching 300m (1,000ft) across, the sinkhole sits in the Mesoamerican reef system that runs 1,000km (600 miles) along the coast of Central America. Coral reefs form when coral larvae attach to underwater rocks along the edge of a landmass.

2 Delta
A tangling network of channels, the great River Ganges creates an abstract jigsaw of islands as it meets the Bay of Bengal. Mature rivers deposit sediment as they slow on their course to the sea. As the sediment builds up, it forms low-lying land – a delta. The soil in a delta is often very fertile because it is rich in organic matter and minerals carried from upstream.

3 Waves
Oceans cover more than two-thirds of Earth's surface, giving our planet its unique, blue-jewel appearance from space. Sea water is constantly moving, and the pattern of currents is governed by the continents, sunlight, Earth's rotation, and the pull of the Moon. Whipped into waves by the wind, the sea in turn shapes the land. Tides, waves, and currents erode, deposit, and transport material, carving out coastlines.

4 Meltwater
Around 80 per cent of Greenland is covered by an ice sheet; it holds about 10 per cent of the world's ice. When temperatures rise, it begins to melt, and meltwater carves deep channels in the remaining ice. This huge ice canyon is 45m (150ft) deep. Ice caps, glaciers, and permanent snow hold almost 70 per cent of Earth's fresh water. Satellite imaging and data are used to track the rate at which the ice is melting.

2
3
4
5

5 Weather
Satellites can track storms from beginning to end. Hurricane Isabel, pictured here over North Carolina, USA, formed over East Africa, and satellites recorded its growth into a tropical cyclone with a wind speed of 267kph (166mph). Cyclones are areas of low atmospheric pressure. Winds rush in to fill a gap and spiral up, pulling energy and moisture from warm seas as they travel across the ocean.

LIFE ON **EARTH**

EARTH IS THE ONLY PLACE IN THE UNIVERSE KNOWN TO HARBOUR LIFE. OTHER SOLAR SYSTEM LOCATIONS, SUCH AS THE SUBSURFACE OCEAN OF JUPITER'S MOON EUROPA, MIGHT THEORETICALLY SUPPORT LIFE, BUT FOR NOW OUR HOME PLANET APPEARS TO BE UNIQUE.

Life has existed on Earth for at least 3.7 billion years. We cannot be sure that it originated on our planet – it might have developed elsewhere and spread to Earth in objects such as comets. The presence on Earth of extremophiles – organisms that can exist in extremely challenging conditions – supports the idea that life may be able to survive in seemingly hostile environments elsewhere in the Universe. However, at present, the consensus is that the life we see on Earth originated here from non-living matter.

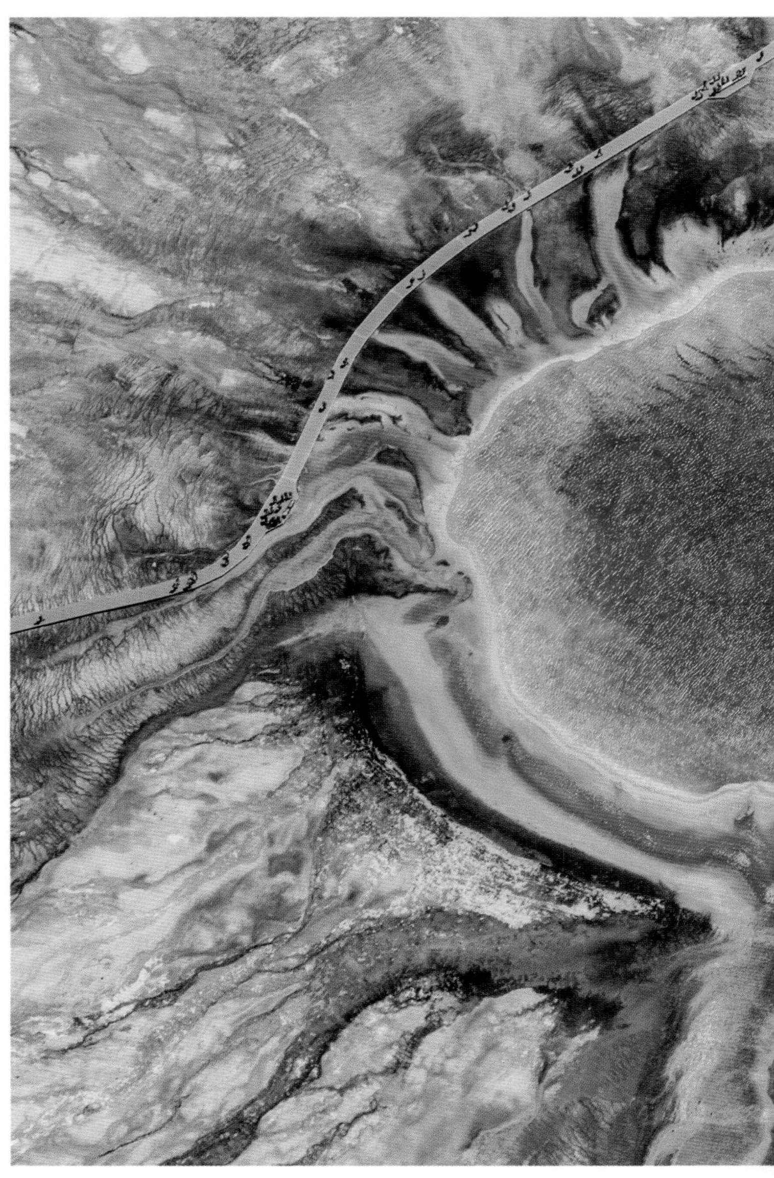

Why Earth?

Life on Earth began almost as soon as the young planet ceased to be bombarded by asteroids, allowing its surface to cool. Since then, our planet has continually provided conditions conducive for living organisms to thrive and evolve. Earth's distance from the Sun puts it in the Solar System's habitable Goldilocks zone. Here, surface temperature and atmospheric pressure conspire to allow water to exist as a liquid on the surface – a prerequisite for life as we know it. Earth also benefits from a rich supply of energy (solar radiation and heat generated from Earth's interior), a protective electromagnetic field (generated by currents in the liquid-iron core), and a large moon, which maintains climatic stability by minimizing swings in the planet's tilt.

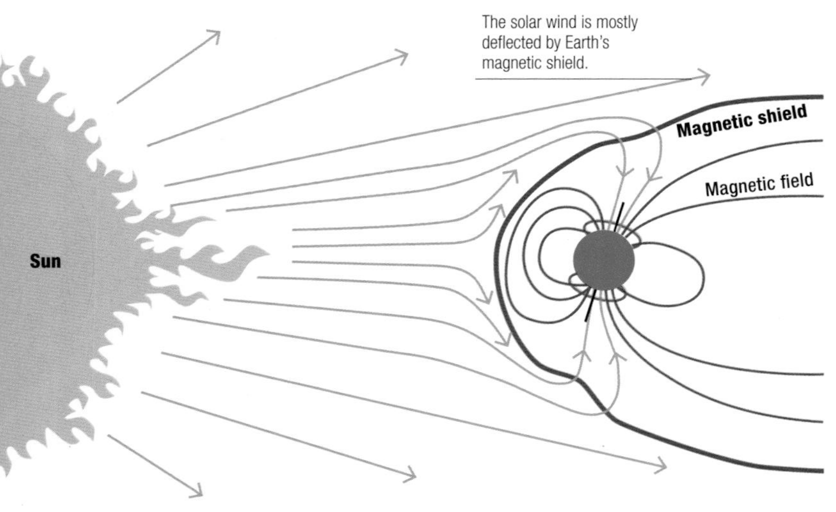
The solar wind is mostly deflected by Earth's magnetic shield.
Magnetic shield
Magnetic field
Sun

△ **Magnetic field**
Earth's strong magnetic field protects life on our planet by creating a shield that prevents most of the potentially harmful particles in the solar wind from reaching the planet's surface. The solar wind consists of a stream of high-energy charged particles, mainly electrons and protons, released from the Sun's upper atmosphere.

How life developed

The precursors of the first life forms were probably complex organic (carbon-containing) molecules that arose by chance in Earth's surface water. At some point, an organic molecule with a unique property appeared: it had the ability to catalyse production of copies of itself. This self-replicating organic molecule was the earliest ancestor of DNA. Through the process of evolution by natural selection, its descendants became more sophisticated, acquiring the ability to manufacture protective structures and substances that helped them survive and multiply – thus becoming primitive cells. Later, the single cells formed intimate, cooperative colonies, giving rise to multicellular organisms. Around a billion years ago, the advent of sexual reproduction sparked off a diversification of these organisms into more complex forms, such as plants and animals, that has continued to the present day.

△ **Extremophiles**
Extremophiles are organisms that thrive in conditions normally inhospitable to life, such as scalding or acidic water, or inside rocks. In Grand Prismatic Hot Spring, the green, yellow, and orange areas are mats of pigmented extremophile bacteria. Different-coloured species favour different temperatures, which reach up to 87°C (188°F) at the centre of the hot, mineral-rich pool.

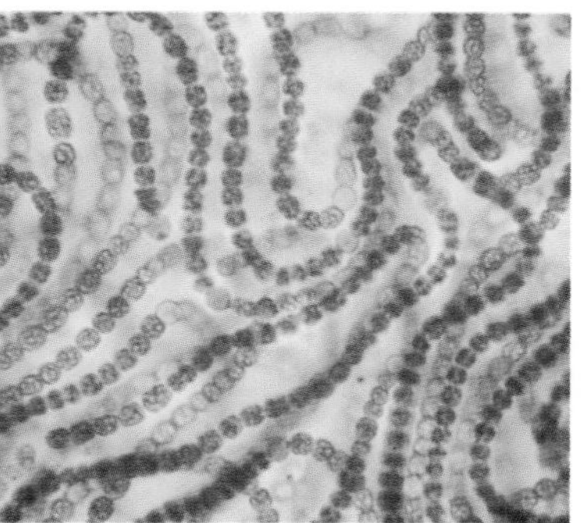

◁ **Cyanobacteria**
Thought to have existed for 3.5 billion years, cyanobacteria are among Earth's oldest life forms. These microbes obtain energy by photosynthesis. By releasing oxygen as a waste product of photosynthesis, ancient cyanobacteria altered Earth's atmosphere, creating a protective blanket of ozone that made the surface habitable and triggering the evolution of oxygen-breathing life forms.

▷ **Hydrothermal vent**
Among the sites where life possibly originated are hydrothermal vents – cracks in the seabed from which gush plumes of hot water containing minerals and some simple dissolved gases, such as ammonia and carbon dioxide. The minerals might have catalysed chemical reactions between the gas molecules, thereby forming the basic building blocks of life.

◁ **Changing life**
Through evolution by natural selection, life on Earth developed from simple early forms, limited in number, to the enormous diversity seen today. Most species that have existed are now extinct, but traces remain preserved in Earth's rocks as fossils. The fossil record reveals that on several occasions in Earth's past, catastrophic events caused mass extinctions that wiped out hundreds of species at once.

Ammonite fossil

▽ **Biodiversity**
The diversity of life within a region is known as its biodiversity. Africa's grasslands are well known for their great diversity of animal species. The Serengeti plains of East Africa, for example, support about 45 mammal species and 500 bird species, to name just a small fraction of the total number present.

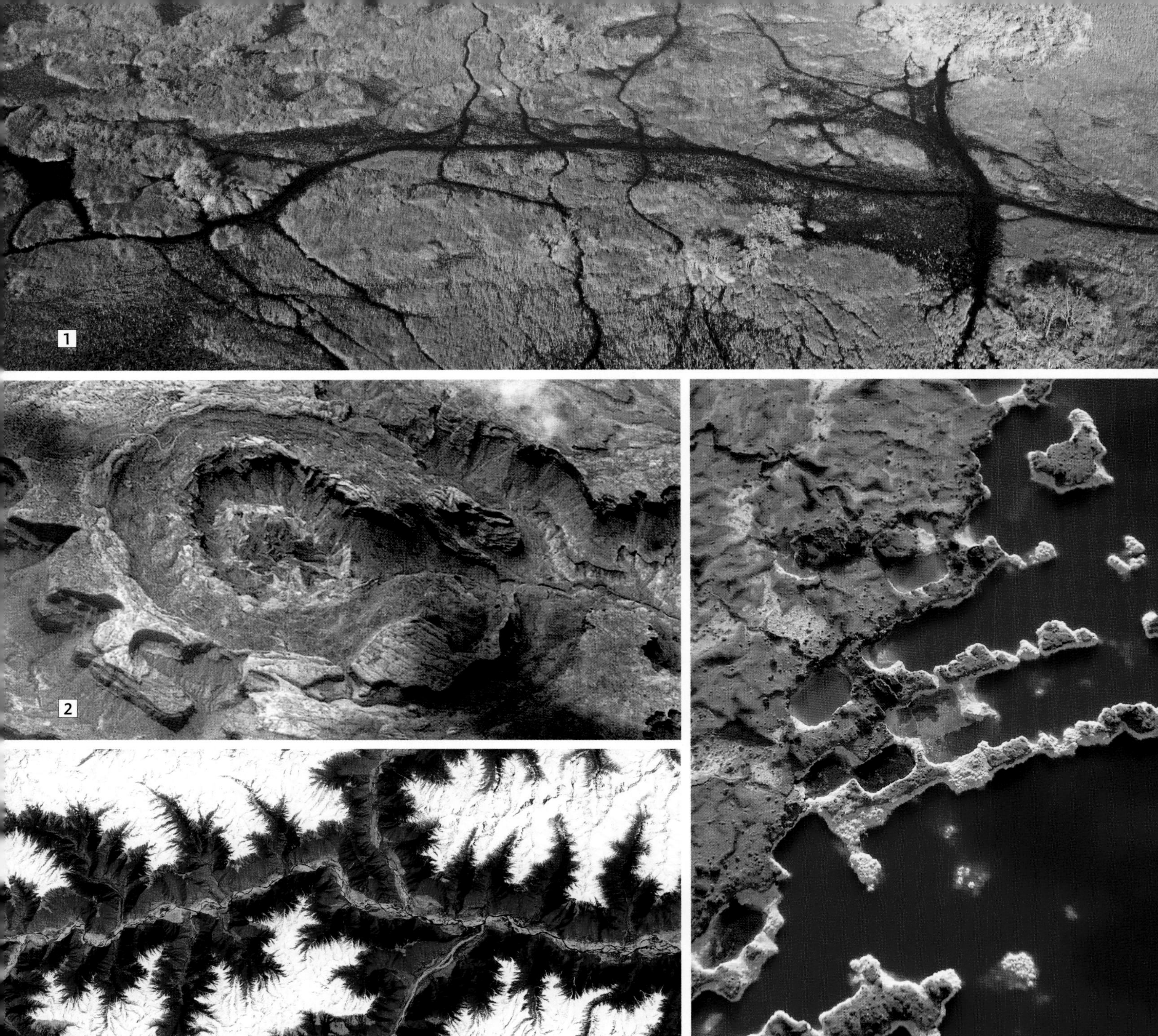
1
2
3
4

EARTH FROM ABOVE

1 Wetlands
Earth's abundance of surface water creates unique habitats such as wetlands. Formed wherever water is slowed on its progress, such as where a mature river meets the sea, wetlands provide a rich source of nutrients for diverse wildlife. This aerial view reveals the flat plains of the Okavango Delta in Botswana as a canvas of lakes, islands, and channels cutting through lush green vegetation.

2 Impact crater
This photograph of Upheaval Dome in Canyonlands National Park, Utah, USA, was taken from the International Space Station (ISS). The origin of the circular structure is uncertain, but the discovery of "shocked quartz" in the rock suggests it is a deeply eroded impact crater, perhaps 60 million years old. An alternative theory is that the dome is the eroded stump of a salt deposit.

3 Mountains
Rising to a towering 5,000m (16,000ft), the snowcapped peaks of the eastern Himalayas in Tibet and southwest China are among the highest on Earth. In this image from the Terra satellite, vegetation on the lower slopes appears red, while rivers are blue. Thrown up by the collisions of the Eurasian and Indian plates 50–70 million years ago, the Himalayas are still rising at the rate of 2cm (¾in) per year.

4 Salt pans
Algae growing in salt evaporation ponds in a coastal lagoon near Alexandria, Egypt, paint the landscape vivid red in this aerial view. Seawater is trapped in ponds for salt extraction; once the water has evaporated, the salt is harvested. As the salinity of the ponds changes, different algae flourish, turning the ponds from green to orange and red.

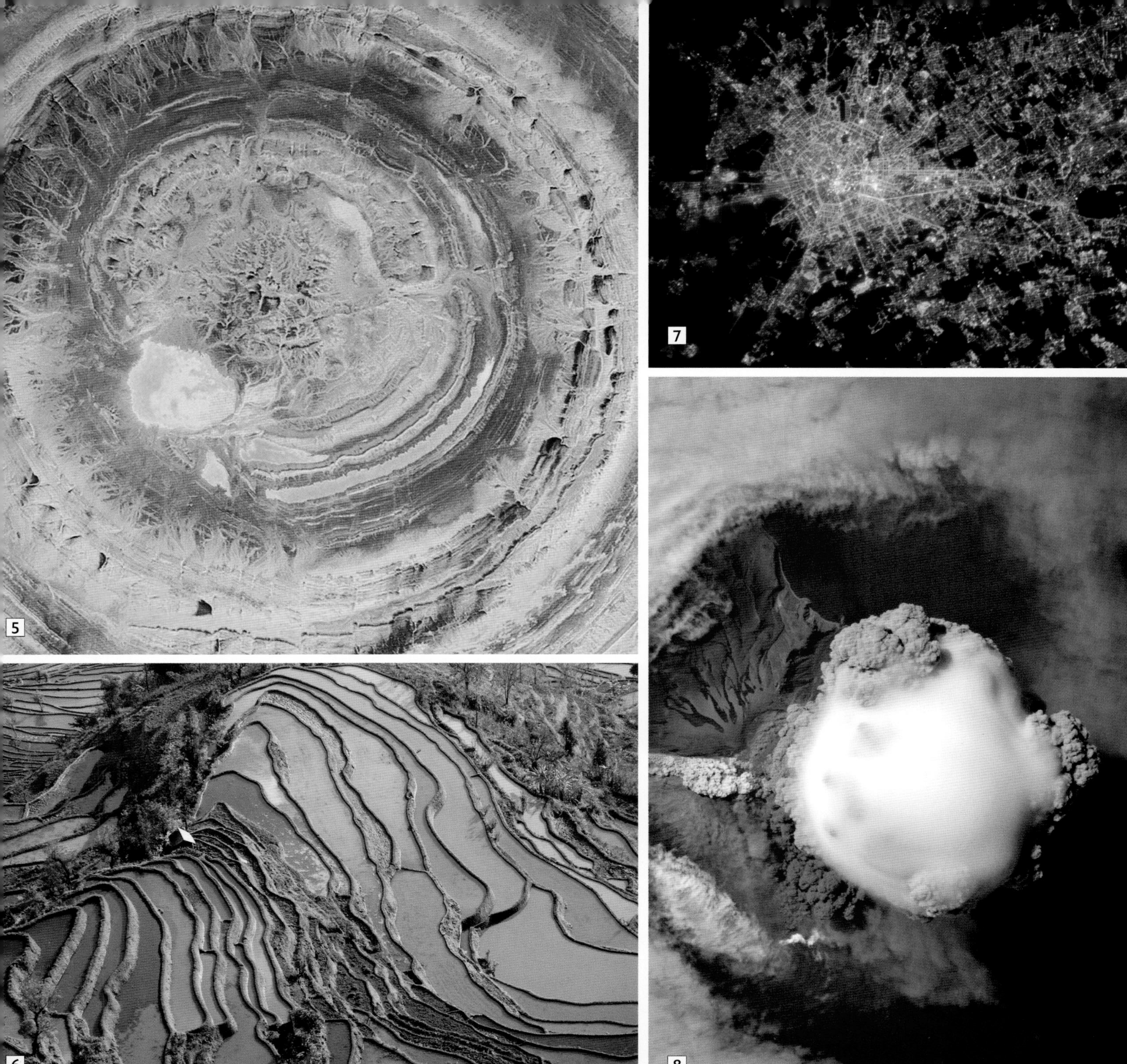

5 Desert
Known as Earth's Bull's-Eye, the Richat Structure in the Sahara desert is a landmark for astronauts. When viewed from space, the 50km (31 mile) wide rock dome stands out amid the otherwise featureless landscape. The circular structure probably formed as a result of uplift of layered sedimentary rock that became exposed to erosion.

6 Farmland
Carved into the mountainsides of Yunnan province, China, terraced fields turn the landscape into an abstract patchwork. The fields at lower altitude are warm enough for rice to flourish, while those at higher elevations are used to grow hardier crops, such as maize. Viewed from above, the extent of human impact on the landscape becomes apparent – the mountain is a monument to agriculture.

7 City
At night, the cities of Earth light up. In this photograph from the ISS, Milan illuminates the region of Lombardy, Italy. From space, the extent of city growth and light pollution is obvious. The brightest areas of Earth are the most urbanized. More than a century after the invention of the electric light, some regions remain unpopulated and entirely unlit – Antarctica is still in the dark.

8 Volcano
Viewed from the safe distance of the International Space Station, Sarychev Peak in the Kuril Islands erupts. At 1,500m (4,900ft), it is dwarfed by the volcano Olympus Mons on Mars, which stands at nearly 22,000m (74,000ft). With around 60 currently active volcanoes, Earth is much quieter, geologically speaking, than Jupiter's moon Io, which has over 400 and is the most volcanically active body in the Solar System.

OUR **PLANET**

FOR THOUSANDS OF YEARS, PEOPLE HAVE TRIED TO UNDERSTAND EARTH'S STRUCTURE AND WORKINGS. KNOWLEDGE HAS ACCUMULATED SLOWLY, WITH MANY KEY THEORIES DEVELOPING IN THE LAST FEW DECADES.

Unlike other celestial bodies, Earth was not visible to people in its entirety until the first camera-carrying satellites were launched in the 1960s. Nevertheless, more than 2,000 years ago the proto-scientists of ancient civilizations worked out that our planet is a sphere and gained some idea of its size and the extent of its oceans. It was not until the 20th century that Earth's age and internal structure were confirmed and the tectonic plates that move continents were discovered.

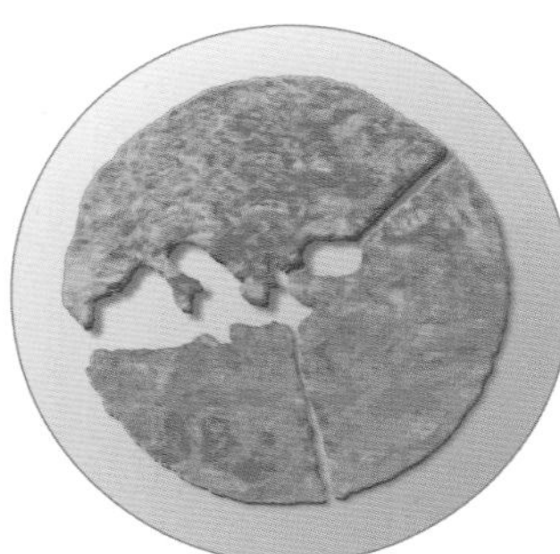

The world as understood by Greek philosopher Anaximander (c.610–546 BCE)

c.3000–500 BCE

Flat Earth
Some ancient Mediterranean societies believe that the world's landmasses sit on the flat surface of a disc, possibly surrounded by sea. The concept of a flat Earth is illustrated in some early maps.

c.330 BCE

Aristotle claims Earth is a sphere
Greek philosopher Aristotle reasons that Earth is a sphere. In support of his theory, he points out that some stars become visible only as a person travels far to the south. If Earth was flat, he argues, the same stars would be visible everywhere.

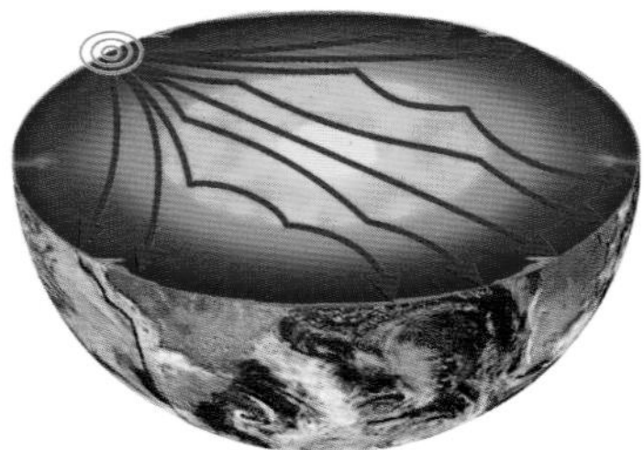

Passage of earthquake waves through Earth

1830s–40s

Ice age theory
Swiss geologist Louis Agassiz and other scientists study glacier-eroded landscapes in the Alpine regions of Europe. Agassiz is the first to propose that Earth has been through an ice age in the relatively recent past.

1906

Evidence for Earth's core
From the study of earthquake waves and their behaviour as they pass through Earth, Irish geologist Richard Oldham concludes that Earth has a distinct core. This, he suggests, is denser than the rest of the planet and slows waves that pass through it.

200 million years ago

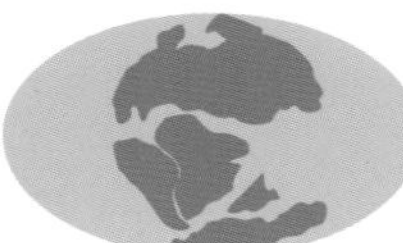

130 million years ago

70 million years ago

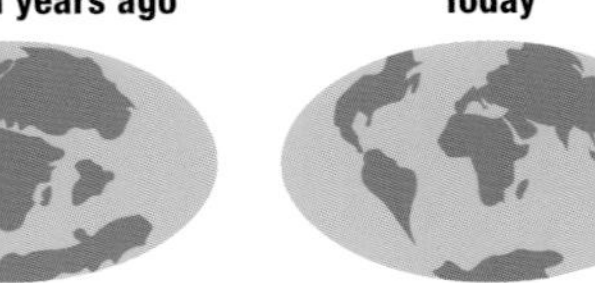

Today

1912

Wegener's continental drift
German scientist Alfred Wegener proposes that all the continents were once joined together and have since moved apart through an unknown mechanism, which he calls "continental drift". His ideas are rejected by most other scientists.

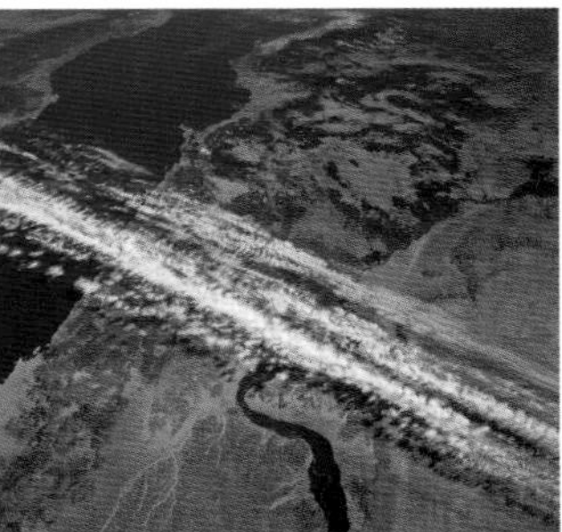

Jet stream clouds over southern Egypt

1920s–30s

Jet streams discovered
From the study of balloon and high-altitude aircraft flights, scientists in Japan, the USA, and Europe understand that fast-moving, narrow air currents flow west to east in Earth's atmosphere. These currents come to be known as jet streams.

1955

Earth's age established
US geochemist Clair Patterson establishes that Earth is 4.55 billion years old, by measuring the ratios of lead isotopes in meteorites that formed in the early Solar System. This is known as radiometric dating.

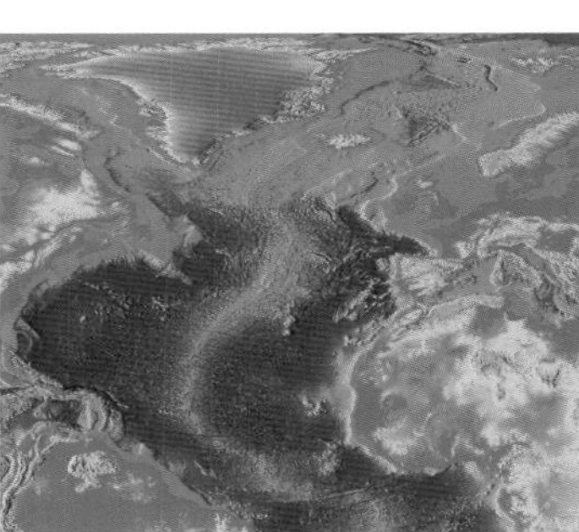

Mid-Atlantic ocean ridge

1960

Seafloor spreading
US geologist Harry Hess proposes that new seafloor is constantly created at mid-ocean ridges, from which it then slowly spreads away. This concept, which is quickly accepted, is key to the later development of the theory of plate tectonics.

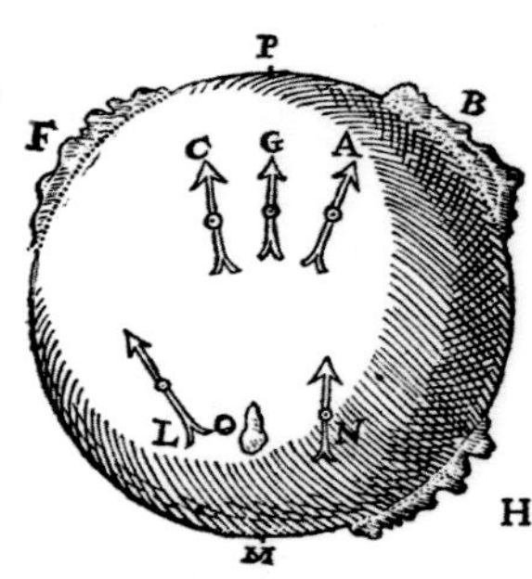
P
B
F
C
G
A
L
N
H
M

Gilbert's model of magnetic Earth

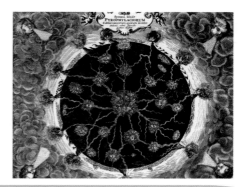

Earth's interior as imagined by Kircher

c.240 BCE

Circumference calculated
Greek scholar Eratosthenes makes the first accurate calculation of Earth's circumference. To do so, he compares the Sun's elevation above the horizon at two different places, one far south of the other, at the same date and time.

1600 CE

Magnetic Earth
After studying the behaviour of compass needles, English scientist William Gilbert, in his book *De Magnete*, suggests that Earth is a giant, spherical magnet. He correctly proposes that its centre is made mostly of iron.

1600s

Looking inwards
Many ideas are advanced about Earth's internal structure. In England, Edmond Halley claims our planet contains concentric, gas-filled spheres, while German scholar Athanasius Kircher thinks it might hold enormous, interlinked, fiery chambers.

Georges Cuvier (1769–1832)

James Hutton (1726–97)

1785

Hutton's geological theory
In his book, *Theory of the Earth*, Scottish scientist James Hutton, considered the father of modern geology, proposes that Earth was shaped entirely by slow-moving forces still in operation today, acting over long periods of time.

1798

Cavendish weighs Earth
English scientist Henry Cavendish calculates Earth's average density by means of gravity-measuring experiments. Using his findings, Earth's mass can also be calculated, so Cavendish is said to have "weighed the world".

1810s–20s

Cuvier's catastrophism
French naturalist Georges Cuvier champions the theory of catastrophism – the idea that many catastrophes have occurred over history, altering our planet suddenly rather than gradually, and killing off large groups of animal species.

Earth's tectonic plates

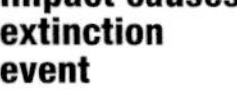

Impact causes extinction event

Late 1960s

Theory of plate tectonics
Building on the ideas of seafloor spreading and continental drift, researchers explore the possibility that Earth's outer shell is split into a dozen or so moving plates. This theory of plate tectonics revolutionizes Earth science.

1980

Explaining the extinction of dinosaurs
US physicist Luis Alvarez and others propose that a large asteroid or comet impacting Earth 65.5 million years ago (at the end of the Cretaceous period) caused extinction of the dinosaurs and many other animal and plant groups.

Late 20th century

Anthropocene
A new name, Anthropocene, is proposed for the modern era during which human activity has begun to have a profound effect on the planet, its climate, and its natural ecosystems.

THE **MOON**

THE MOON, EARTH'S COMPANION IN SPACE, IS OUR PLANET'S LONE SATELLITE. IT IS THE LARGEST AND BRIGHTEST OBJECT IN THE NIGHT SKY AND THE ONLY ONE WHOSE SURFACE FEATURES CAN BE EASILY SEEN WITH THE NAKED EYE.

With a diameter one-quarter of Earth's, the Moon is the largest satellite in the Solar System compared to its parent planet. Earth and the Moon exert a powerful influence on one another through their gravity. Tidal forces have slowed the Moon's rotation so that it spins once on its axis in the same time it takes to orbit Earth (27.32 days), and consequently keeps one face permanently towards our planet.

The Moon is a barren ball of rock that lacks sufficient gravity to hold on to a substantial atmosphere. Exposed alternately to the force of the Sun and the emptiness of space, the lunar surface experiences wild temperature swings, from 120°C (248°F) at local noon to –170°C (–274°F) in the middle of the long lunar night. The floors of permanently shadowed craters get even colder.

With no weather or tectonic activity to erase craters, much of the Moon's battered landscape preserves a barely altered record of conditions in our part of the Solar System over the last 4 billion years.

Hermite Crater, near the lunar north pole, is one of the **coldest places** in the Solar System.

MOON DATA

Average diameter	3,474km (2,159 miles)
Mass (Earth = 1)	0.012
Gravity at equator (Earth = 1)	0.167
Mean distance from Earth	385,000km (239,000 miles)
Axial tilt	1.5°
Rotation period (day)	27.32 Earth days
Orbital period	27.32 Earth days
Minimum temperature	–247°C (–413°F)
Maximum temperature	120°C (248°F)

▷ **Northern hemisphere**
The Moon orbits bolt upright in relation to the Sun, so its polar regions receive horizontal sunlight. As a result, crater floors near the poles can be permanently shadowed and may contain water ice.

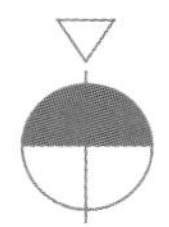

▷ **Far side**
The hemisphere that faces away from Earth is more densely cratered than the near side. It has fewer of the dark lava plains, or maria, that dominate the near side, and those it does have are relatively small.

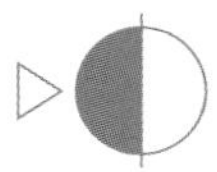

▷ **Southern hemisphere**
The south pole is located at the edge of a vast impact crater called the South Pole–Aitken Basin. Smaller craters within it contain areas of permanent shadow and ice from collisions with comets.

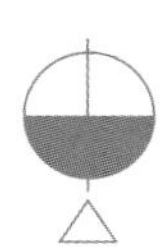

At 1,123km (698 miles) across, the Mare Imbrium (Sea of Rains) is one of the largest lunar maria. It is ringed by mountains thrown up by the meteor strike that formed the Imbrium impact basin.

Oceanus Procellarum (Ocean of Storms)

The Aristarchus Crater is a relatively young impact crater (450 million years old) and one of the Moon's brightest features.

Grimaldi Crater

Copernicus Crater has high central peaks and terraced walls.

Mare Humorum (Sea of Moisture)

Mare Nubium (Sea of Clouds)

The Clavius Crater is a huge ancient crater in the southern highlands. It is 225km (140 miles) in diameter.

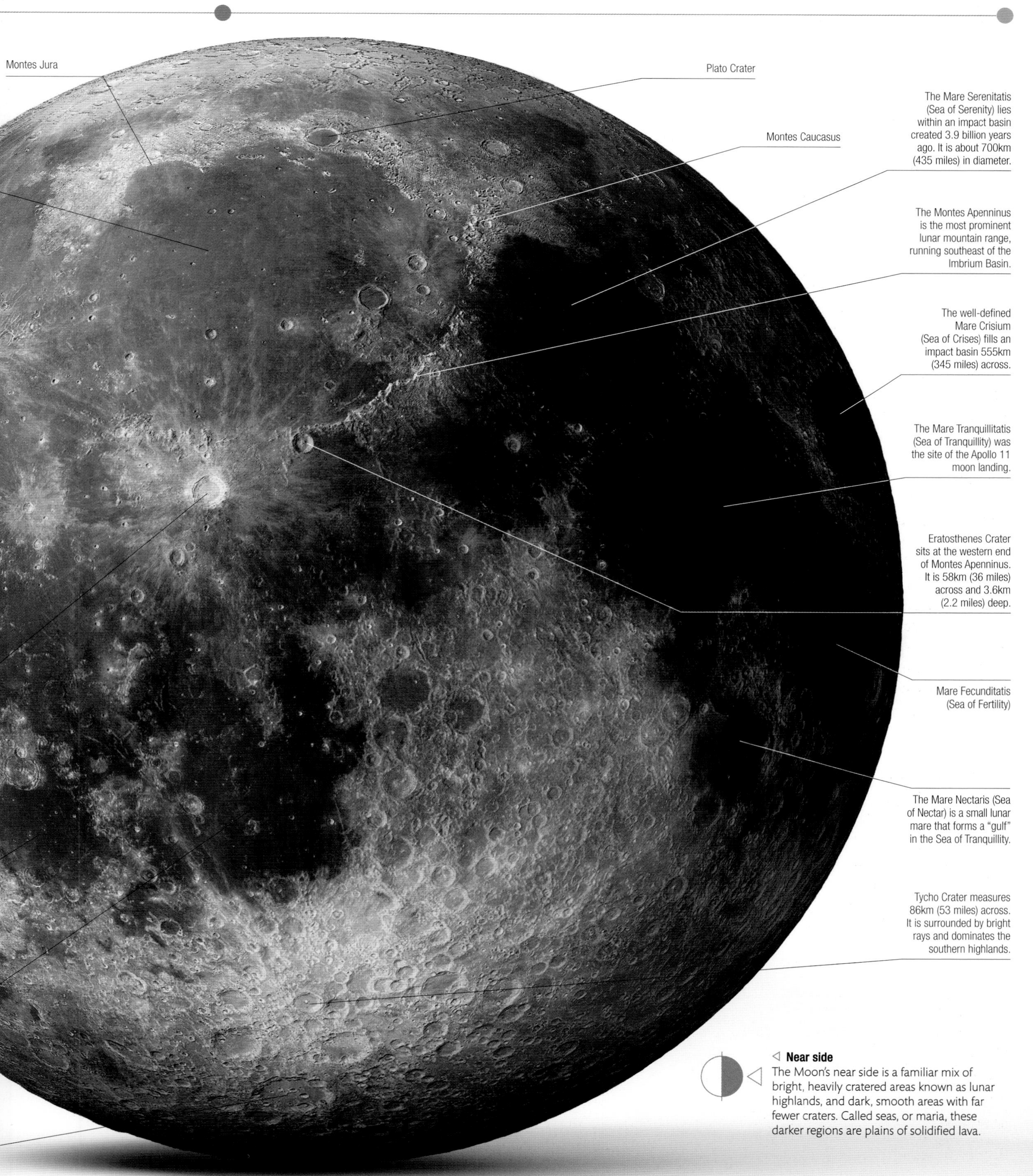
Montes Jura
Plato Crater
Montes Caucasus
The Mare Serenitatis (Sea of Serenity) lies within an impact basin created 3.9 billion years ago. It is about 700km (435 miles) in diameter.
The Montes Apenninus is the most prominent lunar mountain range, running southeast of the Imbrium Basin.
The well-defined Mare Crisium (Sea of Crises) fills an impact basin 555km (345 miles) across.
The Mare Tranquillitatis (Sea of Tranquillity) was the site of the Apollo 11 moon landing.
Eratosthenes Crater sits at the western end of Montes Apenninus. It is 58km (36 miles) across and 3.6km (2.2 miles) deep.
Mare Fecunditatis (Sea of Fertility)
The Mare Nectaris (Sea of Nectar) is a small lunar mare that forms a "gulf" in the Sea of Tranquillity.
Tycho Crater measures 86km (53 miles) across. It is surrounded by bright rays and dominates the southern highlands.

◁ **Near side**
The Moon's near side is a familiar mix of bright, heavily cratered areas known as lunar highlands, and dark, smooth areas with far fewer craters. Called seas, or maria, these darker regions are plains of solidified lava.

MOON STRUCTURE

AS A RELATIVELY SMALL BODY, THE MOON HAS COOLED CONSIDERABLY IN THE 4.5 BILLION YEARS SINCE ITS FORMATION. ITS ROCKY INTERIOR HAS LARGELY SOLIDIFIED AROUND A CORE OF RED-HOT OR PARTIALLY MOLTEN IRON.

The Moon's proximity to Earth has permitted scientists to investigate its inner structure in detail. Using seismometers placed on the surface by astronauts during the Apollo Moon landings, geologists can map the lunar interior by measuring the properties of moonquakes – seismic tremors triggered when tidal forces distort the shape of the Moon, or when meteorite impacts send shock waves through the interior of our satellite.

More recently, spacecraft, including NASA's twin GRAIL (Gravity Recovery and Interior Laboratory) satellites, have mapped the Moon's structure by measuring slight variations in its gravitational field.

Periodic moonquakes occur 1,000km (600 miles) or more below the surface.

The Moon's inner core is remarkably small, only around **240km (150 miles)** across.

◁ **Birth of the Moon**
Studies of lunar rock suggest that the Moon was formed around 4.5 billion years ago, when a Mars-sized world called Theia collided with the still-molten Earth. The impact obliterated Theia and blasted huge amounts of debris into orbit around Earth. Over time, much of this material came together to form a single large satellite – the Moon.

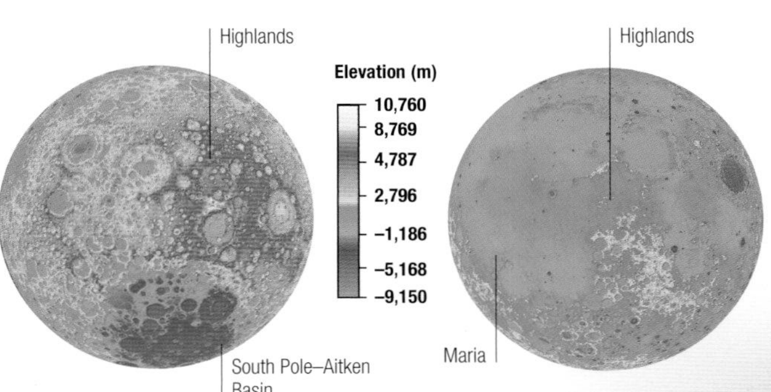
Highlands
Elevation (m)
10,760
8,769
4,787
2,796
–1,186
–5,168
–9,150
South Pole–Aitken Basin
FAR SIDE
Highlands
Maria
NEAR SIDE

◁ **Surface elevation**
The Moon's highest regions are on its far side, which is on average 5km (3 miles) higher than the near side. The lowest region – the 13km (8 mile) deep South Pole–Aitken Basin – is also on the far side. Low-lying lava plains called maria (seas) cover 31 per cent of the Moon's near side.

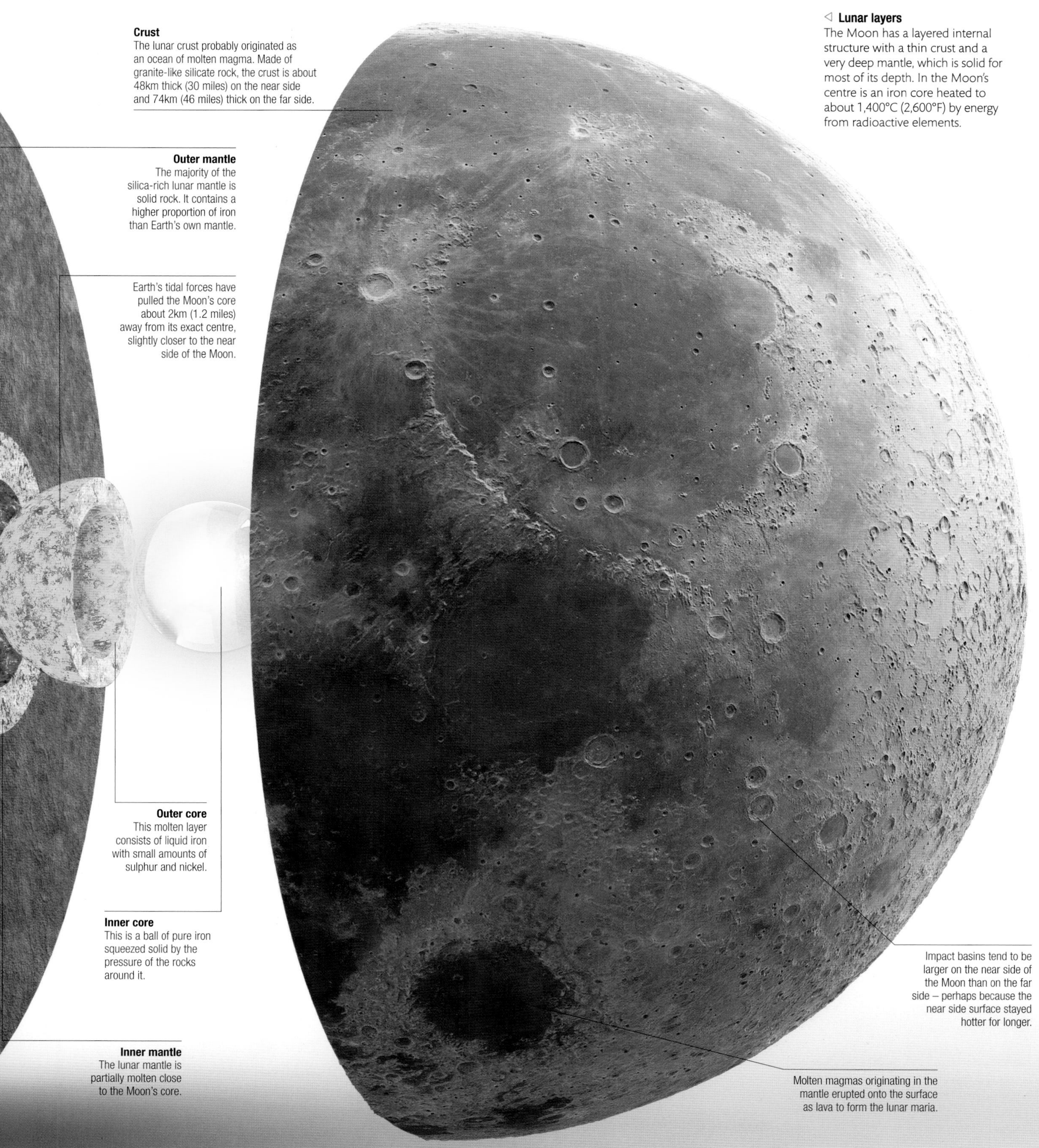
Crust
The lunar crust probably originated as an ocean of molten magma. Made of granite-like silicate rock, the crust is about 48km thick (30 miles) on the near side and 74km (46 miles) thick on the far side.
Outer mantle
The majority of the silica-rich lunar mantle is solid rock. It contains a higher proportion of iron than Earth's own mantle.
Earth's tidal forces have pulled the Moon's core about 2km (1.2 miles) away from its exact centre, slightly closer to the near side of the Moon.
Outer core
This molten layer consists of liquid iron with small amounts of sulphur and nickel.
Inner core
This is a ball of pure iron squeezed solid by the pressure of the rocks around it.
Inner mantle
The lunar mantle is partially molten close to the Moon's core.
Impact basins tend to be larger on the near side of the Moon than on the far side – perhaps because the near side surface stayed hotter for longer.
Molten magmas originating in the mantle erupted onto the surface as lava to form the lunar maria.

◁ **Lunar layers**
The Moon has a layered internal structure with a thin crust and a very deep mantle, which is solid for most of its depth. In the Moon's centre is an iron core heated to about 1,400°C (2,600°F) by energy from radioactive elements.

EARTH'S **COMPANION**

THE MOON IS SO LARGE COMPARED TO EARTH, AND ORBITS SO CLOSE TO ITS PARENT PLANET, THAT THE TWO WORLDS EXERT A CONSIDERABLE INFLUENCE ON ONE ANOTHER THROUGH THE FORCE OF GRAVITY.

The Moon's large size relative to its parent planet is due to the unique way in which it formed. Most natural satellites in the Solar System either formed from leftover debris after the new planet took shape or are small, captured objects such as asteroids. Consequently, moons are usually dwarfed by their parent planet. Earth's moon, in contrast, formed after a collision between Earth and another planet created a huge cloud of debris. Today, separated by an average distance of 384,400km (238,900 miles), Earth and its moon exert a strong gravitational pull on one another that generates tidal forces in both worlds. These forces have slowed the Moon's period of rotation and raise substantial tides in Earth's oceans.

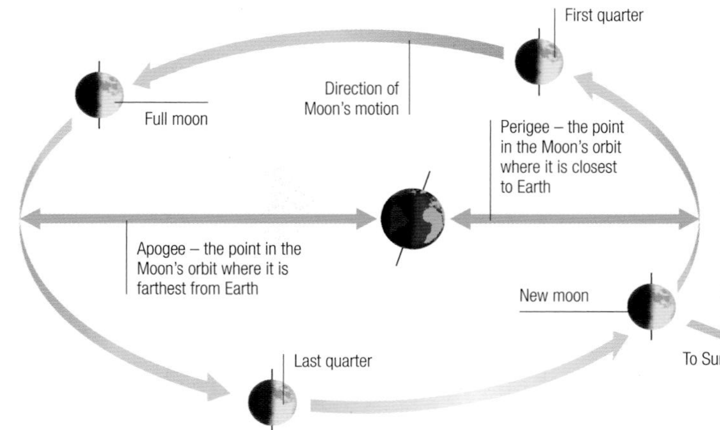
First quarter
Direction of Moon's motion
Full moon
Perigee – the point in the Moon's orbit where it is closest to Earth
Apogee – the point in the Moon's orbit where it is farthest from Earth
New moon
Last quarter
To Sun

△ **Spin and orbit**
Tidal forces pulling at irregularities in the Moon's spherical shape have caused our satellite's rotation to slow and its orbital position to drift slowly outward. The Moon has developed a synchronous rotation, meaning it spins once on its axis with each orbit of Earth. As a result, one hemisphere – the near side – always faces Earth, while the far side is forever turned away.

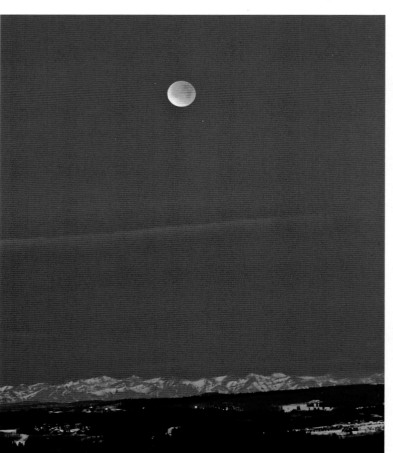

△ **Lunar eclipse**
Lunar eclipses take place when the Moon passes into Earth's shadow and turns a dark reddish colour as it catches sunlight scattered by Earth's atmosphere. Because Earth is much larger than the Moon and its shadow much wider, lunar eclipses are more frequent than solar eclipses.

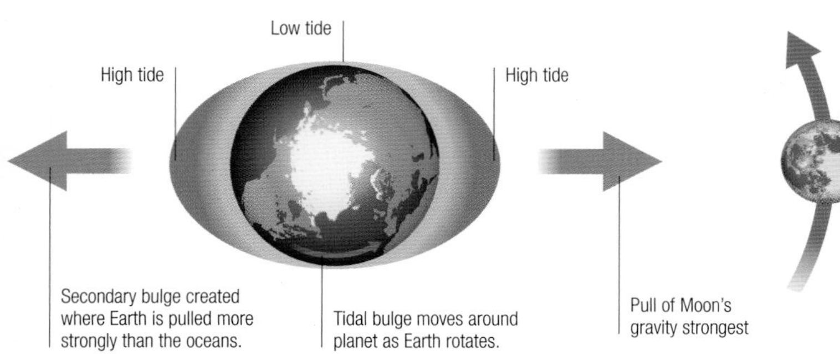
Low tide
High tide
High tide
Secondary bulge created where Earth is pulled more strongly than the oceans.
Tidal bulge moves around planet as Earth rotates.
Pull of Moon's gravity strongest

△ **Tidal forces**
Tidal forces arise because different parts of a celestial body experience different gravitational forces, depending on their distance from another object. Earth's oceans are lifted slightly on the side nearest the Moon, causing a high tide. On the opposite side of the planet, a second bulge occurs when the Moon's gravity is weakest.

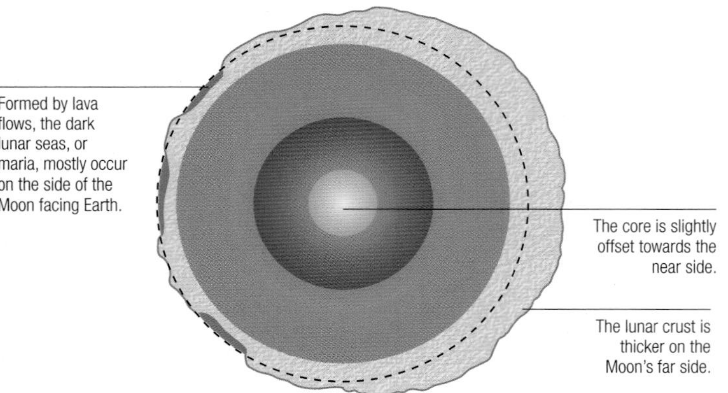
Formed by lava flows, the dark lunar seas, or maria, mostly occur on the side of the Moon facing Earth.
The core is slightly offset towards the near side.
The lunar crust is thicker on the Moon's far side.

△ **Offset structure**
Early in the Moon's history, tidal forces created by Earth's gravity pulled the core about 2km (1.2 miles) closer to the near side. The structures surrounding the core are also offset, with the mantle closer to the near side and the crust thicker on the far side. This may explain why the volcanic eruptions that formed the lunar seas were concentrated on the near side.

The lunar month
The Moon's most obvious feature from Earth is its monthly cycle of phases, waxing (growing) from a dark new moon through crescent, first quarter, and gibbous phases to a brilliant full moon drenched in sunlight, before waning (decreasing) back to another new moon. The entire cycle, known as a synodic or lunar month, takes 29.53 days and sees the Moon make a complete eastward circle around the sky relative to the Sun. The lunar month is slightly longer than the Moon's orbital period of 27.32 days because the Sun is also moving eastwards through Earth's skies, and it takes a little longer for the Moon to catch up and return to the same relative position.

MOON MAPPED

The large lunar seas, or maria, in the centre of the map are familiar features of the Moon's Earth-facing aspect. On the Moon's far side (right on the map), impact craters dominate the terrain.

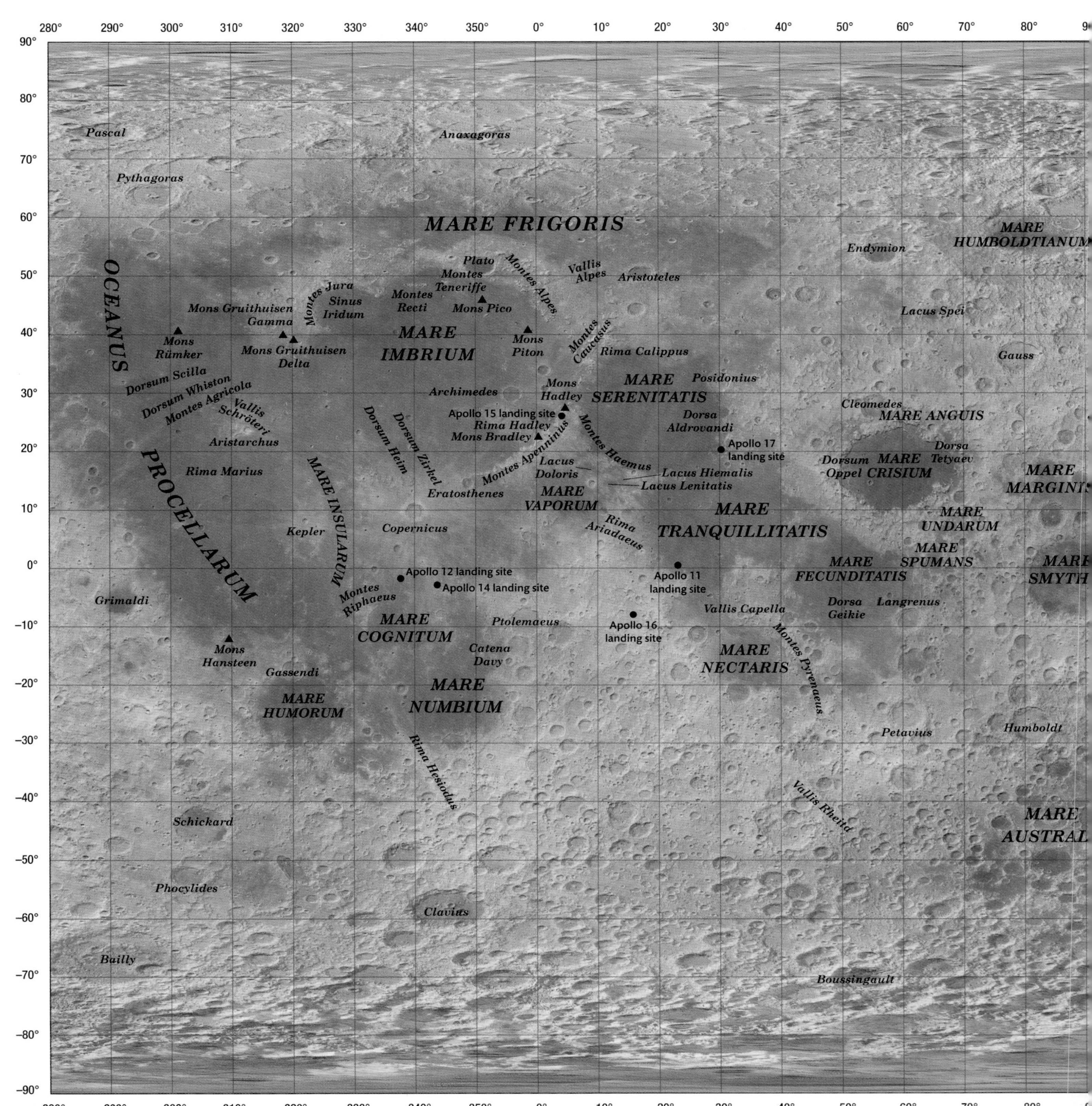

280°
290°
300°
310°
320°
330°
340°
350°
0°
10°
20°
30°
40°
50°
60°
70°
80°
90°
80°
70°
60°
50°
40°
30°
20°
10°
0°
–10°
–20°
–30°
–40°
–50°
–60°
–70°
–80°
–90°
Pascal
Anaxagoras
Pythagoras
MARE FRIGORIS
MARE HUMBOLDTIANUM
Endymion
OCEANUS
Plato
Montes Alpes
Vallis Alpes
Aristoteles
Montes Teneriffe
Montes Jura
Sinus Iridum
Montes Recti
Mons Pico
Mons Gruithuisen Gamma
Lacus Spei
MARE IMBRIUM
Mons Piton
Montes Caucasus
Rima Calippus
Mons Rümker
Mons Gruithuisen Delta
Gauss
Dorsum Scilla
Dorsum Whiston
Montes Agricola
Vallis Schröteri
MARE SERENITATIS
Posidonius
Archimedes
Mons Hadley
Cleomedes
MARE ANGUIS
Apollo 15 landing site
Rima Hadley
Mons Bradley
Dorsum Heim
Dorsum Zirkel
Dorsa Aldrovandi
Aristarchus
Montes Haemus
Apollo 17 landing site
Dorsa Tetyaev
PROCELLARUM
MARE INSULARUM
Montes Apenninus
Lacus Doloris
Lacus Hiemalis
Lacus Lenitatis
Dorsum Oppel
MARE CRISIUM
MARE MARGINIS
Rima Marius
Eratosthenes
MARE VAPORUM
MARE TRANQUILLITATIS
MARE UNDARUM
Rima Ariadaeus
Kepler
Copernicus
MARE SPUMANS
MARE FECUNDITATIS
MARE SMYTHII
Apollo 12 landing site
Apollo 14 landing site
Apollo 11 landing site
Montes Riphaeus
Grimaldi
Vallis Capella
Dorsa Geikie
Langrenus
MARE COGNITUM
Ptolemaeus
Apollo 16 landing site
Mons Hansteen
Catena Davy
Montes Pyrenaeus
MARE NECTARIS
Gassendi
MARE NUMBIUM
MARE HUMORUM
Petavius
Humboldt
Rima Hesiodus
Vallis Rheita
Schickard
MARE AUSTRALE
Phocylides
Clavius
Bailly
Boussingault

Scale 1:23,566,109

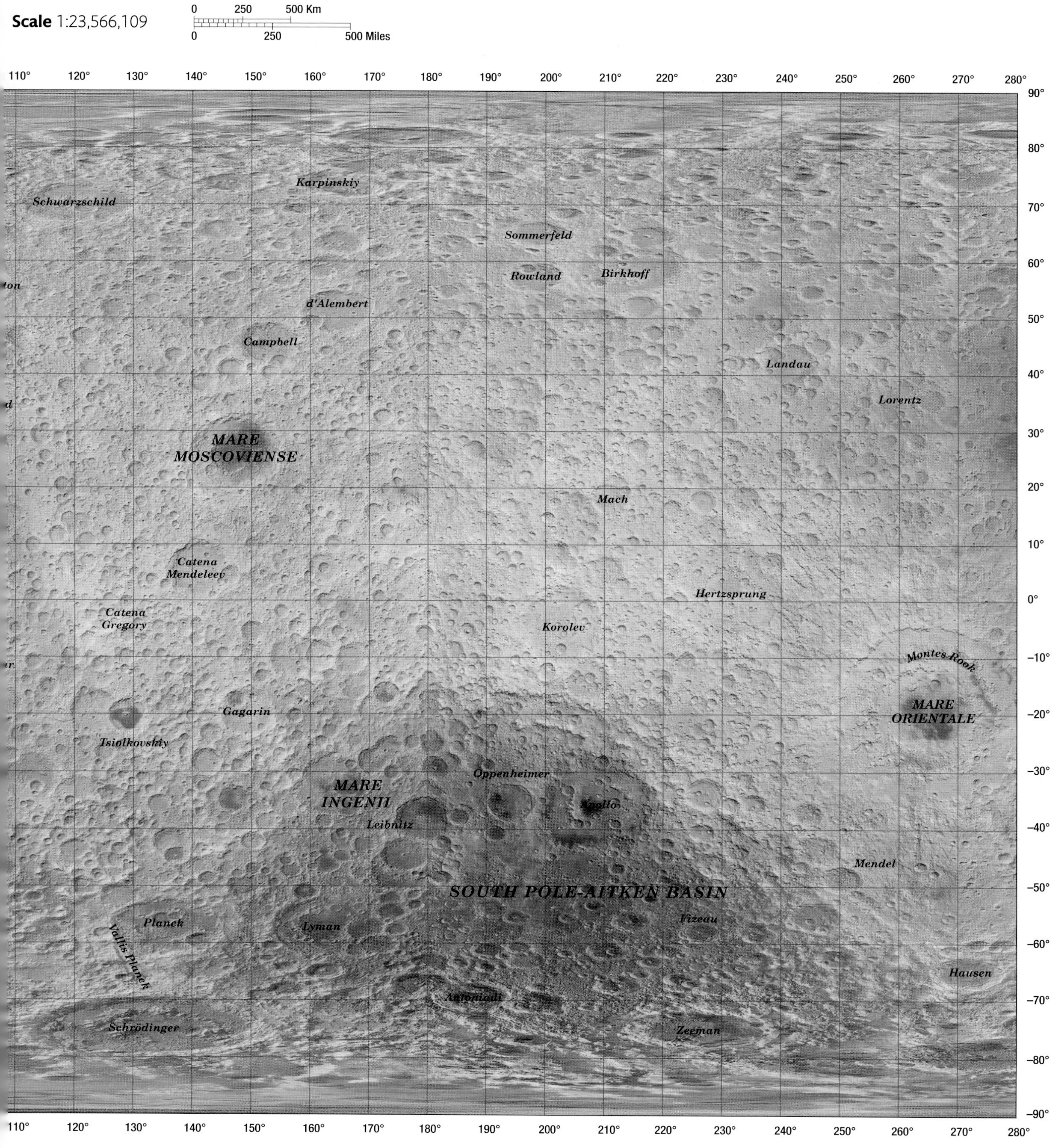
0 250 500 Km
0 250 500 Miles
110° 120° 130° 140° 150° 160° 170° 180° 190° 200° 210° 220° 230° 240° 250° 260° 270° 280°
90° 80° 70° 60° 50° 40° 30° 20° 10° 0° –10° –20° –30° –40° –50° –60° –70° –80° –90°
Karpinskiy
Schwarzschild
Sommerfeld
Rowland
Birkhoff
d'Alembert
Campbell
Landau
Lorentz
MARE MOSCOVIENSE
Mach
Catena Mendeleev
Hertzsprung
Catena Gregory
Korolev
Montes Rook
MARE ORIENTALE
Gagarin
Tsiolkovskiy
Oppenheimer
MARE INGENII
Apollo
Leibnitz
Mendel
SOUTH POLE-AITKEN BASIN
Planck
Lyman
Fizeau
Vallis Planck
Hausen
Antoniadi
Schrödinger
Zeeman

DESTINATION HADLEY RILLE

A STEEP-SIDED VALLEY RUNNING FOR 100KM (60 MILES) ACROSS THE LUNAR LANDSCAPE, HADLEY RILLE IS THE REMNANT OF AN ANCIENT LAVA STREAM THAT FLOWED ACROSS THE MOON'S SURFACE AROUND 3 BILLION YEARS AGO.

Hadley Rille lies on the edge of the Mare Imbrium impact basin at the foot of the Montes Apenninus mountain range. The valley originates at an elongated crater called Bela, from where it winds across a plain known as the Palus Putridinus. The Rille is thought to be a lava channel that formed when lava flowed across the lunar surface like a river. This image was taken in 1971, when Hadley Rille was observed during the Apollo 15 mission. Astronaut David Scott left a memorial sculpture and plaque at the site to commemorate astronauts who had died in training and on missions.

David Scott with a lunar rover at the Apollo 15 landing site, photographed by James Irwin

LOCATION

Latitude 3°E; longitude 26°N

LAND PROFILE

For much of its length, Hadley Rille is around 1.5km (0.9 miles) wide and between 180 and 270m (600 and 900ft) deep.

100
0
−100
−200
−300
−400
−500
Elevation (m)
Profile width (m)
0
800
1600

77 KG (170LB) OF LUNAR MATERIAL WAS RETURNED TO EARTH BY THE APOLLO 15 MISSION.

APOLLO 15

On 30 July 1971, Apollo 15's Lunar Module landed near one of Hadley Rille's deepest points, where the valley plunges to 370m (1,200ft). Using the Lunar Roving Vehicle for the first time, the astronauts made three excursions to explore nearby craters and collect rock samples.

LRV 1
LRV 2
LRV 3
Landing site
Hadley Rille
Earthlight
Dune
St George

EARTHRISE

This awe-inspiring Earthrise – the rising of Earth over the Moon's horizon – was filmed by the Japanese spacecraft Kaguya on 6 April 2008 from an altitude of about 100km (60 miles). For Kaguya to capture this spectacle, the orbits of the Moon, Earth, Sun, and the spacecraft had to line up. Since Earth is almost stationary when viewed from the Moon, an Earthrise is most easily observed from orbiting spacecraft. To see one from the Moon's surface, an astronaut would need to be standing near one of the Moon's poles.

LUNAR CRATERS

THE SURFACE OF THE MOON IS COVERED IN COUNTLESS CRATERS OF ALL SIZES. THEIR FORMATION HAS BEEN THE DRIVING FORCE SHAPING THE LUNAR LANDSCAPE FOR MORE THAN 4.5 BILLION YEARS.

How the Moon's craters formed was not fully understood until the 1960s, when the first robot lunar landers showed that craters of all sizes existed, including tiny ones. This discovery confirmed that the craters must have been caused by impacts from space, rather than by volcanic eruptions.

It's now clear that craters cover all areas of the lunar terrain, although in some places the oldest craters have been covered over by later events, including volcanic eruptions and further impacts. The Moon is not the only heavily cratered body in the Solar System, but it's the one we can study in greatest detail.

▽ **How craters form**
The Moon's well-preserved craters have given astronomers a detailed understanding of the crater formation process. The size and shape of a crater are determined mainly by the kinetic energy of the incoming object (a combination of its speed and mass).

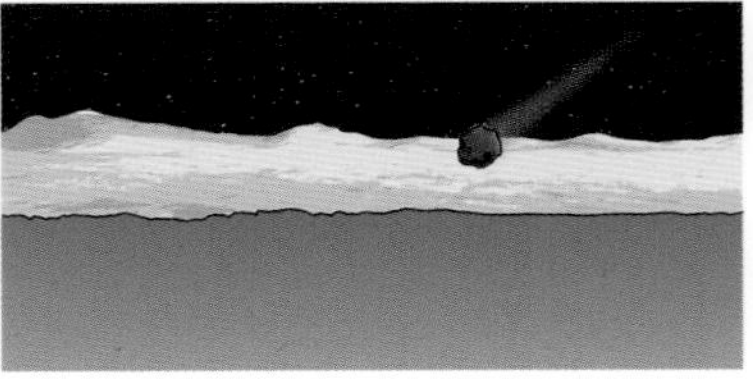

1 Incoming space rock
Meteoroids approach the lunar surface at a variety of speeds, depending on whether they are catching up with the Moon or meeting it head-on.

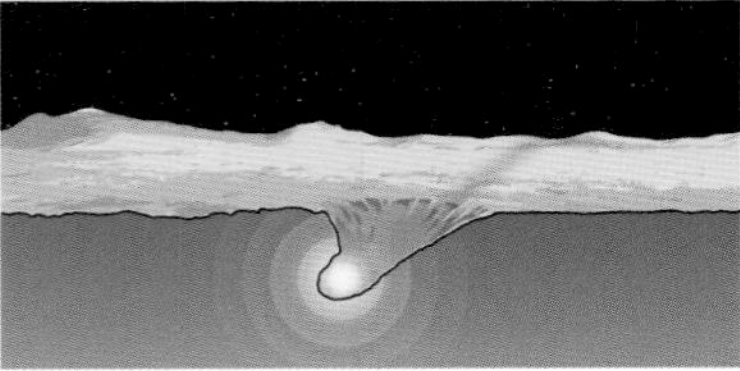

2 Initial impact
The impact creates a shock wave that vaporizes the meteoroid and ripples out into the crust, compressing and heating it along a bowl-shaped shock front.

3 Ejecta blanket
As the shock wave passes, material from the landing site is thrown out, forming a layer of debris on the surrounding landscape known as an ejecta blanket.

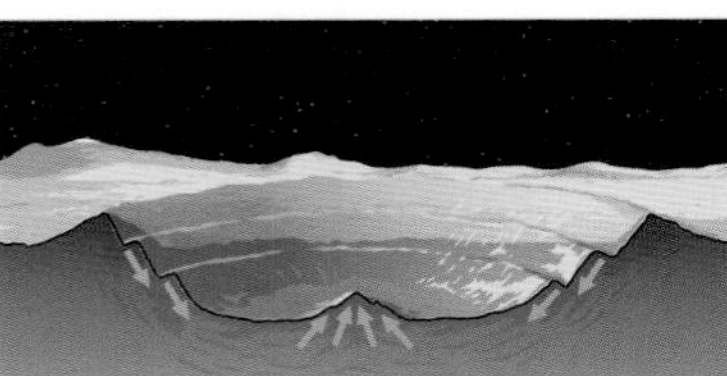

4 Crater
The result is a surface depression. In a large crater, the crust may rebound to form a central peak; the sides may slump under their own weight to form terraces.

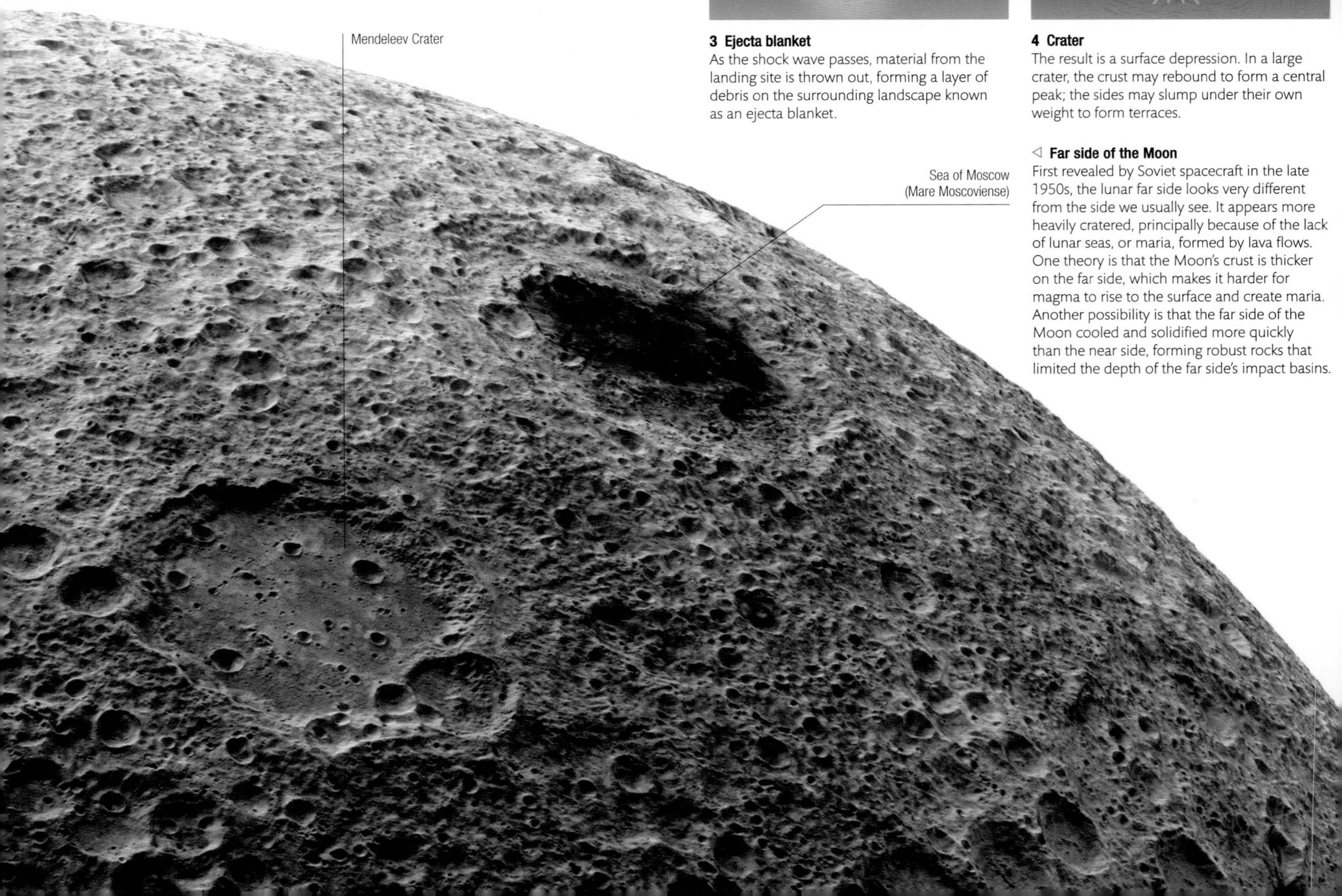

Mendeleev Crater
Sea of Moscow (Mare Moscoviense)

◁ **Far side of the Moon**
First revealed by Soviet spacecraft in the late 1950s, the lunar far side looks very different from the side we usually see. It appears more heavily cratered, principally because of the lack of lunar seas, or maria, formed by lava flows. One theory is that the Moon's crust is thicker on the far side, which makes it harder for magma to rise to the surface and create maria. Another possibility is that the far side of the Moon cooled and solidified more quickly than the near side, forming robust rocks that limited the depth of the far side's impact basins.

▷ **Crater map**
This map, created using data from NASA's Lunar Reconnaissance Orbiter, charts the position and size of over 5,000 large impact craters covering parts of the near and far sides of the Moon. The biggest of them have filled in with lava to form basalt plains, producing the lunar maria. Scientists can estimate the age of different parts of the Moon's surface by counting the craters that accumulated over time.

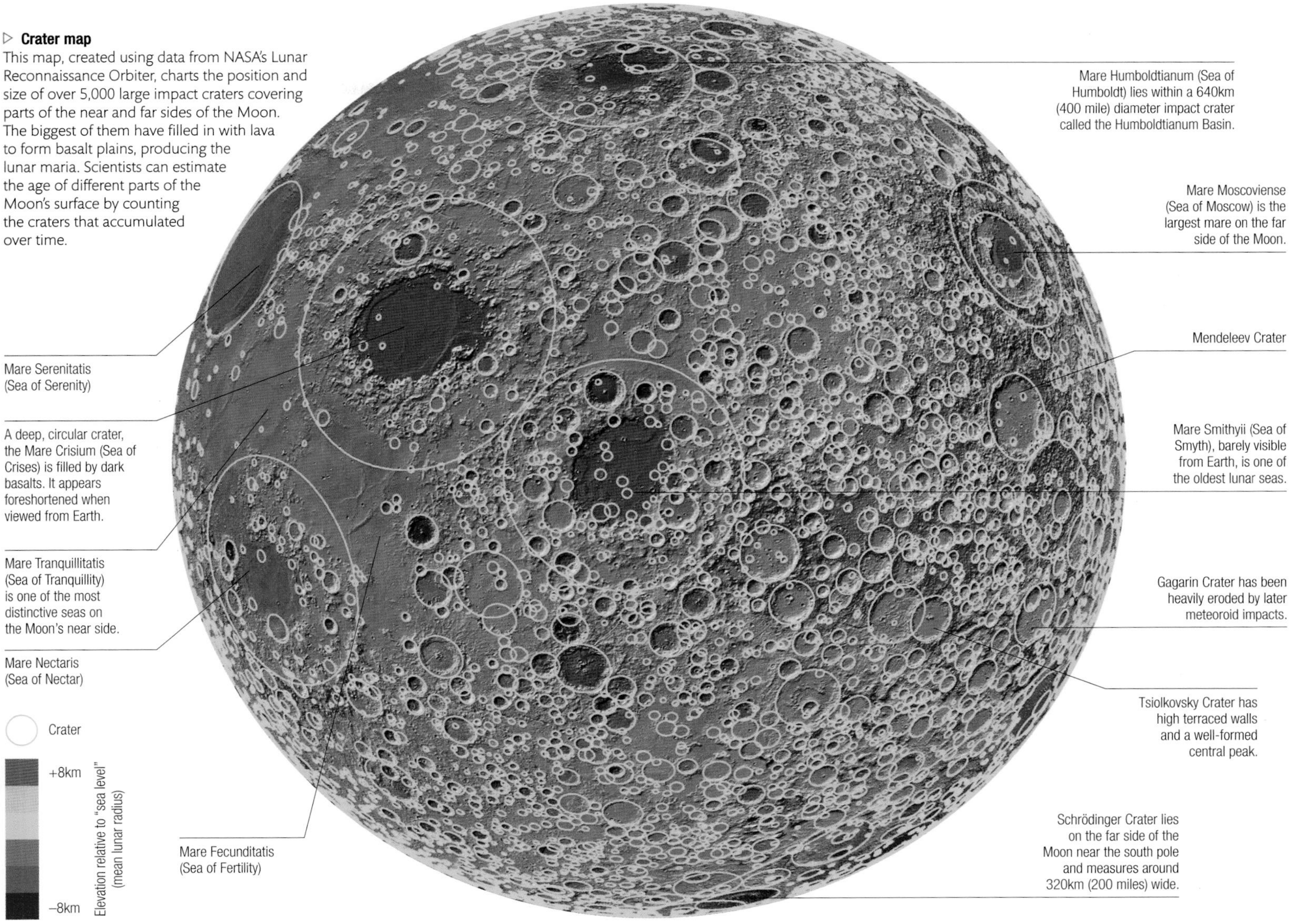

Mare Serenitatis (Sea of Serenity)

A deep, circular crater, the Mare Crisium (Sea of Crises) is filled by dark basalts. It appears foreshortened when viewed from Earth.

Mare Tranquillitatis (Sea of Tranquillity) is one of the most distinctive seas on the Moon's near side.

Mare Nectaris (Sea of Nectar)

Crater

+8km

–8km

Elevation relative to "sea level" (mean lunar radius)

Mare Fecunditatis (Sea of Fertility)

Mare Humboldtianum (Sea of Humboldt) lies within a 640km (400 mile) diameter impact crater called the Humboldtianum Basin.

Mare Moscoviense (Sea of Moscow) is the largest mare on the far side of the Moon.

Mendeleev Crater

Mare Smithyii (Sea of Smyth), barely visible from Earth, is one of the oldest lunar seas.

Gagarin Crater has been heavily eroded by later meteoroid impacts.

Tsiolkovsky Crater has high terraced walls and a well-formed central peak.

Schrödinger Crater lies on the far side of the Moon near the south pole and measures around 320km (200 miles) wide.

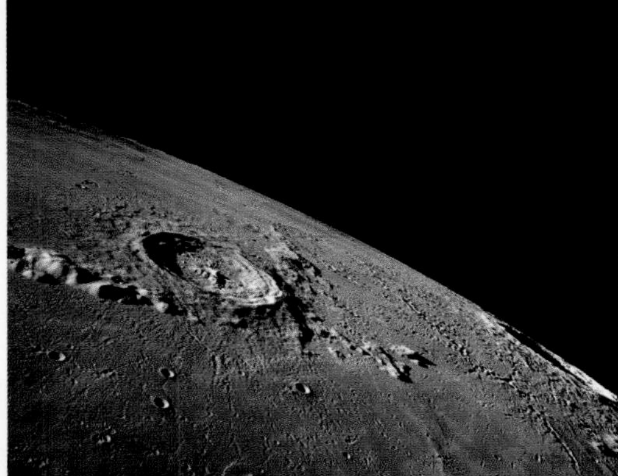

△ **Copernicus Crater**
Easily visible from Earth through binoculars, this young crater, which formed just 800 million years ago, is exceptionally well preserved. Copernicus is surrounded by a ring of enormous, bright rays – debris ejected by the impact – that are most conspicuous at full moon. The crater was the planned landing site for NASA's Apollo 18 manned mission, which was cancelled.

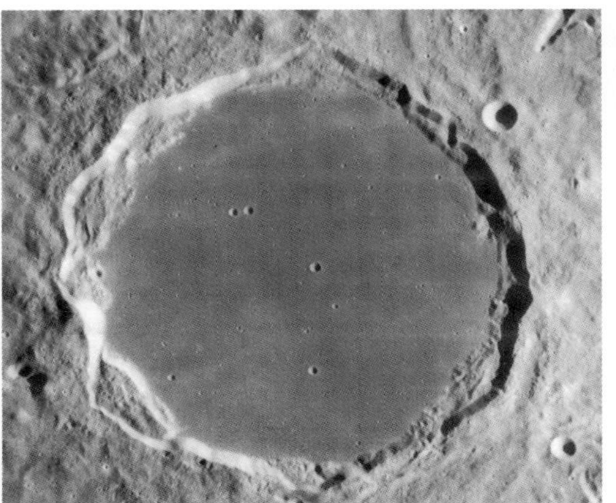

△ **Plato Crater**
This 109km (69 mile) wide crater to the north of the Mare Imbrium has a dark and smooth appearance, thanks to the lavas that flooded its floor. Plato is thought to have formed around 3.84 billion years ago, shortly after the neighbouring Mare Imbrium impact basin. The crater's rim has been shaped by a series of landslides.

△ **Plum Crater**
This small crater, measuring only 36m (118ft) across, was the first geological stop reached by rover during the Apollo 16 mission of 1972. While searching the crater, 1.4km (0.9 miles) from their landing site, the astronauts found Big Muley – a 4-billion-year old boulder weighing 11.7kg (26lb). Big Muley is the largest rock brought back to Earth by Apollo astronauts.

HIGHLANDS AND PLAINS

THE LUNAR LANDSCAPE CAN BE BROADLY DIVIDED INTO TWO DISTINCT TYPES OF TERRAIN: BRIGHT, HEAVILY CRATERED HIGHLANDS AND RELATIVELY SMOOTH, DARK PLAINS KNOWN AS LUNAR SEAS, OR MARIA.

The highlands represent the original ancient crust of the Moon, formed as our satellite's surface began to solidify from a molten magma ocean 4.5 billion years ago. They are dominated by bright silicate minerals similar to those on Earth's crust, and they feature countless craters laid one on top of another over billions of years. The maria, meanwhile, are flat and sparsely cratered plains consisting of dark basaltic lavas. Studies of the boundaries between the two regions show that the lunar maria are later surfaces that have erased all traces of earlier craters.

Mare Frigoris (Sea of Cold)

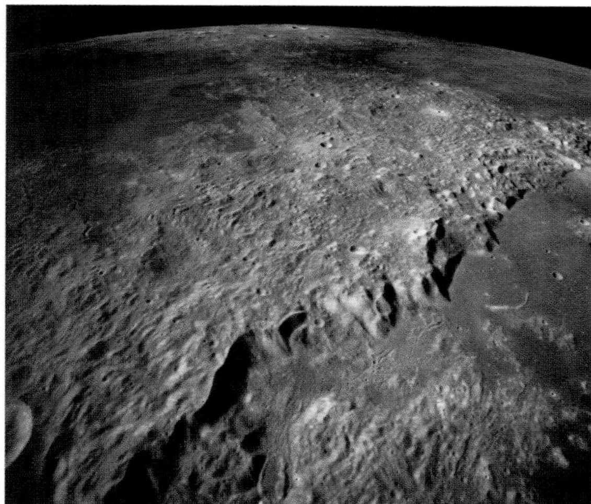

△ **Montes Apenninus**
Named after an Italian mountain range, the lunar Apennines form one of the largest and most prominent mountain chains on the Moon. This range of mountains, approximately 600km (370 miles) long and up to 5km (3.1 miles) high, was thrown up during the formation of the Mare Imbrium basin around 3.9 billion years ago.

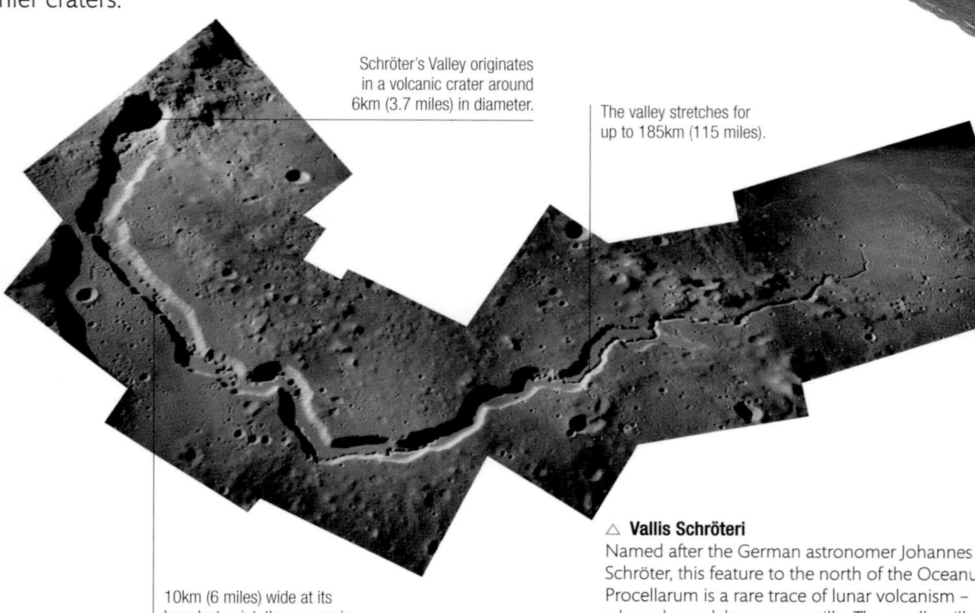
Schröter's Valley originates in a volcanic crater around 6km (3.7 miles) in diameter.
The valley stretches for up to 185km (115 miles).
10km (6 miles) wide at its broadest point, the canyon is up to 1km (0.6 miles) deep.

△ **Vallis Schröteri**
Named after the German astronomer Johannes Schröter, this feature to the north of the Oceanus Procellarum is a rare trace of lunar volcanism – a lava channel, known as a rille. The smaller rille here is from a later lava eruption that flowed along the floor of the original rille, but formed a new channel within the main one. Sinuous rilles occur in several locations on the Moon.

North Massif
Camelot Crater
Sculptured Hills
Lunar rover

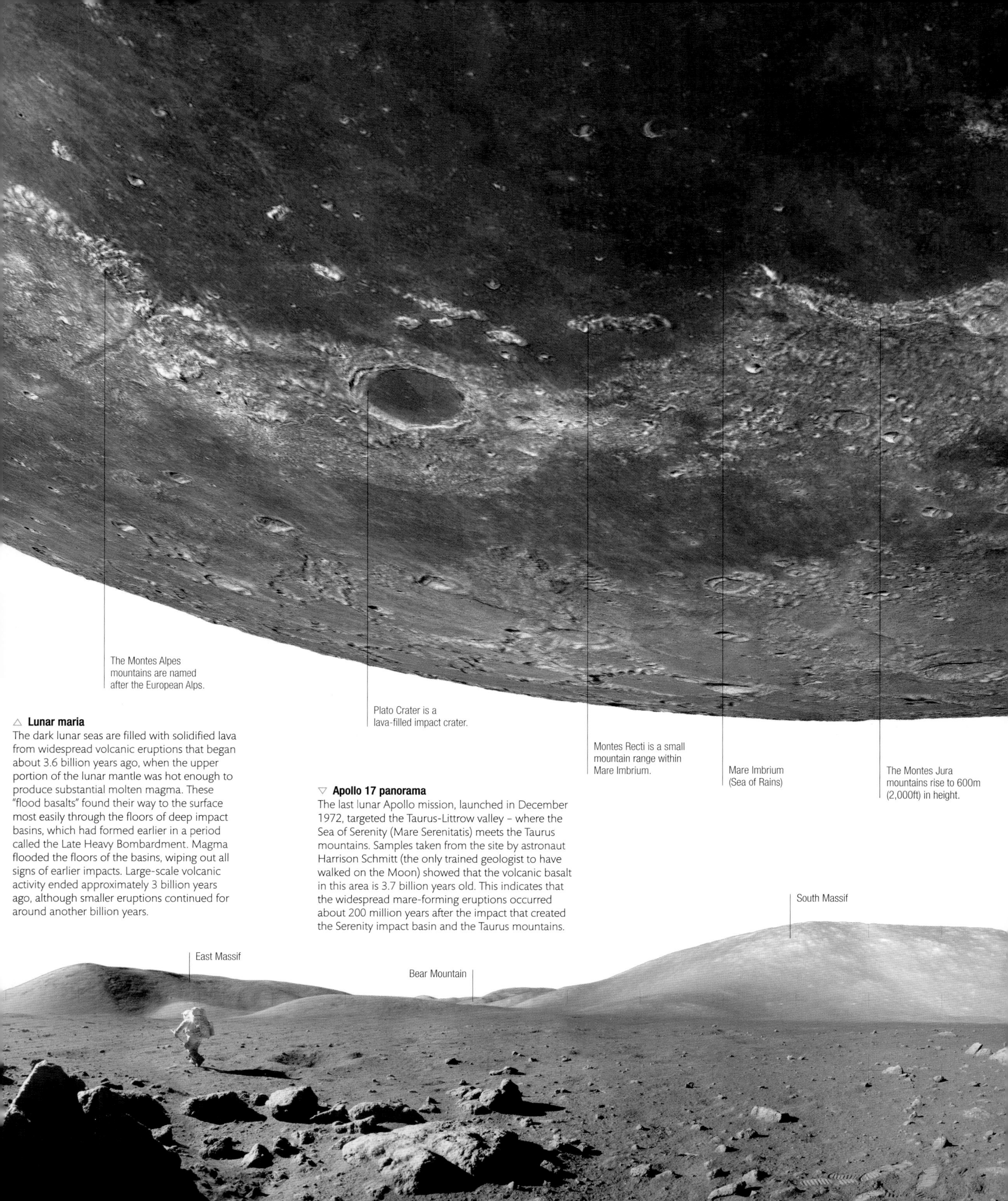
The Montes Alpes mountains are named after the European Alps.
Plato Crater is a lava-filled impact crater.
Montes Recti is a small mountain range within Mare Imbrium.
Mare Imbrium (Sea of Rains)
The Montes Jura mountains rise to 600m (2,000ft) in height.
South Massif
East Massif
Bear Mountain

△ **Lunar maria**

The dark lunar seas are filled with solidified lava from widespread volcanic eruptions that began about 3.6 billion years ago, when the upper portion of the lunar mantle was hot enough to produce substantial molten magma. These "flood basalts" found their way to the surface most easily through the floors of deep impact basins, which had formed earlier in a period called the Late Heavy Bombardment. Magma flooded the floors of the basins, wiping out all signs of earlier impacts. Large-scale volcanic activity ended approximately 3 billion years ago, although smaller eruptions continued for around another billion years.

▽ **Apollo 17 panorama**

The last lunar Apollo mission, launched in December 1972, targeted the Taurus-Littrow valley – where the Sea of Serenity (Mare Serenitatis) meets the Taurus mountains. Samples taken from the site by astronaut Harrison Schmitt (the only trained geologist to have walked on the Moon) showed that the volcanic basalt in this area is 3.7 billion years old. This indicates that the widespread mare-forming eruptions occurred about 200 million years after the impact that created the Serenity impact basin and the Taurus mountains.

STORY OF THE **MOON**

THE BIGGEST AND BRIGHTEST OBJECT IN THE NIGHT SKY HAS ALWAYS BEEN AN INVITING SUBJECT TO STUDY, AND PEOPLE HAVE TRACKED ITS MONTHLY CYCLE OF PHASES SINCE PREHISTORIC TIMES.

Moon-watching was important to the first agricultural societies of the Stone Age because the Moon's phases served as a calendar, telling farmers when to sow and harvest crops. By Babylonian times, astronomers not only understood the phases but could predict lunar eclipses, and by Greek times they knew the Moon was spherical and caused tides. Over the following centuries, our understanding of the Moon progressed in small steps as more details came to light: the nature of its rugged surface, its elliptical orbit, and its lack of air. But the giant leap in understanding came in the 20th century when the Moon became the first alien world people have stepped foot on.

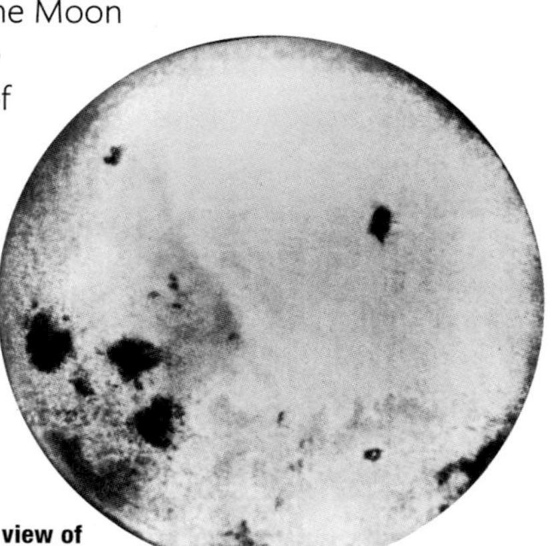

Luna 3 view of the Moon's far side

Lunar eclipse

c.20,000 BCE

Prehistoric calendar
In the Ishango region of central Africa, people mark a bone with a series of notches that appear to track the monthly cycle and phases of the Moon. Modern researchers believe the Ishango bone is an early lunar calendar.

500 BCE

Predicting eclipses
Babylonian astronomers (based in what is now Iraq) keep detailed records of lunar eclipses. They discover that eclipses occur in a repeating cycle and so become able to predict when eclipses will occur.

1757

Moon mass measured
The French astronomer Alexis Clairaut, one of the leading mathematicians of the time, makes the first accurate measurement of the mass of the Moon, using the results of his observations to hone Isaac Newton's early calculations.

Impact craters

1873

Impact theory
English astronomer Richard Proctor proposes that the Moon's craters are caused by meteorite impacts and not, as generally believed, by volcanic activity. Proctor's view is not fully accepted by astronomers until well into the 20th century.

1959

The far side
The Soviet spacecraft Luna 3 returns the first photographs of the far side of the Moon, which has never been seen before. These images reveal a heavily cratered surface that has fewer dark, flat regions, or maria, than the near side.

Luna 9

1966

First soft landing
Another Soviet spacecraft, Luna 9, is the first to make a soft landing on the Moon. It confirms that lunar soil is firm enough to support the weight of a landing craft and that people will be able to walk on the Moon's surface without sinking.

Apollo 17 landing

1969–72

Manned missions
During the Apollo series of lunar missions, US astronauts land on the Moon, place measuring apparatus on its surface, and collect rock samples. Analysis of the samples greatly increases knowledge of the Moon's surface composition, formation, and history.

Lunar formation theory

1980s

Origins understood
There is now agreement among scientists on the origins of the Moon. The favoured hypothesis is that the Moon formed from a ring of debris around Earth – the aftermath of a collision between our planet and a planet the size of Mars.

Hipparchus at the Alexandria Observatory

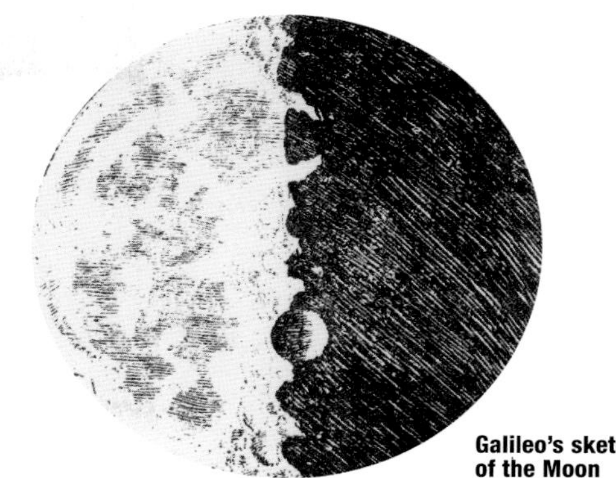
Galileo's sketch of the Moon

c.450 BCE

Moonshine explained
The Greek scholar Anaxagoras makes the first recorded claim that the Moon shines by reflecting light from the Sun. His theories on the cosmos are advanced for the time. His belief that the Moon and Sun are not deities leads to his prosecution for impiety.

c.130 BCE

Distance measured
By comparing observations made at the Egyptian cities of Syene (now Aswan) and Alexandria during a total eclipse of the Sun, Greek astronomer Hipparchus measures the average distance from Earth to the Moon.

1609 CE

First telescopic study
Italian scientist Galileo Galilei is the first person to scrutinize the Moon through a telescope. He notes that its surface is not smooth, as previously thought, but has mountains, craters, and flat, dark areas that are later called maria (seas).

Newton's cannonball diagram

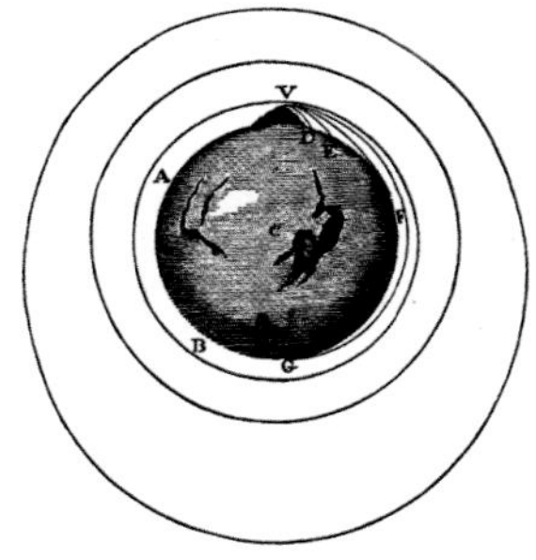

Doppelmayr's comparative map

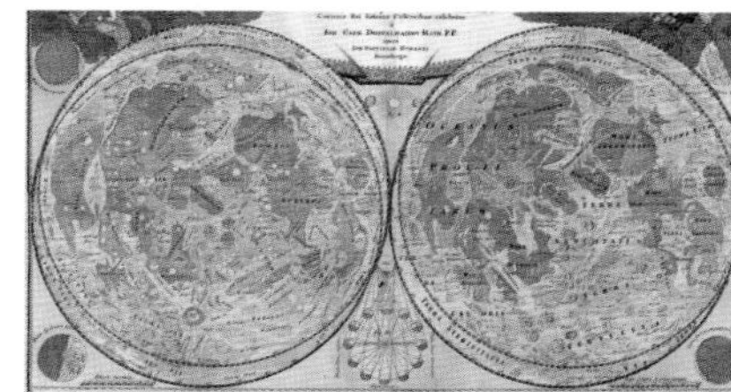

1645–51

First detailed maps
The first detailed Moon maps are made in Germany by Johannes Hevelius and in Italy by Giovanni Riccioli, who includes names still used today. Later (in 1742), German astronomer Johann Doppelmayr makes a comparative map of the two versions.

1680s

Lunar orbit explained
English scientist Isaac Newton develops his theory of gravitation by studying the mathematical properties of elliptical orbits. He uses the analogy of a cannonball to show that the Moon remains in orbit because it is perpetually falling.

1753

Thin atmosphere recognized
Croatian astronomer Roger Boscovich argues that the Moon has a negligible atmosphere. This theory is based on his observation that stars disappear instantly as the Moon passes in front of them, rather than fading over a few seconds.

Excess hydrogen (blue) at south pole

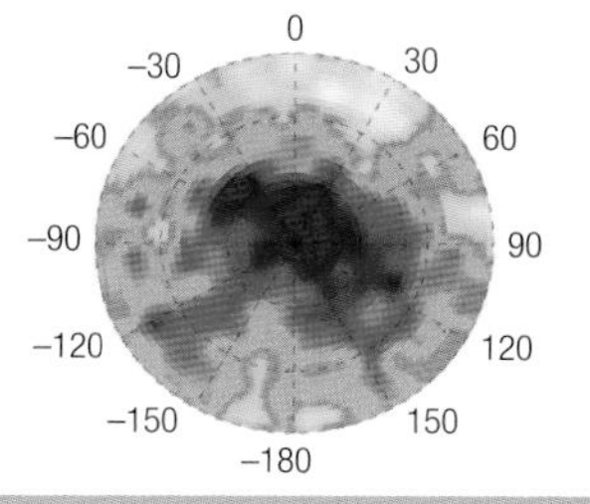
0
30
60
90
120
150
–180
–150
–120
–90
–60
–30

Lunar Reconnaissance Orbiter (USA)

1994

Clementine mission
US orbiter Clementine maps the elevation of the lunar surface in detail and returns ultraviolet and infrared images, which enable scientists to map the concentration of different minerals in the Moon's surface.

1998

Possibility of ice at lunar poles
Another US orbiter, Lunar Prospector, detects excess hydrogen at the Moon's poles. This suggests the presence of water ice in the upper few metres of the lunar surface, within permanently shadowed craters.

2004–present

Further missions
The USA, Japan, China, India, and the European Space Agency send orbiters to the Moon. These return new data about the Moon's internal structure and the distribution of water and other chemicals in or close to the surface.

LANDER
ORBITER
FLYBY
JOURNEY TO THE MOON
EARTH ORBIT
LAUNCH
1958 Pioneer 0
1958 Luna 1958A
1958 Pioneer 1
1958 Luna 1958B
1958 Pioneer 2
1958 Luna 1958C
1958 Pioneer 3
1959 Luna 1
1959 Luna 1959A
1959 Pioneer 4
1959 Luna 2
1959 Luna 3
1959 Pioneer P-3
1960 Pioneer P-30
1960 Pioneer P-31
1961 Ranger 1
1961 Ranger 2
1962 Ranger 3
1962 Ranger 4
1962 Ranger 5
1963 Sputnik 25
1963 Luna 4
1964 Ranger 6
1964 Ranger 7
1965 Ranger 8
1965 Kosmos 60
1965 Ranger 9
1965 Luna 5
1965 Luna 6
1965 Zond 3
1965 Luna 7
1965 Luna 8
1966 Luna 9
1966 Kosmos 111
1966 Luna 10
1966 Surveyor 1
1966 Lunar Orbiter 1
1966 Luna 11
1966 Surveyor 2
1966 Luna 12
1966 Lunar Orbiter 2
1966 Luna 13
1967 Lunar Orbiter 3
1967 Surveyor 3
1967 Lunar Orbiter 4
1967 Surveyor 4
1967 Lunar Orbiter 5
1967 Surveyor 5
1967 Surveyor 6
1968 Surveyor 7
1968 Luna 14
1968 Zond 5

MISSIONS TO THE **MOON**

OUR NEAREST NEIGHBOUR HAS BEEN A TARGET FOR SPACECRAFT FOR OVER 50 YEARS. IT REMAINS THE ONLY DESTINATION BEYOND LOW EARTH ORBIT THAT MANNED CRAFT HAVE VISITED, AND THE ONLY SOLAR SYSTEM BODY BESIDES EARTH THAT PEOPLE HAVE WALKED ON.

After a string of failures in the 1950s, the first craft to reach the Moon's surface was the Soviet probe Luna 2, which deliberately crash-landed in 1959. Three weeks later, Luna 3 returned the first photos of the far side, causing great excitement. Dozens of missions followed as the US and USSR raced to conquer the new frontier of space. More recent missions have aimed to undertake scientific research, but the Moon remains a compelling target for nations eager to demonstrate technological prowess.

KEY

- NASA (USA)
- RFSA (USSR/Russia)
- JAXA (Japan)
- ESA (Europe)
- CNSA (China)
- ISRO (India)
- Destination
- Success
- Failure
- Manned mission

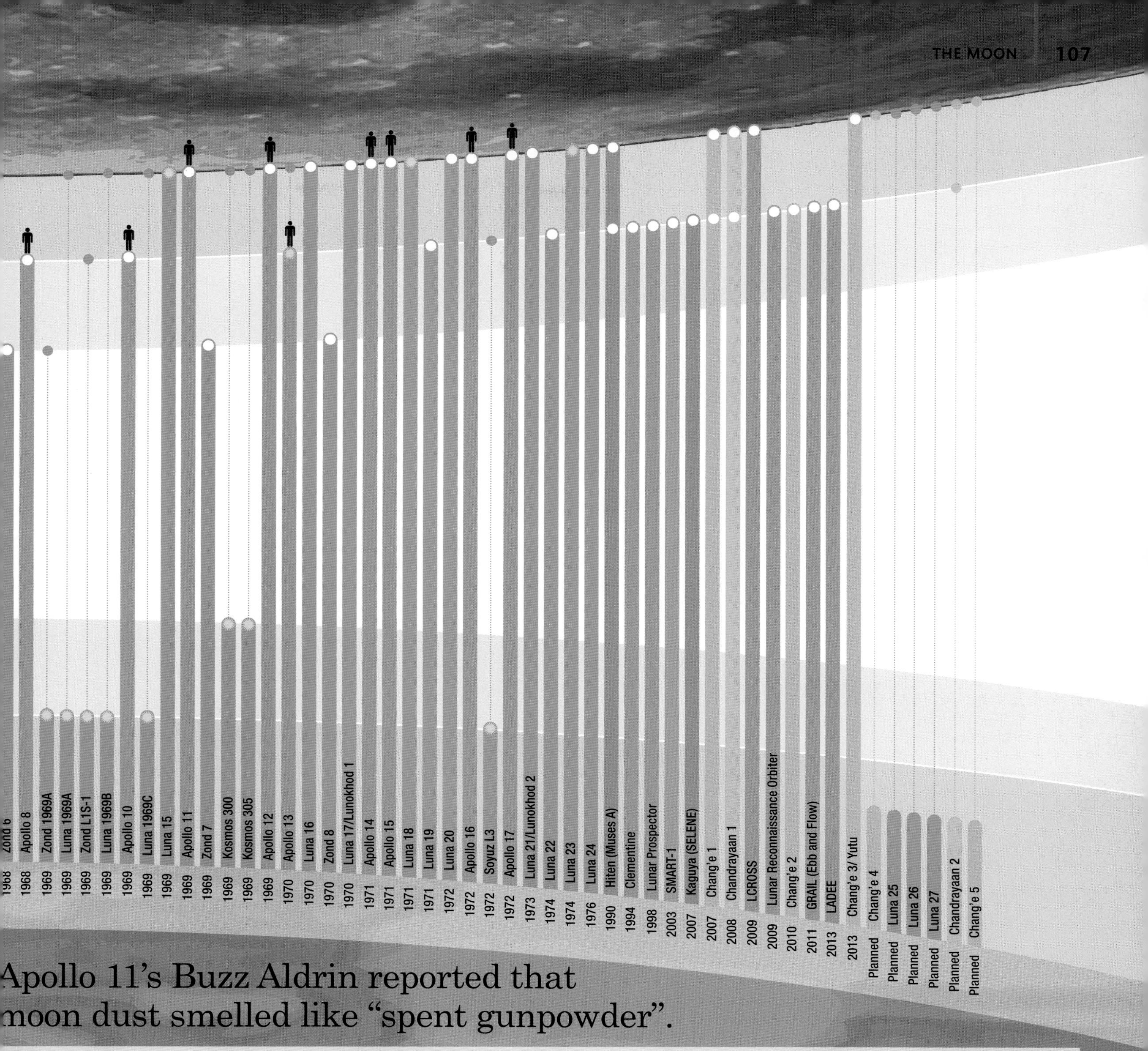

1968 Zond 6
1968 Apollo 8
1969 Zond 1969A
1969 Luna 1969A
1969 Zond L1S-1
1969 Luna 1969B
1969 Apollo 10
1969 Luna 1969C
1969 Luna 15
1969 Apollo 11
1969 Zond 7
1969 Kosmos 300
1969 Kosmos 305
1969 Apollo 12
1970 Apollo 13
1970 Luna 16
1970 Zond 8
1970 Luna 17/Lunokhod 1
1971 Apollo 14
1971 Apollo 15
1971 Luna 18
1971 Luna 19
1972 Luna 20
1972 Apollo 16
1972 Soyuz L3
1972 Apollo 17
1973 Luna 21/Lunokhod 2
1974 Luna 22
1974 Luna 23
1976 Luna 24
1990 Hiten (Muses A)
1994 Clementine
1998 Lunar Prospector
2003 SMART-1
2007 Kaguya (SELENE)
2007 Chang'e 1
2008 Chandrayaan 1
2009 LCROSS
2009 Lunar Reconnaissance Orbiter
2010 Chang'e 2
2011 GRAIL (Ebb and Flow)
2013 LADEE
2013 Chang'e 3/ Yutu
Planned Chang'e 4
Planned Luna 25
Planned Luna 26
Planned Luna 27
Planned Chandrayaan 2
Planned Chang'e 5

Apollo 11's Buzz Aldrin reported that moon dust smelled like "spent gunpowder".

Lunar rovers
The vast majority of soft landings on the Moon have involved static spacecraft, but several mobile vehicles have also explored the lunar surface. The first of these was NASA's Lunar Roving Vehicle (LRV) – a "moon buggy" driven by astronauts on the later Apollo missions. The Soviet Union landed two remote-controlled Lunokhod rovers on the Moon in the early 1970s, and in 2013 China landed its Yutu ("Jade Rabbit") vehicle.

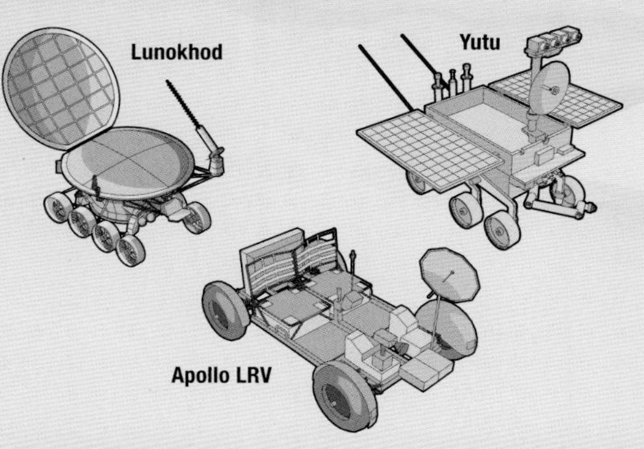
Lunokhod
Yutu
Apollo LRV

Landing sites
The first unpiloted soft landers on the Moon were designed to test surface conditions, amid fears that the soil, having been pulverized by countless impacts, might be too weak to support the weight of a large spacecraft. Later missions, including the Apollo manned landings, aimed for specific areas and types of lunar landscape in order to collect data that might shine light on the Moon's formation and early history.

15
17
11
12
14
16
Apollo landing sites

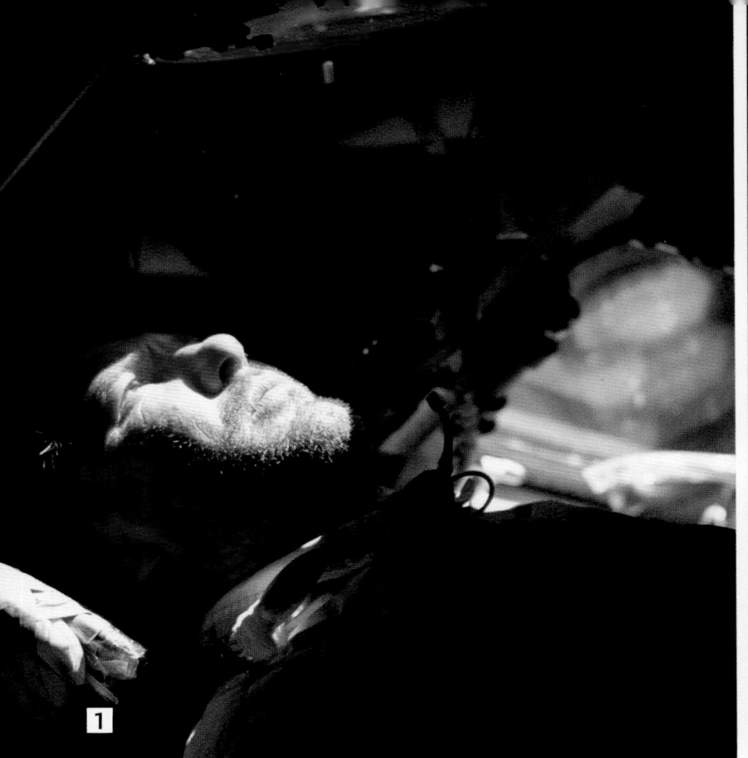
1

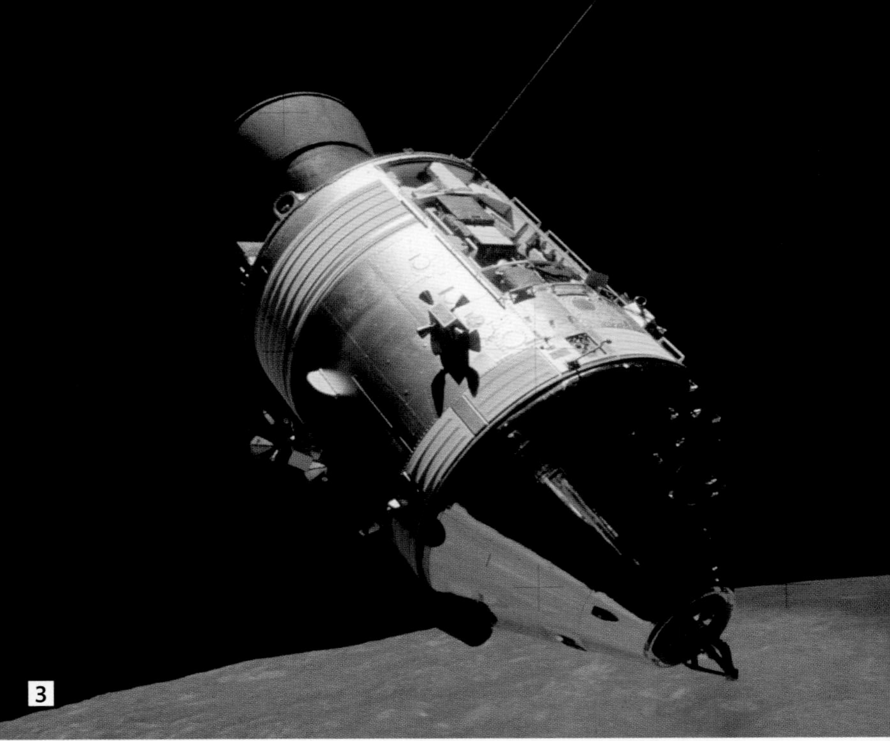
3

2

5

APOLLO PROJECT

1 Test flight

The United States' Apollo project of the 1960s and 70s was the only series of missions to put people on another world. The first successful manned flight was Apollo 7, launched in October 1968 under commander Walter Schirra (pictured). This was a test run for the spacecraft's command and service modules, satisfactorily completed after 163 Earth orbits and nearly 11 days in space.

2 Stepping outside

The task of Apollo 9, launched in March 1969, was crucial to the entire project. On this flight, the lunar landing module was manned in space for the first time. During their ten-day orbit of Earth, the crew undocked and redocked the lander, tested their equipment and support systems, and performed a spacewalk. Pilot David Scott is seen here emerging into space from the command module.

3 Command and service module

The Apollo spacecraft was made up of three parts: a command module, which served as control centre; a service module, which carried a rocket engine, fuel, and oxygen; and a lunar module, which landed on the Moon. Only the cone-shaped command module returned to Earth. Here the combined command/service module of Apollo 17 is seen in lunar orbit prior to rendezvous with the returning lunar module.

4 Mission accomplished

On 20 July 1969, the Apollo project achieved its aim as Neil Armstrong and Buzz Aldrin of the Apollo 11 mission became the first people on the Moon. Planting his boots on the surface at Tranquility Base (above), Aldrin was intrigued to note that when lunar dust is kicked "every grain of it lands nearly the same distance away". The astronauts spent 21 hours on the Moon, taking photographs and collecting samples.

UNITED STATES

5 Flying the flag
On every one of the six Apollo moon landings, it has been a tradition for the astronauts to plant an American flag in lunar soil. Here, near the Moon's Apennine Mountains, Commander David Scott does his duty on the Apollo 15 mission of 1971. Behind him are the landing craft, poised on spider-like legs, and a small, battery-powered lunar roving vehicle, used for the first time on this mission.

6 Last lunar excursions
Apollo 17's lunar module, Challenger, landed astronauts Eugene Cernan (right) and Harrison Schmitt (reflected in Cernan's helmet) in the Moon's Taurus-Littrow valley. They made long excursions, exploring the terrain and collecting a record number of rock and soil samples. With the cancellation of further planned Apollo missions, nobody has set foot on the Moon since Cernan and Schmitt in 1972.

6

MARS

MARS IS A BITTERLY COLD DESERT WORLD, STAINED A RUSTY RED BY IRON-RICH DUST ON ITS SURFACE. THOUGH HALF THE DIAMETER OF EARTH AND MUCH FURTHER FROM THE SUN'S WARMTH, MARS SHOWS MANY STRIKING SIMILARITIES TO OUR HOME PLANET.

Images of Mars returned by NASA spacecraft reveal a world that looks eerily familiar, with rock-strewn deserts, rolling hills, spectacular canyons, and a hazy sky flecked by occasional white clouds. Mars has a 25-hour day, polar ice caps that wax and wane like Earth's, an axis tilted only two degrees steeper than ours, and dry riverbeds that hint at the past presence of water. Volcanoes and rift valleys suggest tectonic forces were once generated by a hot interior.

Yet despite the many parallels, Mars and Earth are worlds apart. With only a tenth of Earth's mass, Mars lacks the gravity to hold on to a dense atmosphere, and its tenuous air is almost devoid of oxygen. While Earth's large molten core keeps the planet's fractured crust in motion and generates a protective magnetic shield, Mars's smaller core has cooled and at least partially solidified. Its crust has frozen solid, and its magnetism is too weak to deflect solar radiation.

At one time Mars may have been warm and wet, but today it is an uninhabitable and barren wasteland.

Dust clouds on Mars can reach 1,000m (3,000ft) in height and last for **several weeks.**

MARS DATA

Average diameter	6,780km (4,213 miles)
Mass (Earth = 1)	0.11
Gravity at equator (Earth = 1)	0.38
Mean distance from Sun (Earth = 1)	1.5
Axial tilt	25.2°
Rotation period (day)	24.6 hours
Orbital period (year)	687 Earth days
Minimum temperature	–143°C (–225°F)
Maximum temperature	35°C (95°F)
Moons	2

▷ **Northern hemisphere**
A permanent ice cap called the Planum Boreum (Northern Plain) sits on the north pole of Mars. Around 1,000km (620 miles) across, its perimeter is formed from lobes of ice separated by deep, canyon-like troughs.

▷ **Lava plains**
Enormous lava-covered plains dominate Mars's northern regions. In the south is Hellas Planitia, the largest impact crater on Mars at more than 2,000km (1,243 miles) wide.

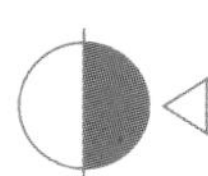

▷ **Southern hemisphere**
At Mars's south pole is the Planum Australe (Southern Plain), an ice cap with an upper layer of carbon-dioxide ice. Beyond it are huge areas of permafrost – water and soil frozen as hard as rock.

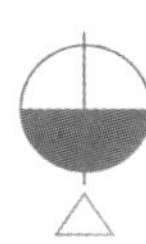

The Alba Mons is an enormous flat volcano surrounded by extensive lava fields.

This is the Tharsis region, a huge domed plateau about 4,000km (2,485 miles) wide and home to giant volcanoes.

Olympus Mons is the largest volcano on Mars.

The southernmost of the three giant Tharsis volcanoes is Arsia Mons.

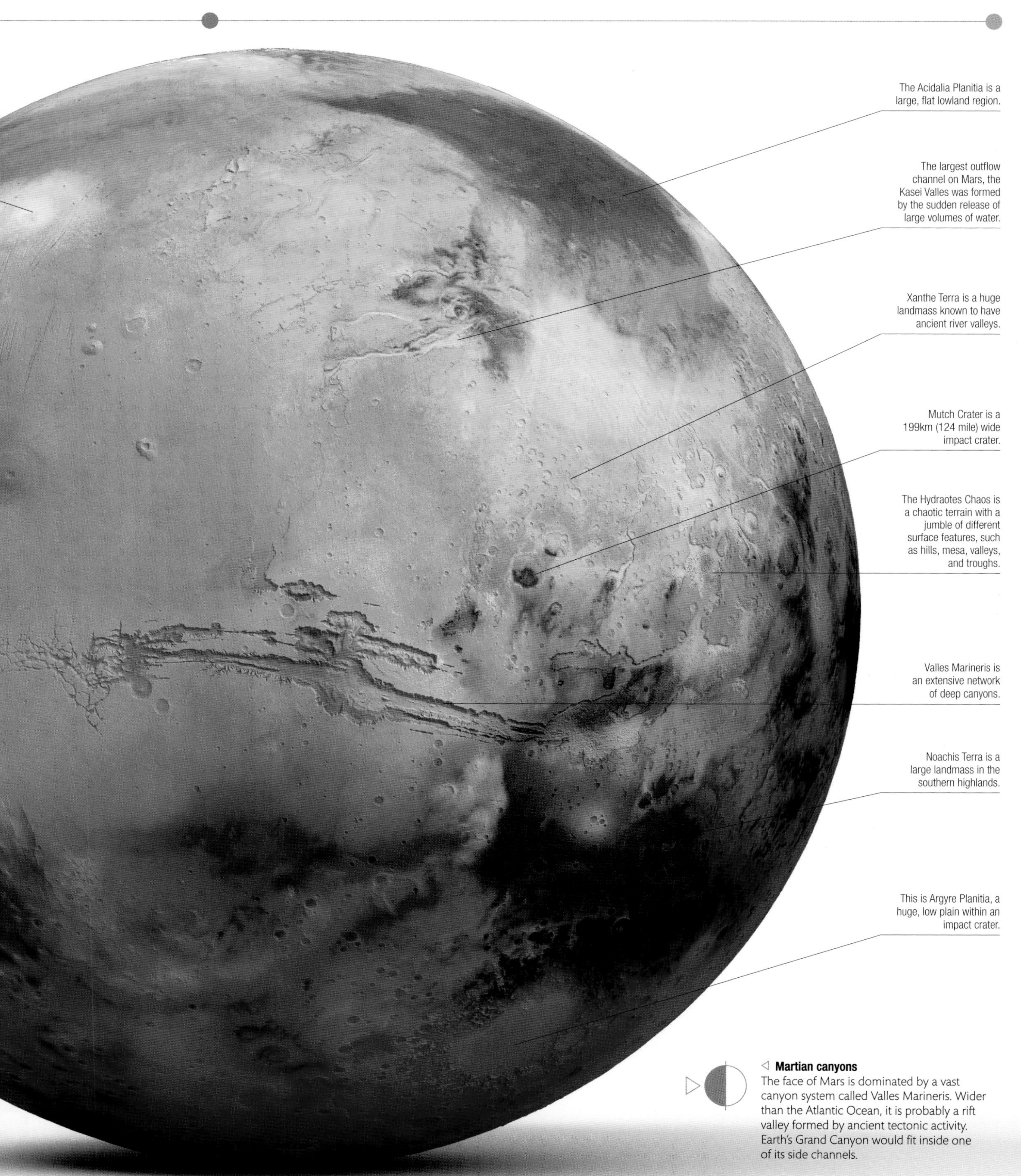
The Acidalia Planitia is a large, flat lowland region.
The largest outflow channel on Mars, the Kasei Valles was formed by the sudden release of large volumes of water.
Xanthe Terra is a huge landmass known to have ancient river valleys.
Mutch Crater is a 199km (124 mile) wide impact crater.
The Hydraotes Chaos is a chaotic terrain with a jumble of different surface features, such as hills, mesa, valleys, and troughs.
Valles Marineris is an extensive network of deep canyons.
Noachis Terra is a large landmass in the southern highlands.
This is Argyre Planitia, a huge, low plain within an impact crater.

◁ **Martian canyons**
The face of Mars is dominated by a vast canyon system called Valles Marineris. Wider than the Atlantic Ocean, it is probably a rift valley formed by ancient tectonic activity. Earth's Grand Canyon would fit inside one of its side channels.

MARS STRUCTURE

NO ONE KNOWS EXACTLY WHAT THE INTERIOR OF MARS IS LIKE, BUT THROUGH VARIOUS STUDIES, INCLUDING UNMANNED SPACECRAFT MISSIONS, SCIENTISTS HAVE BUILT UP A THEORETICAL PICTURE OF THE PLANET'S STRUCTURE.

As a young planet, Mars cooled down more rapidly than Earth, because it is smaller and further from the Sun, although the outer region of its iron core is thought to still be partially molten. A rocky crust of variable thickness forms the outermost layer of the planet. This is in one solid piece, rather than split into separate moving plates as on Earth. Beneath the crust is a deep mantle of silicate rock, once a fluid layer that was in constant motion. As the mantle shifted, it changed the face of Mars, causing great rifts in the crust and breaking through the surface to form gigantic volcanoes.

Core
Probably partly liquid, the small core of Mars is believed to be composed predominantly of iron. While Mars was still in a molten state, heavy metals sank to the centre of the planet and started to solidify as they cooled.

Enormous surface rifts were caused by past movements of the mantle.

▷ **Mars layer by layer**
The outer layer of Mars is a crust of solid rock about 80km (50 miles) thick in the southern regions and around 35km (22 miles) in the northern hemisphere. Below the crust is a mantle of solid silicate rock. Deeper still is the small core of the planet, which is probably composed of iron as well as lighter materials, including iron sulphide.

Surface temperatures on Mars can be as low as **–143°C (–225°F).**

Mantle
Less dense than the core, the mantle is the middle layer of Mars. At the beginning of the planet's life, the mantle was in a liquid state and its movements and outpourings helped to shape the appearance of the Martian surface. There is now no evidence of activity.
Crust
The outer layer, or crust, of Mars is composed largely of volcanic rock and was formed in one solid piece. Its surface, deeply smothered in soft red dust, bears evidence of a turbulent past marked by volcanic action, flowing water, weathering, and meteoroid impacts.
The highest atmospheric layer, the exosphere, merges into space.
In the upper atmosphere, the gases are rarefied.
The middle atmosphere contains thin snowflake clouds of frozen carbon dioxide and water ice.
The lower atmosphere is laden with windswept dust.

▽ **Atmosphere**
Mars's atmosphere is 95.3 per cent carbon dioxide, with small amounts of other gases, notably nitrogen and argon, and traces of water vapour. Atmospheric pressure varies considerably with the seasons, decreasing in winter as carbon dioxide is locked into ice at the poles and increasing in summer when carbon dioxide returns into the atmosphere as vapour.

MARS MAPPED

Between the seasonally ice-capped poles, the surface of Mars shows dramatic variation. The northern hemisphere mainly comprises flat lava plains; vast volcanoes dominate the equatorial region; and southwards are older, crater-pitted highlands.

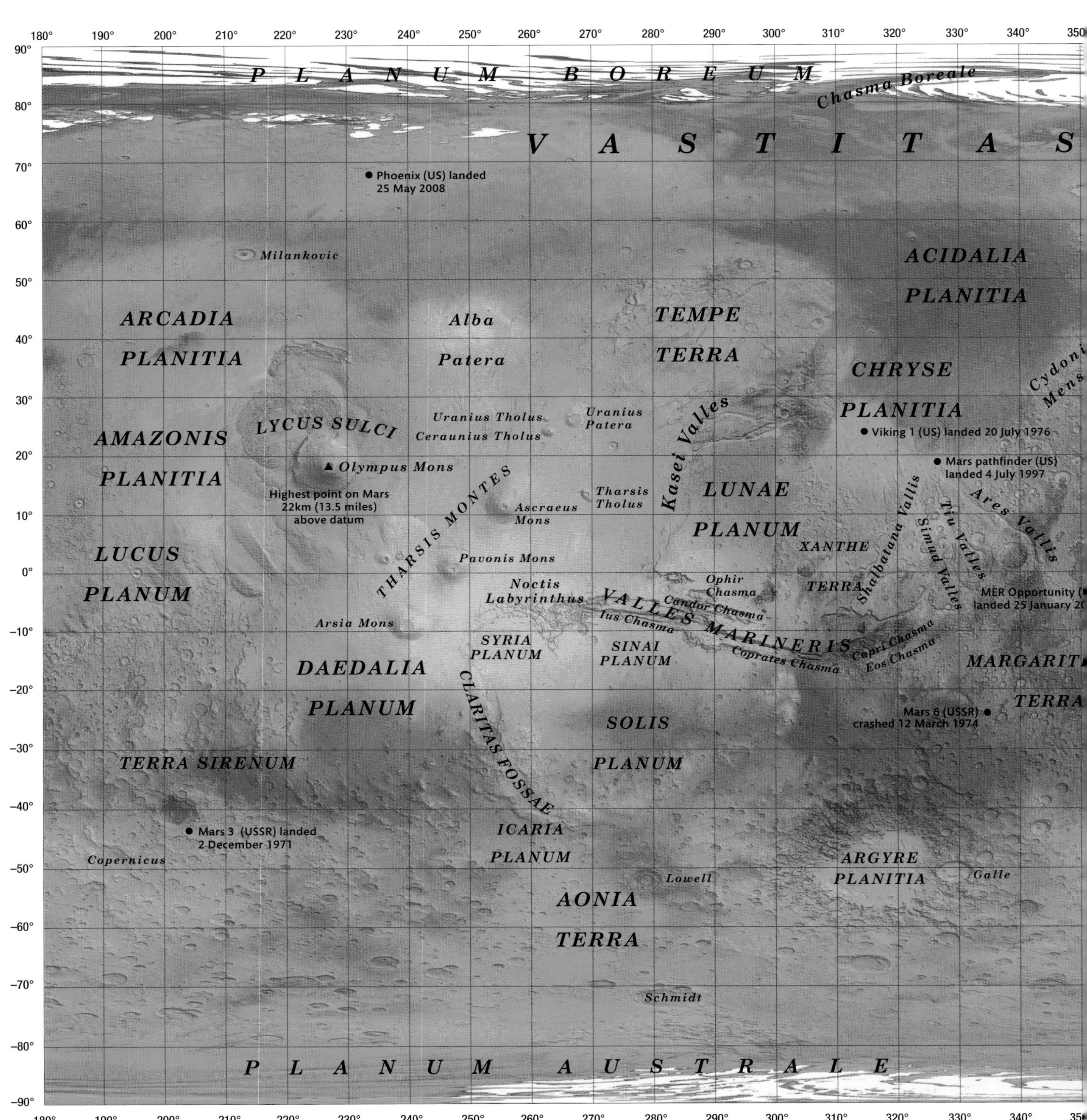
PLANUM BOREUM
Chasma Boreale
VASTITAS
Phoenix (US) landed 25 May 2008
Milankovic
ACIDALIA PLANITIA
ARCADIA PLANITIA
Alba Patera
TEMPE TERRA
CHRYSE PLANITIA
Cydonia Mensae
AMAZONIS PLANITIA
LYCUS SULCI
Uranius Tholus
Ceraunius Tholus
Uranius Patera
Kasei Valles
Viking 1 (US) landed 20 July 1976
Olympus Mons
Highest point on Mars 22km (13.5 miles) above datum
THARSIS MONTES
Ascraeus Mons
Tharsis Tholus
LUNAE PLANUM
Mars pathfinder (US) landed 4 July 1997
Ares Vallis
Shalbatana Vallis
Simud Valles
Tiu Valles
XANTHE TERRA
LUCUS PLANUM
Pavonis Mons
Noctis Labyrinthus
Ophir Chasma
Candor Chasma
VALLES MARINERIS
Ius Chasma
MER Opportunity landed 25 January
Arsia Mons
SYRIA PLANUM
SINAI PLANUM
Coprates Chasma
Capri Chasma
Eos Chasma
MARGARITIFER TERRA
DAEDALIA PLANUM
CLARITAS FOSSAE
SOLIS PLANUM
Mars 6 (USSR) crashed 12 March 1974
TERRA SIRENUM
Mars 3 (USSR) landed 2 December 1971
ICARIA PLANUM
Copernicus
ARGYRE PLANITIA
Galle
Lowell
AONIA TERRA
Schmidt
PLANUM AUSTRALE

Scale 1:45,884,054

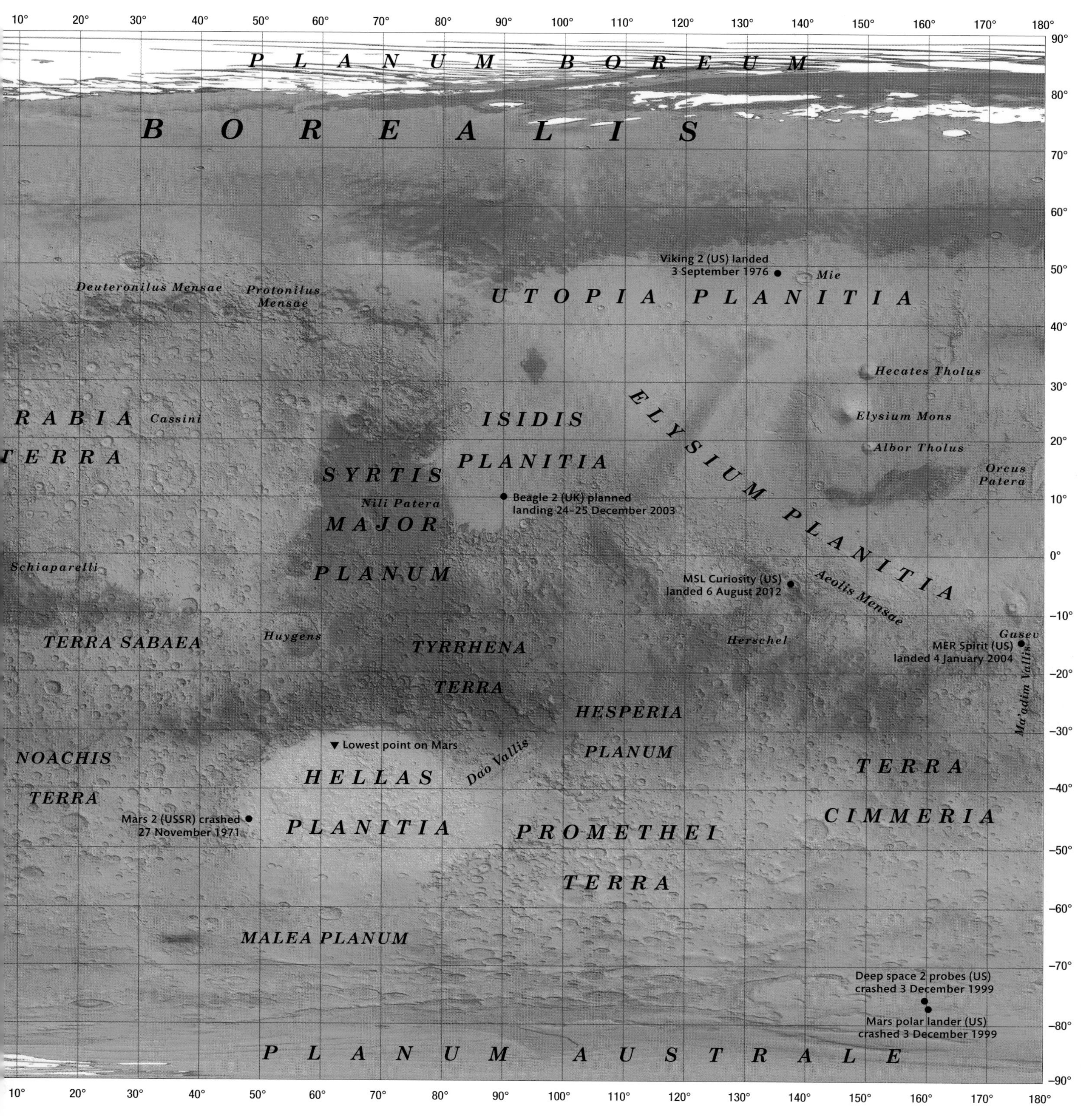
0 250 500 750 1000 Km
0 250 500 750 1000 Miles
PLANUM BOREUM
BOREALIS
Deuteronilus Mensae
Protonilus Mensae
Viking 2 (US) landed 3 September 1976
Mie
UTOPIA PLANITIA
Hecates Tholus
Elysium Mons
Albor Tholus
Orcus Patera
ARABIA
Cassini
TERRA
ISIDIS PLANITIA
ELYSIUM PLANITIA
SYRTIS MAJOR PLANUM
Nili Patera
Beagle 2 (UK) planned landing 24-25 December 2003
Schiaparelli
MSL Curiosity (US) landed 6 August 2012
Aeolis Mensae
Gusev
MER Spirit (US) landed 4 January 2004
Ma'adim Vallis
TERRA SABAEA
Huygens
TYRRHENA TERRA
Herschel
HESPERIA PLANUM
Lowest point on Mars
Dao Vallis
NOACHIS TERRA
HELLAS PLANITIA
TERRA CIMMERIA
Mars 2 (USSR) crashed 27 November 1971
PROMETHEI TERRA
MALEA PLANUM
Deep space 2 probes (US) crashed 3 December 1999
Mars polar lander (US) crashed 3 December 1999
PLANUM AUSTRALE

WATER ON **MARS**

MARS IS A DRY WORLD. IT HAS WATER ABOVE, ON, AND UNDER ITS SURFACE, BUT THE WATER IS IN THE FORM OF VAPOUR OR ICE. LIQUID WATER WAS ONCE ABUNDANT ON MARS, AND ITS EFFECT ON THE LANDSCAPE IS STILL EVIDENT.

Today, liquid water cannot exist on the Martian surface because of the low temperature and atmospheric pressure. However, sedimentary rocks built up by water-deposited material, minerals formed by standing water, and landscape features shaped by flowing water all point to the fact that Mars may once have had large volumes of liquid water.

Ancient water

Billions of years ago, when Mars was a warmer planet, river beds and channel-like valleys hundreds of kilometres long formed as fast-flowing water carved through the landscape, and catastrophic floods covered vast areas, leaving floodplains behind. Valleys such as Kasei Valles, the site of two giant waterfalls eight times the height of Earth's Niagara Falls, are now dry. So too are Mars's deltas, lakes, and shallow seas. Increasing our knowledge of the planet's watery past helps in our search for life. Liquid water is essential for life – if it once existed on Mars, then perhaps life did too.

△ **Outflow channel**
The surface of Mars features outflow channels – vast swathes of water-scoured ground. The largest and longest of these is Kasei Valles, at over 2,400km (1,500 miles) long. It was created by a huge outpouring of fast-flowing water. In this view, the water flowed towards the bottom left, and created an island in the centre of the channel.

◁ **Evidence in rocks**
These grey balls, each about 4mm (0.2in) wide, lie scattered over a rocky outcrop in Eagle Crater. Analysis by the Opportunity rover in 2004 showed the balls consist of an iron mineral called hematite. Originally embedded in the outcrop, they collect on the ground after the softer rock erodes away. On Earth, hematite typically forms in lakes, so the same could have occurred on Mars. The circular patch is where Opportunity analysed the underlying rock for comparison.

▽ **Impact meltwater**
Some of the water that flowed on Mars was released by volcanic activity or asteroid impact. This false-colour image shows Hephaestus Fossae, a region of impact craters and channels. The impact that created the large crater penetrated the surface and melted underground ice, apparently causing a catastrophic flood.

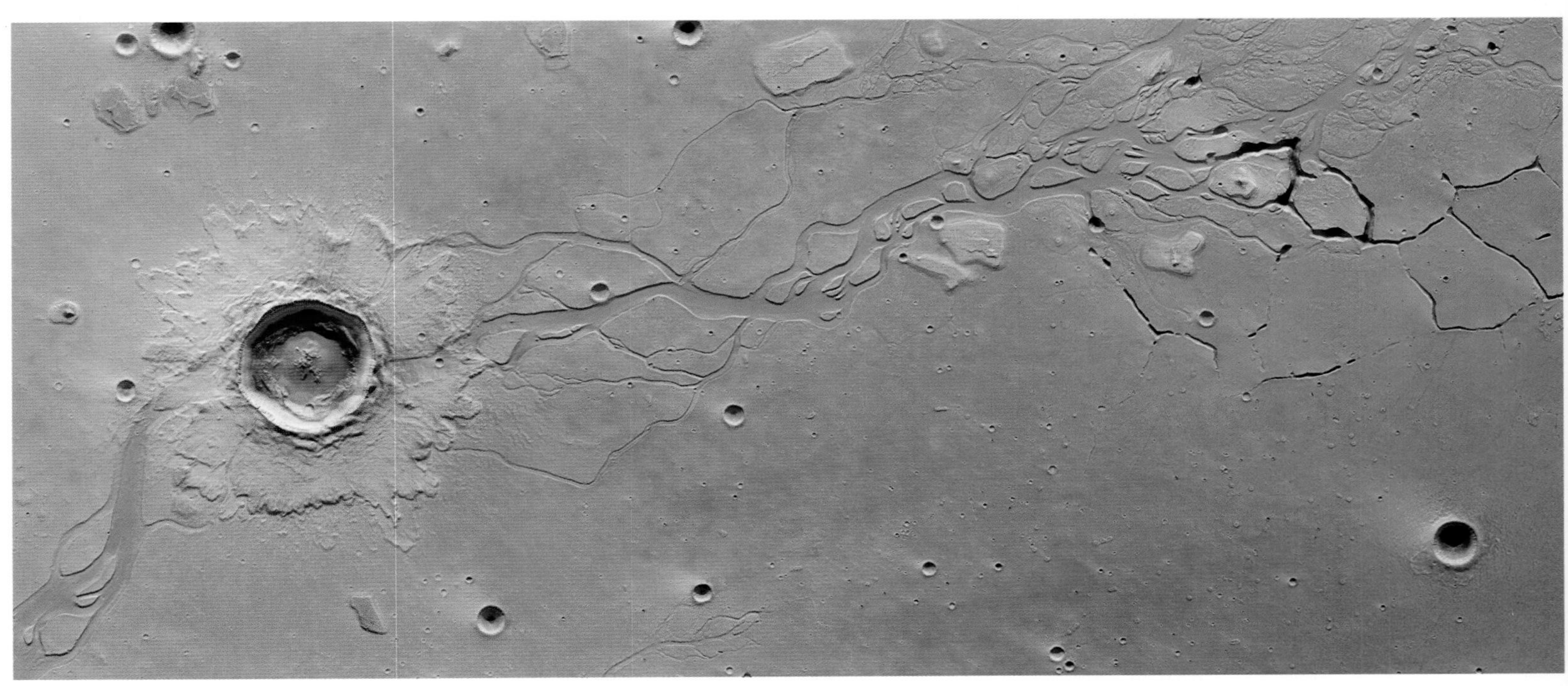

Water today

Most of the water on Mars today is locked within its frozen ice caps or held as vapour in its atmosphere. Orbiting spacecraft have also detected ice below the surface in other locations. Recently formed gullies on crater walls could be evidence of liquid groundwater released onto the surface.

▽ **Water ice**
This huge sheet of water ice is a permanent feature in an unnamed crater near the Martian north pole. The ice is 15km (9 miles) across and sits on a field of sand dunes. Water ice is also visible on parts of the crater's rim and wall.

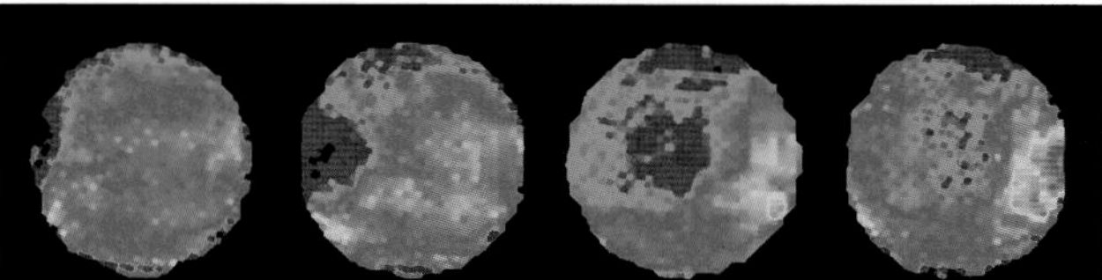

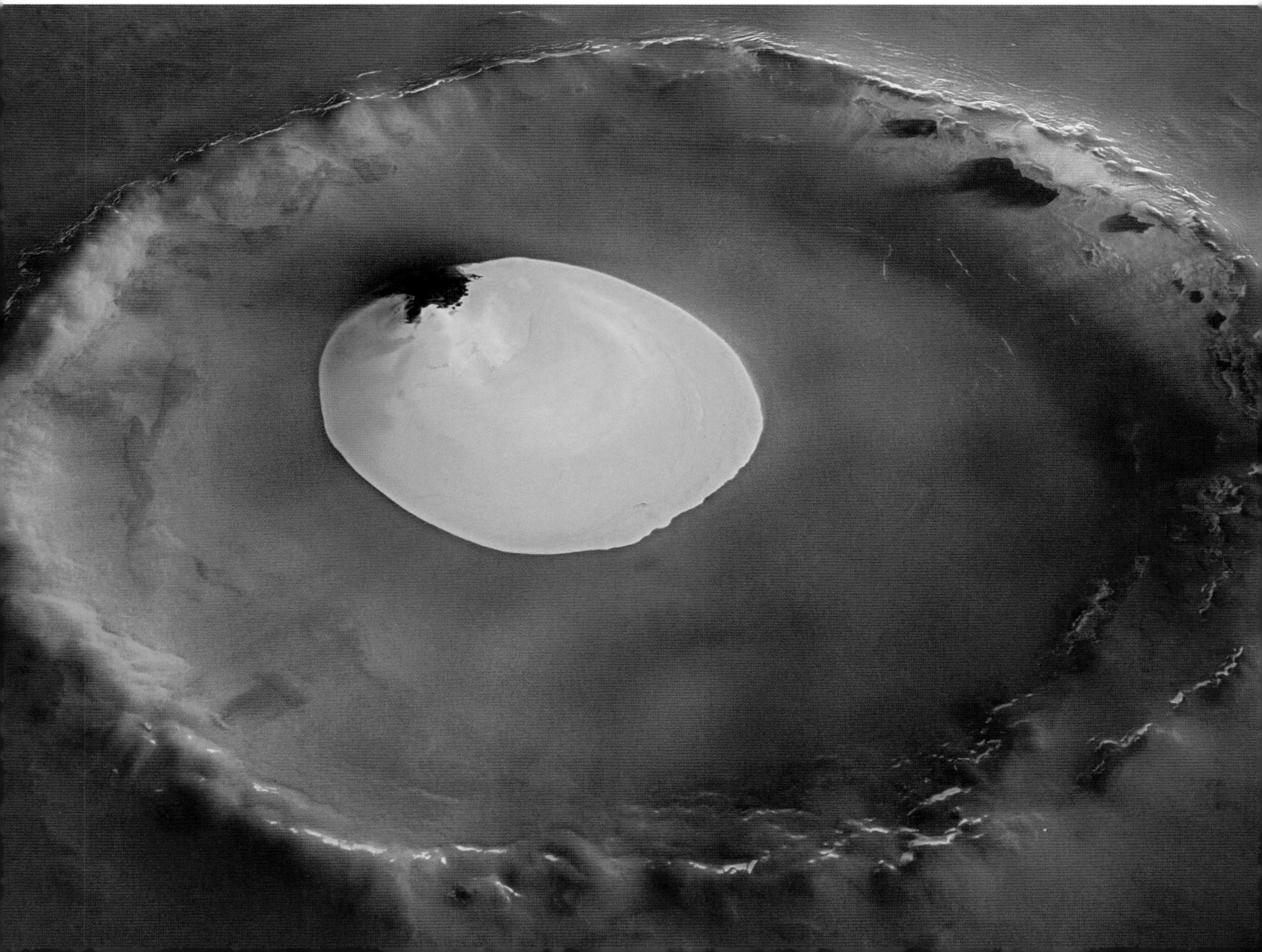

△ **Clouds on Mars**
Four Mars Global Surveyor images show the progression of water-ice clouds (in blue) across the planet. These occasional, wispy, cirrus-type clouds occur when atmospheric water vapour forms ice crystals. Water vapour can also form low-lying mist and early morning frost.

◁ **Ice under the surface**
The Phoenix Mars Lander was the first craft to explore Mars's arctic region on the ground. In 2008, it landed near the northern polar cap. Using its robotic arm, it dug into the ground, exposing ice just centimetres below the surface. Four days later, the ice had vaporized.

△ **Gullies**
Root-shaped gullies on the walls of impact craters may indicate that water still flows. Observations show that the gullies change with the seasons. Mars is too cold for pure water to be liquid, but briny groundwater, which has a lower freezing point, may be released to briefly carry fine-grained sediment down the walls.

DESTINATION
VALLES MARINERIS

FIVE TIMES DEEPER AND NEARLY TEN TIMES LONGER THAN EARTH'S GRAND CANYON, VALLES MARINERIS STRETCHES ACROSS THE FACE OF MARS LIKE A VAST WOUND.

Named after the Mariner spacecraft that discovered it, Valles Marineris (Mariner Valleys) is a rift valley system that runs nearly a fifth of the way around the Martian equator. While Earth's Great Rift Valley was created by tectonic plate movements, Valles Marineris is thought to have formed as a result of upheaval and collapse of the static Martian crust several billion years ago. Marsquakes, meteorite impacts, and water floods have since triggered numerous landslides in the canyon walls, widening the valley and creating some of the most spectacular terrain in the Solar System.

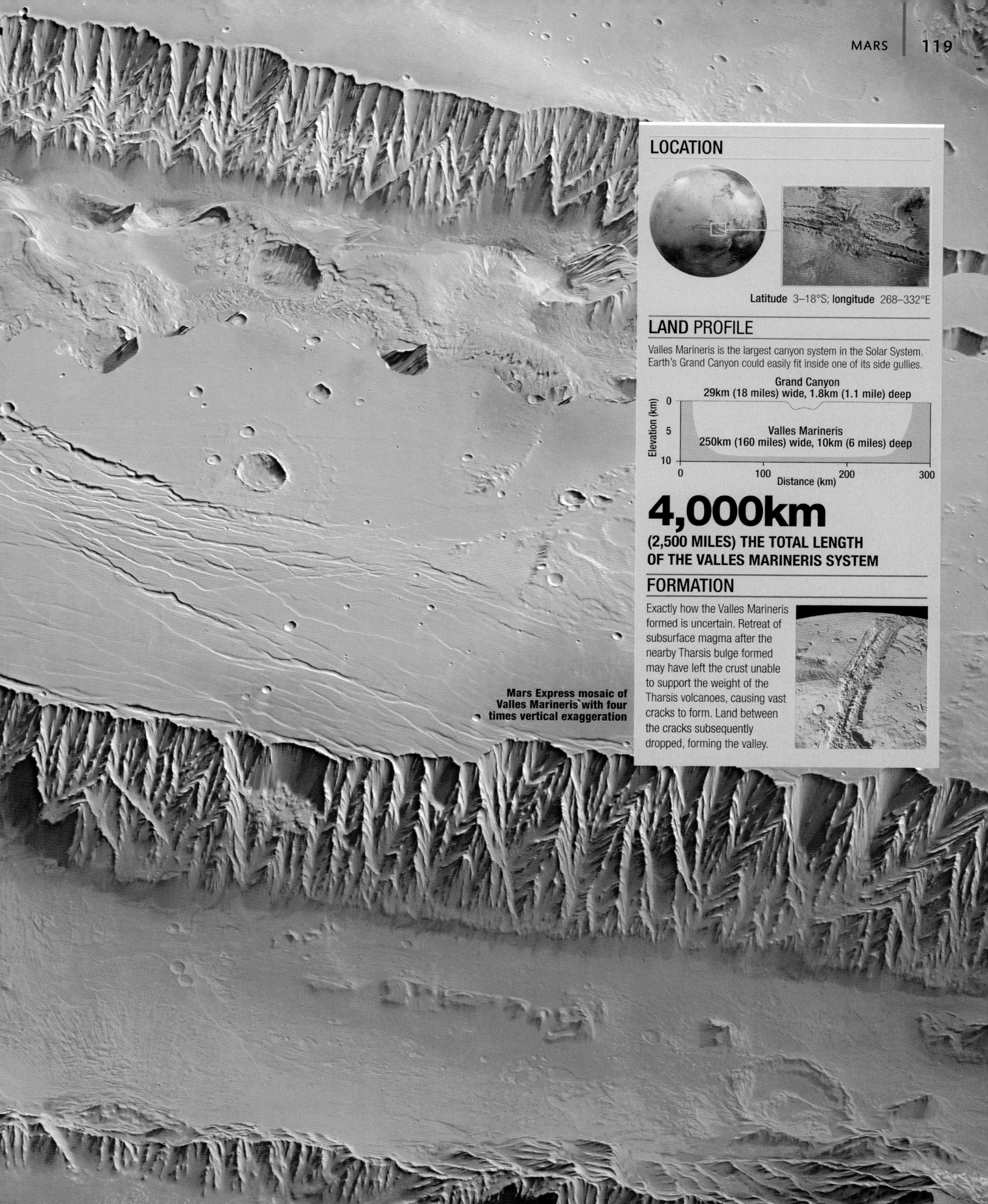
Grand Canyon
29km (18 miles) wide, 1.8km (1.1 mile) deep
Elevation (km)
0
5
10
Valles Marineris
250km (160 miles) wide, 10km (6 miles) deep
0
100
200
300
Distance (km)

Mars Express mosaic of Valles Marineris with four times vertical exaggeration

LOCATION

Latitude 3–18°S; **longitude** 268–332°E

LAND PROFILE

Valles Marineris is the largest canyon system in the Solar System. Earth's Grand Canyon could easily fit inside one of its side gullies.

4,000km

(2,500 MILES) THE TOTAL LENGTH OF THE VALLES MARINERIS SYSTEM

FORMATION

Exactly how the Valles Marineris formed is uncertain. Retreat of subsurface magma after the nearby Tharsis bulge formed may have left the crust unable to support the weight of the Tharsis volcanoes, causing vast cracks to form. Land between the cracks subsequently dropped, forming the valley.

MARTIAN **VOLCANOES**

MUCH OF MARS IS DOMINATED BY VOLCANIC LANDSCAPES. GIANT VOLCANOES – THE LARGEST IN THE SOLAR SYSTEM – TOWER ABOVE EXTENSIVE LAVA FLOWS AND VAST VOLCANIC PLAINS.

Volcanoes and lava plains are evidence of sporadic volcanic activity in Mars's past. The most recent major volcanic event occurred 2 million years ago, but astronomers believe there will be more activity in the future. The largest volcanic region on Mars is the Tharsis Bulge, a huge, elevated plain that straddles the equator to the west of the Valles Marineris canyon system. Some 4,000km (2,500 miles) wide and up to 8km (5 miles) high, it formed more than 3 billion years ago through crustal uplift during a period of volcanic activity that lasted hundreds of millions of years. It is home to the largest volcanoes on Mars – the Martian shield volcanoes, or montes.

Formation and types

Martian volcanoes come in various shapes and sizes (right), from steep domes and flat saucers to large shield volcanoes like those on Earth. Although much larger than Earth's shield volcanoes, the Martian ones are similar in shape, with shallow, sloping flanks and summit calderas (craters). Such volcanoes form when low-viscosity (runny) lava flows out with little explosiveness. The lava disperses over a wide area and builds up in a shallow dome. On Mars, lower gravity results in larger magma chambers and in longer, more widespread lava flows. The lack of tectonic plate movement also allows the volcanoes to grow much larger than on Earth (below).

△ Mons (shield)
Shaped like shields, montes volcanoes have broad bases with shallow, steadily sloping sides. They develop from successive outpourings of runny lava, and reach enormous sizes. The summits of montes volcanoes feature huge craters called calderas.

△ Tholus (dome)
Tholi are small and dome-shaped. They are thought to be the tops of buried shield volcanoes. The flanks rise steeply, and the caldera is large in relation to the base.

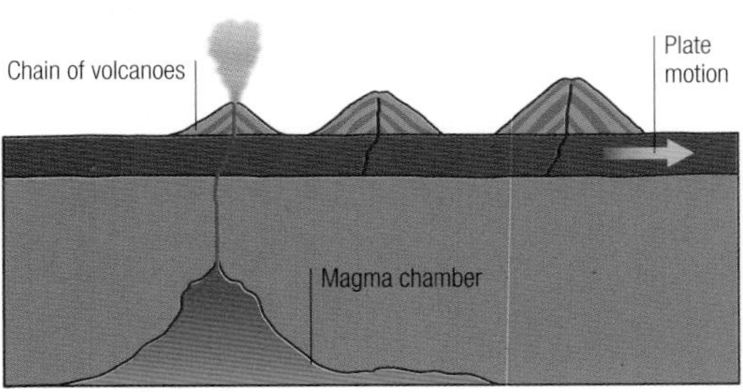
Chain of volcanoes
Plate motion
Magma chamber

△ Earth
The Hawaiian shield volcanoes formed over a hot spot in Earth's mantle. As the ocean crust has slowly moved over the hot spot, a chain of shield volcanoes has grown, forming the Hawaiian Islands.

▽ Mars
Because Mars's crust is in one solid piece with no moving plates, shield volcanoes such as Olympus Mons sit stationary over a hot spot and grow to a vast size over millions of years.

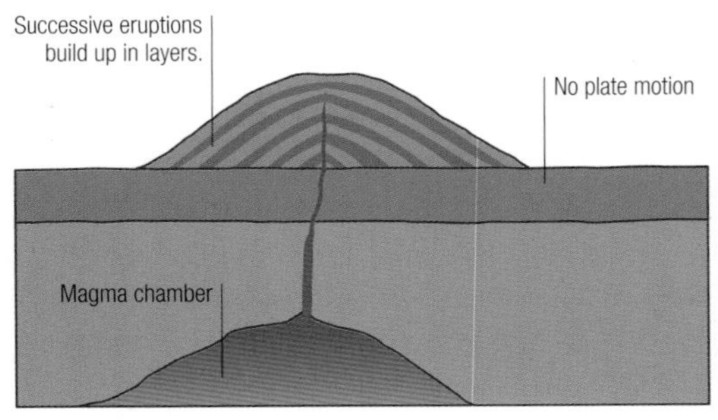
Successive eruptions build up in layers.
No plate motion
Magma chamber

The partially collapsed caldera on the summit is 32km (20 miles) across.

△ Tharsis Tholus
A mid-range volcano on Mars, Tharsis Tholus would be a giant on Earth, at 8km (5 miles) tall and 150km (95 miles) across. Colours in this image represent altitude – light brown at the peak and blue at the base.

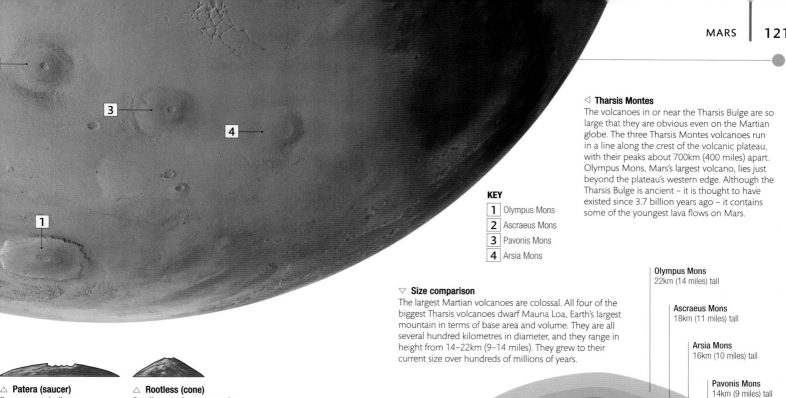

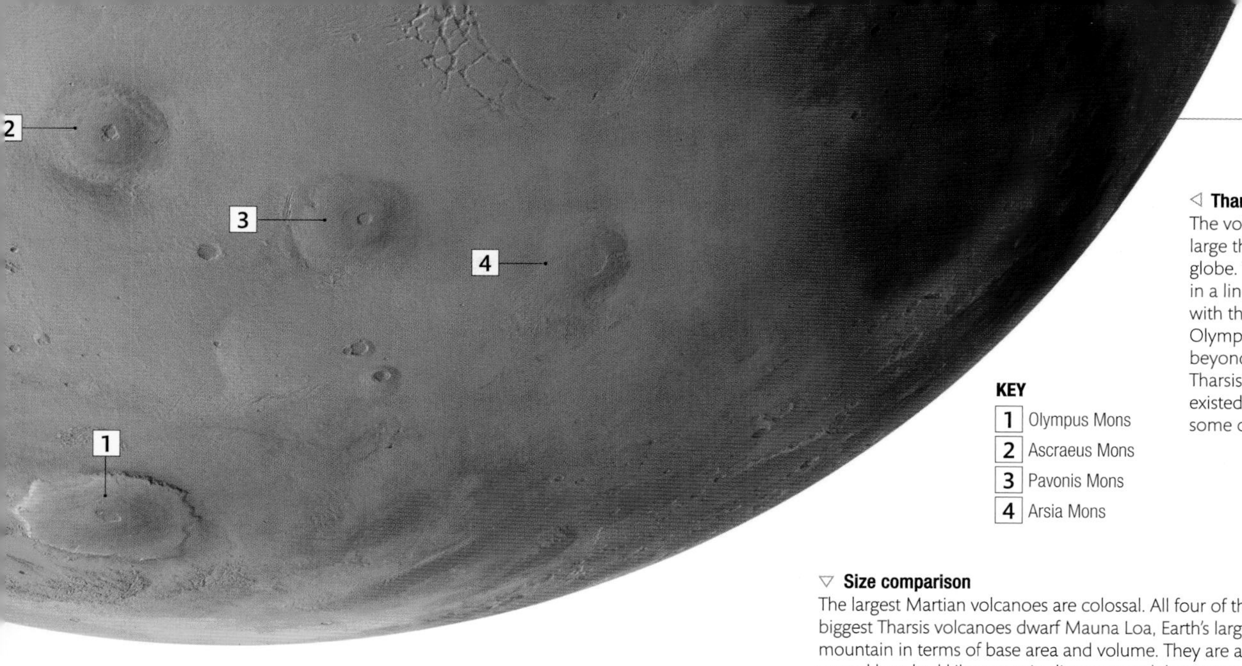

◁ **Tharsis Montes**
The volcanoes in or near the Tharsis Bulge are so large that they are obvious even on the Martian globe. The three Tharsis Montes volcanoes run in a line along the crest of the volcanic plateau, with their peaks about 700km (400 miles) apart. Olympus Mons, Mars's largest volcano, lies just beyond the plateau's western edge. Although the Tharsis Bulge is ancient – it is thought to have existed since 3.7 billion years ago – it contains some of the youngest lava flows on Mars.

KEY
1 Olympus Mons
2 Ascraeus Mons
3 Pavonis Mons
4 Arsia Mons

▽ **Size comparison**
The largest Martian volcanoes are colossal. All four of the biggest Tharsis volcanoes dwarf Mauna Loa, Earth's largest mountain in terms of base area and volume. They are all several hundred kilometres in diameter, and they range in height from 14–22km (9–14 miles). They grew to their current size over hundreds of millions of years.

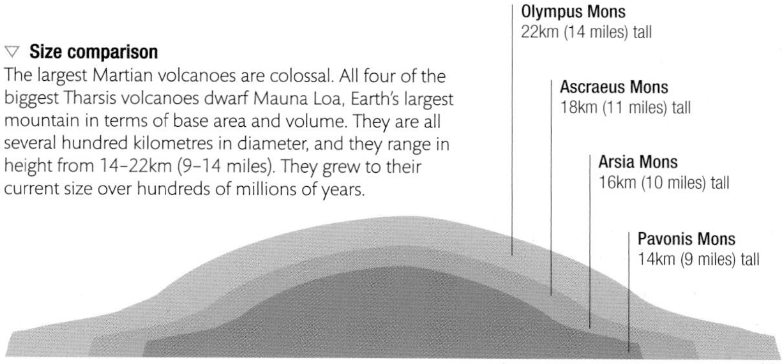

Olympus Mons
22km (14 miles) tall

Ascraeus Mons
18km (11 miles) tall

Arsia Mons
16km (10 miles) tall

Pavonis Mons
14km (9 miles) tall

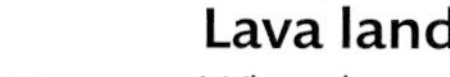

△ **Patera (saucer)**
Paterae are shallow, saucer-shaped bumps in the Martian surface. Like tholi, they may be the tops of buried shield volcanoes, but with larger calderas.

△ **Rootless (cone)**
Small conical structures, less than 250m (800ft) wide, are volcanic cones that form on the surface of fresh lava flows. They are rootless as they are not above a magma source.

The flanks of Tharsis Tholus are among the steepest on Mars, with an average slope of 10°.

Impact crater

Lava lands

When lava spills out of Martian volcanoes, it runs down their gentle slopes in sinuous channels before spreading out across the lowlands. Such eruptions leave distinctive formations in the landscape, such as lava tubes and lava plains. Lava tubes form when hot lava continues to flow beneath a solidified crust, like an underground river. When the source is exhausted, an empty tunnel is left behind, the roof of which may later collapse. Lava plains are ancient floods that have cooled and solidified.

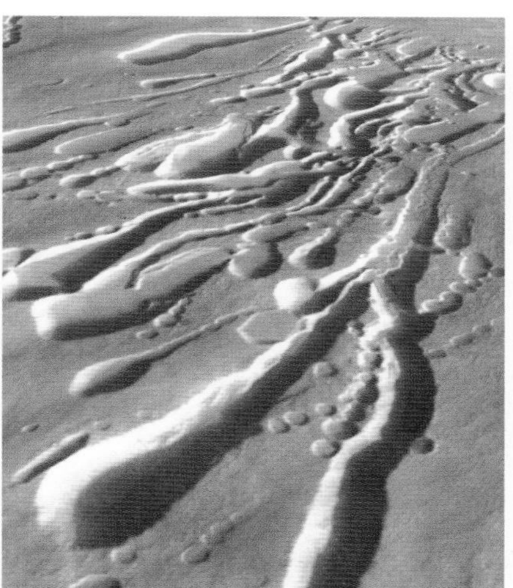

△ **Lava tubes**
Ancient lava tubes have been identified on the slopes of the biggest shield volcanoes. These lava tubes occur on the flanks of Pavonis Mons – the longest of them stretches 60km (40 miles) from end to end. When the surface of an empty lava tunnel collapses, these long depressions are left behind. Such features indicate that the lava was relatively fluid.

△ **Lava flows**
Hesperia Planum is a 1,600km (1,000 mile) wide lava plain in the southern highlands of Mars. Here, a flood of lava spilled across the land, partially filling a 24km (15 mile) long impact crater. The crater's elliptical shape, formed by a strike at a low angle, is still evident.

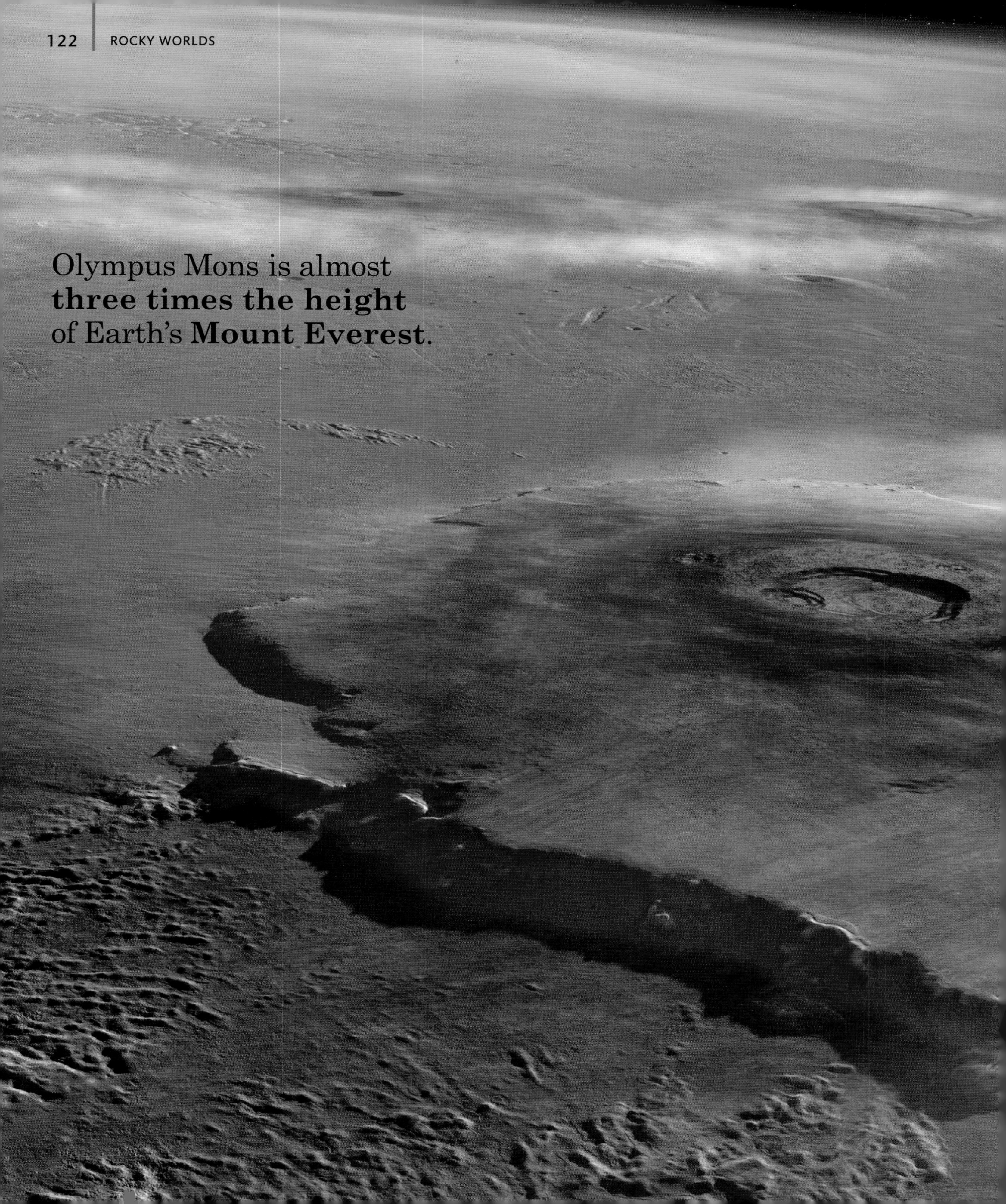

Olympus Mons is almost **three times the height** of Earth's **Mount Everest**.

DESTINATION **OLYMPUS MONS**

THE LARGEST VOLCANO IN THE SOLAR SYSTEM, OLYMPUS MONS RISES 22KM (14 MILES) ABOVE THE MARTIAN PLAINS. IT IS MARS'S TALLEST FEATURE, BUT IT IS SO WIDE THAT A VISITOR LANDING ON THE SUMMIT WOULD SEE NO END TO ITS SHALLOW SLOPES.

Almost as wide as France, Olympus Mons measures 610km (380 miles) across. It grew to its great size over millions of years as thousands of successive lava flows piled one upon another. Because Mars's crust is stationary, unlike Earth's, the volcano stays permanently over a hot spot in the planet's mantle. The summit plateau is surrounded by steep, 6km (3 mile) tall cliffs over which lava has cascaded like a waterfall to spill onto the surrounding plain. Olympus Mons is dormant at present but could easily erupt again. Originally discovered by astronomers in the 19th century, this Martian giant was not recognized as a volcano until the Mariner 9 spacecraft went into orbit around Mars in 1971.

3D reconstruction from MOLA (Mars Orbiter Laser Altimetre) elevation data with accurate vertical relief

LOCATION

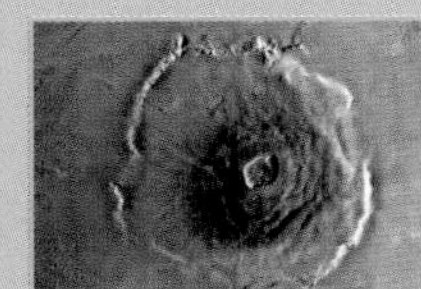

Latitude 19°N; **longitude** 226°E

LAND PROFILE

Olympus Mons dwarfs Earth's tallest volcano, Mauna Kea in the Hawaiian Islands. Both are asymmetrically shaped shield volcanoes with an average hill slope of about 5 degrees.

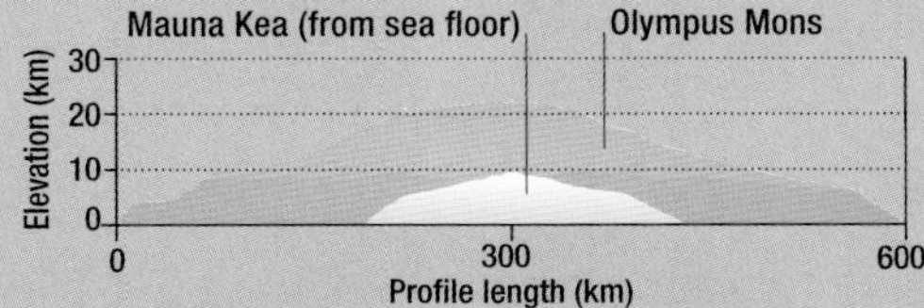
Mauna Kea (from sea floor)
Olympus Mons
Elevation (km)
30
20
10
0
0
300
600
Profile length (km)

CALDERA

The summit caldera is about 60km (37 miles) across. It contains at least six individual craters that formed after lava flow ceased and the magma chambers below collapsed. The figures are the craters' approximate ages in millions of years.

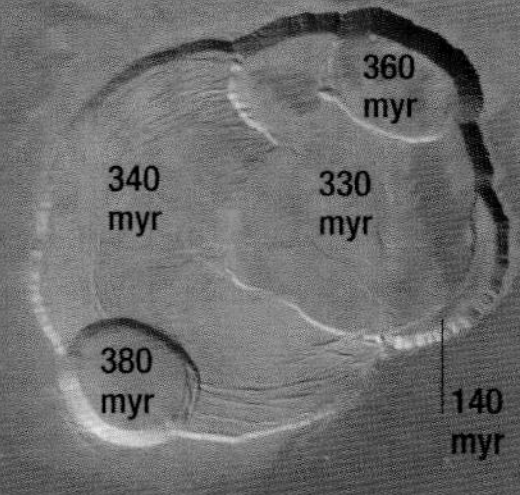
360 myr
340 myr
330 myr
380 myr
140 myr

1

DUNES OF **MARS**

1 Noachis Terra
Orbiting cameras have captured many of Mars's stunningly beautiful dune fields, which are created by wind-blown surface materials forming rippling patterns. This false colour image shows sand dunes trapped inside an impact crater in Noachis Terra, a region in the southern hemisphere of the planet.

2 North Polar Erg
Fantastically sculptured dunes created from grains of basalt and gypsum decorate an icy plain in the high northern region known as the North Polar Erg. The Erg, or sand sea, encircles the north polar ice cap and contains immense dune fields. The crescent formations seen here occur when the sand cover is relatively thin.

3 Seasonal changes
The apparent tree plantation on this dune field in the northern polar region is an illusion. The dark shapes are streaks of black, basaltic sand next to gaps in the carbon dioxide frost that covers the dunes in winter. The phenomenon occurs in spring as the ice layer thins and wind catches the underlying sand.

4 Dunes on the move
Like sand dunes on Earth, those on Mars show significant movement, reflecting the effect of local winds. In this image, the dunes are gradually migrating from left to right. The dark arcs in the lower right are barchans – wind-sculpted, crescent-shaped dunes that also form in sandy deserts on Earth.

2

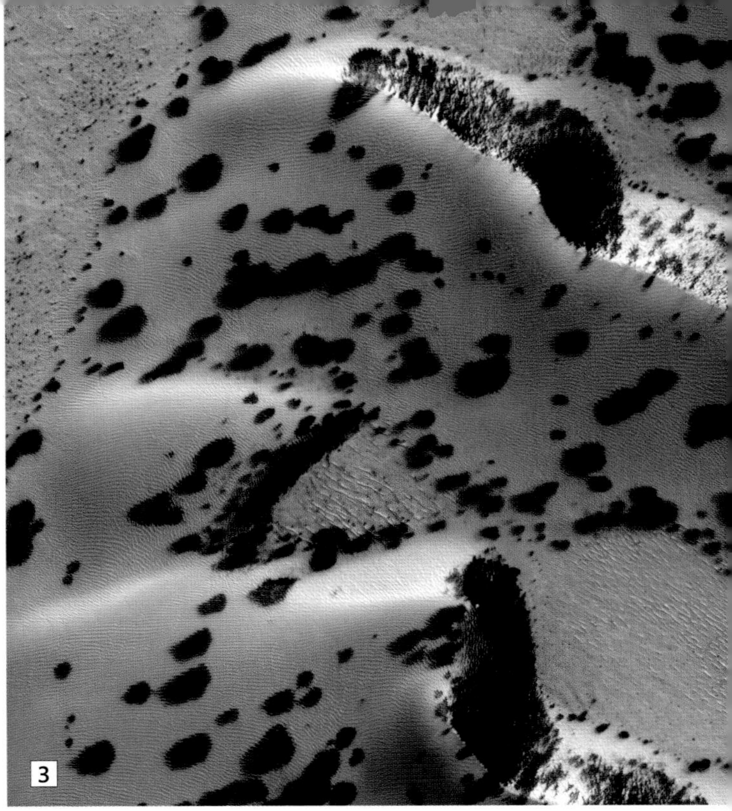

3

4

POLAR **CAPS**

A WHITE CAP MADE PREDOMINANTLY OF FROZEN WATER SITS ON EACH OF MARS'S POLES. ALTHOUGH THESE ALMOST CIRCULAR CAPS ARE A PERMANENT FEATURE OF THE MARTIAN LANDSCAPE, BOTH CHANGE WITH THE SEASONS.

The polar caps are huge mounds of ice that stand proud of the land that surrounds them. Cliffs at their edges reveal that the caps are made of layer upon layer of ice, sand, and dust laid down over millions of years. In winter, the caps extend as they are covered with new deposits of carbon dioxide snow and ice. With rising temperatures in summer, the carbon dioxide returns to the atmosphere as gas and the caps shrink.

North cap

The northern cap, Planum Boreum (Northern Plain), is the larger of the two – about 1,000km (620 miles) across and 2km (1.2 miles) thick – and is 90 per cent water ice. Data on the thickness and composition of the cap's layers, collected by NASA's Mars Reconnaissance Orbiter, is being used to study the planet's history of climate change.

▷ **Seasonal change**
These two images of the north cap from the Hubble Space Telescope show the change from winter to spring. By late winter, the ice extends southwards to almost 60°N latitude – nearly its maximum extent. Three months later, it is warmer and the carbon dioxide ice and frost south of 70°N have evaporated. By early summer, only the remnant core of water ice will remain.

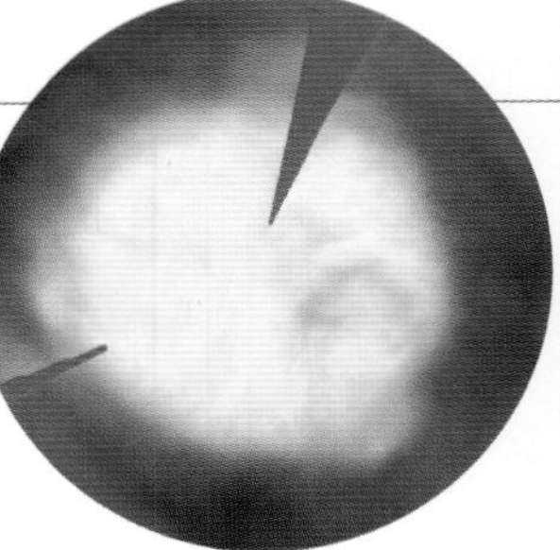

Late winter

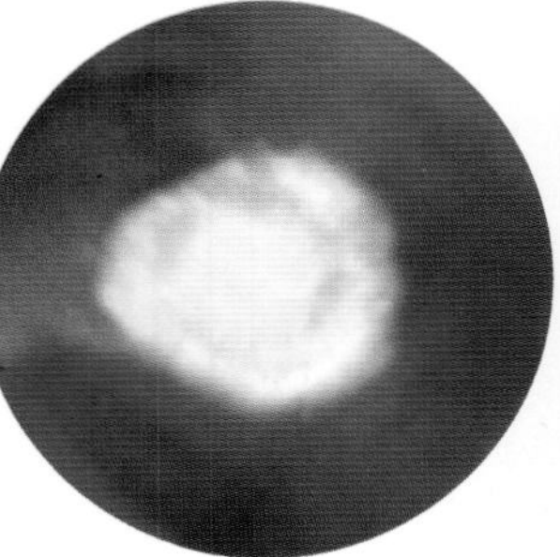

Mid spring

▽ **Chasma Boreale**
This 3D reconstruction looks into Chasma Boreale, the northern cap's largest canyon. It is about 570km (350 miles) long – a little longer than Earth's Grand Canyon – and up to 1.4km (0.87 miles) deep. At its mouth it is 120km (75 miles) wide, tapering as it runs into the cap. The walls are stacked layers of ice, and the dark terrain is frozen sand.

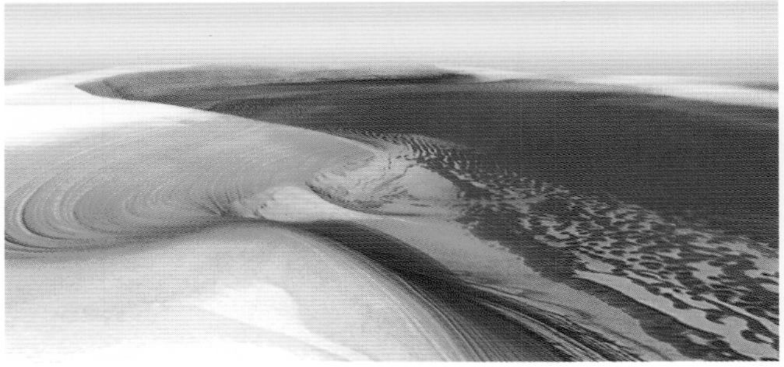

▽ **Spiral pattern**
The distinctive spirals of dark troughs at the north cap were caused by strong polar winds over millions of years. The troughs probably began as slight depressions that gradually deepened into valleys. The vast dark sea of dunes extending from the cap formed when Mars was warmer and still ice-free.

Chasma Boreale, a huge canyon that cuts into the north cap, was carved by polar winds.

Sand dunes shaped by polar winds surround the pole.

South cap

The south cap, Planum Australe (Southern Plain), has a thick base of water ice topped with an 8m (25ft) layer of carbon dioxide ice. At its minimum size in summer, it measures about 420km (260 miles) across. During the southern winter, the cap is in permanent darkness, the temperature drops, and carbon dioxide both freezes as frost and falls as snow.

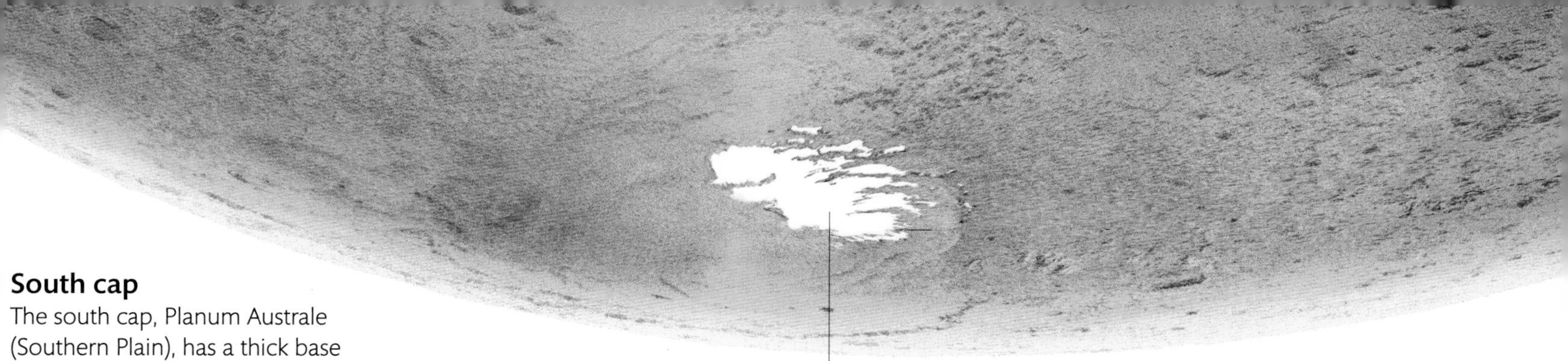

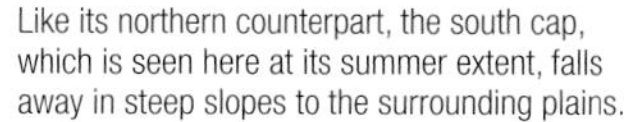

Like its northern counterpart, the south cap, which is seen here at its summer extent, falls away in steep slopes to the surrounding plains.

△ **Frozen solid**
The south cap is the only place on Mars where carbon dioxide, which freezes at around −125°C (−193°F), persists as ice on the surface all year round. As in the north, the south polar region is encircled by a vast area of permafrost (water ice mixed with soil and frozen to the hardness of solid rock).

▷ **Starburst**
In springtime, as carbon dioxide gas beneath the seasonal ice makes its way to the surface, it carves out troughs in the ground. These troughs form branch-like patterns often referred to as starbursts or spiders. In some locations, dust carried by the gas falls to the ice surface in fan-shaped deposits.

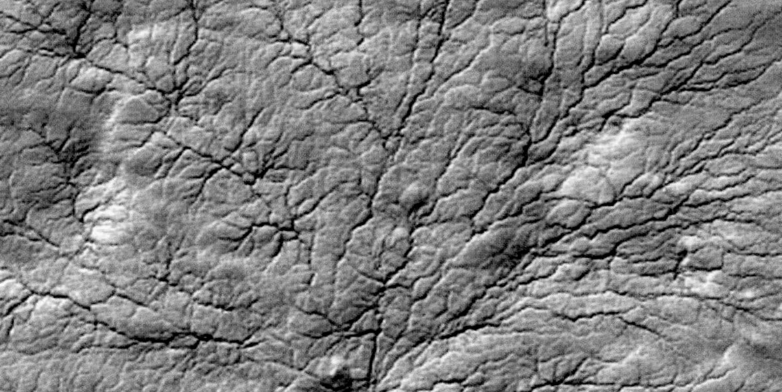

▽ **Icy pits**
This view shows an effect created in the late summer in the southern polar region. The carbon dioxide ice is here about 3m (10 ft) thick and penetrated by flat-floored pits. For most of the year the pit walls are covered by bright frost. But an upper layer of the ice has turned to gas, revealing the edges of the pits. The smallest of the pits are roughly the size of a sports stadium – about 60m (195ft) across.

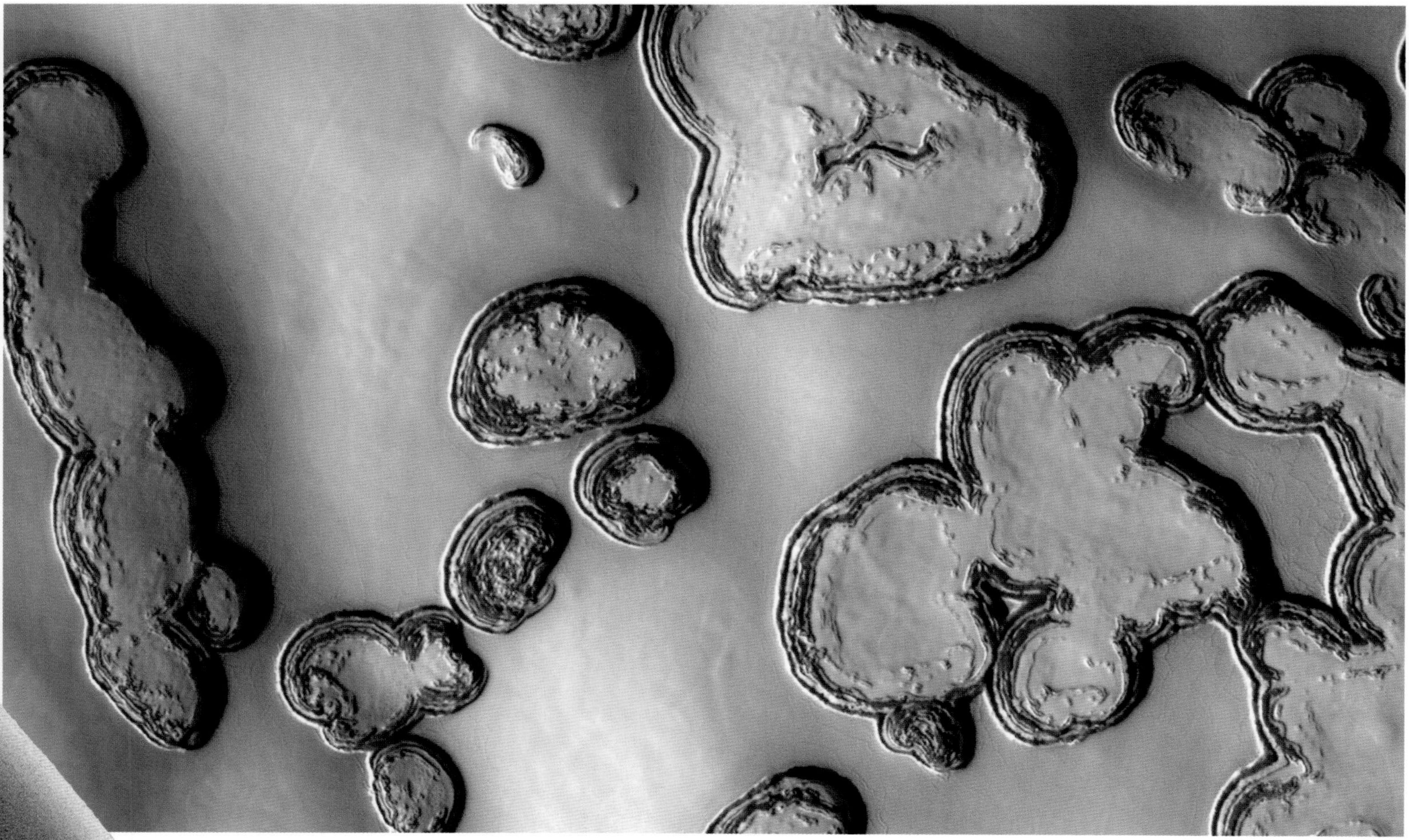

THE MOONS OF **MARS**

On **Phobos**, the temperature in the shade is **–112°C (–170°F).**

MARS HAS TWO MOONS, PHOBOS AND DEIMOS. THEY ARE IRREGULARLY SHAPED, ROCKY LUMPS WITH CRATERED SURFACES. TINY COMPARED TO EARTH'S MOON, THEY HURTLE AROUND MARS IN LESS THAN A DAY AND A HALF.

The two moons were discovered within days of each other by American astronomer Asaph Hall in 1877 and were named after characters in Greek mythology. Phobos was the god of fear and Deimos the god of terror; the two brothers accompanied their father Ares, the god of war, into battle. The moons have been imaged in detail only in relatively recent times. Phobos has been studied most closely: it was the subject of a series of flybys by Mars Express in 2010. The origin of the moons is uncertain. Some astronomers think the pair are asteroids captured by Mars's gravity; others that Phobos formed from debris left over from the formation of Mars.

Earth's Moon (diameter)
3,476km
2,160 miles

Phobos (average width)
22.2km
13.8 miles

Deimos (average width)
12.4 km
7.7 miles

△ **Comparing the moons of Mars and Earth**
Earth's Moon is around 155 times wider than Phobos and 280 times larger than Deimos. But Mars's two moons are much closer to their parent planet than the Moon is to Earth. An observer on the Martian surface would see Phobos at just over a third of the size that the Moon appears in Earth's sky.

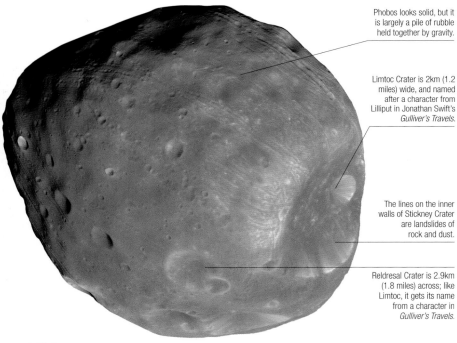

Phobos looks solid, but it is largely a pile of rubble held together by gravity.

Limtoc Crater is 2km (1.2 miles) wide, and named after a character from Lilliput in Jonathan Swift's *Gulliver's Travels.*

The lines on the inner walls of Stickney Crater are landslides of rock and dust.

Reldresal Crater is 2.9km (1.8 miles) across; like Limtoc, it gets its name from a character in *Gulliver's Travels.*

△ **Phobos**
The larger of Mars's two moons, Phobos is a cavity-ridden rocky body about 27km (17 miles) long. Its heavily cratered, barren surface is covered in a thick, loose layer of fine dust. Almost all of its 20 named surface features are craters. The largest, Stickney, is about 9km (5.5 miles) across. The grooves and rows of craters surrounding it could have been formed by the impact that created Stickney or by debris ejected from Mars when meteoroids hit the planet's surface.

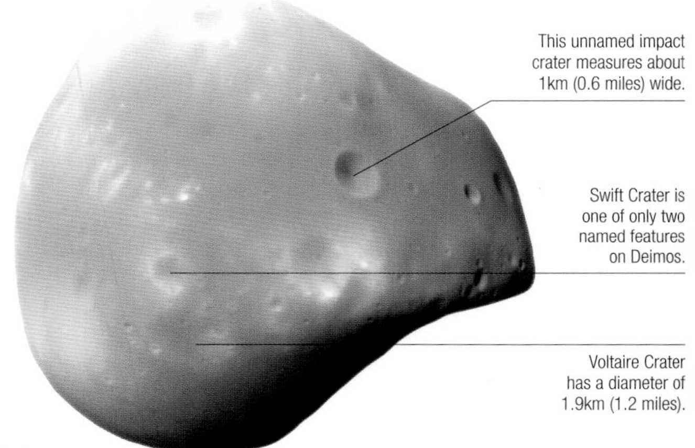

This unnamed impact crater measures about 1km (0.6 miles) wide.

Swift Crater is one of only two named features on Deimos.

Voltaire Crater has a diameter of 1.9km (1.2 miles).

△ **Deimos**
At 15km (9 miles) long, Deimos is about half the size of Phobos. Like its bigger companion, it is a rocky body blanketed in a reddish soil of rock fragments and dust. It has fewer craters; all but the most recent contain soil, giving Deimos a smoother surface. The surface colour varies: it is least red around the freshest craters, where the soil has slipped down the slopes and exposed the bedrock.

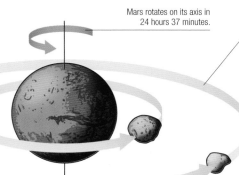

Mars rotates on its axis in 24 hours 37 minutes.

Deimos orbits Mars in 30 hours 18 minutes.

One orbit of Mars by Phobos takes 7 hours 39 minutes.

◁ **Moon orbit and spin**
Phobos and Deimos follow near-circular orbits above Mars's equator. Phobos is closest, at 9,376km (5,826 miles) from Mars, and it is getting closer by a few centimetres each year. In 50 million years' time, it will have either crashed into Mars or, more likely, disintegrated through the stress of being pulled by Mars's gravity. Deimos is 23,458km (14,576 miles) away, over twice the distance of Phobos. Both moons are in synchronous orbits, keeping the same face pointed to Mars at all times.

△ **Phobos over Mars**
When the Viking 1 orbiter was imaging the surface of Mars as it flew around the planet in September 1977, it took a snapshot of the largest Martian moon. Seen here as an almost black ball, Phobos was between Viking 1 and the surface when the picture was taken. Phobos orbits the planet faster than Mars spins on its axis. Anyone on the surface would see Phobos rise in the west, move rapidly across the sky, and then set in the east – a feat it performs twice each Martian day.

THE **RED PLANET**

MARS HAS BEEN KNOWN SINCE ANCIENT TIMES. EARLY ASTRONOMERS NOTED ITS COLOUR AND MOVEMENT ACROSS THE SKY. TELESCOPES LATER REVEALED SURFACE DETAIL.

The colour of Mars led the ancient Greeks and Romans to associate the planet with blood and war. It wasn't until much later that telescopes revealed more than just a reddish point of light. The mistaken sighting of channels led to the idea that Mars might be home to an advanced civilization, but when spacecraft visited they found a dry, lifeless desert. Nevertheless, evidence suggests that Mars had a watery past. Several generations of rover have now explored the surface, and Mars is the planet most likely to be visited by people in the future.

Mars, Roman god of war

500 BCE

The red planet
Mars, the red planet, is named after the Roman god of war. Astrologically, the planet becomes associated with passion, fighting, and lust. Apparent variations in its movements and brightness baffle astronomers until the 17th century.

Johannes Kepler's illustration of Mars's orbit

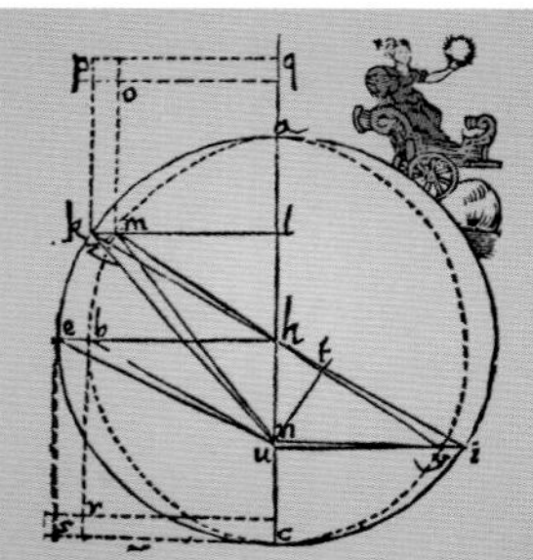

1609 CE

Orbit calculation
German astronomer Johannes Kepler works out the shape of Mars's orbit. Kepler realizes that planets have elliptical rather than circular orbits, and he derives three laws of planetary motion. These will later inspire Isaac Newton's revolutionary work on gravity.

Orson Welles in the CBS radio studio

1938

Mars and science fiction
The idea that Mars is inhabited is popular in science fiction. On 30 October Orson Welles makes a radio broadcast of H.G. Wells' *War of the Worlds*. Presented in the style of a news bulletin, it convinces some listeners that Martian invaders are taking over Earth.

1947

Atmosphere
US astronomer Gerard Kuiper working at the Yerkes Observatory in Wisconsin, USA, finds that the thin atmosphere of Mars consists mainly of carbon dioxide. The discovery helps overturn the widespread belief that Mars is like Earth.

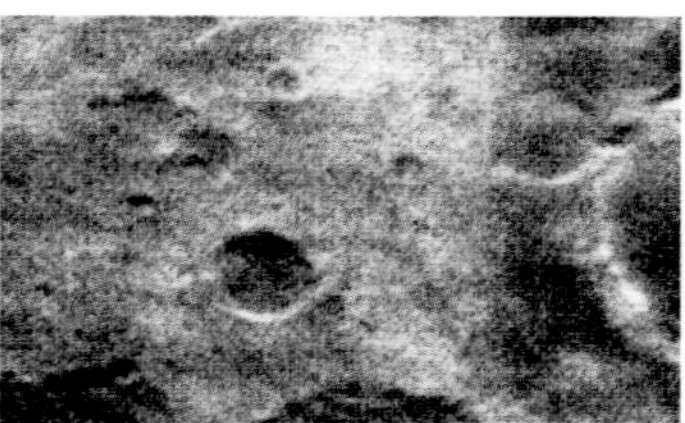

Mariner 4 image of cratered surface

1965

First spacecraft and surface photos
NASA's Mariner 4 spacecraft performs the first successful flyby of Mars, passing within 9,846km (6,118 miles) of the surface. It takes 21 images of the southern hemisphere. The area imaged is billions of years old and cratered much like Earth's moon.

Summit of Olympus Mons volcano

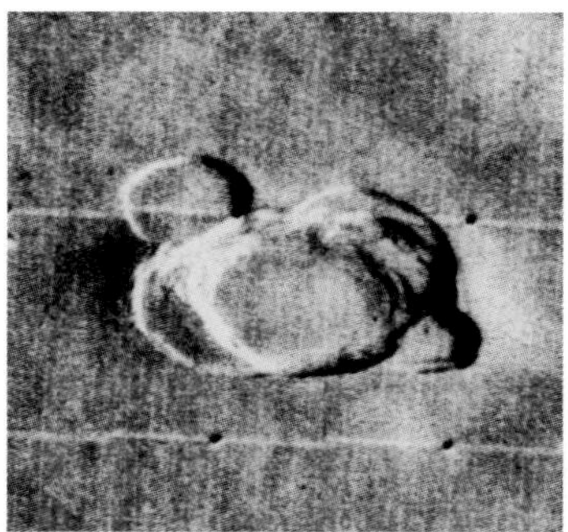

1971

First orbiter
Mariner 9 is the first spacecraft to orbit a planet other than Earth. It finds huge, dormant volcanoes, a giant system of canyons, and signs of erosion by fluids. The southern hemisphere is more cratered than the younger northern hemisphere.

Viking 2 lander on Utopia Planitia

1975

Landers on Mars
Two identical Viking craft leave Earth for Mars. Each consists of an orbiter and a lander. The Viking 1 lander is the first to the surface, and within five minutes of touchdown it returns the first images from the ground. Both landing craft search for evidence of life, past and present. The orbiters see what appear to be dried-up, branching river beds.

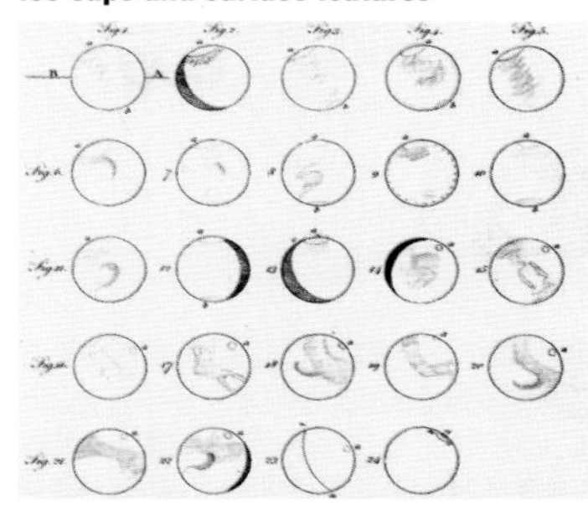
Herschel's 1784 drawings of Mars show ice caps and surface features

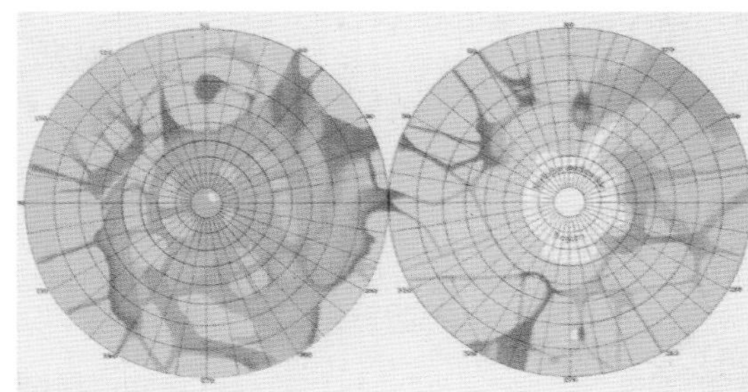
The two hemispheres of Mars by Schiaparelli

1659

First surface observations

Dutch scientist Christiaan Huygens looks at Mars through a telescope and sees markings on the surface. By watching them disappear and reappear he finds that Mars spins on its axis every 24 hours and 40 minutes. In 1672, Huygens discovers Mars's polar caps.

1784

Seasons on Mars

English astronomer William Herschel improves the measurement of Mars's rotation period and finds that its axis is tilted by 25.2°. As a result, Mars has seasons. Herschel notes that the size of Mars's ice caps changes with the seasons.

1863

First maps

Italian astronomer Angelo Secchi produces the first colour map of Mars. Then, in 1879, fellow Italian Giovanni Schiaparelli produces more detailed maps that include fine lines labelled *canali* – Italian for channels. English versions mistranslate the word as "canals".

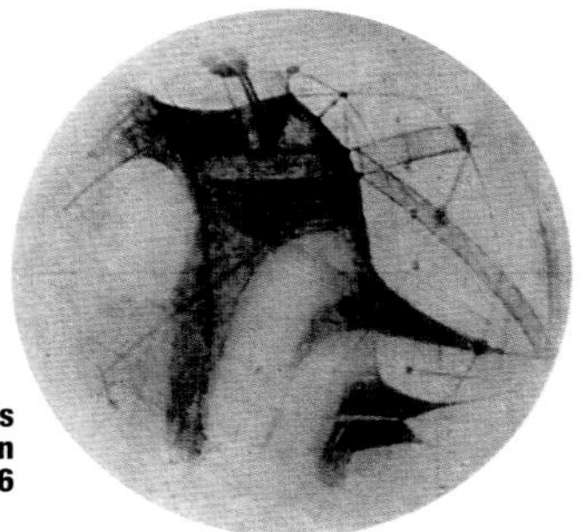
One of Percival Lowell's drawings of Martian canals, 1896

US Naval Observatory 66cm (26in) refracting telescope

1877

Discovery of moons

With Mars in a favourable position, US astronomer Asaph Hall discovers its two moons, Phobos and Deimos. He uses the largest telescope in the world at the time, a 66cm (26in) refractor at the US Naval Observatory, Washington DC.

1896

Intelligent life on Mars

Using the 60cm (24in) refractor at his private observatory in Arizona, USA, astronomer Percival Lowell maps Mars. Inspired by Schiaparelli's "canals", he argues in his book *Mars as the Abode for Life* that the planet is inhabited by intelligent beings.

1924

Temperature

Using the Hooker telescope on Mount Wilson, California, US astronomers Edison Pettit and Seth Nicholson measure Mars's surface temperature. It is 7°C (45°F) at the equator and –68°C (–90°F) at the pole. The wind and temperature vary seasonally.

Three generations of rovers: Sojourner (front), Opportunity (left), and Curiosity (right)

1984

Martian meteorite

Meteorite ALH84001 is found on Earth, in the Allan Hills region of Antarctica. It was ejected from Mars 16 million years ago, reaching Earth 13,000 years ago. It contains structures that look like fossilized microbes.

2012

Rovers on Mars

Curiosity, the latest and largest of the four rovers to roam on Mars, arrives in Gale Crater. Sojourner was the first and explored the floodplain Chryse Planitia in 1996, staying close to its mothercraft. The twin rovers Spirit and Opportunity arrived in 2004 and covered many miles as they explored the planet.

LAUNCH — EARTH ORBIT — JOURNEY TO MARS

Year	Mission
1960	Mars 1M1
1960	Mars 1M2
1962	Sputnik 22
1962	Mars 1
1962	Sputnik 24
1964	Mariner 3
1964	Mariner 4
1964	Zond 2
1969	Mariner 6
1969	Mars 1969A
1969	Mariner 7
1969	Mars 1969B
1971	Mariner 8
1971	Kosmos 419
1971	Mars 2
1971	Mars 3
1971	Mariner 9
1973	Mars 4
1973	Mars 5
1973	Mars 6
1973	Mars 7
1975	Viking 1
1975	Viking 2
1988	Phobos 1
1988	Phobos 2
1992	Mars Observer
1996	Mars Global Surveyor
1996	Mars 96
1996	Mars Pathfinder and Sojourner
1998	Nozomi
1998	Mars Climate Orbiter
1999	Mars Polar Lander and Deep Space 2
2001	Mars Odyssey
2003	Mars Express and Beagle 2
2003	MER-A Spirit
2003	MER-B Opportunity
2005	Mars Reconnaissance Orbiter
2007	Phoenix
2011	Phobos-Grunt and Yinghuo 1
2011	MSL Curiosity
2013	Mars Orbiter Mission
2013	MAVEN
Planned	ExoMars Orbiter
Planned	InSight
Planned	ExoMars Rover
Planned	Mars 2020 Rover Mission

KEY

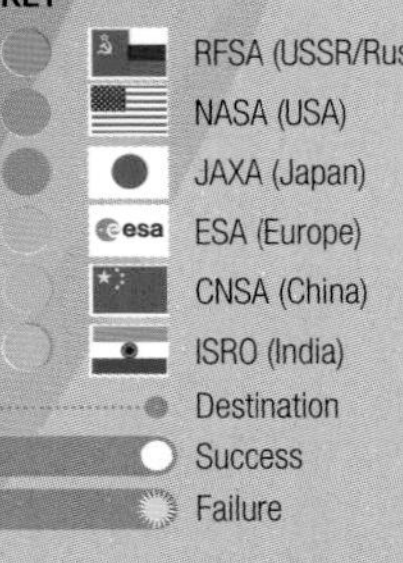
RFSA (USSR/Russia)
NASA (USA)
JAXA (Japan)
esa
ESA (Europe)
CNSA (China)
ISRO (India)
Destination
Success
Failure

▷ **Landing sites**
Seven craft have touched down successfully on Mars. Three stayed where they landed and investigated their immediate surroundings. These were Viking 1 and 2, which arrived in 1976, and Phoenix in 2008. The other four craft, two of which are still working, were rovers designed to drive over the Martian landscape, stopping now and then to investigate.

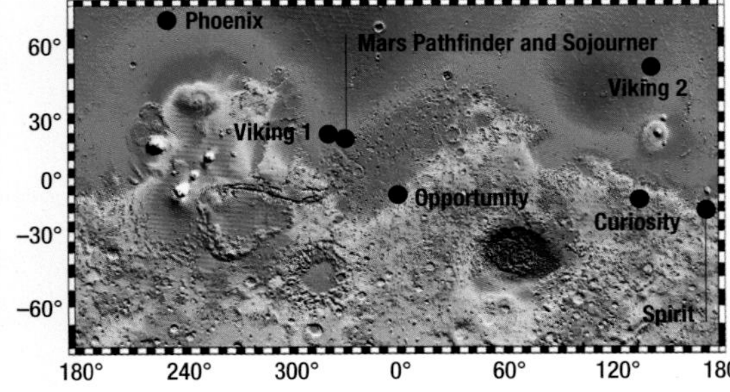
Phoenix
Mars Pathfinder and Sojourner
Viking 2
Viking 1
Opportunity
Curiosity
Spirit
60°
30°
0°
-30°
-60°
180°
240°
300°
0°
60°
120°
180°

▷ **First surface image**
The USA's Viking 1 was the first craft to return images from Mars's surface. Although the earlier Soviet craft Mars 3 had a TV camera on board, it stopped transmitting seconds after landing and nothing was seen of its surroundings. Viking 1 took its first image (right) just after it arrived on 20 July 1976; one of the craft's footpads is seen in the photograph.

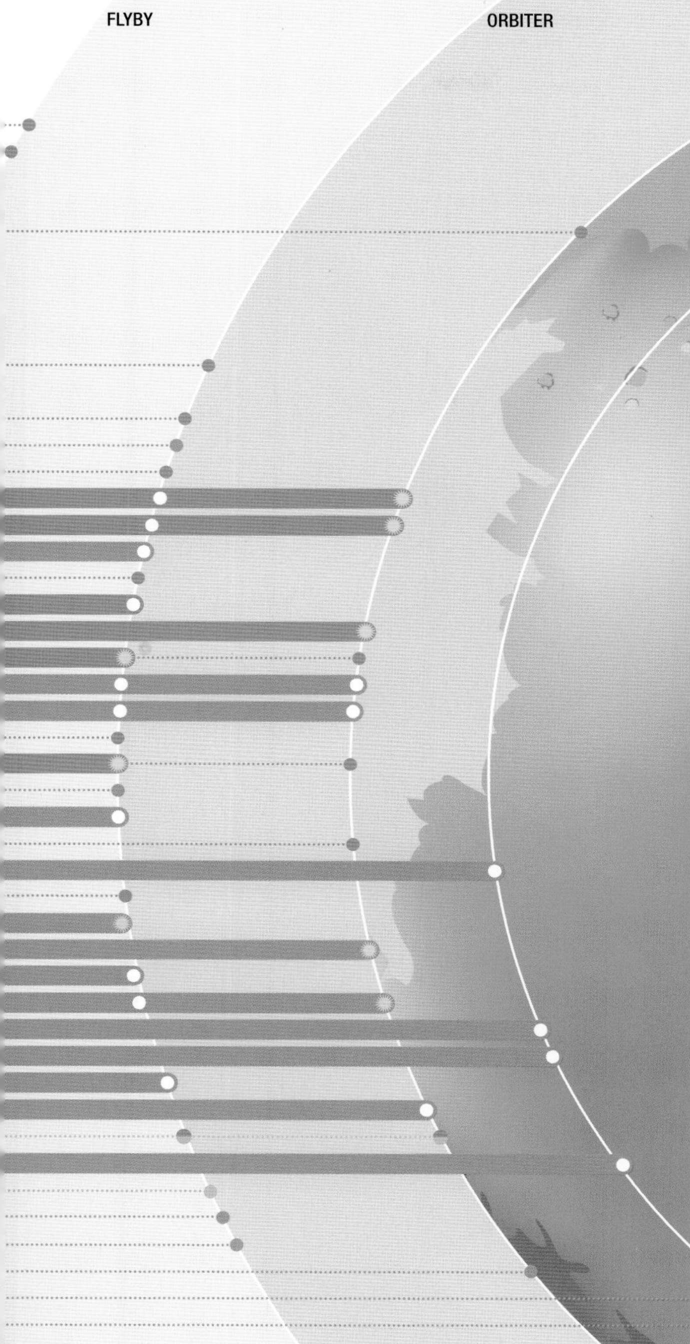

FLYBY

ORBITER

LANDER

ROVER

MISSIONS TO **MARS**

IN THE PAST 60 YEARS, MORE THAN 40 MISSIONS HAVE BLASTED OFF FROM EARTH FOR MARS. THE PLANET HAS BEEN FLOWN BY, ORBITED, LANDED ON, AND ROVED OVER, AND WAS THE FIRST PLANET EVER SEEN IN CLOSE-UP.

Missions sent to Mars in the 21st century have been extraordinarily successful, sometimes far exceeding expectations. But success has been built on earlier disappointments, with more than half of all Mars missions either failing to get away from Earth or losing contact with their controllers as they closed in on their target. The first attempts at Martian exploration were undertaken by the USA and the then Soviet Union in the 1960s and 70s, after which there was little interest in Mars until the mid 1990s. Now, six countries have sent craft to Mars, more missions are planned, and a privately funded project is underway to develop a space flight system capable of taking a human crew to Mars.

▷ **Landmark missions**
The American Mariner series provided the first successful missions to Mars. Mariner 4 was the first craft to fly by the planet and to take close-up images. Mariner 9 was the first craft to orbit Mars. The first soft-landing on Mars was made by the Soviet craft Mars 3, but no data was returned.

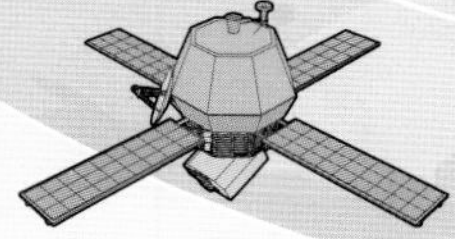

Mariner 9
The first craft to orbit any planet, Mariner 9 arrived in 1971 and provided the first global map of Mars.

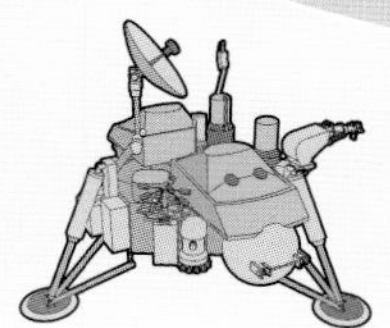

Viking 1 and 2
Twin craft, each consisting of an orbiter and a lander, reached Mars in 1976 and made soil tests.

Sojourner
The size of a microwave oven, Mars's first rover worked for almost three months from July 1997.

Mars Express
The orbiter, Europe's first planetary mission, has been mapping Mars since December 2003.

ROVING ON **MARS**

MARS IS THE ONLY PLANET TO HAVE BEEN EXPLORED BY ROBOTIC ROVERS. FOUR HAVE SUCCESSFULLY VISITED THE PLANET: SOJOURNER, SPIRIT, OPPORTUNITY, AND CURIOSITY. WE NOW KNOW MORE ABOUT THE SURFACE OF MARS THAN ANY OTHER PLANET EXCEPT EARTH.

Designed to drive across alien terrain, robotic rovers are mobile science labs that hunt out interesting sites and conduct on-the-spot investigations. With their own power supply, they are operated by on-board computers and armed with scientific instruments, including cameras and rock analysis tools. Back on Earth, ground controllers decide where the rovers should go and what they should do. Directions take a few minutes to get through. Collected data is relayed directly to Earth or via orbiters like Mars Reconnaissance Orbiter, a spacecraft circling the planet.

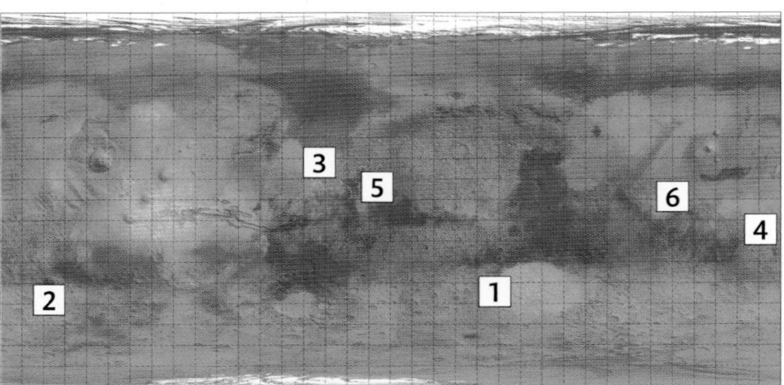
3
5
6
4
2
1

KEY
1 Mars 2 (1971)
2 Mars 3 (1971)
3 Sojourner (1997)
4 Spirit (2004)
5 Opportunity (2004)
6 Curiosity (2012)

△ **Rover sites**
The first two attempts to put rovers on Mars ended in failure. The Soviet Mars 2 lander, carrying a tethered rover equipped with skis, crash-landed. Its twin Mars 3 failed seconds after touchdown. Since then, four rovers have made successful landings. They have explored a variety of terrains, all low-lying for ease of landing and smooth enough to drive over.

▽ **Opportunity**
Opportunity touched down in Meridiani Planum in 2004, and has investigated sites including four impact craters – Endurance, Erebus, Victoria, and Endeavour. It travels at around 1cm (0.5in) per second, sending back images of the terrain and results of its rock analysis. Designed to operate for about three months, it is now in its eleventh year of work.

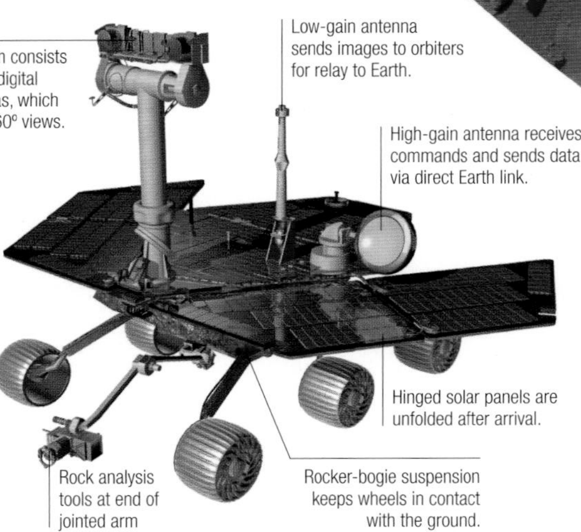
Pancam consists of two digital cameras, which take 360° views.
Low-gain antenna sends images to orbiters for relay to Earth.
High-gain antenna receives commands and sends data via direct Earth link.
Hinged solar panels are unfolded after arrival.
Rocker-bogie suspension keeps wheels in contact with the ground.
Rock analysis tools at end of jointed arm

▽ **Martian rovers**
The first rover, Sojourner, was the size of a microwave oven. It stayed close to its landing site and worked for about three months. The twin craft Spirit and Opportunity arrived on opposite sides of Mars in 2004. Spirit no longer works but Opportunity continues to explore. Curiosity is the size of a small car and has a laser tool to gauge the composition of a rock in seconds.

Sojourner July–September 1997
Distance travelled: 100m (330ft)

Spirit January 2004–March 2010
7.7km (4.75 miles)

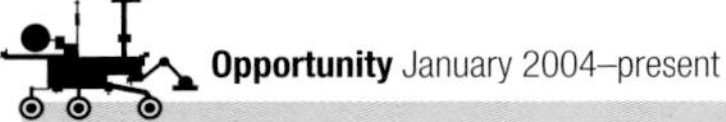
Opportunity January 2004–present
38.7 km (24 miles)

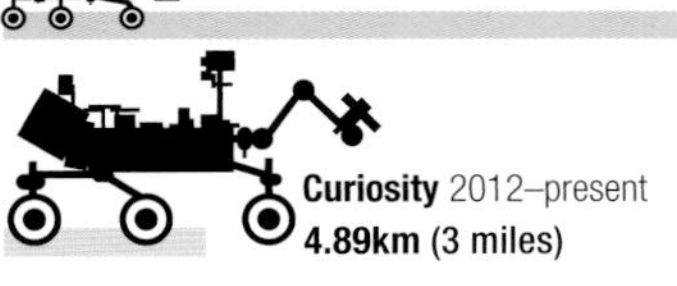
Curiosity 2012–present
4.89km (3 miles)

▷ **Curiosity self-portrait**
Curiosity is investigating the floor of Gale Crater, a 154km (96 mile) wide impact crater formed more than 3 billion years ago. This self-portrait shows the rover in the Yellowknife Bay area of the crater where sedimentary rocks called mudstones indicate an ancient lake bed. The image is a mosaic of dozens of individual views taken in February 2013 using MAHLI (Mars Hand Lens Imager), one of Curiosity's 17 cameras.

This patch of flat outcrop is named John Klein and was the site of Curiosity's first rock drilling.

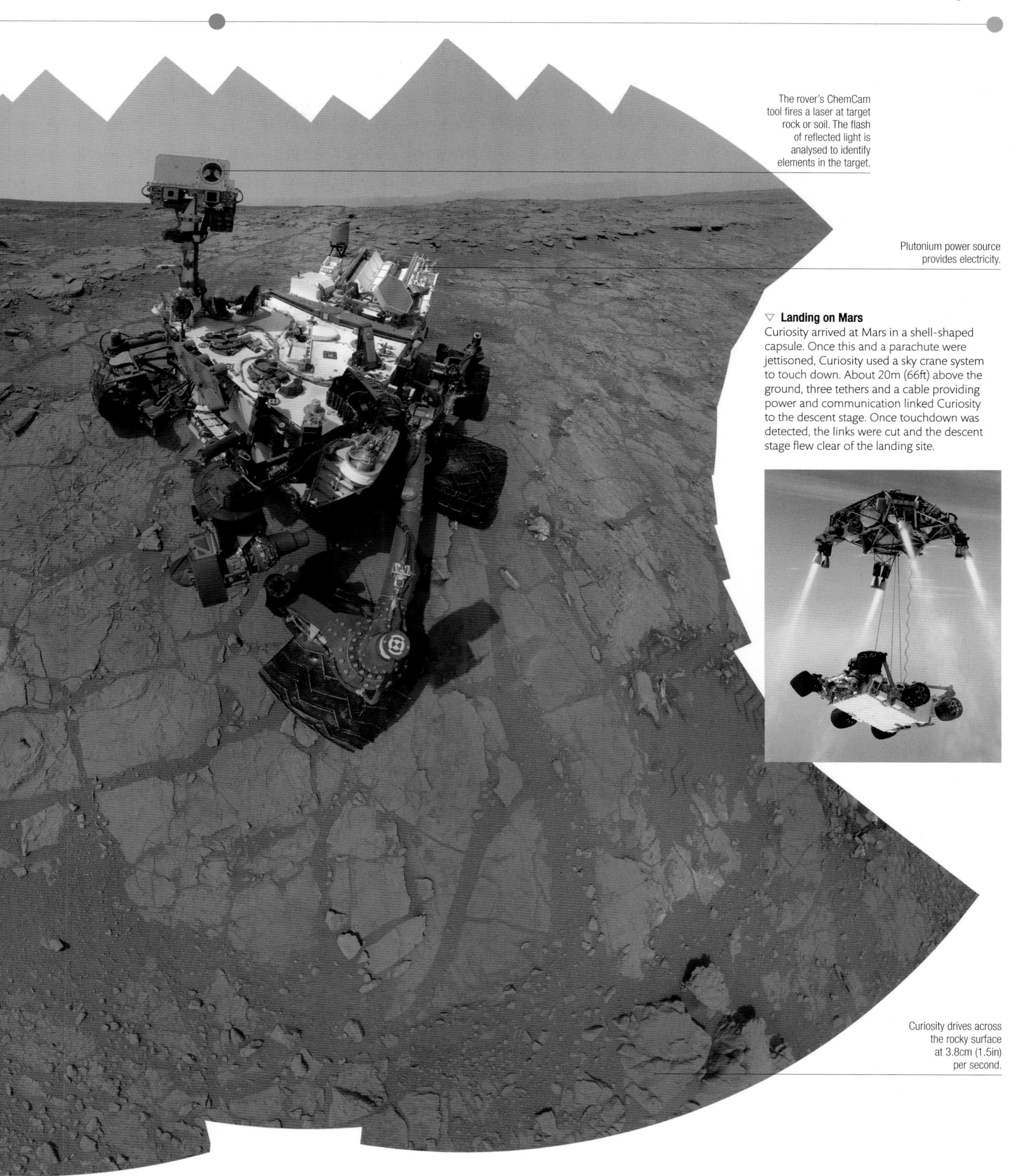

The rover's ChemCam tool fires a laser at target rock or soil. The flash of reflected light is analysed to identify elements in the target.

Plutonium power source provides electricity.

▽ **Landing on Mars**
Curiosity arrived at Mars in a shell-shaped capsule. Once this and a parachute were jettisoned, Curiosity used a sky crane system to touch down. About 20m (66ft) above the ground, three tethers and a cable providing power and communication linked Curiosity to the descent stage. Once touchdown was detected, the links were cut and the descent stage flew clear of the landing site.

Curiosity drives across the rocky surface at 3.8cm (1.5in) per second.

EXPLORING **MARS**

1 Endurance Crater
This view of wind-whipped sand dunes inside Endurance Crater is one of many incredible views of Mars returned by Opportunity – the longest-running rover on Mars. Opportunity was unable to ride directly over the sand because of the risk of becoming stuck – a fate that befell its twin, the Spirit rover, in 2009.

2 Santa Maria Crater
This montage of images from Opportunity reveals the view east across the 90m (295ft) wide Santa Maria Crater, with the rim of Endurance Crater visible in the far distance. Camera filters were used to highlight different rocks and soils in false colour; to human eyes, the scene would appear reddish-brown.

3 Gale Crater
The rolling hills on the horizon in this image from NASA's Curiosity rover are part of the rim of Gale Crater. Curiosity touched down in this ancient, 154km (96 mile) wide meteor crater in 2012. The site was chosen because it may once have contained running water and, perhaps in the distant past, microbial life.

4 Home Plate
The Spirit rover visited this rust-red plateau, named for its similarity to the home plate in a baseball pitch, in 2006. The plateau is thought to have formed in an ancient volcanic explosion, perhaps when lava came into contact with water. One of Spirit's radio antennae is visible on the right.

5

5 Payson Outcrop
Captured by the Opportunity rover's panoramic camera, this image shows Payson Outcrop – the crumbling, eroded wall of Erebus Crater. False colours have been used to enhance subtle differences in layers of rock and soil. The outcrop is about 1m (3ft) deep and 25m (82ft) long.

ASTEROIDS

ASTEROIDS ARE ROCKY BODIES THAT VARY IN SIZE FROM A FEW MILLIMETRES TO HUNDREDS OF KILOMETRES WIDE. THEY EXIST THROUGHOUT THE SOLAR SYSTEM BUT MOST ARE FOUND IN THE ASTEROID BELT BETWEEN MARS AND JUPITER.

Sometimes called minor planets, asteroids orbit the Sun in the same direction as planets, but only the very largest have sufficient mass to pull themselves into a regular, rounded shape.

Asteroids were much more numerous in the Solar System's early years. As they orbited the Sun, they collided and sometimes joined through gravity, accumulating to form larger bodies. Some of these embryonic worlds were destined to become today's terrestrial planets, but those near Jupiter's orbit were disturbed by the giant planet's powerful gravity, which caused them to crash violently and fragment. As a result, a ring of rocky debris has remained between the orbits of Mars and Jupiter ever since, forming the Asteroid Belt.

Today, the Asteroid Belt is sparsely populated; the total mass of the Main Belt is equal to only 4 per cent of the Moon's mass. Collisions dominate this part of the Solar System, and most asteroids are fragments of larger bodies that were destroyed.

253 Mathilde
(NEAR Shoemaker image)

△ **Carbonaceous asteroids (C-type)**
Asteroids can be classified by the materials they are made up of. About 75 per cent of all known asteroids are carbonaceous. These carbon-rich asteroids have very dark surfaces, typically reflecting only 3–10 per cent of the light that falls on them. Carbonaceous asteroids are found in the outer regions of the main Asteroid Belt.

▷ **Many sizes**
The largest body in the Asteroid Belt is Ceres, which is 952km (592 miles) wide and classed as a dwarf planet because of its spherical shape. While there are few very large asteroids in the belt, there are an estimated 200 million asteroids larger than 1km (0.6 miles) in diameter, and millions of smaller ones. They are irregular in shape and bear the scars of repeated impacts and collisions. The smallest asteroids are just millimetres across; smaller still are countless specks of asteroid dust.

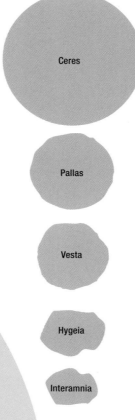

Ceres

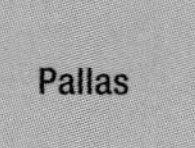
Pallas

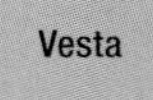
Vesta

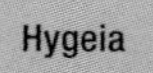
Hygeia

Interamnia

Europa

Largest asteroids by diameter

The Moon

A series of concentric troughs circle Vesta's equator. These are fractures produced when the largest craters formed.

433 Eros
(NEAR Shoemaker image)

△ **Grey silicaceous asteroids (S-type)**
These rocky bodies consist mainly of iron and magnesium silicates – the same materials that makes up Earth's mantle. Their surfaces reflect 10–22 per cent of the light that falls on them, and they make up about 17 per cent of the Asteroid Belt. Eros, the asteroid visited and orbited in 2000 by the NEAR Shoemaker spacecraft, is an S-Type.

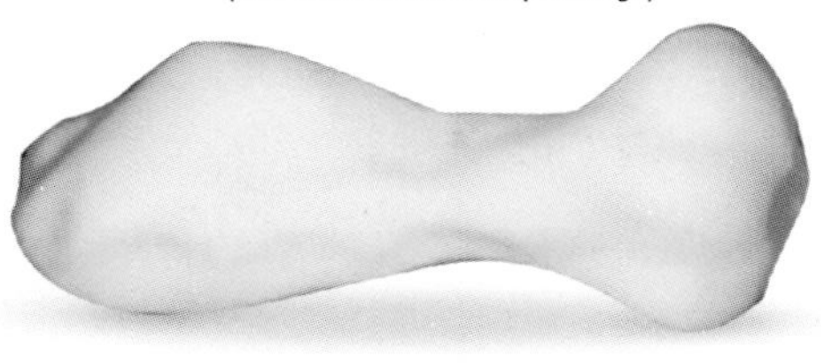
216 Kleopatra
(Arecibo radio telescope image)

△ **Metallic asteroids (M-type)**
These bodies appear to be a mixture of iron and nickel, similar in composition to Earth's core. This material has been molten and well mixed in the past, and then slowly cooled. The 1.2km (0.75 mile) diameter Barringer Crater in Arizona, USA, was formed 50,000 years ago when a 50m (164ft) wide M-type asteroid hit Earth at about 50,000kph (30,000mph).

▽ **Asteroid evolution**
If an asteroid grows sufficiently large, heat released inside it by decay of radioactive elements can cause it to melt. The molten materials then separate out due to gravity, heavy elements such as iron sinking to form a core, and more lightweight rocky minerals settling on top as mantle and crust. An asteroid continues to evolve as a result of impacts with other asteroids. Small impacts merely break off fragments, which become new asteroids. A large impact can smash an asteroid, scattering the fragments, but the parts may slowly reaggregate under gravitational attraction to form a loose mass of rubble.

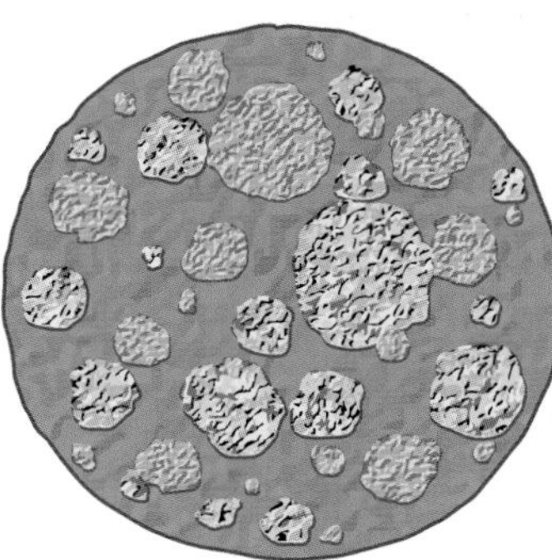
Accretion of smaller bodies

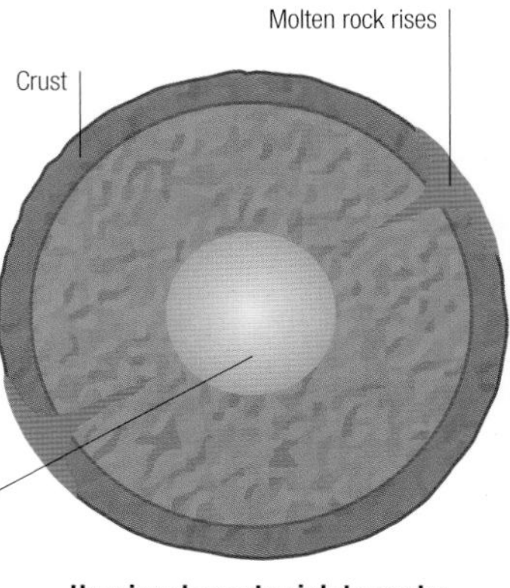
Molten rock rises
Crust
Iron-nickel core
Heavier elements sink to centre

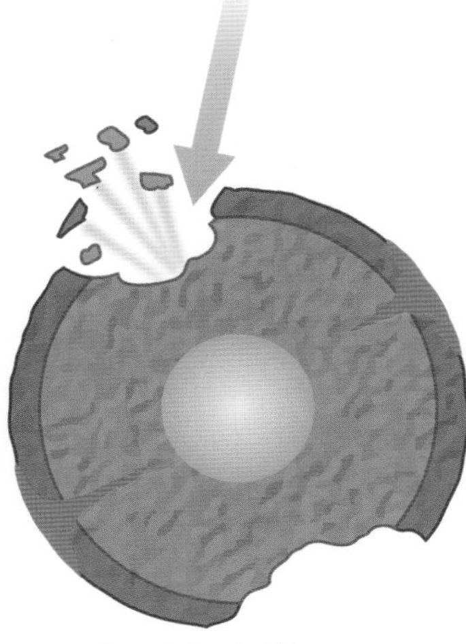
Impacts break off fragments

◁ **Vesta**
The second most massive member of the Asteroid Belt, Vesta rotates once every 5.3 hours and is 525km (326 miles) wide. Its surface is extensively cratered, and ejecta from these impacts has subsequently fallen to Earth, creating around 1,200 meteorites. Vesta is large enough to have melted completely as a result of radioactive heating and to have separated into a rocky mantle and metallic core. It was visited by NASA's Dawn spacecraft between July 2011 and September 2012.

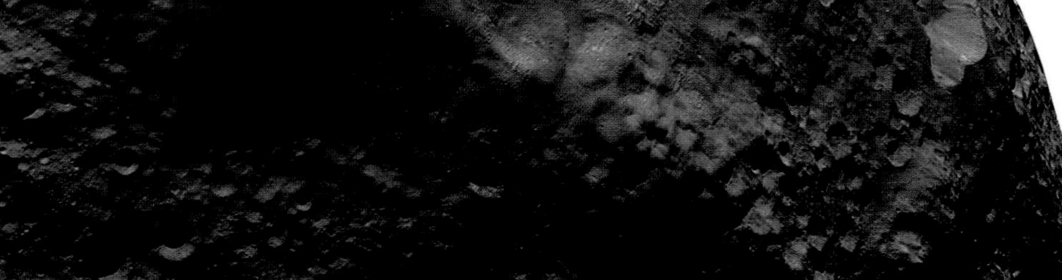
The Snowman craters are thought to have formed when another asteroid hit Vesta's surface. The largest of them is 70km (43 miles) across.

THE **ASTEROID BELT**

THERE ARE MILLIONS OF ASTEROIDS. MOST ARE IN THE ASTEROID BELT – A DOUGHNUT-SHAPED RING BETWEEN MARS AND JUPITER. EACH ONE FOLLOWS ITS OWN PATH AROUND THE SUN, BUT THEY ALL SHARE A COMMON ORIGIN.

The Asteroid Belt, also called the Main Belt, stretches between 315 and 480 million km (195 and 300 million miles) from the Sun. Frequent collisions send asteroids hurtling out of the Belt – its overall mass has decreased with time. Today, the combined mass of its asteroids amounts to 4 per cent of that of the Moon. The largest asteroid of all, Ceres, lies within the Belt, and this single body makes up 30 per cent of the Belt's mass. It is one of only eight asteroids that measure more than 300km (186 miles) across and are spherical. The rest are irregular and much smaller.

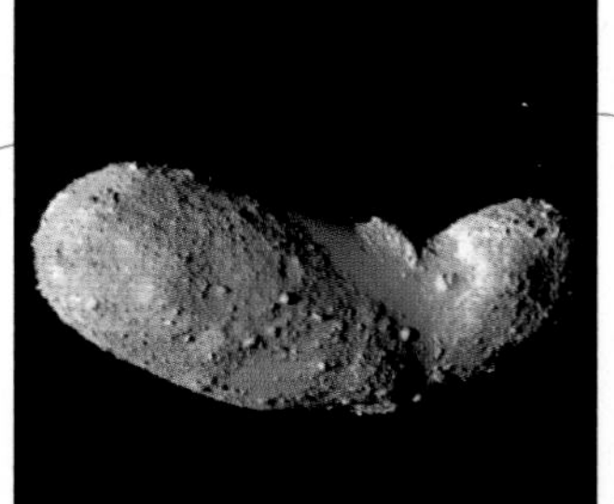

Itokawa
This near-Earth asteroid orbits outside the Belt. It is 5.4km (3.4 miles) in length and orbits in 1.52 years.

A near-Earth asteroid, Eros is 34km (21 miles) long and takes 1.76 years to orbit the Sun.

The Asteroid Belt is about 2.8 times further from the Sun than Earth.

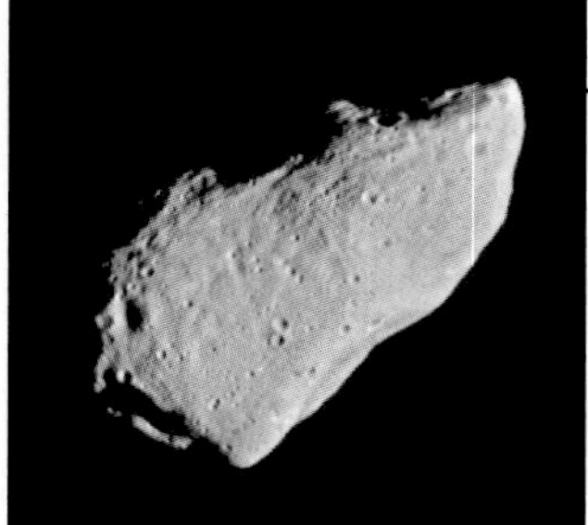

Gaspra
Measuring 18km (11.2 miles) long, Gaspra orbits every 3.29 years, near the inner edge of the Belt. Its surface is pitted with craters from collisions with other asteroids.

Toutatis is a 4.3km (2.7 miles) long near-Earth asteroid. Its orbit is outside the Belt and takes 4.03 years to complete.

Belt profile

Around 200,000 Belt asteroids are bigger than 10km (6 miles) across, 200 million are over 1km (0.6 miles) wide, and billions more are smaller still. They orbit the Sun in the same direction as the planets – that is, anticlockwise if they were seen from above. Their individual orbits are non-circular and slightly inclined to the plane of the planetary orbits, making the Asteroid Belt not flat but doughnut-shaped. One orbit of the Sun typically takes four to five years to complete. Jupiter's gravitational pull can change asteroid orbits, pushing or pulling them out of the Belt. Asteroids outside the Belt include near-Earth asteroids, and several thousand Trojans – two swarms of asteroids with orbits similar to that of Jupiter.

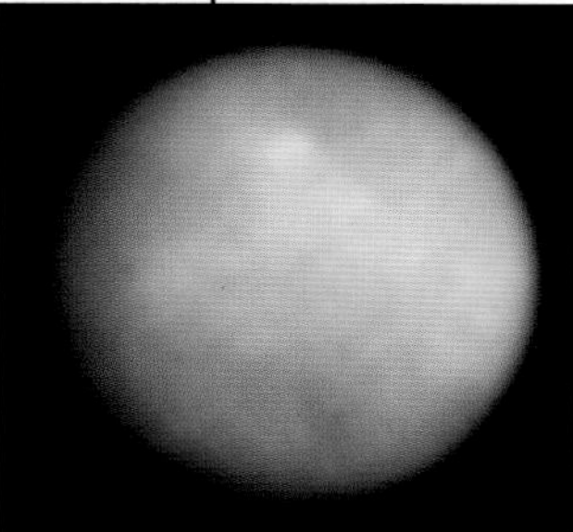

Ceres
The largest asteroid, Ceres, is classed as a dwarf planet. Its orbit takes 4.6 years to complete and is inclined by 10.6°.

These Trojans move 60° behind Jupiter.

Origins and collisions

Astronomers think that the Belt asteroids are the remains of a planet that began to form between Mars and Jupiter when the Solar System was young. At that time, the gap between Mars and Jupiter contained about 1,000 times more material than it does now, or four times as much matter as makes up Earth. This rocky and metallic debris began to accrete to form larger masses, but the gravity of the young Jupiter disrupted the process by changing the orbital paths of the growing bodies, causing them to collide and break up. Asteroids were thrown out of the Belt and destroyed when they struck planets and moons. Collisions still occur in the Belt today. They result in impact craters and, less frequently, the internal fracturing of asteroids; rarely, an asteroid may shatter and disperse. Most collisions occur at thousands of kilometres an hour. A collision's outcome depends mainly on the sizes of the bodies involved.

Both sets of Trojans orbit in roughly the same time as Jupiter – 11.8 years. This group travels 60° in front of Jupiter.

Ida, which is 60km (37 miles) long, orbits the Sun in 4.84 years.

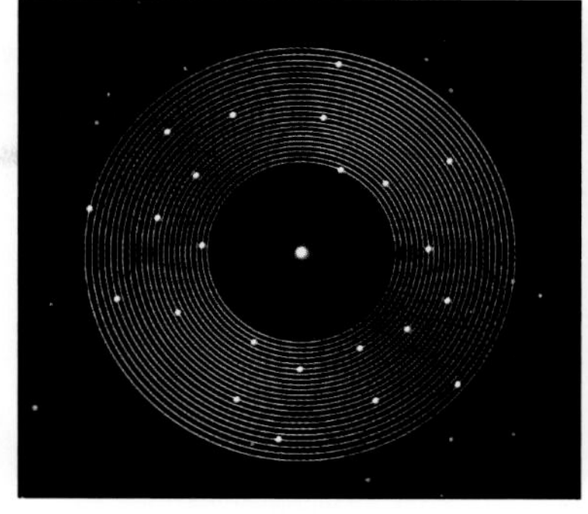

△ **Orbits before Jupiter formed**
The chunks of material between Mars and Jupiter initially followed near-circular orbits. Collisions between them were at relatively low speeds, so material stuck together until some bodies grew as big as Mars.

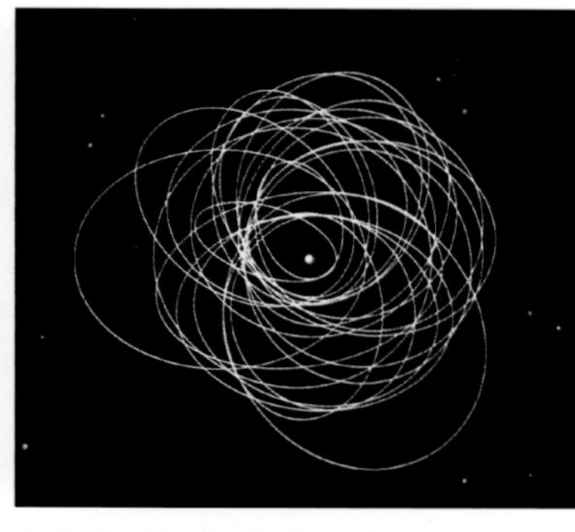

△ **Orbits after Jupiter formed**
Jupiter's gravity pulled at the bodies and changed their orbits into ellipses. This caused collisions to occur at much higher velocities. As a result, the impacting bodies smashed into pieces, producing a belt of asteroids.

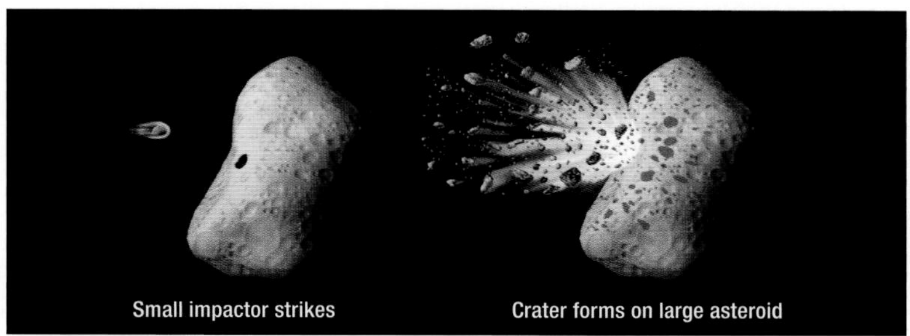
Small impactor strikes
Crater forms on large asteroid

△ **Cratering**
Most collisions involve a small asteroid striking a larger one. The small asteroid is destroyed, leaving a crater in the large asteroid's surface that measures about ten times the size of the impactor. Most of the material blasted from the crater moves into its own orbit around the Sun.

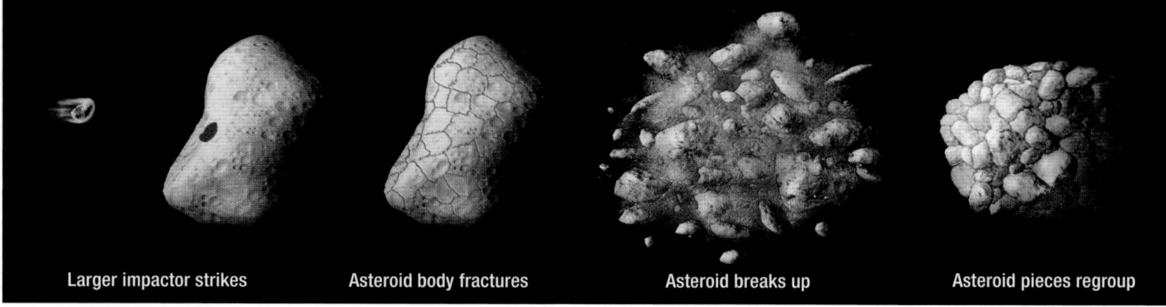
Larger impactor strikes
Asteroid body fractures
Asteroid breaks up
Asteroid pieces regroup

△ **Rubble pile**
When the impacting asteroid is bigger – about one fifty-thousandth the size of the large asteroid – it strikes with greater force, and the body of the large asteroid breaks up. The combined gravitational pull of the pieces soon pulls them back together. The result is an asteroid that is not one solid body but a ball of rubble.

▽ **Asteroid family**
An even bigger impactor – over one fifty-thousandth the size of the large asteroid – is more devastating. The large asteroid shatters, but the combined gravitational pull of the fragments cannot pull them back together. Instead, they form a family of asteroids that spreads around the orbit of the original large asteroid.

Very large impactor strikes
Large asteroid shatters
Family of asteroids forms

NEAR-EARTH **ASTEROIDS**

THOUSANDS OF ASTEROIDS PASS CLOSE TO EARTH ON THEIR JOURNEYS AROUND THE SOLAR SYSTEM, AND SOME POSE A GENUINE DANGER TO OUR PLANET. HUGE CRATERS ON EARTH'S SURFACE ARE THE SCARS OF PAST ENCOUNTERS.

Near-Earth asteroids (NEAs) started life in the Asteroid Belt. At some point, Jupiter's gravitational pull or collisions with other asteroids set them in new orbits that now bring them within 194.5 million km (121 million miles) of the Sun, which is classed as being "near" to Earth. Asteroids closer to Earth than 7.5 million km (4.7 million miles) – less than 20 times the average Moon-Earth distance – and at least 150m (500ft) across are called potentially hazardous asteroids (PHAs). Anything this size or larger would have a devastating impact on Earth, producing a huge tsunami if it landed in the ocean or vaporizing an area the size of Manhattan, USA, if it struck land.

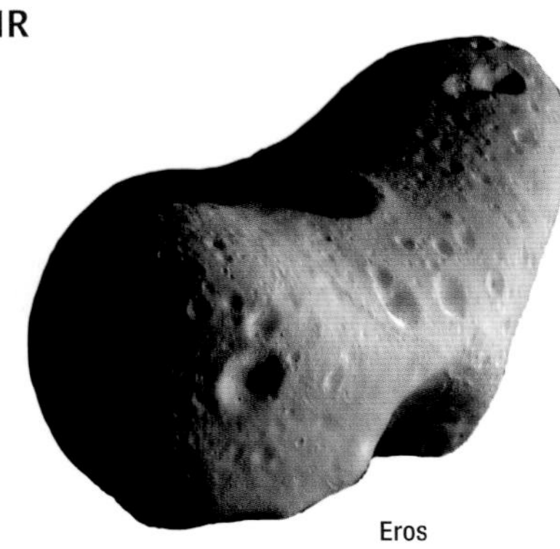
Eros

△ **Close enough**
Eros is a NEA and a member of the Amor group (see right). In January 2012, it passed within 26.7 million km (16.6 million miles) of Earth. In the same month, an 8m (26ft) wide Aten asteroid, 2012 BX34, made one of the closest recorded flybys, at a distance of 65,000km (40,400 miles) – one-sixth of the Earth-Moon distance.

▽ **Orbit types**
Near-Earth asteroids are classified by their orbital paths. The estimated 5,200 Apollo asteroids follow paths that cross Earth's orbit. The 750 or so members of the Aten group have orbits that stay mainly inside Earth's orbit. The Atiras, a small subgroup of the Atens, travel entirely within Earth's orbit. The orbits of the Amor group lie mostly between Earth and Mars.

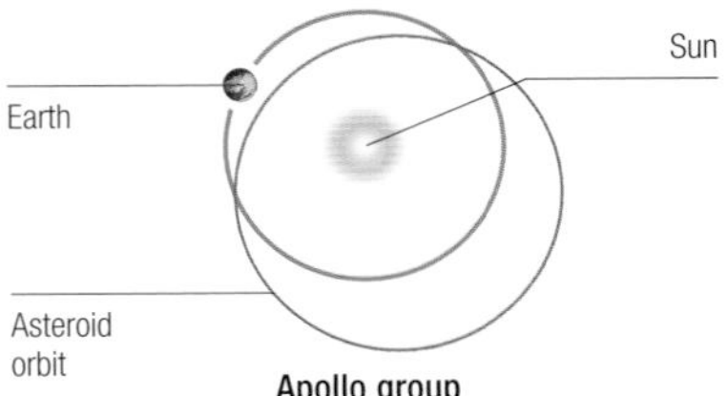
Sun
Earth
Asteroid orbit
Apollo group

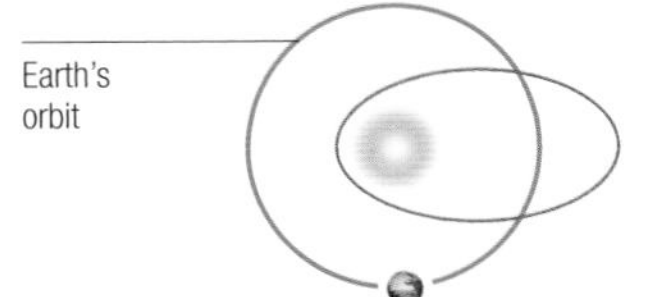
Earth's orbit
Aten group

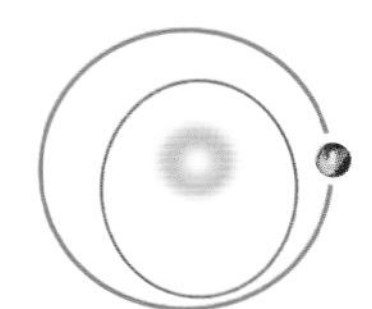
Atira subgroup

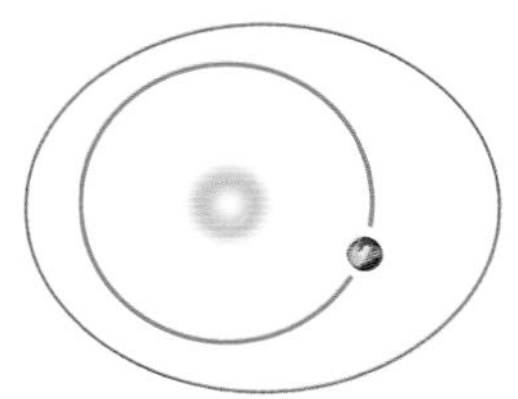
Amor group

▷ **Mapping asteroids**
In this edge-on view of the Solar System, tiny dots are NEAs that scientists believe exist. The data is from the NEOWISE survey, which was carried out by the Wide-field Infrared Survey Explorer telescope between 2010 and 2011. Astronomers have discovered 10,000 NEAs at least 1km (0.6 miles) across – perhaps 90 per cent of the total number. There are thought to be about 5,000 PHAs. In early 2014, around 1,500 PHAs were being monitored.

KEY
- Earth's orbit
- Potentially hazardous asteroids
- Near-Earth asteroids

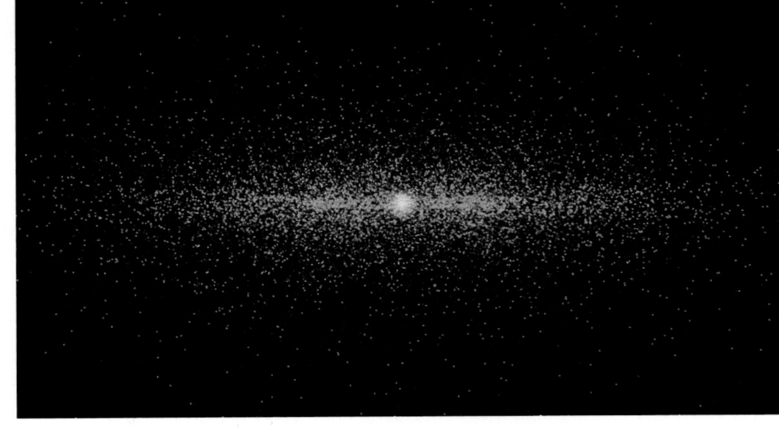

◁ **Chelyabinsk meteorite**
In February 2013, a brilliant fireball blazed across the morning sky over the city of Chelyabinsk, Russia. It was a previously undetected asteroid, 18m (60ft) across and with a mass of 11,000 tonnes, speeding through Earth's atmosphere. The asteroid exploded at an altitude of 23km (14 miles), producing a shower of pieces that fell to the ground as meteorites. It was the largest object to enter Earth's atmosphere since a similar event occurred over Tunguska, SIberia, in 1908.

▽ **Detection and monitoring**
Astronomers use optical telescopes to detect and track NEAs and PHAs, and radio telescopes to image any PHAs that get close enough. Once detected, an object is verified and catalogued by the Minor Planet Center, Massachusetts, USA. Its orbital path is updated, and improved predictions are made about the asteroid's future close approaches to Earth.

Impact on Earth

Thousands of tonnes of asteroid material enter Earth's atmosphere each year. Most are small pieces that burn up before reaching the ground. Pieces big enough to survive the journey are known as meteorites. Earth was heavily bombarded by asteroids when it was young. The rate of impact has decreased, but it hasn't stopped: an asteroid at least 150m (450ft) wide strikes roughly every 10,000 years, and one more than 1km (0.6 miles) wide hits Earth every 750,000 years.

Earth is **twice as likely** to be hit by something we **don't know** as by something we do.

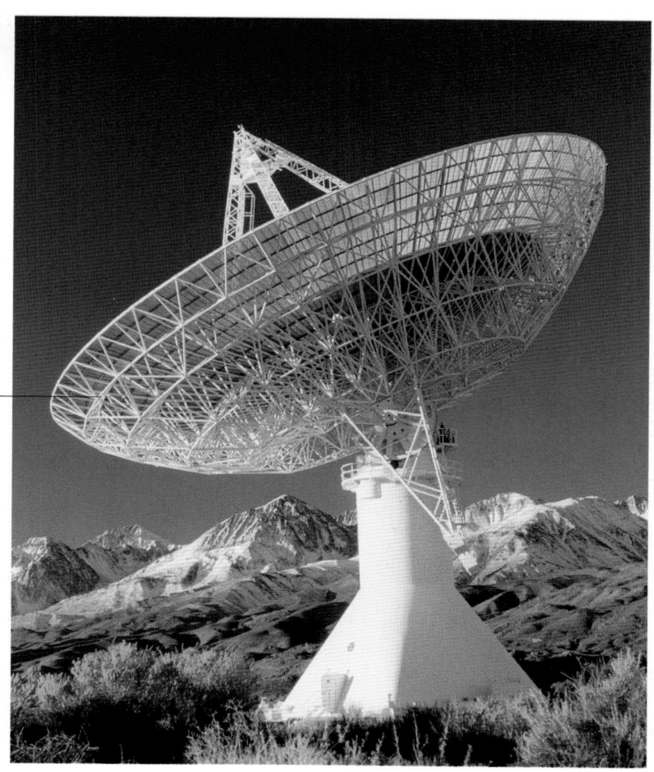

The telescope sends out radio waves, and the dish collects the "echoes" that bounce back off objects, such as asteroids, in space.

▽ **Earth's impact craters**
Measuring 1.2km (0.7 miles) across, the Barringer Crater in Arizona, USA (shown below), was created by a 50m (165ft) wide meteorite. The largest of Earth's 180 known impact craters is Vredefort in South Africa, which was 300km (185 miles) wide when it formed over 2 billion years ago. Many other craters have been wiped out by volcanic or tectonic resurfacing, and by erosion.

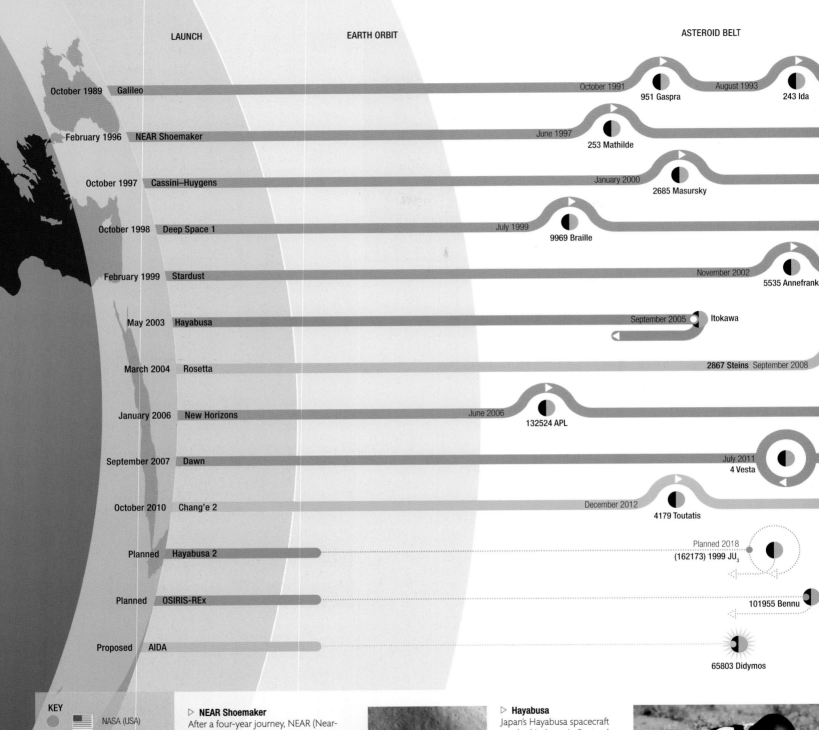

LAUNCH	Mission	EARTH ORBIT	ASTEROID BELT
October 1989	Galileo		October 1991 951 Gaspra; August 1993 243 Ida
February 1996	NEAR Shoemaker		June 1997 253 Mathilde
October 1997	Cassini–Huygens		January 2000 2685 Masursky
October 1998	Deep Space 1		July 1999 9969 Braille
February 1999	Stardust		November 2002 5535 Annefrank
May 2003	Hayabusa		September 2005 Itokawa
March 2004	Rosetta		2867 Steins September 2008
January 2006	New Horizons		June 2006 132524 APL
September 2007	Dawn		July 2011 4 Vesta
October 2010	Chang'e 2		December 2012 4179 Toutatis
Planned	Hayabusa 2		Planned 2018 (162173) 1999 JU_3
Planned	OSIRIS-REx		101955 Bennu
Proposed	AIDA		65803 Didymos

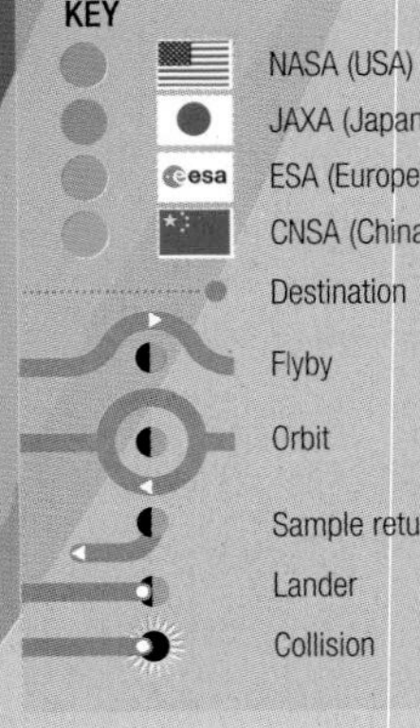
KEY
NASA (USA)
JAXA (Japan)
esa
ESA (Europe)
CNSA (China)
Destination
Flyby
Orbit
Sample return
Lander
Collision

▷ NEAR Shoemaker
After a four-year journey, NEAR (Near-Earth Asteroid Rendezvous) Shoemaker arrived at Eros in February 2001 and moved into orbit around the asteroid. Over the next 12 months, its orbit took it ever closer to the surface of Eros, enabling the craft to capture increasingly detailed images. Planned and built as an orbiter, NEAR Shoemaker's mission was later changed and it made a soft landing on Eros – the first landing on an asteroid.

Eros surface from NEAR Shoemaker

▷ Hayabusa
Japan's Hayabusa spacecraft reached Itokawa in September 2005. It surveyed the asteroid from several kilometres away and then touched down to collect a surface specimen. The craft broke up on re-entry into Earth's atmosphere, but the previously ejected sample capsule made a parachute landing in the South Australian outback on 13 June 2010.

Retrieving the sample capsule

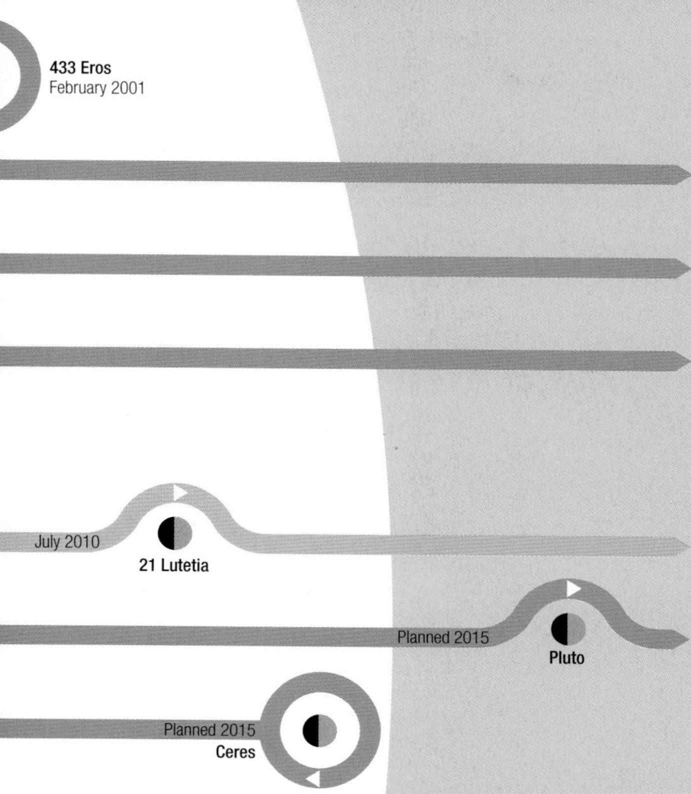
433 Eros
February 2001
July 2010
21 Lutetia
Planned 2015
Pluto
Planned 2015
Ceres

MISSIONS TO **ASTEROIDS**

MORE THAN A DOZEN ASTEROIDS HAVE BEEN VISITED BY SPACECRAFT, BUT ONLY FOUR MISSIONS HAVE BEEN DEDICATED TO STUDYING THESE ROCKY BODIES. THE MOST RECENT SUCCEEDED IN RETURNING A SAMPLE TO EARTH.

The first close-up image of an asteroid came in 1991 when the Galileo spacecraft sent back remarkable images of Gaspra – an 18km (11.2 mile) long, crater-covered boulder – during the spacecraft's journey to Jupiter. The first dedicated asteroid mission was NEAR Shoemaker, which landed on Eros in 2001. Nearly five years later, the Japanese spacecraft Hayabusa touched down on the 1km (0.6 mile) wide asteroid Itokawa, collected a sample, and brought it back. After orbiting Vesta, Dawn is on target for a 2015 encounter with the largest and first discovered asteroid, Ceres. Even more ambitious projects are under discussion, including a NASA mission to capture an asteroid and tow it into lunar orbit, where astronauts can visit it.

Hayabusa brought back around **1,500 particles of asteroid** dust.

The small, transparent container held dust grains less than a tenth of a millimetre wide.

△ **Itokawa dust sample**
Analysis of the asteroid dust returned by Hayabusa's sample capsule showed that it had lain on Itokawa's surface for about 8 million years. It also revealed that Itokawa probably formed from the fragments of a larger asteroid that broke up in a collision.

▽ **Dawn**
Dawn's mission is to orbit the two most massive asteroids, Vesta and Ceres. The craft entered orbit around Vesta in July 2011 after a voyage that took it past Mars. It returned thousands of images that have enabled scientists to study the geology of Vesta's surface in detail. Dawn left for Ceres in September 2012 and will image the dwarf planet's entire surface.

With solar arrays extended, Dawn is 20m (65ft) wide.

◁ **Asteroid capture**
NASA is considering a mission to capture a near-Earth asteroid about 500 tonnes in weight and 8m (25ft) wide. The asteroid would be towed into a lunar orbit, where a manned Orion capsule could dock with the capture craft, allowing astronauts to study the rock. Lunar orbit would be safer than Earth orbit as the risk of accidental collision with Earth would be lower.

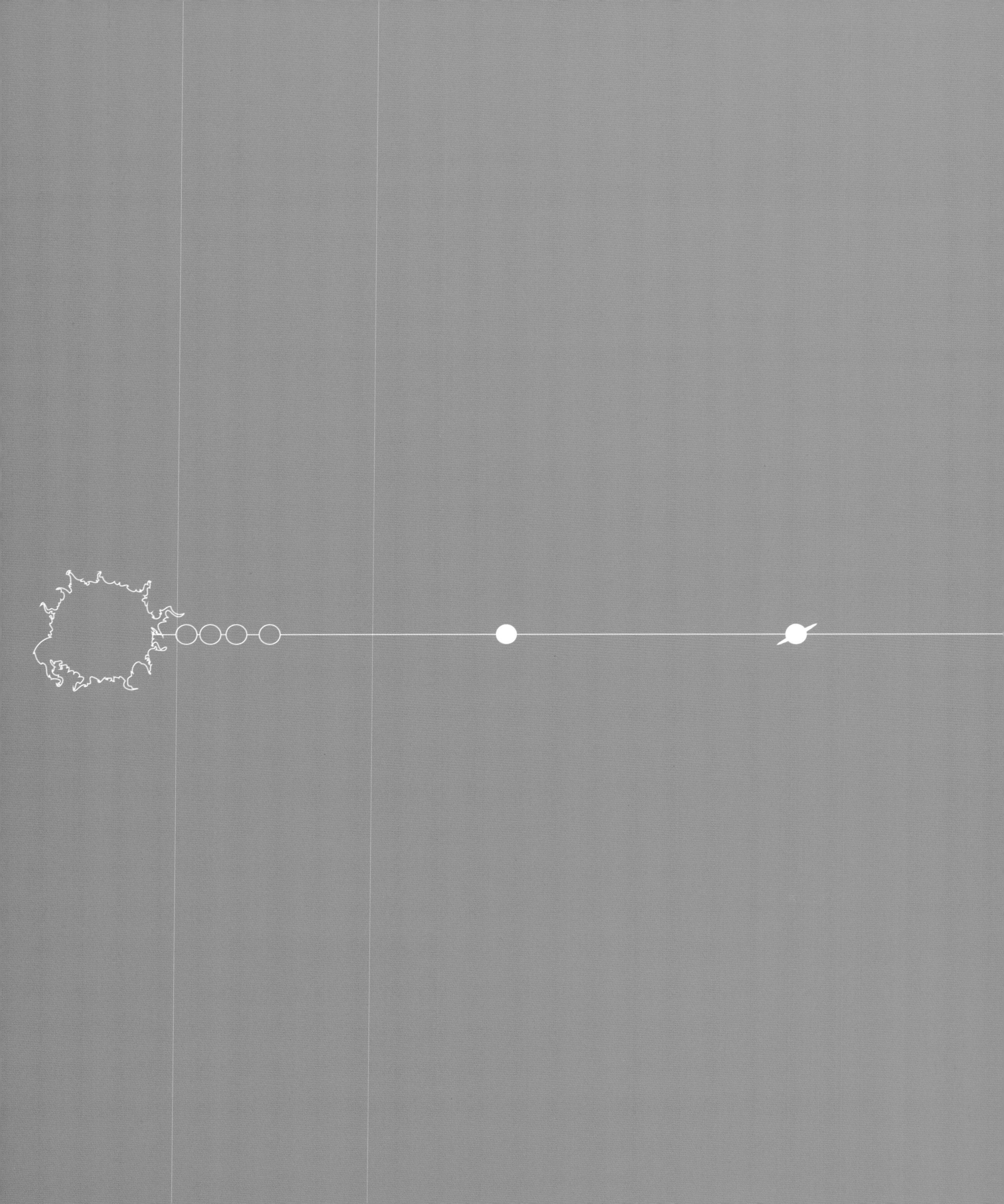

GAS **GIANTS**

The planets of the cold outer reaches of the Solar System are not worlds on which a spacecraft could ever land. Jupiter, Saturn, Uranus, and Neptune, known collectively as the gas giants, are colossal globes of hydrogen and helium that are solid only at their cores. They formed towards the far edge of the spinning nebula of dust from which our Sun was born. At first mere clumps of rock and ice, they

REALM OF **GIANTS**

grew big enough to exert gravitational pull, ballooning into huge planets as they attracted layer after layer of gases. While the Sun contains 98 per cent of all matter in the Solar System, vast Jupiter, biggest of the four giants, comprises nearly all the rest. The outer planets take their time to circle our star: Jupiter's year is nearly 12 Earth years, Neptune's almost 165. These are incredibly active worlds whose hot interiors generate phenomenal cosmic weather. Jupiter's much-photographed Great Red Spot is a gigantic storm system three times the size of Earth. On Neptune, the fastest recorded winds in the Solar System rage at over 2,000kph (1,200mph). All of the gas giants are surrounded by rings of debris, the most famous being the rings of Saturn. These form a gleaming disc visible through binoculars; if placed around Earth they would stretch nearly all the way to the Moon. And each of the outer planets is attended by an orbiting retinue of moons of diverse shapes and sizes.

◁ **Far-away worlds**
In the outer Solar System there are small worlds as well as large ones. In this dramatic photograph taken by NASA's Cassini spacecraft, Io, the innermost of Jupiter's major moons, appears as an insignificant dot against the swirling cloud bands of its giant parent.

JUPITER

THE LARGEST OBJECT IN THE SOLAR SYSTEM AFTER THE SUN, JUPITER IS A BLOATED BALL OF GAS STREAKED WITH MULTICOLOURED CLOUDS. THIS RAPIDLY SPINNING PLANET IS CIRCLED CEASELESSLY BY WINDS AND STORMS.

The first of the giant planets beyond the Asteroid Belt, Jupiter is nearly five times further away from the Sun than Earth. Composed of gas at increasingly high pressure towards the core, almost like a miniature star, it has a gravitational pull strong enough to have captured a large family of moons. Even with the naked eye, Jupiter is easily identifiable as one of the brightest objects in the night sky.

Rotating on its axis in just under ten hours, Jupiter has the shortest day of all the planets in the Solar System. The planet spins so fast that its equator is forced outwards in a noticeable bulge. The zones of high and low atmospheric pressure wrapped around the planet, identifiable by the different colours of cloud found within them, are stretched out by the rapid rotation. Nonstop winds race in both directions, stirring up giant storms large enough to obliterate Earth. The Great Red Spot, Jupiter's most prominent feature, is a storm that has been raging for more than 300 years.

Winds in Jupiter's equatorial region can reach speeds in excess of **400kph (250mph).**

JUPITER DATA

Equatorial diameter	142,984km (88,846 miles)
Mass (Earth = 1)	318
Gravity at equator (Earth = 1)	2.36
Mean distance from Sun (Earth = 1)	5.20
Axial tilt	3.1°
Rotation period (day)	9.93 hours
Orbital period (year)	11.86 Earth years
Cloud-top temperature	–108°C (–162°F)
Moons	67+

▷ **Northern hemisphere**
Until 2003, Jupiter's north polar regions hid a secret – a dark spot twice the size of the planet's best-known feature, the Great Red Spot. The dark spot, which is visible only intermittently, appears to be in the highest layers of Jupiter's atmosphere.

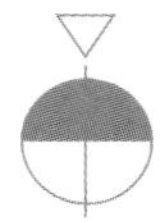

▷ **Tilt**
Jupiter orbits with almost no tilt in its axis, so it has no seasons, and the equator always receives much more heat from solar radiation than the poles. This may contribute to the planet's remarkably stable large-scale weather systems.

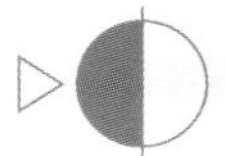

Jupiter has a thin, barely discernible ring system with four distinct regions.

▷ **Southern hemisphere**
Both of Jupiter's poles are partly obscured by a haze, caused by radiation making chemical changes in atmospheric gases. Enormous electrical energy at the poles creates aurorae thousands of times more extensive than those seen in polar latitudes on Earth.

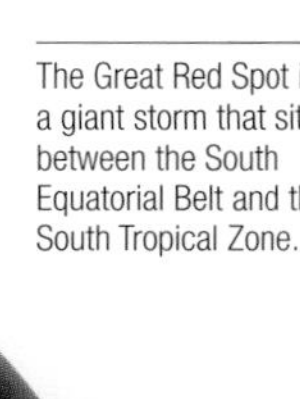

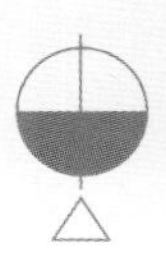

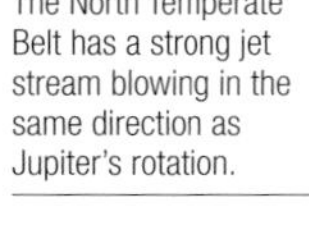

The North Temperate Belt has a strong jet stream blowing in the same direction as Jupiter's rotation.

The Great Red Spot is a giant storm that sits between the South Equatorial Belt and the South Tropical Zone.

The South Tropical Zone is Jupiter's most active weather region, with a strong jet stream moving in the opposite direction to the planet's rotation.

Complex, ribbon-like features called festoons form in the turbulent boundaries between belts and zones.
The North Equatorial Belt marks a clearing of the atmosphere, where darker clouds are seen deeper down.
The Equatorial Zone is a belt of bright, high-altitude clouds.
The South Equatorial Belt is usually the broadest and darkest cloud band on the planet.

◁ **Stormy face**
Jupiter's turbulent cloud belts and zones are very long-lived features, but their intensity varies according to weather conditions and the changing combinations of chemicals dredged up from the interior.

Atmosphere
Jupiter's atmosphere, mostly hydrogen gas with some helium, extends upwards for more than 5,000km (3,100 miles) to merge with interplanetary space.

JUPITER STRUCTURE

GIGANTIC THOUGH JUPITER IS, THE MATERIALS THAT FORM THE PLANET ARE COMPARATIVELY LIGHT. DESPITE THIS, FORCES OF GRAVITATIONAL CONTRACTION DEEP INSIDE JUPITER TURN THE PLANET'S INTERIOR INTO A POWERHOUSE OF ENERGY.

While Jupiter's interior is almost entirely pure hydrogen, the planet's upper layers are enriched with more complex gases that form the well-defined striped atmosphere. Around 1,000km (620 miles) below this apparent "surface", pressures are high enough to transform hydrogen gas into liquid. Some 20,000km (12,500 miles) further inwards, pressure is so intense – many millions of times the atmospheric pressure on Earth – that it tears the hydrogen atoms apart, freeing their hold over electrons and causing the hydrogen to behave like liquid metal.

Within the planet, denser materials sink downwards, while the lighter materials rise up. The power this generates allows Jupiter to pump out more energy than it receives from the Sun, mostly in the form of heat and radio waves. Huge electrical currents in the metallic hydrogen layer create the most powerful magnetic field of any planet in the Solar System.

Jupiter has **2.5 times the mass** of all the other planets **put together.**

Core
The existence of a solid core at Jupiter's heart is unproven but likely. It could be the original seed around which the planet coalesced, or possibly a growing nucleus formed by Jupiter's ongoing contraction.

Liquid metallic hydrogen layer
Liquid hydrogen atoms break down under heat and pressure to create a layer of liquid metallic hydrogen. This fluid, produced under extreme conditions, never occurs naturally on Earth.

Liquid layer
Below Jupiter's cloud layer, increasing pressure gradually causes the planet's hydrogen to act like a liquid rather than a gas.

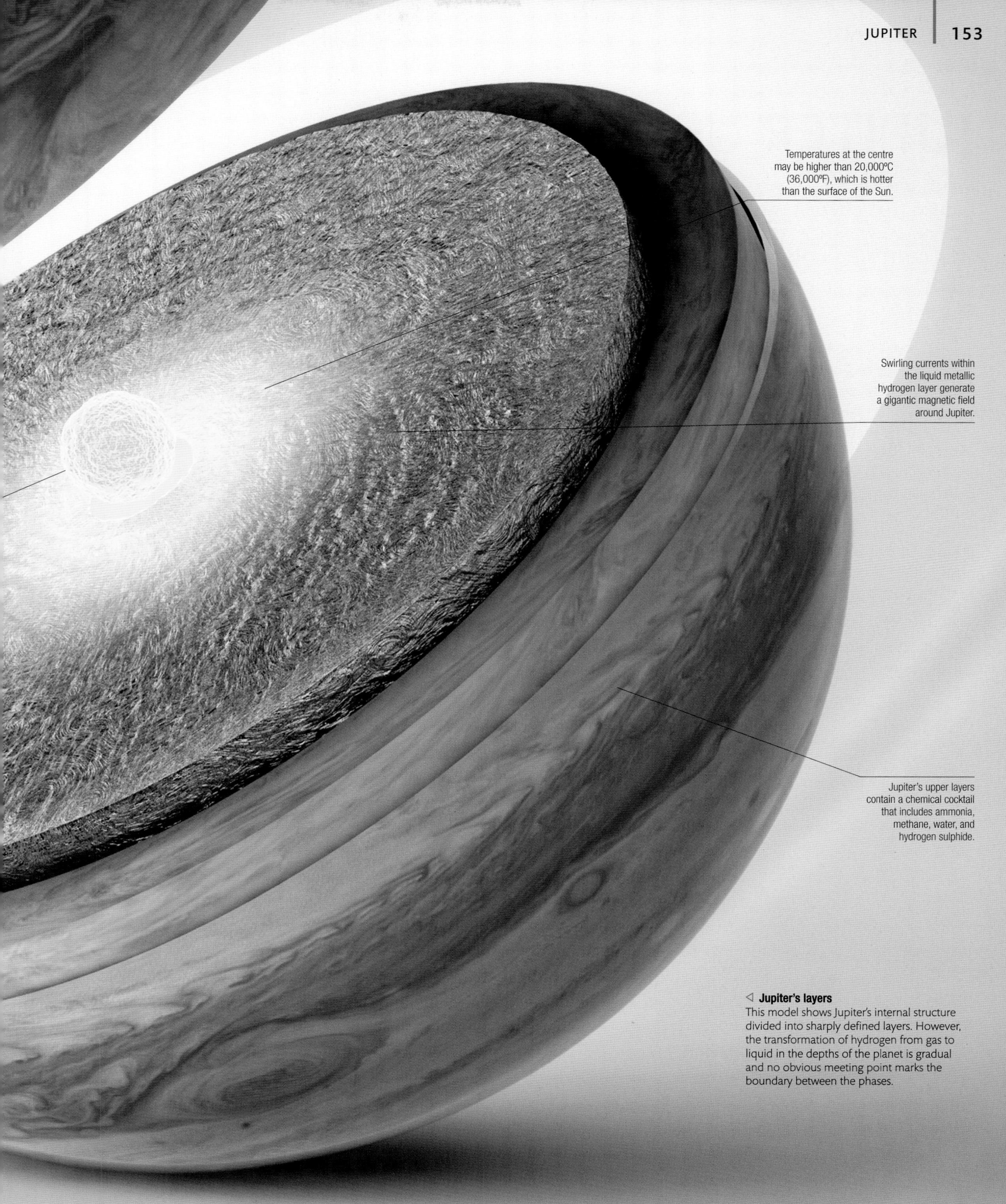
Temperatures at the centre may be higher than 20,000ºC (36,000ºF), which is hotter than the surface of the Sun.
Swirling currents within the liquid metallic hydrogen layer generate a gigantic magnetic field around Jupiter.
Jupiter's upper layers contain a chemical cocktail that includes ammonia, methane, water, and hydrogen sulphide.

◁ **Jupiter's layers**
This model shows Jupiter's internal structure divided into sharply defined layers. However, the transformation of hydrogen from gas to liquid in the depths of the planet is gradual and no obvious meeting point marks the boundary between the phases.

JUPITER UP CLOSE

ALTHOUGH JUPITER HAS NO SOLID SURFACE, THE TURBULENT CLOUDS THAT COVER ITS FACE ARE PACKED WITH DETAIL, AND INDIVIDUAL WEATHER SYSTEMS CAN PERSIST FOR YEARS OR EVEN CENTURIES IN THE SWIRLING ATMOSPHERE.

Jupiter's most conspicuous features are the bands of cloud that encircle the planet parallel to its equator. Astronomers classify them as either light-coloured zones or dark-coloured belts. Zones are high-pressure areas where clouds pile up at high altitude, while belts are low-pressure clearings in which sinking, cloud-free air provides a window through to darker clouds below. Storms, such as the Great Red Spot, are areas of high pressure where the clouds tower high above everything else.

The giant planet's weather is created by the interaction of a number of different factors, including heat rising from Jupiter's deep interior, the differential rotation that causes equatorial regions to move faster than polar latitudes, and convection in the upper atmosphere, which redistributes heat between Jupiter's warm equator and its colder poles.

The complex boundaries between belts and zones are shaped by powerful jet-stream winds that blow in opposite directions around the planet. These winds cause the zones to flow in an eastward direction (with the planet's rotation) and the belts, in contrast, to flow in a westward (or retrograde) direction. The general system of belts and zones appears to be stable over long periods of time, although the width of specific bands can vary significantly, as can the hue and intensity of the clouds in the belts.

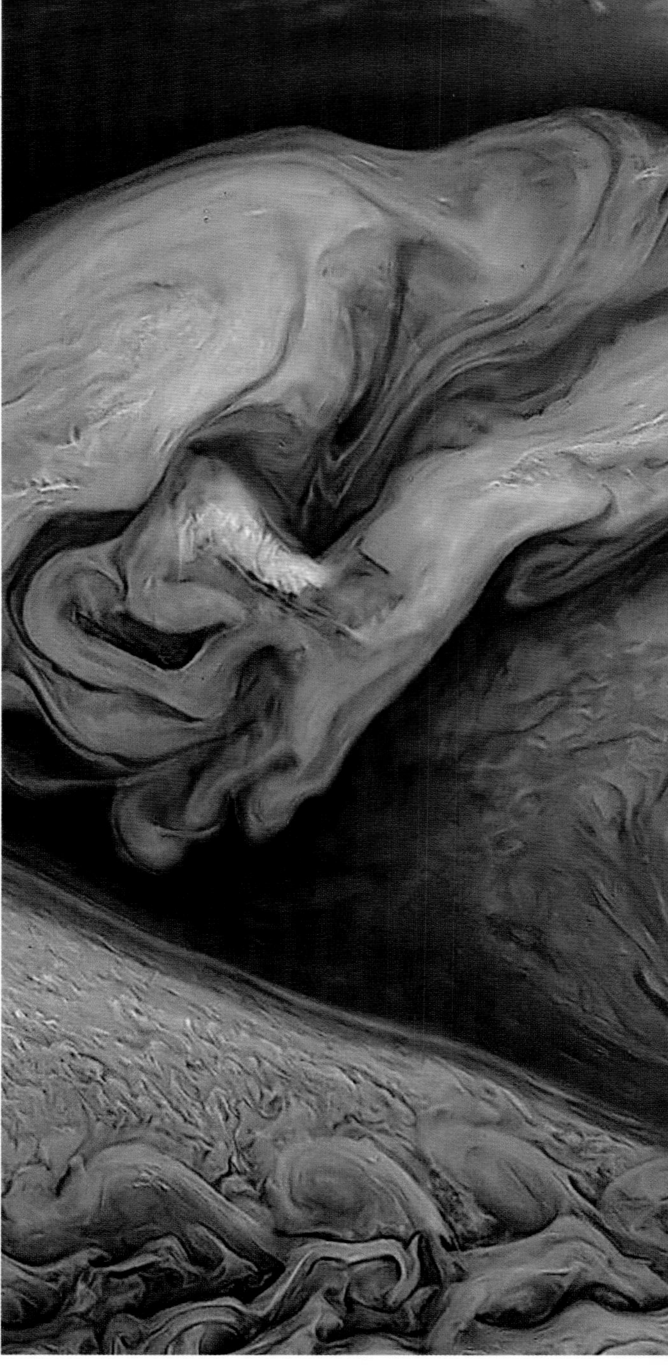

▷ **Great Red Spot**
Jupiter's most spectacular feature is the Great Red Spot, observed since at least 1830 and possibly since the 17th century. It is an anticyclonic (anticlockwise-rotating), hurricane-like weather system, twice the size of Earth and with a high-pressure centre. The origins of its colour are uncertain, but its intensity can vary substantially and seems to be linked to the appearance of the neighbouring South Equatorial Belt.

▽ **Banded planet**
Individual belts and zones are named according to their geographical location, such as the North Temperate Belt and the Equatorial Zone. Jupiter's rotation can be measured approximately by monitoring the movement of the dark cloud belts, but scientists can obtain more accurate results by measuring the rotation of the planet's magnetosphere.

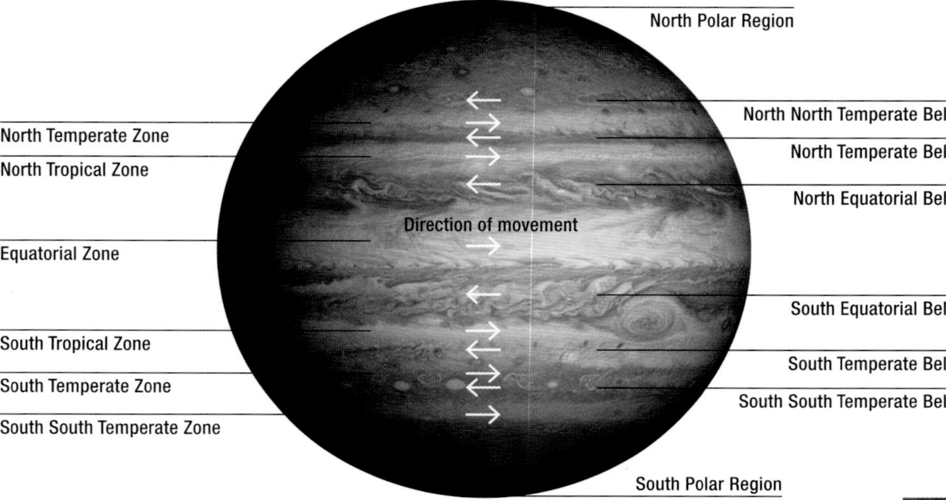
North Polar Region
North North Temperate Belt
North Temperate Zone
North Temperate Belt
North Tropical Zone
North Equatorial Belt
Direction of movement
Equatorial Zone
South Equatorial Belt
South Tropical Zone
South Temperate Belt
South Temperate Zone
South South Temperate Belt
South South Temperate Zone
South Polar Region

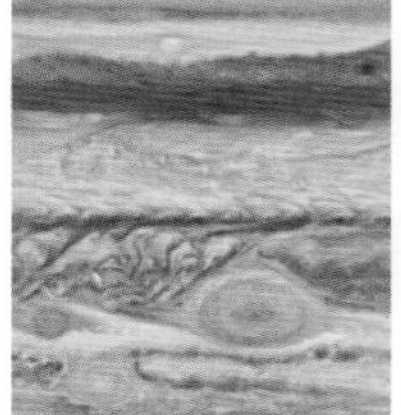
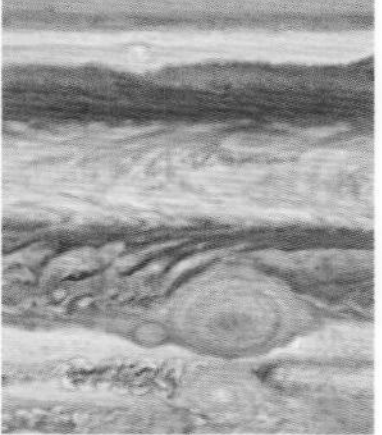
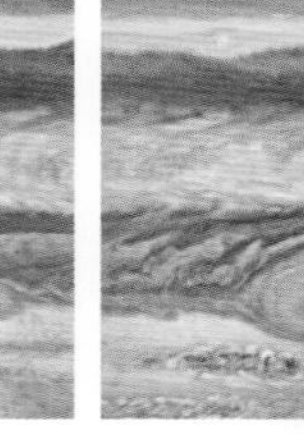

△ **Baby spots**
This sequence of images from the Hubble Space Telescope shows a succession of close encounters between Jupiter's Great Red Spot and two smaller storms in summer 2008. Red Spot Junior (bottom) survived unscathed after passing the Great Red Spot several times, but the Baby Red Spot (smallest spot) was captured and destroyed by the giant storm.

◁ Cloud temperature and height
This infrared image from the Gemini Observatory shows temperature differences in colour. Zones appear blue because they are higher and colder than the belts, which are reddish. The cloud tops in the Great Red Spot and other high-altitude storms appear white because they are even higher and colder than the zones.

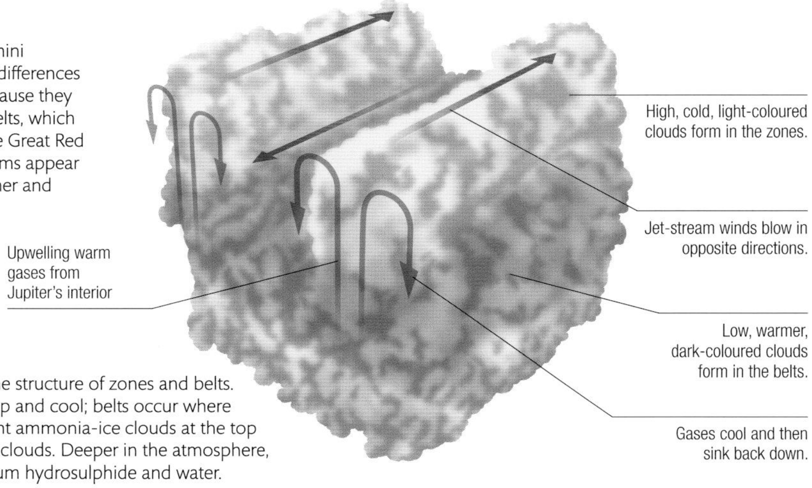

Upwelling warm gases from Jupiter's interior

High, cold, light-coloured clouds form in the zones.

Jet-stream winds blow in opposite directions.

Low, warmer, dark-coloured clouds form in the belts.

Gases cool and then sink back down.

▷ Convection cycle
Convection of gases maintains the structure of zones and belts. Zones occur where clouds well up and cool; belts occur where they descend and warm up. Bright ammonia-ice clouds at the top of the zones hide the underlying clouds. Deeper in the atmosphere, the clouds are made of ammonium hydrosulphide and water.

THE **JUPITER** SYSTEM

FITTINGLY FOR THE LARGEST PLANET IN THE SOLAR SYSTEM, JUPITER ALSO HAS THE BIGGEST FAMILY OF SATELLITES – AT LEAST 67 ARE KNOWN AT PRESENT. HOWEVER, JUST FOUR OF THESE ARE PLANET-SIZED AND DOMINATE THE JUPITER SYSTEM.

Jupiter's satellites are divided into three major groups: four small inner satellites, sometimes called the Amalthea group; the four huge Galilean moons (discovered in 1610 by Italian astronomer Galileo Galilei); and 59 or more small outer moons, most of which are just a few kilometres across, though some are much larger. The Amalthea group and the Galilean moons are together referred to as regular satellites, which means they orbit in the same direction as Jupiter's rotation and are all on roughly the same plane. The outer, irregular satellites are small bodies captured by Jupiter's gravity throughout its life.

Moons to scale
The four Galilean moons account for most of the material in Jupiter's satellite system. The other, irregular satellites include captured asteroids, centaurs, and comets. Most are lumps of ice or rock, but a few are tens of kilometres across or even bigger.

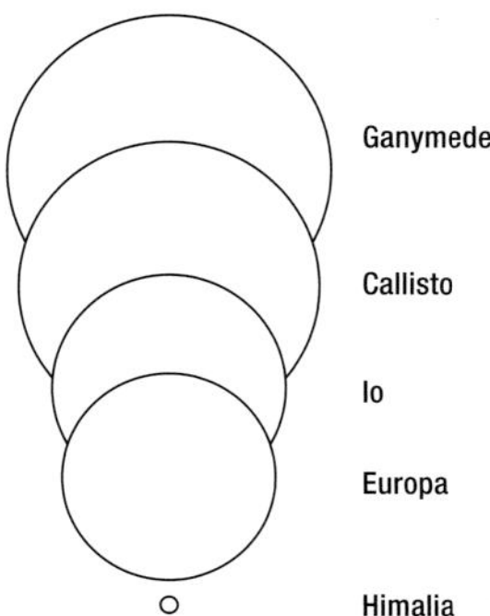
Ganymede
Callisto
Io
Europa

Himalia
Amalthea
Thebe
Elara
Pasiphaë
Carme
Metis
Sinope
Lysithea
Ananke
Adrastea
Leda
Callirrhoe
Themisto
Praxidike
Iocaste
Taygete
Kalyke
Megaclite
S/2000 J11
Helike
Harpalyke
Hermippe
Thyone
Chaldene
Aoede
Eukelade
Isonoe
S/2003 J5
Autonoe
Carpo
Euanthe
Aitne
Erinome
Eurydome
Hegemone
Arche
Euporie
S/2003 J3
S/2003 J18
Thelxinoe
Orthosie
S/2003 J16
Mneme
Herse
Kale
S/2003 J19
S/2003 J15
S/2003 J10
S/2003 J23
Kallichore
Pasithee
S/2010 J1
Kore
Cyllene
S/2003 J4
Sponde
S/2003 J2
S/2003 J12
S/2001 J1
S/2010 J2
S/2011 J2
S/2003 J9

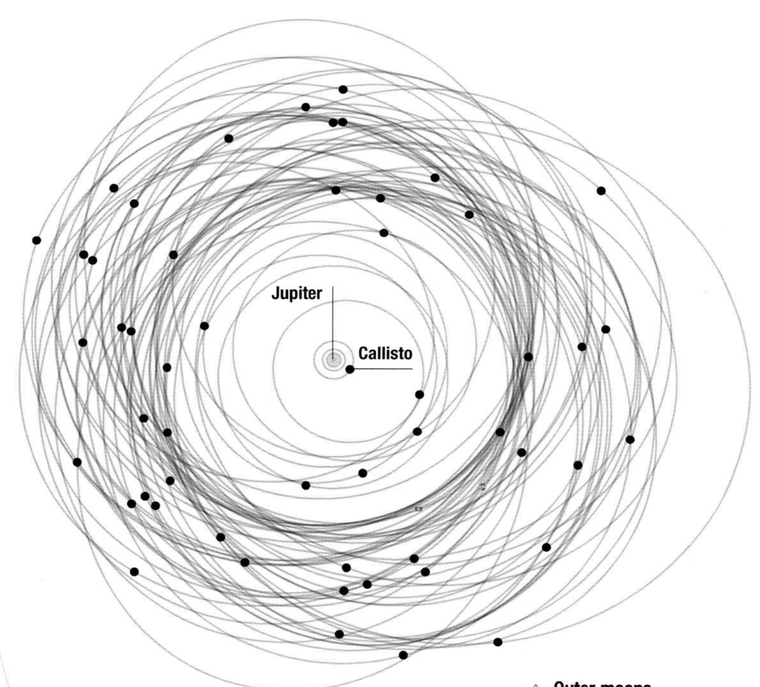
Jupiter
Callisto

Ganymede
Ganymede, the Solar System's largest moon, is locked in orbital resonance with other moons, orbiting Jupiter in 7 days 3.7 hours – twice the period of Europa and four times that of Io. Ganymede doesn't experience significant tidal heating but its surface shows signs that it did so in the past.

Callisto
The outermost Galilean moon orbits Jupiter in 16 days 16.5 hours, at a distance of almost 1.9 million km (1.2 million miles). Its heavily cratered surface shows it never suffered the extreme tidal heating that probably caused the widespread resurfacing evident on the other Galileans.

△ **Outer moons**
The orbits of the irregular satellites trace a chaotic cloud around Jupiter, some following Jupiter's rotation and others orbiting the opposite way. There are distinct groups among the outer moons. The Himalia, Carme, Ananke, and Pasiphaë groups all consist of a single large moon and a number of smaller ones in related orbits. Each group probably formed from the break-up of a larger object.

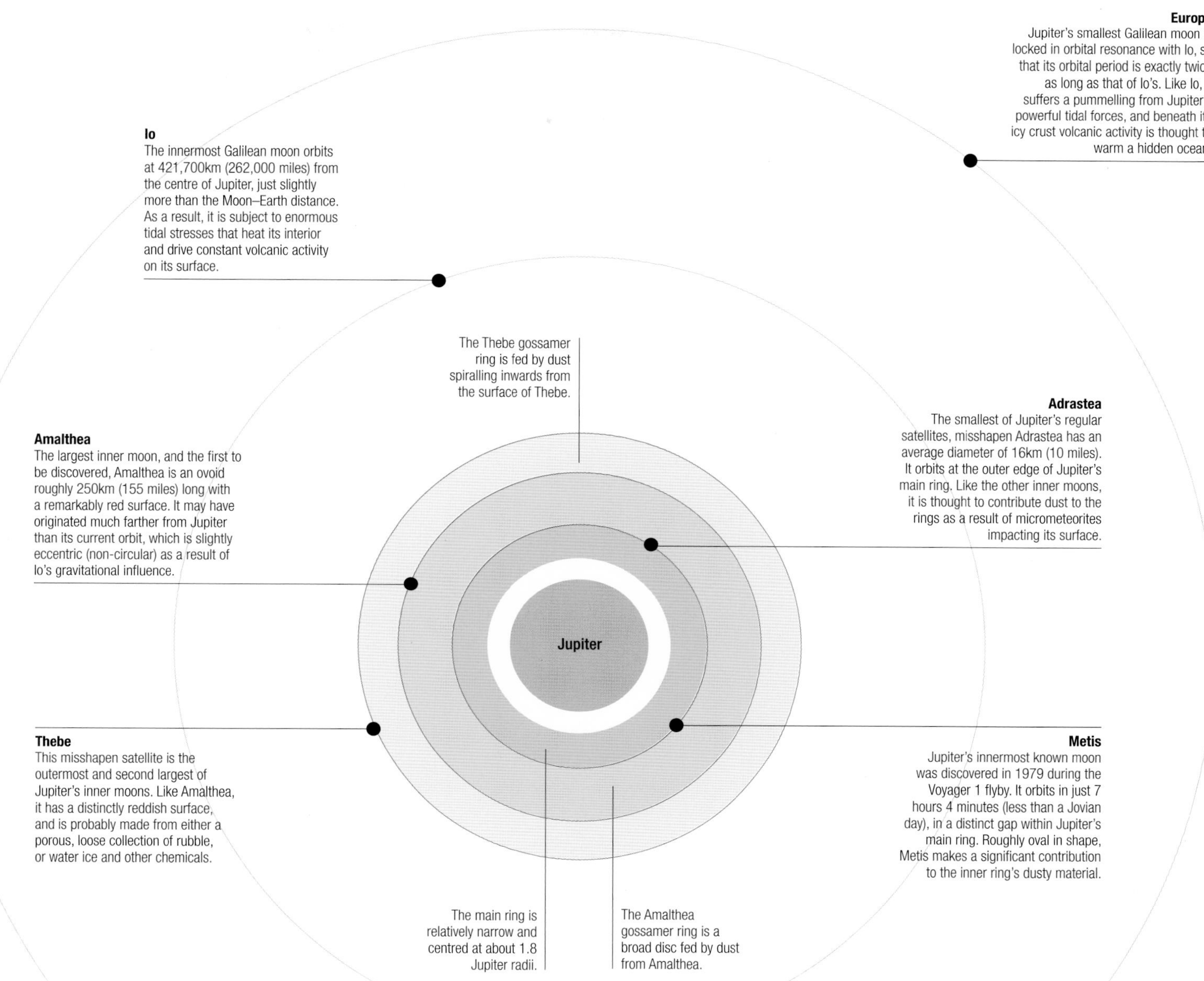
Europa
Jupiter's smallest Galilean moon is locked in orbital resonance with Io, so that its orbital period is exactly twice as long as that of Io's. Like Io, it suffers a pummelling from Jupiter's powerful tidal forces, and beneath its icy crust volcanic activity is thought to warm a hidden ocean.
Io
The innermost Galilean moon orbits at 421,700km (262,000 miles) from the centre of Jupiter, just slightly more than the Moon–Earth distance. As a result, it is subject to enormous tidal stresses that heat its interior and drive constant volcanic activity on its surface.
The Thebe gossamer ring is fed by dust spiralling inwards from the surface of Thebe.
Adrastea
The smallest of Jupiter's regular satellites, misshapen Adrastea has an average diameter of 16km (10 miles). It orbits at the outer edge of Jupiter's main ring. Like the other inner moons, it is thought to contribute dust to the rings as a result of micrometeorites impacting its surface.
Amalthea
The largest inner moon, and the first to be discovered, Amalthea is an ovoid roughly 250km (155 miles) long with a remarkably red surface. It may have originated much farther from Jupiter than its current orbit, which is slightly eccentric (non-circular) as a result of Io's gravitational influence.
Jupiter
Thebe
This misshapen satellite is the outermost and second largest of Jupiter's inner moons. Like Amalthea, it has a distinctly reddish surface, and is probably made from either a porous, loose collection of rubble, or water ice and other chemicals.
Metis
Jupiter's innermost known moon was discovered in 1979 during the Voyager 1 flyby. It orbits in just 7 hours 4 minutes (less than a Jovian day), in a distinct gap within Jupiter's main ring. Roughly oval in shape, Metis makes a significant contribution to the inner ring's dusty material.
The main ring is relatively narrow and centred at about 1.8 Jupiter radii.
The Amalthea gossamer ring is a broad disc fed by dust from Amalthea.

Ganymede is larger than Mercury and almost the size of Mars. It **would be classified as a planet** if it were orbiting the Sun rather than Jupiter.

△ **Inner moons**
Jupiter's inner moons include four small satellites associated with the tenuous ring system, and the four giant Galilean moons – Ganymede, Callisto, Io, and Europa. The large size of the Galilean moons makes them vulnerable to tidal forces. Io, Europa, and Ganymede have settled into resonant orbits, in which their mutual gravitational tugs help to keep the orbits of Io and Europa stable.

IO

THE INNERMOST OF JUPITER'S LARGE GALILEAN MOONS IS A HELLISH WORLD TORTURED BY TIDAL FORCES AND WRACKED BY POWERFUL VOLCANIC ERUPTIONS.

Io is the third largest of Jupiter's moons. Its location near the centre of the Jovian system puts it in the middle of a gravitational tug-of-war between Jupiter and the large moons Europa and Ganymede orbiting farther out. Powerful tides squeeze the moon in various directions, flexing its surface by as much as 100m (330ft). In comparison, the most dramatic tidal range of the sea on Earth is just 18m (60ft). Io's tidal activity heats the moon's interior, which consists of sulphurous rock with a much lower melting point than the silicate rocks of Earth. As a result, Io is the most volcanically active world in the Solar System, with numerous volcanoes pouring sulphur-rich magma onto the surface or launching geyser-like plumes of sulphurous chemicals as high as 300km (190 miles) into the sky. Io owes its colourful, pizza-like appearance to the unique properties of the element sulphur, which can take several different forms (allotropes) with different physical properties. The moon has little atmosphere – only a thin layer of gases, mostly sulphur dioxide, surrounds it.

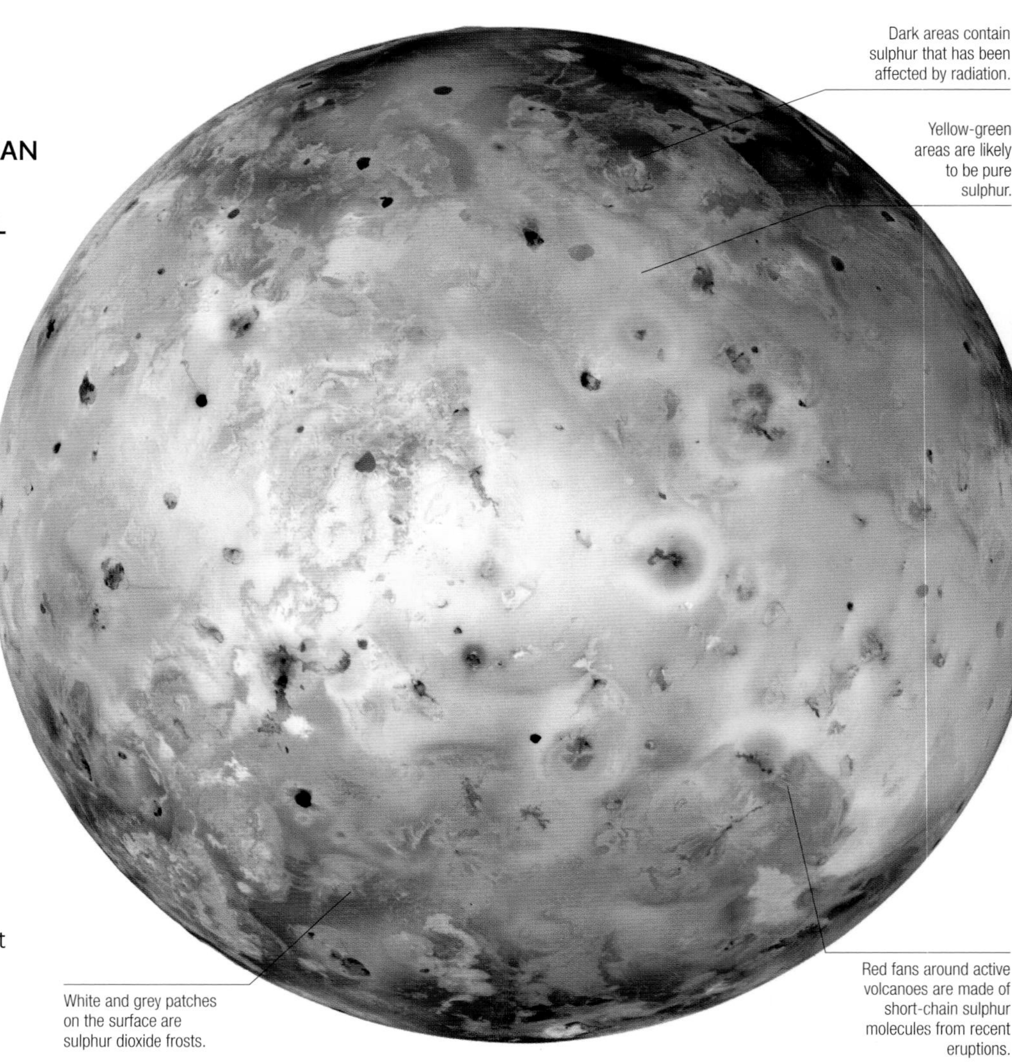

Dark areas contain sulphur that has been affected by radiation.

Yellow-green areas are likely to be pure sulphur.

White and grey patches on the surface are sulphur dioxide frosts.

Red fans around active volcanoes are made of short-chain sulphur molecules from recent eruptions.

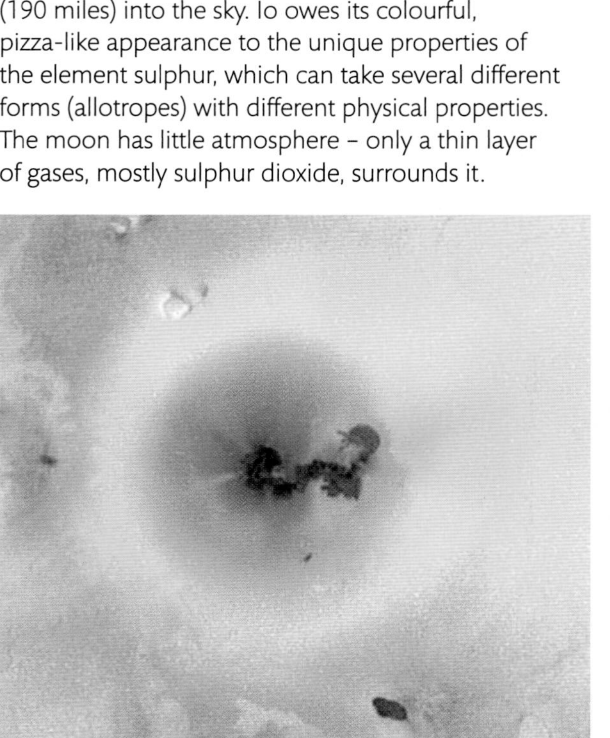

△ **Volcanic plume**
A volcanic feature known as Prometheus has been nicknamed Old Faithful on account of its reliable outbursts. Prometheus sends geyser-like plumes of molten sulphur up into the sky, and the fallout creates an ever-changing halo of colour around the vent.

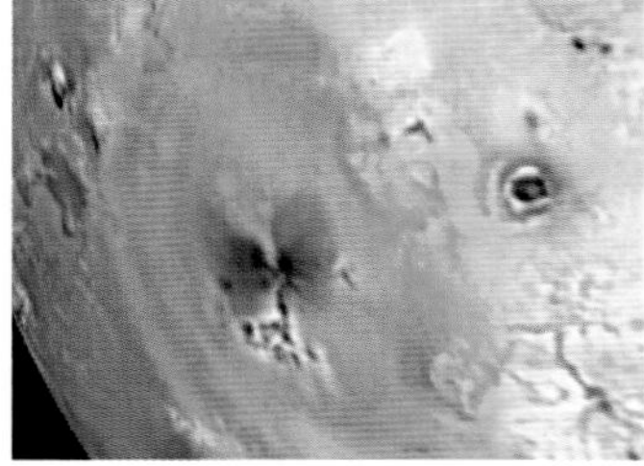

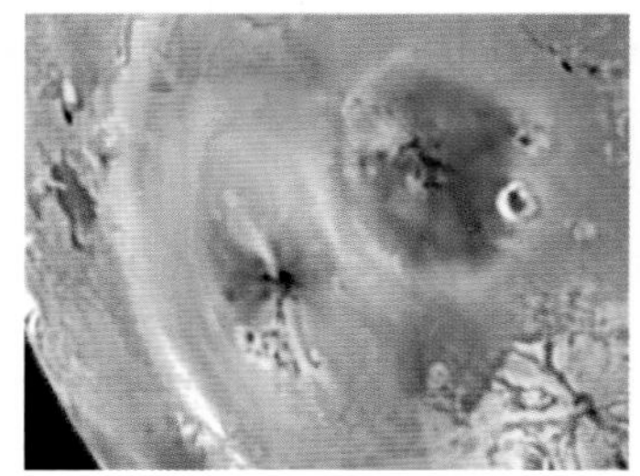

△ **A new eruption**
Io's landscape is dynamic. These images from the Galileo orbiter, taken five months apart, show the growth of a 400km (250 mile) dark spot on Pillan Patera volcano.

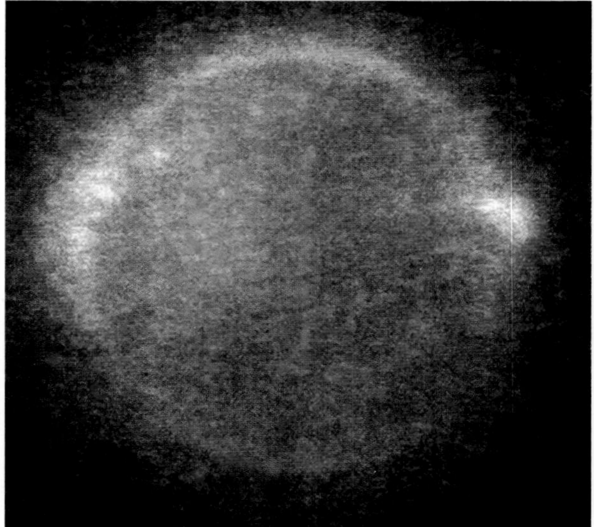

△ **Aurorae on Io**
Io's location within Jupiter's magnetic field means that it is constantly bombarded by high-energy particles trapped in the planet's radiation belts. When the particles collide with gases in Io's thin atmosphere, they produce glowing aurorae with vivid red and green colours.

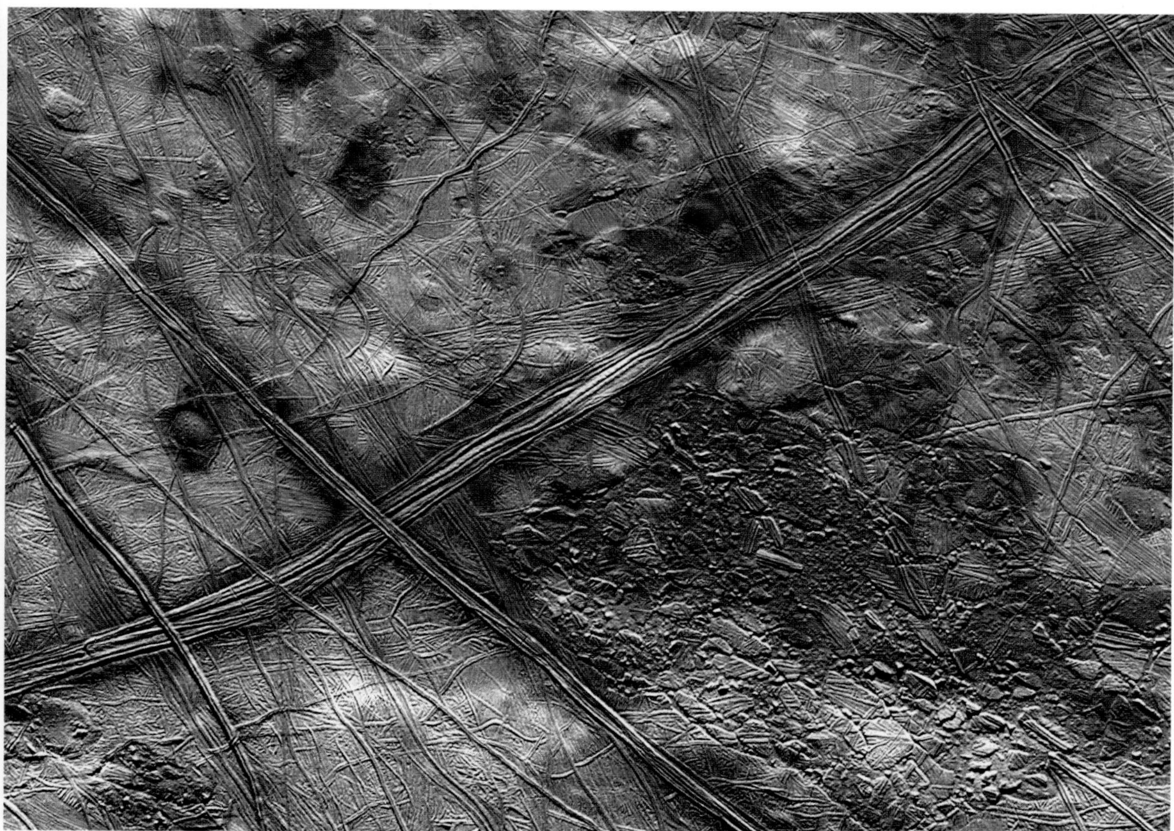

◁ **Cracking ice**
The way features on opposite sides of lineae match reveals that Europa's icy crust is being pulled apart as the moon flexes under changing tidal forces. Warmer ice, stained red by salts and sulphur, wells up from beneath and heals the cracks, but liquid water sometimes also erupts violently, gushing out to form huge plumes more than 200km (125 miles) high.

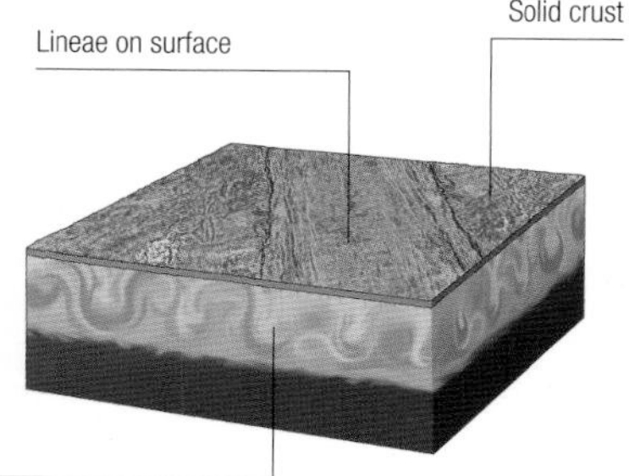
Lineae on surface
Solid crust
Liquid water or a slushy layer of convective ice lies below the surface.

△ **Water world**
The ocean beneath Europa's crust is thought to be around 100km (62 miles) deep, but it is covered by a crust of solid ice that may be tens of kilometres thick. The recent discovery of liquid water eruptions suggests the crust could be thinner in places, though it is not clear whether the eruptions are fed by the ocean or isolated pockets of water in the crust.

EUROPA

THE SMALLEST OF JUPITER'S GALILEAN MOONS, EUROPA HIDES ITS INTERNAL RESEMBLANCE TO ITS VOLCANIC NEIGHBOUR IO BENEATH A SUPERFICIALLY PLACID ICY SURFACE.

Europa's icy crust gives it the smoothest surface of any large world in the Solar System. Any significant features – formed, for example, by impact craters – gradually slump back to the average surface level. Enhanced-colour images, however, reveal networks of discoloured lines called lineae crisscrossing the ground, showing that Europa is far from dormant. Like Io, this moon is squeezed and stretched by competing tidal forces – from Io and Jupiter on the one side and planet-sized Ganymede on the other. The volcanic activity this generates is thought to warm a vast ocean of liquid water trapped beneath the frozen crust. This hidden sea may be one of the few places in the Solar System that is hospitable to life.

Europa is one of the **main targets** in the **search for life** beyond Earth.

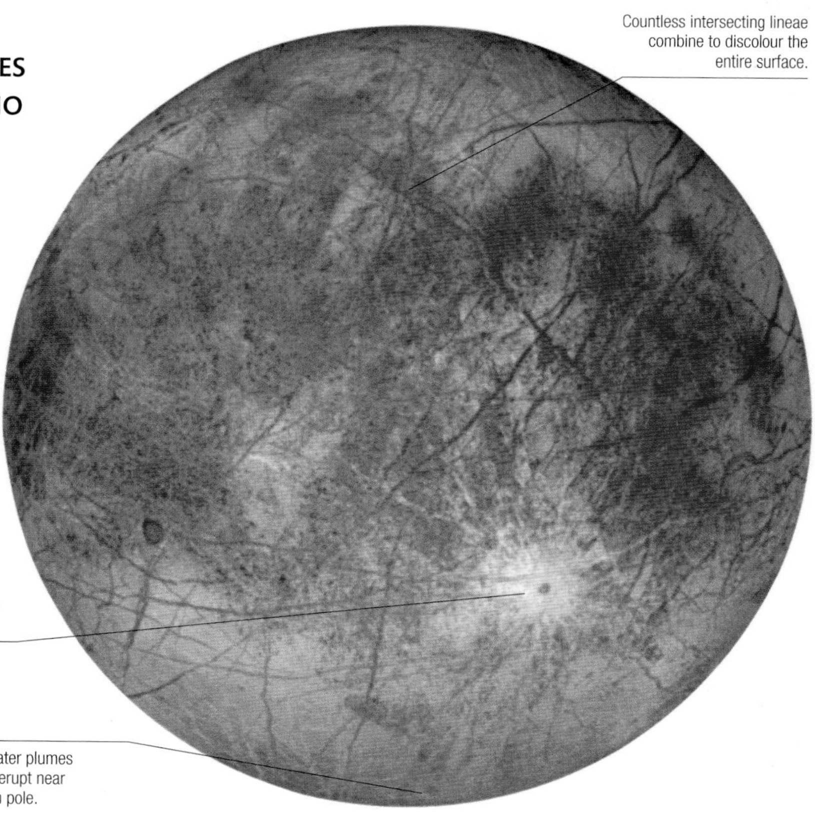

Countless intersecting lineae combine to discolour the entire surface.

Pwyll is Europa's most prominent crater and one of its youngest features.

Liquid water plumes seem to erupt near the south pole.

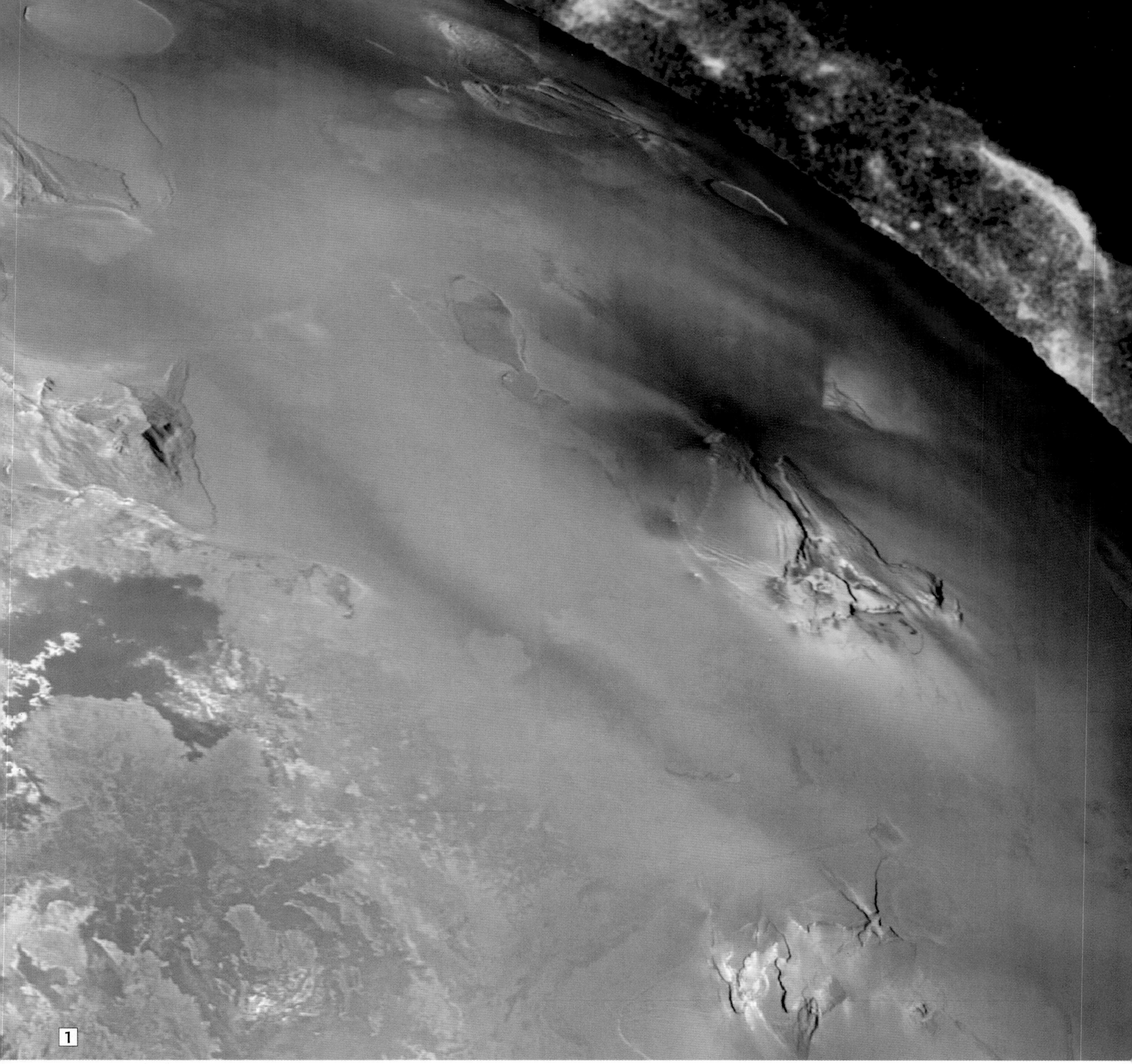

1

THE **GALILEAN MOONS**

1 Pele erupts on Io
This Voyager 1 image shows the eruption of Io's huge volcano, Pele. A plume of gas and dust rises from the volcano's vent to a height of 300km (185 miles). The plume, invisible against the surface, can be seen as a bright umbrella shape against the dark sky. Fallout from the plume covers a heart-shaped area around Pele the size of Alaska.

2 Europa
When Galileo imaged Europa, it revealed vast plains of bright ice crisscrossed by cracks snaking away to the horizon, and dark patches that probably contain both ice and dirt. There are few highlands or big impact craters. Plumes of water vapour 200km (125 miles) tall have been seen spurting from Europa's surface, and oceans of briny liquid water – and perhaps even life – may exist below the icy exterior.

3 Ganymede
In this Voyager 2 view from a range of 300,000km (185,000 miles), the ancient dark area of Galileo Regio is at the upper right. In the lower centre is a relatively young impact crater, surrounded by white rays of water-ice debris. The lighter regions – the younger parts of the surface – have grooves and ridges caused by tectonic activity. Like Europa and Callisto, Ganymede probably has subsurface salt water.

4 Callisto
Despite Callisto forming at the same time as Io, the two moons are very different. While Io's surface is young, constantly renewed by volcanism, Callisto's surface is old, scarred by the highest density of impact craters in the Solar System and devoid of volcanoes and large mountains. In fact, it is one vast ice field, laced with cracks and craters from billions of years of collisions with interplanetary debris.

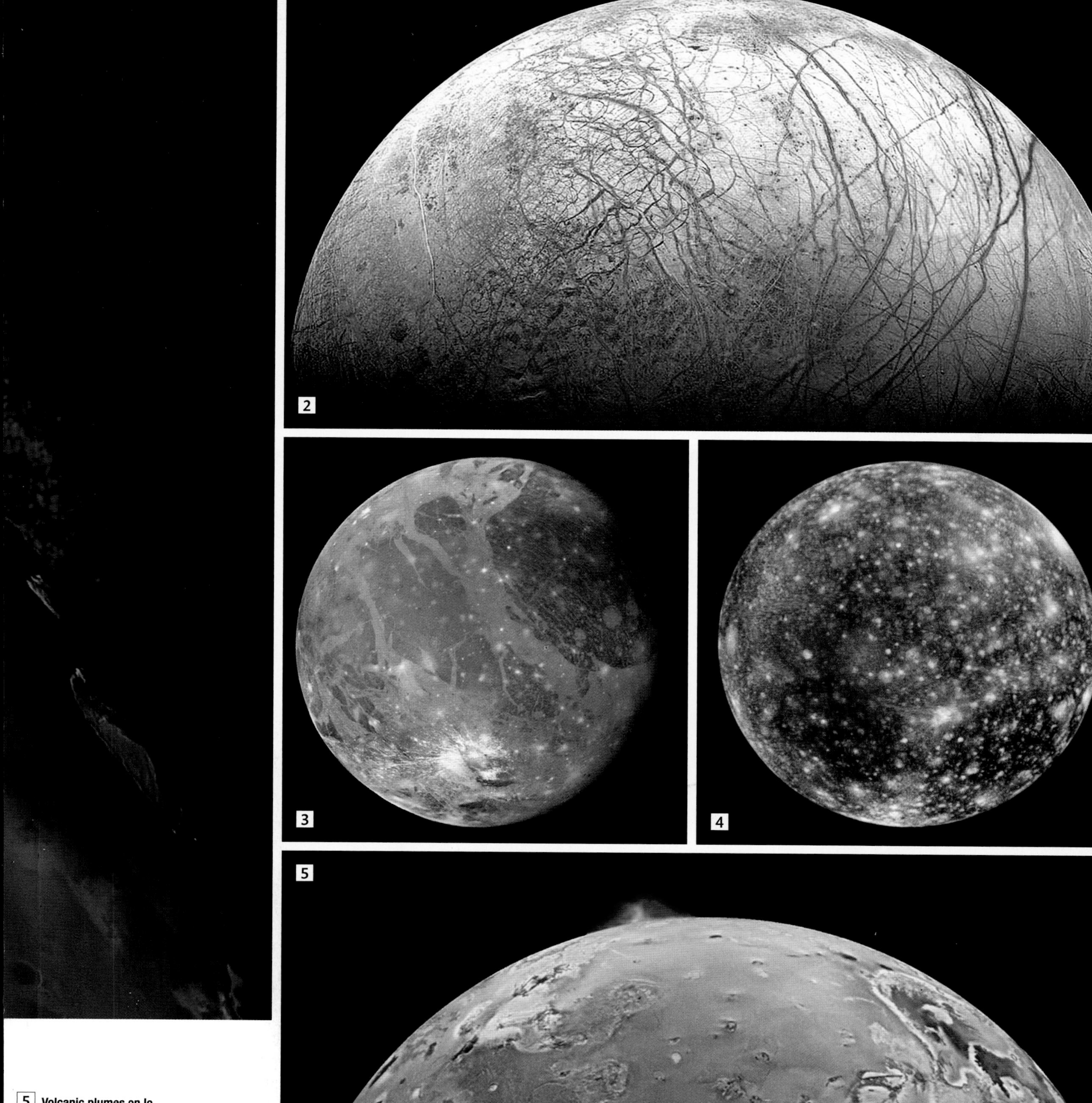

2
3
4
5

5 Volcanic plumes on Io
Io's surface has virtually no impact craters, and is continually being repaved by lava from its many volcanoes. Two sulphurous eruptions are visible in this Galileo image. At the top, on Io's limb, a bluish plume towers about 140km (97 miles) above Pillan Patera, a volcanic caldera. At bottom centre, a ring-shaped plume can be seen over the vent of the volcano Prometheus, rising about 75km (47 miles) into space.

GANYMEDE

THE LARGEST MOON IN THE SOLAR SYSTEM, GANYMEDE IS BIGGER THAN THE PLANET MERCURY. WHILE IT SHOWS FEW SIGNS OF ACTIVITY TODAY, ITS SURFACE – A JIGSAW OF DIVERSE TERRAIN – BEARS THE SCARS OF A COMPLEX HISTORY.

With a diameter of 5,268km (3,272 miles), Ganymede is 8 per cent wider than Mercury and 25 per cent larger in terms of volume. However, its much lower density suggests it consists of a rock–ice mix similar to its inner neighbour, the moon Europa. Ganymede has a thin atmosphere dominated by oxygen, and its landscape is a jumble of bright and dark regions, with far fewer impact craters in the bright regions. This suggests that the dark areas have been exposed to bombardment from space for significantly longer than the lighter patches, which have been resurfaced. The lighter areas are scarred by parallel grooves and ridges – evidence of tectonic activity.

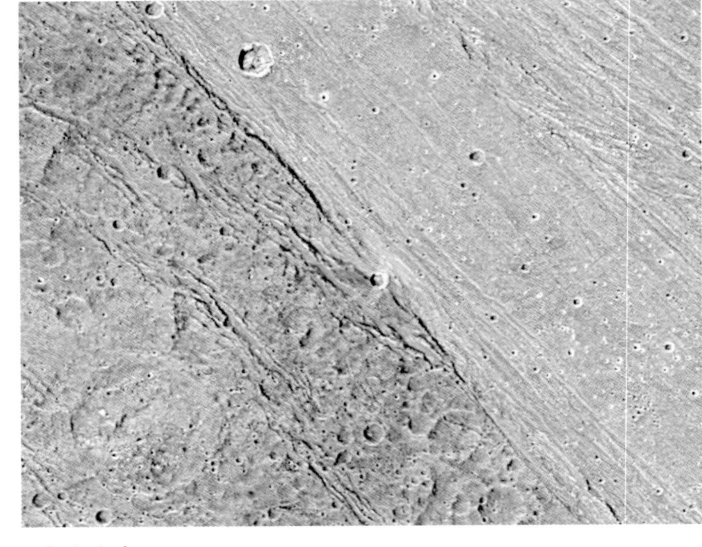

△ **Icy tectonics**
Ganymede's surface probably solidified early in its history, though Jupiter's tidal pull caused the moon's interior to remain molten. The crust split into tectonic plates like those on Earth, and a slushy mix of rock and ice welled up to bridge the gap between moving plates, forming grooved terrain similar to younger parts of Earth's crust.

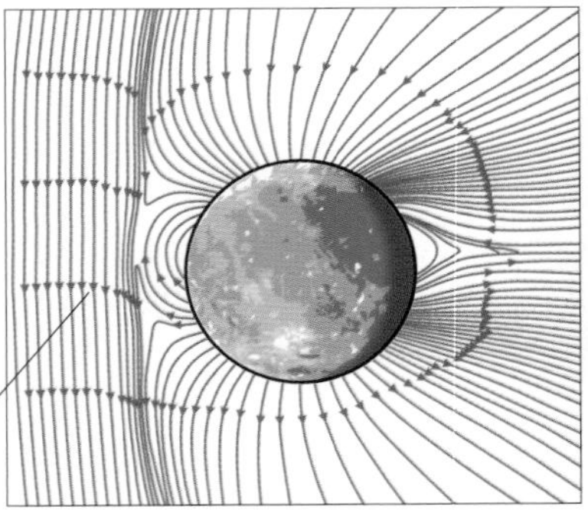

Ganymede's magnetic field interacts with that of Jupiter's.

△ **Magnetic moon**
Ganymede is the only moon in the Solar System known to have a significant magnetic field – evidence of an interior with distinct layers and a core that likely contains liquid iron. In 2002, scientists detected features in the magnetic field that suggest the presence of an ocean layer roughly 200km (125 miles) below the surface, between layers of ice.

Lighter patches form where the dark plates have drifted apart.

Relatively young craters expose fresh ice at the surface.

Dark cratered areas are Ganymede's oldest terrain.

Water ice accounts for some **90 per cent of** Ganymede's surface terrain.

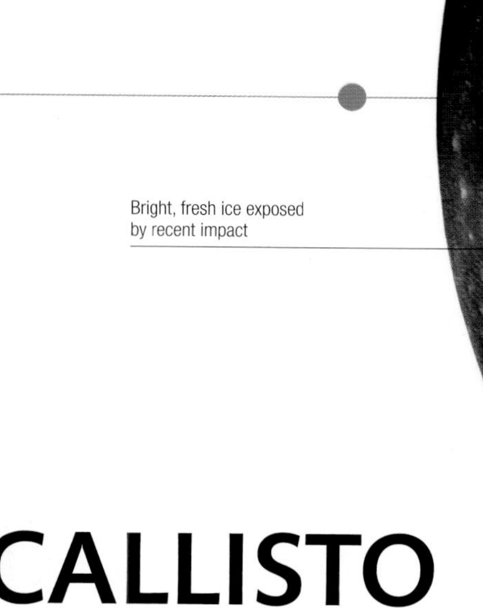

Bright, fresh ice exposed by recent impact
Major impact basins are surrounded by concentric rings
Valhalla is Callisto's largest impact crater.
Fresh ice has welled up to fill the centre of the basin.

CALLISTO

THE OUTERMOST GALILEAN MOON IS A DARK, HEAVILY CRATERED BALL OF ICE AND ROCK, CONTRASTING IN STRUCTURE AND APPEARANCE WITH ITS INNER NEIGHBOURS.

Callisto seems to have changed relatively little since its formation, and spacecraft images show a surface covered in craters accumulated over 4.5 billion years of Solar System history. The largest features are enormous, ringed impact basins such as those named Asgard and Valhalla. Solar radiation has caused the surface of the moon to darken gradually over time, making the youngest impact craters look like bright starbursts on the otherwise dull landscape.

Callisto is the least dense of the Galilean moons, indicating that it contains more ice and less rock than its neighbours. It is thought to be a relatively homogenous blend of rock and ice throughout, a structure that may have been common to all the Galilean moons before tidal heating took hold and caused the interiors of the other moons to melt and separate into layers.

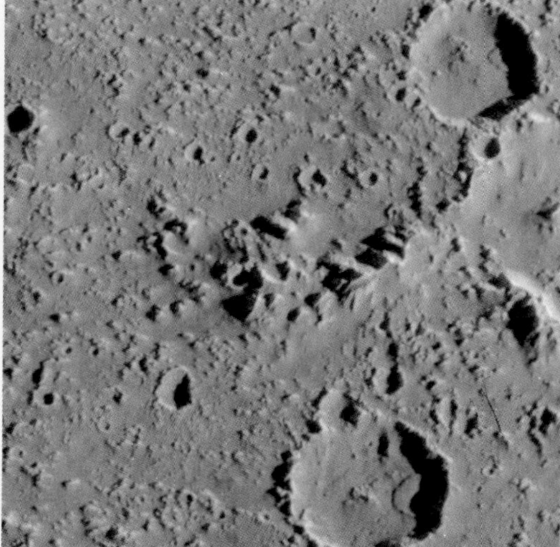

△ **Craters**
Callisto's location close to Jupiter puts it directly in the firing line for comets and asteroids pulled to their doom by the giant planet's gravity. As a result, Callisto is often described as the most heavily cratered world in the Solar System.

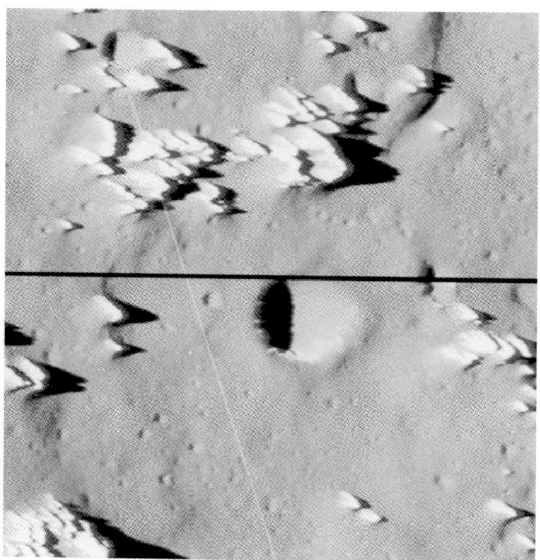

△ **Jagged hills**
Erosion by solar radiation has caused much of the ice in raised crater rims to evaporate from the rock–ice mix, degrading their structure and leaving chains of jagged, knob-like peaks across the land. Landslips in the remaining material are common.

△ **Scarps**
Callisto's largest impact basins contain long scarps – cliffs separating areas of different elevation. The scarps mark the top of deep faults where the crust has fractured after impact and blocks of terrain have shifted vertically in relation to each other.

Jupiter's gravity pulls comets and asteroids **to their doom**, shredding them into fragments that **collide with its moons**.

Artist's impression based on NASA images

LOCATION

Latitude 39°N; **longitude** 14°W

FORMATION

The comet or asteroid that formed Enki Catena was probably drawn into orbit around Jupiter before its break-up and impact.

1. Object strays too close to Jupiter.
2. Object breaks up, and fragments spread out along orbit.
3. Collision with Ganymede.

Jupiter
Ganymede
1.
2.
3.

CRATER CHAIN

Icy debris flung out during the impact surrounds one end of Enki Catena, where the underlying surface is younger. Darker material in older terrain may disguise the ejecta.

No ejecta on older, darker landscape
Bright ejecta on young, light terrain

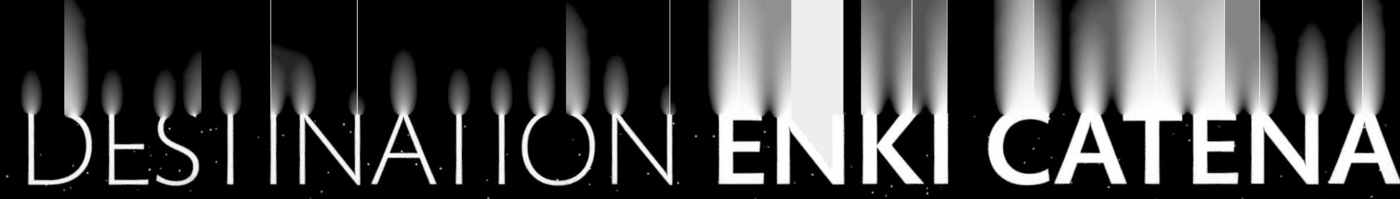

DESTINATION **ENKI CATENA**

A SPECTACULAR CHAIN OF CRATERS MARCHES IN A STRAIGHT LINE ACROSS 160KM (100 MILES) OF GANYMEDE'S SURFACE. THIS REMARKABLE FEATURE IS THE RESULT OF A SERIES OF IMPACTS IN THE MOON'S RELATIVELY RECENT PAST.

Enki Catena consists of at least 13 overlapping craters, each around 10km (6 miles) or more in diameter, running diagonally across a boundary between darker and lighter areas of Ganymede's terrain (see page 162). The chain is the most prominent of several such features identified on Ganymede and Callisto. It almost certainly formed from the near-simultaneous impact of fragments of a comet or asteroid, broken apart under the force of Jupiter's gravitational pull in the same way as Comet Shoemaker-Levy 9, which struck the giant planet itself in 1994.

KING OF THE PLANETS

JUPITER'S BRIGHTNESS AND STATELY MOVEMENT THROUGH EARTH'S SKIES LED EARLY STARGAZERS TO GIVE IT A PROMINENT PLACE IN THEIR MYTHOLOGY. FROM THE DAWN OF SCIENTIFIC ASTRONOMY, IT HAS PLAYED A PIVOTAL ROLE IN MANY DISCOVERIES.

Because of its great size, Jupiter is visible as a disc rather than a point through even a basic telescope, and its four largest moons are easy to observe. However, the planet's shifting surface markings mystified early astronomers, and it was not until the 20th century that Jupiter's gaseous nature was widely accepted. Since the 1970s, spacecraft such as Galileo have revealed many more of the Jupiter system's secrets.

Zeus

c.500 BCE

Ruling planet
The ancient Greeks and Romans associate the planet with the king of the gods, known as Zeus to the Greeks and Jupiter or Jove to the Romans. Long before, astronomers in Babylon associated Jupiter with Marduk, the ruling god in the Babylonian pantheon.

Galileo's record of Jovian moons

1610 CE

Galilean moons
Italian scientist Galileo Galilei studies Jupiter with his telescope and sees four faint "stars" nearby, which prove to be satellites. The existence of moons around other worlds contradicts the prevailing idea that everything in the Universe circles Earth.

PIONEER ★ JUPITER
US
10c

Stamp commemorating Pioneer 10

1973

Jupiter flyby
Launched in 1972, Pioneer 10 flies close to Jupiter the following year and returns the first close-up images of the planet. It suffers radiation damage while passing through Jupiter's magnetic equator, confirming the great strength of Jupiter's magnetic field.

Voyager images of the Galilean moons Io, Europa, Ganymede, and Callisto

1979

Voyagers
The Voyager 1 and 2 spacecraft provide the first detailed views of Jupiter's Galilean moons, revealing four complex worlds, each the size of a small planet. Voyager 1 also discovers a tenuous ring system, composed of sparse particles, encircling Jupiter.

Volcanic eruption on Io

1979

Volcanoes over Io
Voyager 2 captures an image of a huge plume of material arching high above the surface of Io. This moon is the most volcanically active body in the Solar System, with sulphurous eruptions driven by heat generated by Jupiter's tidal forces.

Aftermath of Shoemaker–Levy impact

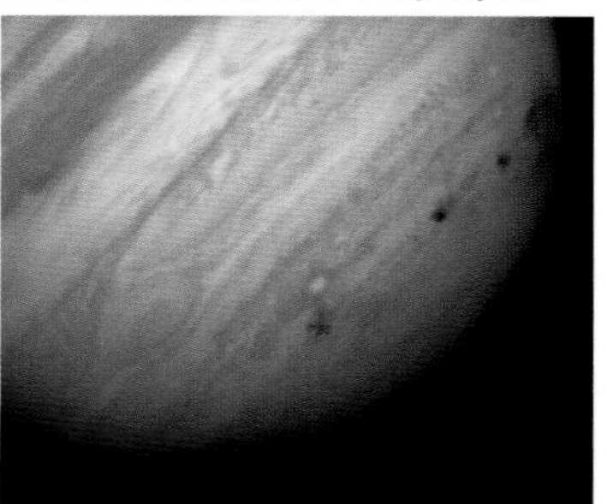

1994

Comet impact
Fragments of the comet Shoemaker–Levy 9 strike Jupiter, creating fireballs larger than Earth and stirring up material from deep inside the planet. The resulting "bruises" on Jupiter's face provide an insight into the planet's internal chemistry.

1995

Probing the atmosphere
NASA's Galileo spacecraft releases a probe that plunges into Jupiter's clouds. The probe sends back data about weather conditions and atmospheric chemistry as it descends 156km (97 miles) through the upper atmosphere, until contact is lost.

Close-up of Europa's surface

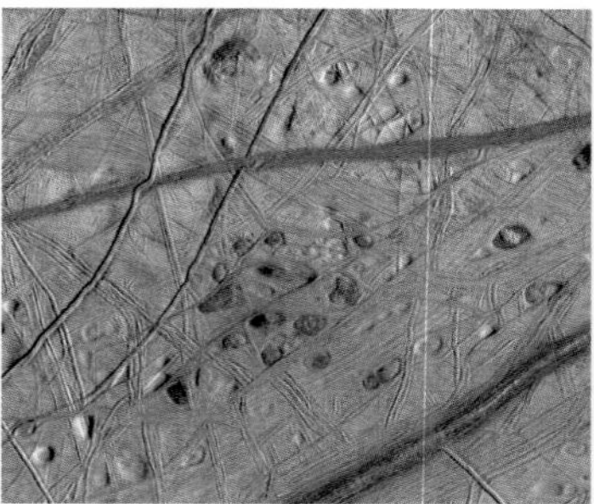

1995–2003

Orbiting Jupiter
The Galileo orbiter studies the Jovian system for over eight years, investigating the planet and its major moons in detail and making countless discoveries. It finds evidence of a liquid-water ocean deep under the icy surface of the Galilean moon Europa.

Cassini's sketches of Jupiter

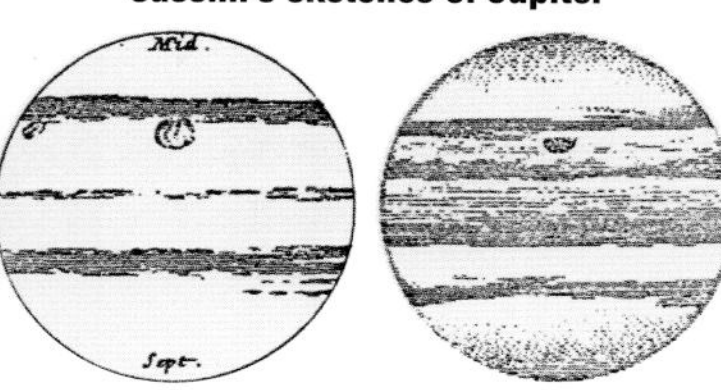

Ole Rømer observing Jupiter

1665–90

Jovian weather
Italian-French astronomer Giovanni Cassini makes sketches of Jupiter's atmosphere and identifies cloud bands and spots, which he uses to measure the planet's rotation. By 1690 he has concluded that different parts of Jupiter rotate at different rates.

1676

Measuring the speed of light
Danish astronomer Ole Rømer notices that eclipses and transits of Jupiter's moons don't always occur at predicted times, because of variations in the time it takes for light to reach Earth. This allows him to make the first estimate of the speed of light.

1733

Calculating Jupiter's diameter
English astronomer James Bradley measures the size of Jupiter's disc through a telescope and uses his result to calculate the planet's immense diameter. Bradley also tracks the movements of Jupiter's moons and studies their shadows and eclipses.

A 19th century map of Jupiter

1830

Great Red Spot
Giovanni Cassini and English scientist Robert Hooke may have seen the giant storm called the Great Red Spot in the 1660s, but the first confirmed sighting is made by German astronomer Heinrich Schwabe in 1830. It has been regularly viewed ever since.

1903

Jupiter is a gas giant
American astronomer George W. Hough states that Jupiter is dominated by a deep envelope of gases, transforming into liquid at great depth and high pressure – the first suggestion that Jupiter is a gas giant and not a solid body with a thin atmosphere.

Jupiter's magnetic field

1955

Jupiter's magnetic field
In the USA, Kenneth Franklin and Bernard Burke detect bursts of radio waves, known as synchrotron radiation, coming from Jupiter. This shows that Jupiter has a magnetosphere, since this type of radiation is emitted when high-speed electrons spin in a magnetic field.

Io and Jupiter from Cassini

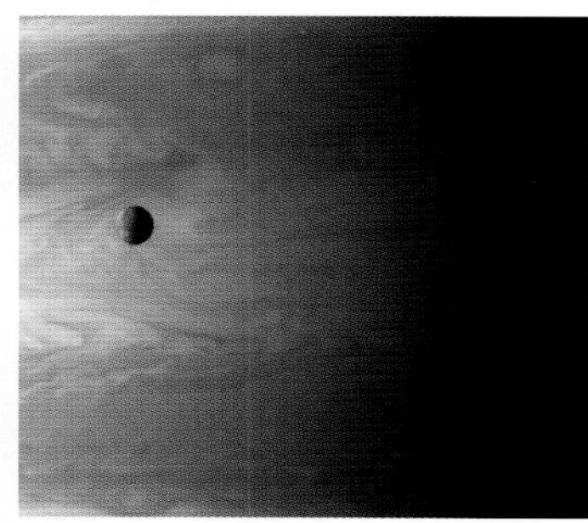

2000

Cassini flyby
The Cassini spacecraft takes 26,000 images of Jupiter from a distance of 10 million km (6.2 million miles) during a flyby en route to Saturn. Together with Galileo's close-ups, the Cassini images lead to new findings about the giant planet's weather systems.

Three red spots (Junior at lower left)

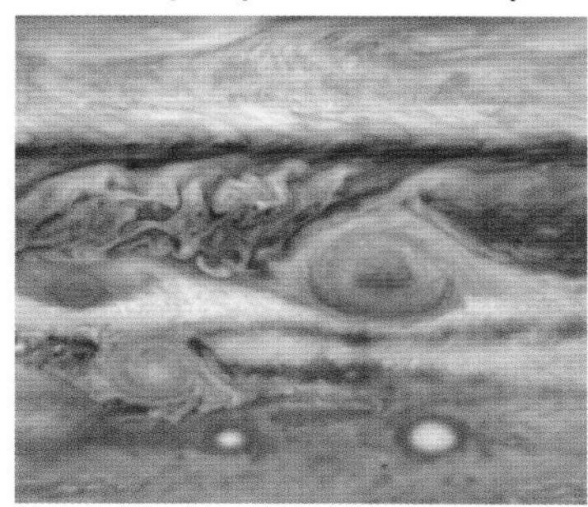

2006

Red Spot Junior
Astronomers notice that a large storm, formed by the merging of three smaller white storms in 1998–2000, is turning red. Over the next few years, "Red Spot Junior" grows to more than half the size of the more famous Great Red Spot.

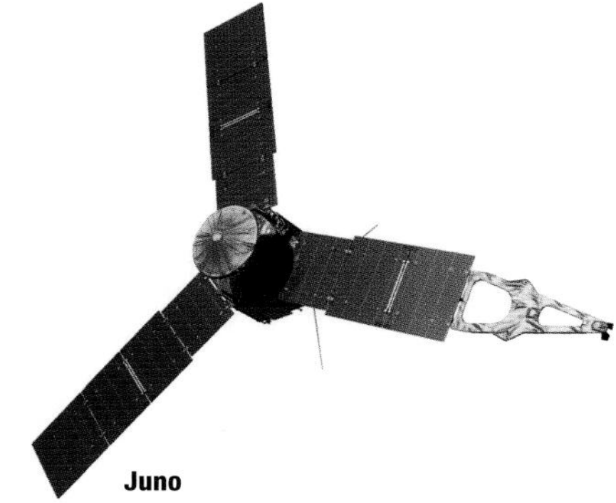

Juno

2011

Launch of Juno
Upon arrival in 2016, NASA'S Juno will map Jupiter's magnetic field, measure atmospheric levels of water and ammonia, observe Jupiter's aurorae, and investigate whether Jupiter has a solid core. It is hoped that Juno's findings will reveal much about how giant planets form.

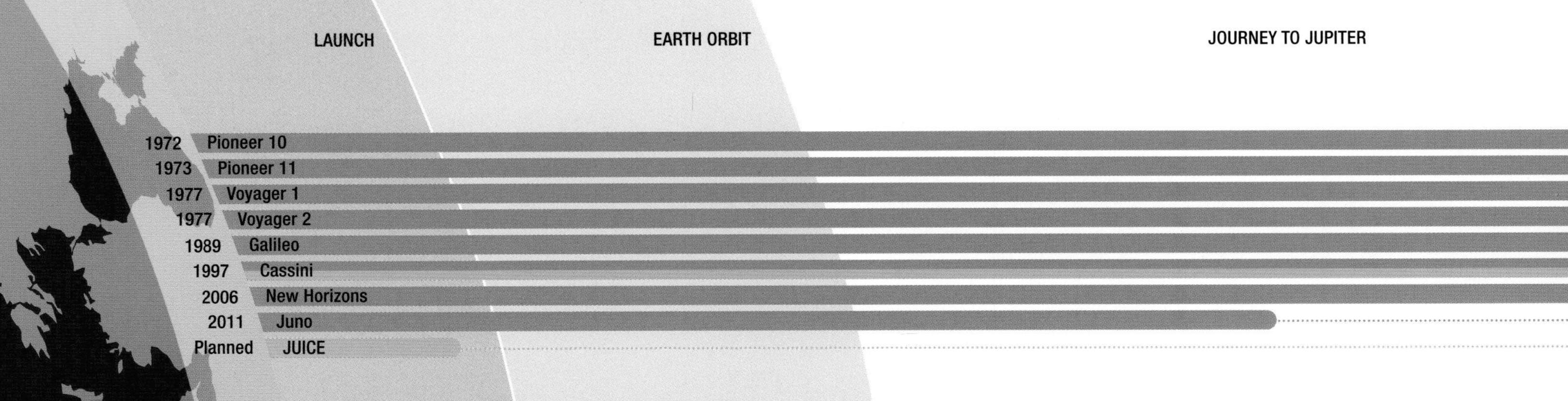
LAUNCH
EARTH ORBIT
JOURNEY TO JUPITER
1972 Pioneer 10
1973 Pioneer 11
1977 Voyager 1
1977 Voyager 2
1989 Galileo
1997 Cassini
2006 New Horizons
2011 Juno
Planned JUICE

MISSIONS TO JUPITER

MOST OF THE SPACECRAFT THAT HAVE VISITED JUPITER HAVE MADE ONLY A BRIEF FLYBY DURING A GRAVITY-ASSIST MANOEUVRE ON THE WAY TO ANOTHER PLANET. ONLY ONE SPACECRAFT HAS GONE INTO ORBIT AROUND JUPITER ITSELF.

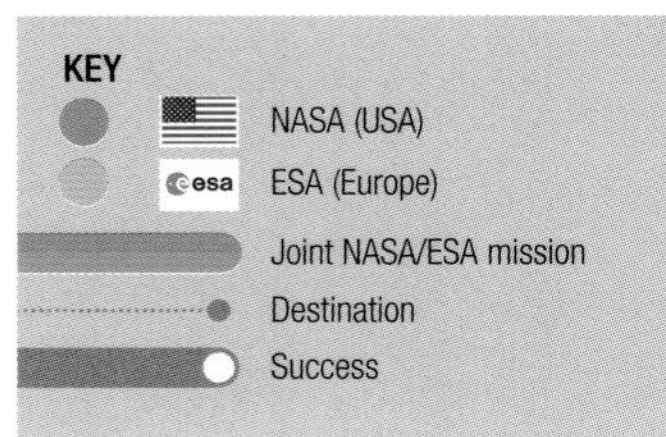
KEY
NASA (USA)
esa
ESA (Europe)
Joint NASA/ESA mission
Destination
Success

The first spacecraft to journey beyond the inner Solar System were Pioneers 10 and 11. After proving that the Asteroid Belt could be safely crossed, they sent back the first close-ups of Jupiter in 1973 and 1974. They were followed by the more sophisticated Voyagers 1 and 2, which returned breathtaking images of Jupiter's moons. The Galileo spacecraft entered orbit in 1995 and spent eight years surveying the Jupiter system in great detail, before self-destructing. Cassini and New Horizons, bound for Saturn and Pluto respectively, followed later.

Jupiter's rings from Voyager 2

△ Voyager 1 and 2
The two Voyager flybys of Jupiter provided the first detailed views of the giant planet and its major moons. These missions confirmed the existence of a tenuous ring system around Jupiter (above) and discovered three new inner moons orbiting among the rings. The Voyager spacecraft returned beautiful images of Io's active volcanoes and Europa's fractured, icy crust. Time-lapse movies of Jupiter brought the planet's swirling cloud bands and rotating Great Red Spot to life.

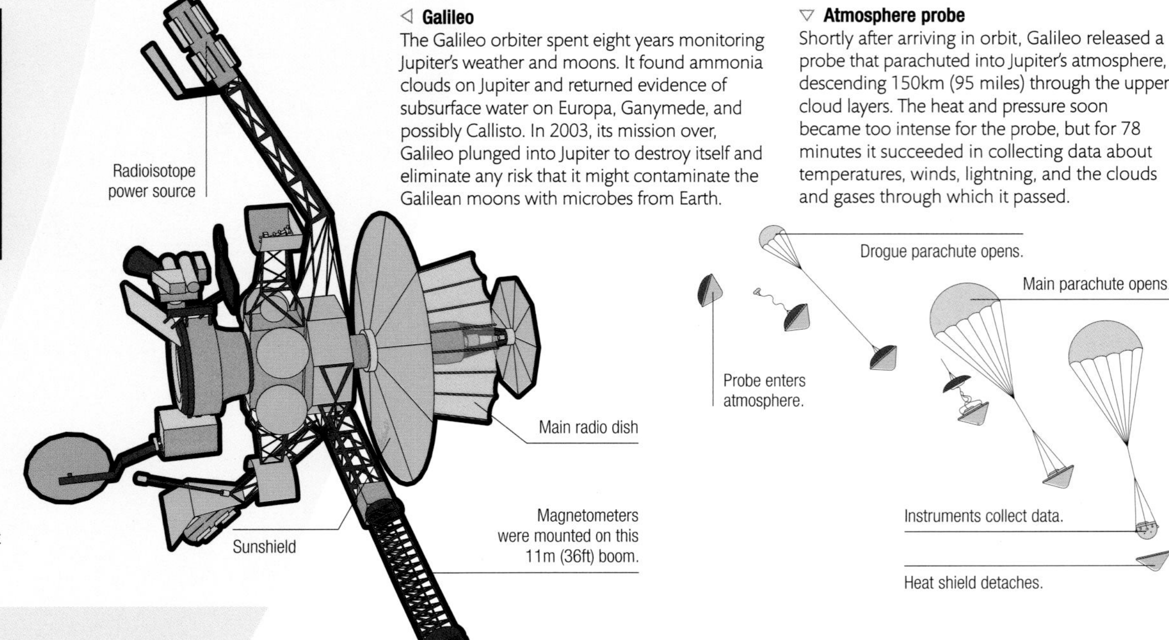
Radioisotope power source
Sunshield
Main radio dish
Magnetometers were mounted on this 11m (36ft) boom.
Drogue parachute opens.
Main parachute opens.
Probe enters atmosphere.
Instruments collect data.
Heat shield detaches.

◁ Galileo
The Galileo orbiter spent eight years monitoring Jupiter's weather and moons. It found ammonia clouds on Jupiter and returned evidence of subsurface water on Europa, Ganymede, and possibly Callisto. In 2003, its mission over, Galileo plunged into Jupiter to destroy itself and eliminate any risk that it might contaminate the Galilean moons with microbes from Earth.

▽ Atmosphere probe
Shortly after arriving in orbit, Galileo released a probe that parachuted into Jupiter's atmosphere, descending 150km (95 miles) through the upper cloud layers. The heat and pressure soon became too intense for the probe, but for 78 minutes it succeeded in collecting data about temperatures, winds, lightning, and the clouds and gases through which it passed.

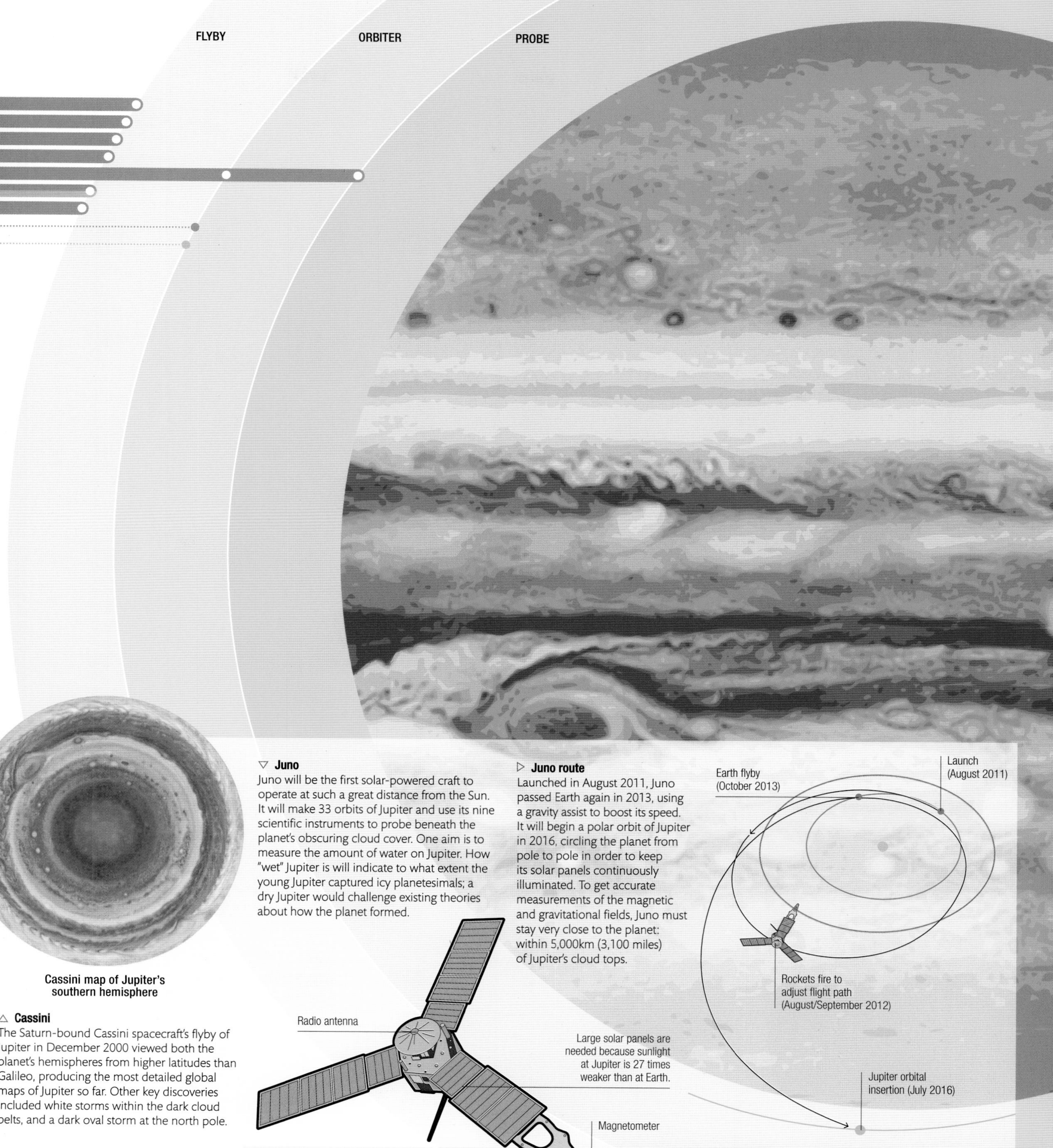
FLYBY
ORBITER
PROBE
Earth flyby
(October 2013)
Launch
(August 2011)
Rockets fire to
adjust flight path
(August/September 2012)
Jupiter orbital
insertion (July 2016)
Radio antenna
Large solar panels are
needed because sunlight
at Jupiter is 27 times
weaker than at Earth.
Magnetometer

Cassini map of Jupiter's southern hemisphere

△ **Cassini**
The Saturn-bound Cassini spacecraft's flyby of Jupiter in December 2000 viewed both the planet's hemispheres from higher latitudes than Galileo, producing the most detailed global maps of Jupiter so far. Other key discoveries included white storms within the dark cloud belts, and a dark oval storm at the north pole.

▽ **Juno**
Juno will be the first solar-powered craft to operate at such a great distance from the Sun. It will make 33 orbits of Jupiter and use its nine scientific instruments to probe beneath the planet's obscuring cloud cover. One aim is to measure the amount of water on Jupiter. How "wet" Jupiter is will indicate to what extent the young Jupiter captured icy planetesimals; a dry Jupiter would challenge existing theories about how the planet formed.

▷ **Juno route**
Launched in August 2011, Juno passed Earth again in 2013, using a gravity assist to boost its speed. It will begin a polar orbit of Jupiter in 2016, circling the planet from pole to pole in order to keep its solar panels continuously illuminated. To get accurate measurements of the magnetic and gravitational fields, Juno must stay very close to the planet: within 5,000km (3,100 miles) of Jupiter's cloud tops.

SATURN

SATURN IS A LONG WAY FROM THE SUN. VIEWED FROM EARTH, IT IS EASILY OUTSHONE IN THE NIGHT SKY BY SUCH LUMINARIES AS JUPITER AND VENUS. BUT SEEN FROM SPACE, IT IS ARGUABLY THE MOST BEAUTIFUL OF ALL THE PLANETS.

Data	
Equatorial diameter	120,536km (74,898 miles)
Mass (Earth = 1)	95.2
Gravity at equator (Earth = 1)	1.02
Mean distance from Sun (Earth = 1)	9.58
Axial tilt	26.7°
Rotation period (day)	10.66 hours
Orbital period (year)	29.46 Earth years
Cloud-top temperature	–140°C (–220°F)
Moons	62+

Clothed in a creamy-white blanket of high-altitude ammonia cloud, with softly muted colour bands just visible through the hazy cover, Saturn looks deceptively placid. But beneath this disguise is a turbulent atmosphere. Saturn spins fast, generating high winds that race nonstop around the planet. Colossal electrical storms occur frequently and can last for months, hurling down bolts of lightning thousands of times more powerful than those on Earth.

All the giant planets have ring systems, but Saturn's is the glory of the Solar System. These concentric disc-like platters are composed of countless ringlets, each of which consists of millions of orbiting ice fragments of varying size and composition.

Saturn's **density** is less than water – placed in a large enough ocean, the planet **would float.**

Saturn's rapid rotation forces its gases outwards, causing a distinct bulge at the equator.

▽ **Northern hemisphere**
Saturn's north polar region is remarkable for a long-lived hexagonal cloud structure, more than 27,000km (17,000 miles) across, with a huge storm at its centre. This weather system, which is different from any other so far seen in the Solar System, is thought to be caused by a circumpolar jet stream.

▽ **Tilted axis**
Saturn's axis of rotation is tilted at an angle of 26.7°, so we view the planet and its rings at different angles throughout its 29.5-Earth-year orbit, as either the north or south pole tips towards the Sun. When the rings lie edge-on, they are invisible to observers on Earth.

▽ **Southern hemisphere**
The south polar region of Saturn is dominated by a hurricane-like storm almost the diameter of Earth and rotating about 550kph (340mph) faster than the planet itself. The eye of the storm is ringed by clouds up to 75km (45 miles) high.

The polar regions acquire a blue tinge in winter.
Saturn is encircled by broad cloud bands running parallel to the equator.
Though vast in terms of diameter, the main rings are just tens of metres thick.

◁ **Rings and bands**
Like Jupiter, Saturn has a distinctive banded appearance, although with much paler colours. The enormous ring system extends far beyond the planet; its main elements have a total diameter of over 270,000km (170,000 miles).

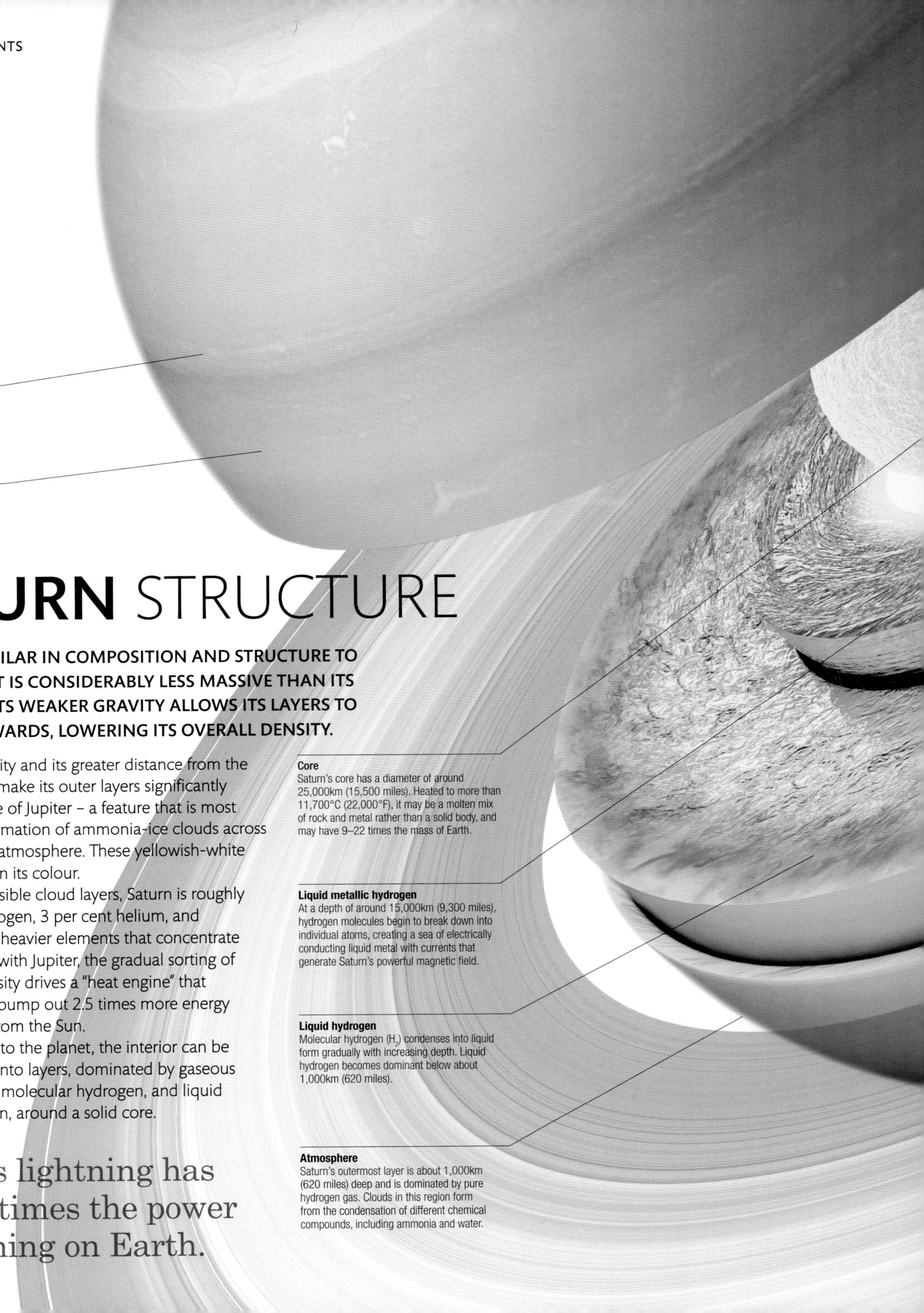

Upper atmosphere gas forms bands that encircle the planet. Clouds and storms are generated within them.

High winds reach speeds of up to 1,800kph (1,120mph).

SATURN STRUCTURE

SATURN IS SIMILAR IN COMPOSITION AND STRUCTURE TO JUPITER, BUT IT IS CONSIDERABLY LESS MASSIVE THAN ITS NEIGHBOUR. ITS WEAKER GRAVITY ALLOWS ITS LAYERS TO EXPAND OUTWARDS, LOWERING ITS OVERALL DENSITY.

Saturn's low density and its greater distance from the Sun combine to make its outer layers significantly cooler than those of Jupiter – a feature that is most evident in the formation of ammonia-ice clouds across the entire upper atmosphere. These yellowish-white clouds give Saturn its colour.

Beneath the visible cloud layers, Saturn is roughly 96 per cent hydrogen, 3 per cent helium, and 1 per cent other, heavier elements that concentrate at the centre. As with Jupiter, the gradual sorting of elements by density drives a "heat engine" that allows Saturn to pump out 2.5 times more energy than it receives from the Sun.

Descending into the planet, the interior can be broadly divided into layers, dominated by gaseous hydrogen, liquid molecular hydrogen, and liquid metallic hydrogen, around a solid core.

Saturn's lightning has **10,000** times the power of lightning on Earth.

Core
Saturn's core has a diameter of around 25,000km (15,500 miles). Heated to more than 11,700°C (22,000°F), it may be a molten mix of rock and metal rather than a solid body, and may have 9–22 times the mass of Earth.

Liquid metallic hydrogen
At a depth of around 15,000km (9,300 miles), hydrogen molecules begin to break down into individual atoms, creating a sea of electrically conducting liquid metal with currents that generate Saturn's powerful magnetic field.

Liquid hydrogen
Molecular hydrogen (H_2) condenses into liquid form gradually with increasing depth. Liquid hydrogen becomes dominant below about 1,000km (620 miles).

Atmosphere
Saturn's outermost layer is about 1,000km (620 miles) deep and is dominated by pure hydrogen gas. Clouds in this region form from the condensation of different chemical compounds, including ammonia and water.

Hydrogen molecules break down into metallic form under pressures equal to 1 million Earth atmospheres.
Temperatures at the base of the liquid hydrogen layer reach 6,000°C (10,800°F).
The ring system consists of many individual rings and a number of gaps between them.

◁ **Complex atmosphere**
Saturn's placid appearance belies its dynamic interior and stormy atmosphere. Enhanced-colour images from spacecraft have revealed the presence of turbulent cloud layers beneath the outer ammonia haze. These cloud layers are dominated by ammonium hydrogen sulphide at high altitudes and by water ice at lower levels.

SATURN'S RINGS

SATURN IS ENCIRCLED BY THE LARGEST RING SYSTEM IN THE SOLAR SYSTEM. THE SPECTACULAR STRUCTURES VISIBLE FROM EARTH CONSIST ALMOST ENTIRELY OF ICE FRAGMENTS THAT WHIRL AROUND THE PLANET IN CONCENTRIC RINGLETS.

Saturn's rings contain billions of pieces of ice, varying from house-sized boulders to minute crystals. Jostling together, these particles are constrained by the planet's gravity to orbit in a flat plane above Saturn's equator. The system is complex, with each large ring being made up of many narrow ringlets. Several distinct gaps between the rings are created by the gravitational pull of Saturn's more distant moons and the clumping together of material within the rings themselves. The particles consist predominantly of water ice, which makes them naturally reflective. Although their surfaces become dust-coated over time, constant collisions within the rings cause them to fracture, exposing bright new facets.

The origin of the rings is something of a mystery. They may be the remains of a small, icy moon that was either torn apart by Saturn's powerful gravity or destroyed in a collision with another body.

In places, Saturn's **main rings** are a mere **10m (33ft)** thick.

← Colombo Gap

D ring → ← C
74,700km (46,300 miles) from Saturn's centre

▷ **Rings within rings**
Astronomers have identified at least nine major rings. The A and B rings are the brightest and contain the largest ice particles; white and purple denote particles larger than 5cm (2 in) in this false-colour image. A wide gap called the Cassini Division separates the A and B rings. The paler C and D rings extend inwards from the B ring and contain particles less than 5cm (2in) in size (colour coded green and blue).

▷ **Ringside view**
Spacecraft can see far more detail in the rings than could ever be seen from Earth, though even the best images cannot resolve individual ring particles. In this ultraviolet image of Saturn's outer C (left) and inner B (right) rings from the Cassini spacecraft, chemical and physical properties are highlighted in colour. Dust-covered ice particles appear red, whereas purer water ice is turquoise. The more densely packed B ring appears cleaner and purer, indicating that collisions between ice particles are more frequent here, repeatedly opening up fresh new surfaces where the ice has fractured.

▽ **Shepherd moons**
Small satellites orbiting within the rings, or very close to them, are known as shepherd moons. The gravitational influence of these bodies can create complex structures within the ring plane, including fine, braided ringlets, narrow gaps, and even vertical bumps. At Saturn's equinox, these inner satellites can cast long shadows across the rings, as shown below in an image of Daphnis, a small moon that maintains the Keeler Gap within the A ring.

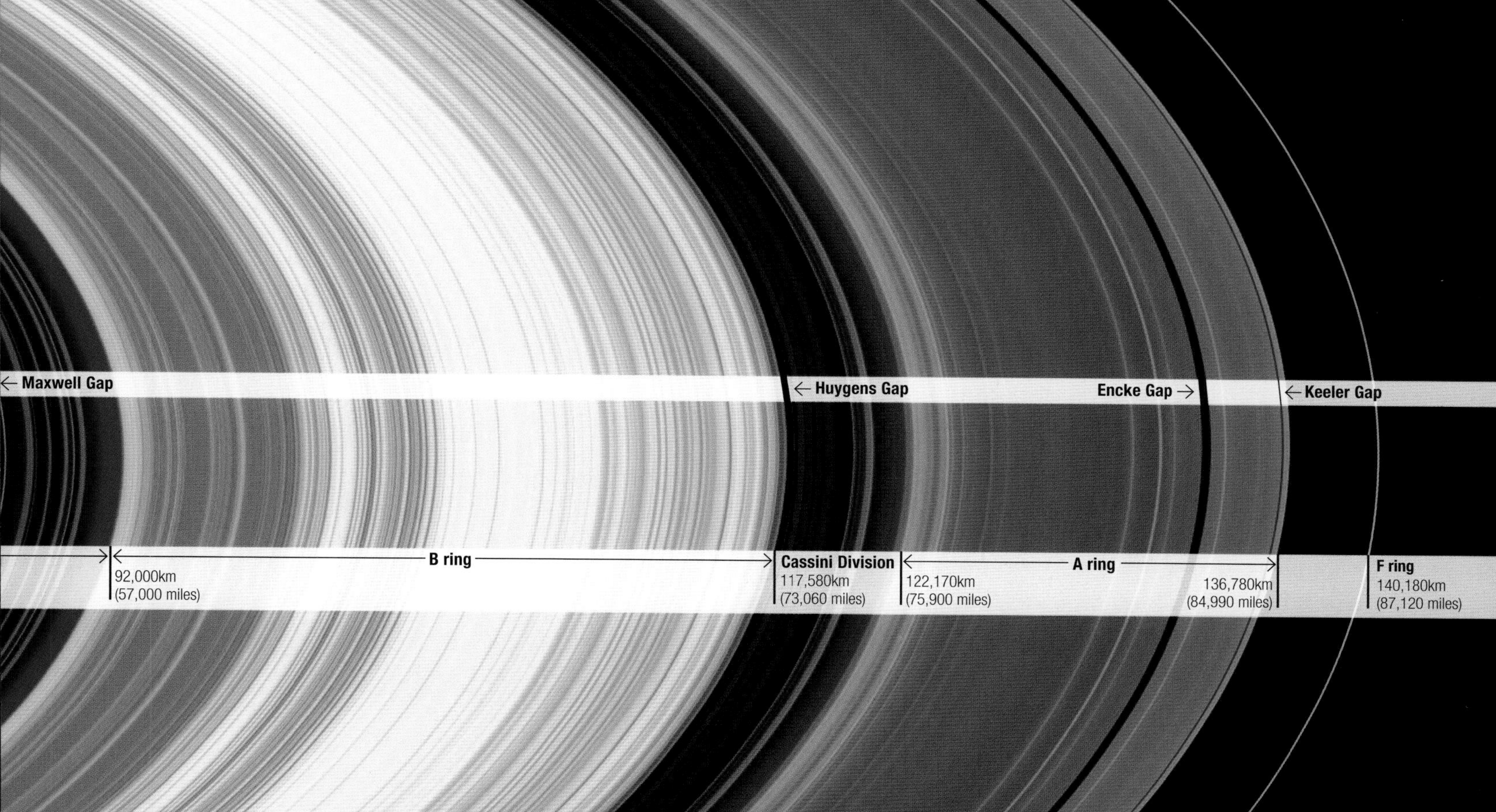

← Maxwell Gap
← Huygens Gap
Encke Gap →
← Keeler Gap
92,000km
(57,000 miles)
B ring
Cassini Division
117,580km
(73,060 miles)
122,170km
(75,900 miles)
A ring
136,780km
(84,990 miles)
F ring
140,180km
(87,120 miles)

▽ Outer rings
Beyond Saturn's familiar main rings are several hazier, darker, and much less sharply defined outer rings. These tenuous haloes of dust and ice become visible only with the use of special imaging techniques. Below, a backlit view of Saturn, with the Sun obscured by the planet's disc, reveals the faint E ring. This cloud of microscopic particles is fed by the plumes of ice that erupt from the surface of Enceladus, one of Saturn's most interesting moons. Unlike the slim main rings, the E ring is more than 2,000km (1,250 miles) thick.

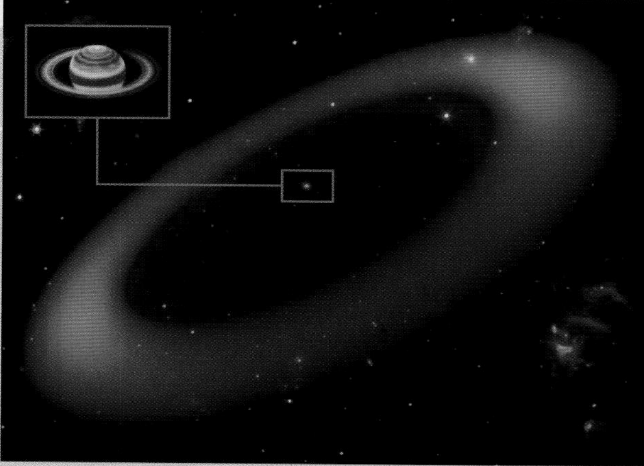

◁ The Phoebe ring
In 2009, astronomers using NASA's infrared Spitzer Space Telescope discovered a vast ring of dust thought to be produced by meteor impacts on one of Saturn's outer moons, Phoebe. Tilted at 27 degrees to the other rings, the Phoebe ring begins at around 4 million km (2.5 million miles) from Saturn and extends outwards for more than three times that distance.

DESTINATION
SATURN'S RINGS

THE B RING IS THE LARGEST, BRIGHTEST, AND MOST DENSELY PACKED OF SATURN'S RINGS. HERE, GIANT BOULDERS OF SPARKLING ICE FLOAT ALONGSIDE ONE ANOTHER IN A SEEMINGLY IMPOSSIBLE ORBITAL BALLET. THE DENSE DISC OF DEBRIS SPELLS DOOM FOR ANYTHING THAT ATTEMPTS TO CROSS ITS PATH.

While the plane of particles orbiting Saturn extends to many times the planet's own diameter, and contains trillions of objects, the particles' individual paths are remarkably uniform – each follows a near-perfect circular orbit in a plane directly above Saturn's equator. Objects straying into more elliptical orbits or attempting to cross the plane soon collide with their neighbours and are nudged back into more orderly paths. Fragments produced by recent collisions are everywhere, gleaming brightly in the sunlight as they slowly attempt to reassemble under their own gravitational attraction.

Artist's impression of B ring

The main rings lie within Saturn's **Roche lobe** – a region where the planet's gravity prevents them from coalescing into a **single moon.**

LOCATION

B ring, 50,000km (31,000 miles) above Saturn's cloud tops

SPIRAL WAVES

Material in the B ring is not uniform – it is spread out unevenly due to density waves. These are caused by changes in Saturn's gravity, when the planet is shaken by internal tremors.

30 MILLION BILLION TONNES – THE TOTAL MASS OF SATURN'S RINGS

CLUMPING

This computer simulation, based on observations by Cassini, shows how ring particles gradually coalesce. They slowly clump together to form more substantial moonlets that are eventually shattered in collisions, thus causing the cycle to repeat.

SATURN UP CLOSE

BENEATH AN OUTER HAZE OF BRIGHT AMMONIA CLOUDS THAT GIVE THE ENTIRE PLANET A SEPIA TINT, SATURN'S DEEP GASEOUS ATMOSPHERE IS JUST AS ACTIVE AND TURBULENT AS THAT OF ITS INNER NEIGHBOUR, JUPITER.

Orbiting almost twice as far from the Sun as Jupiter, Saturn receives only a quarter as much solar heat, and so the upper layers of its atmosphere are considerably colder, averaging about –140°C (–220°F). At such low temperatures, atmospheric ammonia freezes into ice crystals, cloaking the planet in a layer of thin, hazy cloud. Beneath this outer cloud layer, however, Saturn is wracked by storms, high winds, and lightning, driven not only by heat from the Sun but also by Saturn's own internal energy.

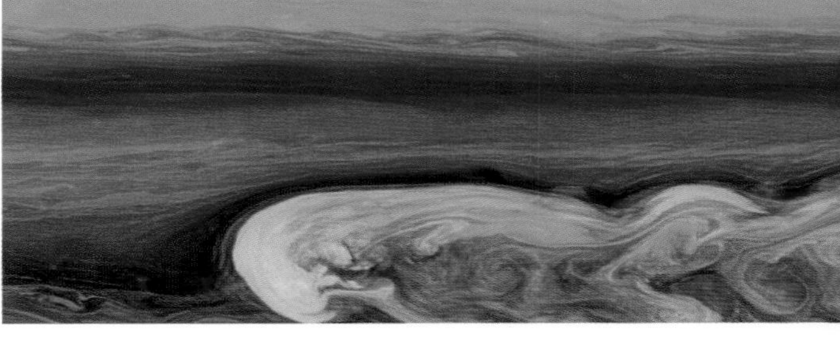

△ **Colourful stream**
This infrared image from the Cassini spacecraft unwraps the full extent of a great white spot that appeared in 2010 and grew rapidly through 2011. High clouds at the head of the storm system (left) suggest that the original spot formed from an upwelling of warm material from inside the planet, perhaps linked to seasonal changes.

▽ **White storms**
Saturn's most prominent weather features are large white spots that periodically erupt in its northern hemisphere. The spots recur roughly every 29 years and usually coincide with the onset of the northern summer, suggesting they are triggered by an increase in heat from the Sun. As they develop, the spots can wrap themselves around the planet to form pale, turbulent bands.

Stormy skies

Saturn's atmosphere has a banded appearance with some resemblance to that of Jupiter, albeit with broader bands and less contrast between light and dark regions. Hidden within these bands, long-lived storms crackle with powerful lightning. They can be detected from the radio signals they emit, but occasionally the storms also erupt into visibility on Saturn's surface as seasonal "great white spots".

△ **Cloud bands**
Saturn's bluish-coloured clouds tend to be made up of water vapour, while the higher red-orange ones are largely formed from ammonium hydrosulphide. Colour and temperature variations are exaggerated in this Cassini infrared image. Dark and light bands seem to move in opposite directions, but this is an illusion caused by their rotation at different rates.

Saturn's winds are the second fastest in the Solar System.

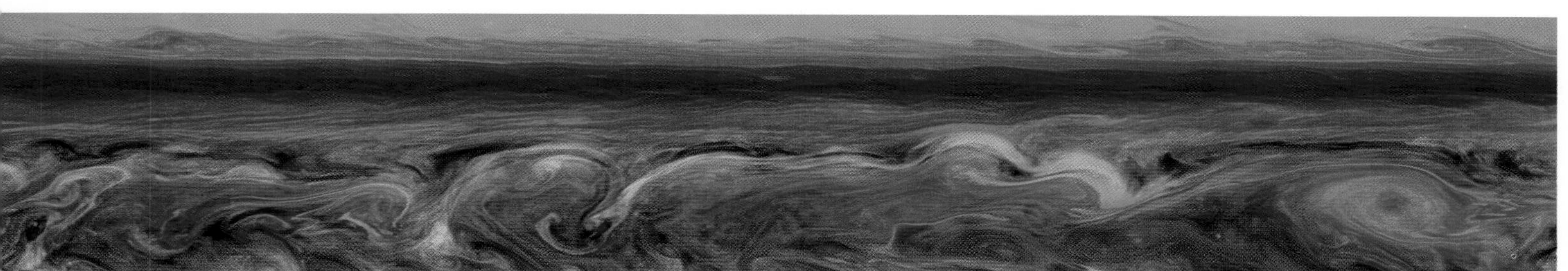

Polar regions

Saturn's axis of rotation is tilted at a similar angle to that of Earth, giving it a cycle of seasons like our own planet's, with each pole spending roughly half of Saturn's long year in permanent darkness. This gives polar regions very different weather from the rest of the planet. Each pole is dominated by a swirling, hurricane-like vortex with a cloudless "eye" at its centre.

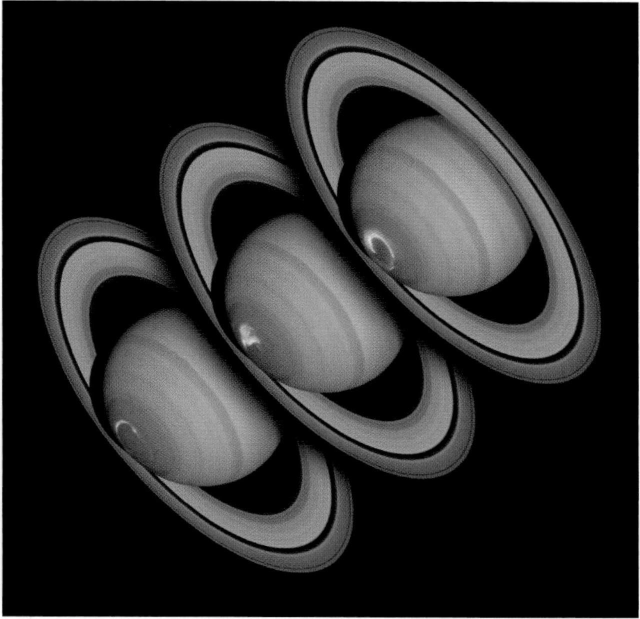

▷ **Southern lights**
Saturn's powerful magnetic field draws in charged particles from the solar wind and channels them into the upper atmosphere around the poles. There they collide with gas molecules, causing the molecules to emit light and produce beautiful aurorae, as seen in these images from the Hubble Space Telescope.

▷ **Southern hot spot**
This infrared image from Cassini reveals heat emanating from deep inside Saturn, with colder, overlying cloud bands revealed in silhouette. Powered by internal contraction, Saturn radiates 2.5 times more energy than it receives from the Sun, but astronomers are not sure why so much of it escapes around the south pole.

△ **Northern rose**
This Cassini close-up focuses on the eye of Saturn's north polar vortex, revealing the sharp division between high surrounding clouds (colour-coded green in the image) and the much deeper clouds within the eye (red). The eye is an impressive 2,000km (1,250 miles) across, and wind speeds around it reach 530kph (330mph).

▽ **Hexagonal hurricane**
Saturn's north polar vortex is surrounded by a remarkable hexagonal cloud structure that has persisted at least since the Voyager flybys of the early 1980s. The geometric pattern is thought to arise at the boundary between different atmospheric zones that are moving at contrasting speeds. Each side of the hexagon is longer than the diameter of Earth.

SATURN IN THE SPOTLIGHT

This remarkable, natural-colour view of Saturn and its rings is a mosaic of more than 120 photographs. The images were captured by the NASA spacecraft Cassini in 2004, a few months after it arrived at Saturn to begin an initial four-year study of the gas giant and its system of rings and moons. Still in orbit today, Cassini is the first and only spacecraft to orbit Saturn and has returned images of unprecedented detail and clarity. At the top of this image, shadows cast by the rings can be seen sharply etched across the north polar region. When these photographs were taken, Saturn had just passed its northern winter solstice, and the pole had assumed the azure-blue tint characteristic of Saturnian winters. The pale blue oval spots just discernible in a band around the southern hemisphere are storms in Saturn's atmosphere.

THE **SATURN** SYSTEM

A HUGE FAMILY OF MOONS SURROUND SATURN. THEY RANGE FROM PLANET-SIZED WORLDS WITH COMPLEX ATMOSPHERES AND ACTIVE SURFACES TO SMALL LUMPS OF ROCK AND ICE TRAPPED IN ORBIT BY THE PLANET'S GRAVITY.

Saturn has 62 officially recognized satellites, 53 of which have been named. The dividing line between moons, "moonlets", and large particles of ring material is not clear cut, so a precise count of Saturn's moons may never be agreed. The innermost moons orbit within the planet's ring system, sitting in small gaps in the rings that are kept clear by the moons' gravity; these are known as shepherd moons. The outermost moons follow wildly eccentric orbits that can take them tens of millions of kilometres away from Saturn. In contrast, Saturn's largest moons mostly follow circular orbits relatively close to the planet, but outside the main rings.

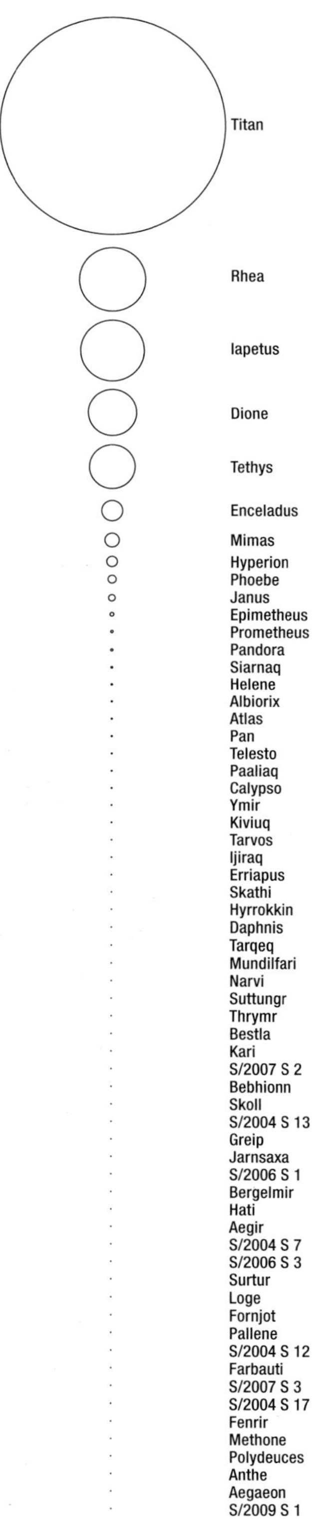
Titan
Rhea
Iapetus
Dione
Tethys
Enceladus
Mimas
Hyperion
Phoebe
Janus
Epimetheus
Prometheus
Pandora
Siarnaq
Helene
Albiorix
Atlas
Pan
Telesto
Paaliaq
Calypso
Ymir
Kiviuq
Tarvos
Ijiraq
Erriapus
Skathi
Hyrrokkin
Daphnis
Tarqeq
Mundilfari
Narvi
Suttungr
Thrymr
Bestla
Kari
S/2007 S 2
Bebhionn
Skoll
S/2004 S 13
Greip
Jarnsaxa
S/2006 S 1
Bergelmir
Hati
Aegir
S/2004 S 7
S/2006 S 3
Surtur
Loge
Fornjot
Pallene
S/2004 S 12
Farbauti
S/2007 S 3
S/2004 S 17
Fenrir
Methone
Polydeuces
Anthe
Aegaeon
S/2009 S 1

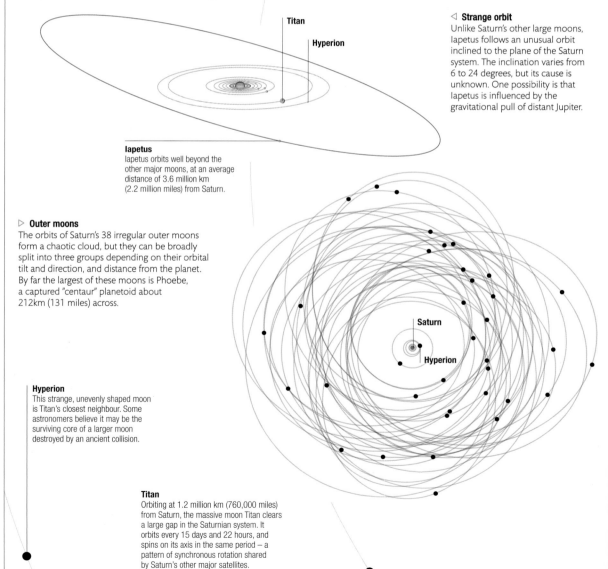

Moons to scale
Saturn's satellites are dominated by the huge bulk of Titan. All the other moons are far smaller, and scientists speculate that Titan's formation stunted the growth of its neighbours.

◁ **Strange orbit**
Unlike Saturn's other large moons, Iapetus follows an unusual orbit inclined to the plane of the Saturn system. The inclination varies from 6 to 24 degrees, but its cause is unknown. One possibility is that Iapetus is influenced by the gravitational pull of distant Jupiter.

Iapetus
Iapetus orbits well beyond the other major moons, at an average distance of 3.6 million km (2.2 million miles) from Saturn.

▷ **Outer moons**
The orbits of Saturn's 38 irregular outer moons form a chaotic cloud, but they can be broadly split into three groups depending on their orbital tilt and direction, and distance from the planet. By far the largest of these moons is Phoebe, a captured "centaur" planetoid about 212km (131 miles) across.

Hyperion
This strange, unevenly shaped moon is Titan's closest neighbour. Some astronomers believe it may be the surviving core of a larger moon destroyed by an ancient collision.

Titan
Orbiting at 1.2 million km (760,000 miles) from Saturn, the massive moon Titan clears a large gap in the Saturnian system. It orbits every 15 days and 22 hours, and spins on its axis in the same period – a pattern of synchronous rotation shared by Saturn's other major satellites.

More than **150 moonlets** have been detected within Saturn's rings.

▽ **Inner moons**
Saturn's inner 24 moons mostly follow regular orbits, moving in the same direction as Saturn's rotation and staying in the same plane as the rings. These regular moons likely formed from material left over from Saturn's formation, unlike the irregular outer moons, which were captured later. The inner moons include seven major moons, the largest of which – Titan – is bigger than Mercury.

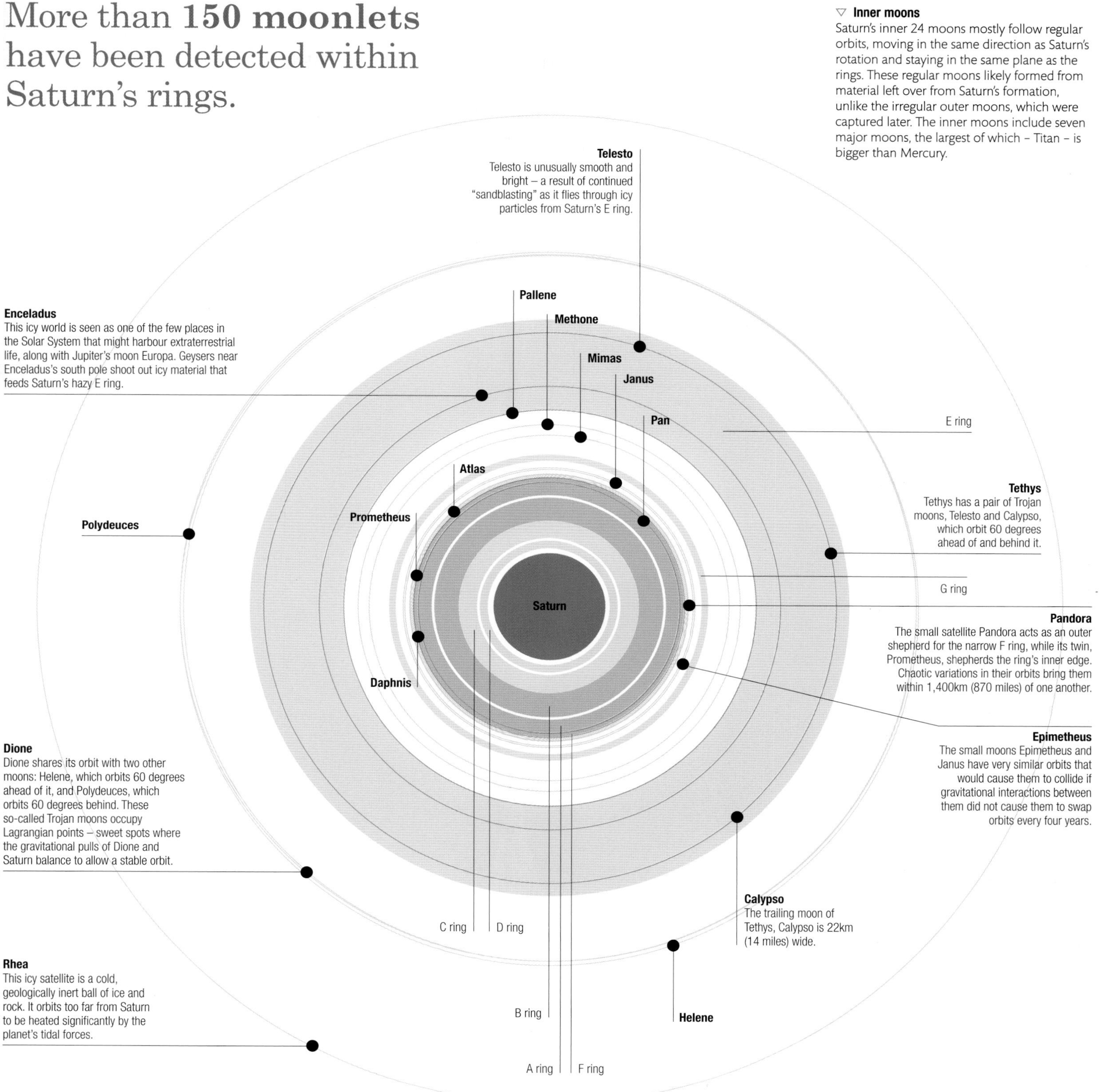
Telesto
Telesto is unusually smooth and bright – a result of continued "sandblasting" as it flies through icy particles from Saturn's E ring.
Enceladus
This icy world is seen as one of the few places in the Solar System that might harbour extraterrestrial life, along with Jupiter's moon Europa. Geysers near Enceladus's south pole shoot out icy material that feeds Saturn's hazy E ring.
Pallene
Methone
Mimas
Janus
Pan
E ring
Atlas
Prometheus
Polydeuces
Tethys
Tethys has a pair of Trojan moons, Telesto and Calypso, which orbit 60 degrees ahead of and behind it.
G ring
Saturn
Pandora
The small satellite Pandora acts as an outer shepherd for the narrow F ring, while its twin, Prometheus, shepherds the ring's inner edge. Chaotic variations in their orbits bring them within 1,400km (870 miles) of one another.
Daphnis
Epimetheus
The small moons Epimetheus and Janus have very similar orbits that would cause them to collide if gravitational interactions between them did not cause them to swap orbits every four years.
Dione
Dione shares its orbit with two other moons: Helene, which orbits 60 degrees ahead of it, and Polydeuces, which orbits 60 degrees behind. These so-called Trojan moons occupy Lagrangian points – sweet spots where the gravitational pulls of Dione and Saturn balance to allow a stable orbit.
Calypso
The trailing moon of Tethys, Calypso is 22km (14 miles) wide.
C ring
D ring
Rhea
This icy satellite is a cold, geologically inert ball of ice and rock. It orbits too far from Saturn to be heated significantly by the planet's tidal forces.
B ring
Helene
A ring
F ring

SATURN'S MAJOR MOONS

SEVEN OF SATURN'S MOONS ARE LARGE ENOUGH FOR GRAVITY TO HAVE PULLED THEM INTO ROUGHLY SPHERICAL SHAPES. SOME OF THESE HAVE BEEN DEAD WORLDS FOR BILLIONS OF YEARS, BUT OTHERS ARE GEOLOGICALLY ACTIVE.

Saturn's major moons are named after giants in Greek mythology. In order of distance from the planet, they are Mimas, Enceladus, Tethys, Dione, Rhea, Titan, and Iapetus. They range in size from Mimas, which is a mere 396km (246 miles) wide, to mighty Titan, which at 5,150km (3,200 miles) in diameter is 50 per cent wider than Earth's moon. Titan was the first Saturnian moon to be discovered, in 1655. By 1789 all seven major moons had been located and named.

Dense atmosphere

The dark regions on Titan's surface may be dry seabeds.

Light areas are regions of higher ground.

▷ **Titan**
Larger than Mercury and Pluto, Titan is the only moon in the Solar System with a significant atmosphere, and the only body besides Earth with nitrogen-rich "air". Composed of rock and ice, it has an average surface temperature of around −180 °C (−292 °F). Despite the cold, its dense atmosphere traps enough heat energy to drive a complex weather cycle, with liquid methane on the surface evaporating and raining back down like water on Earth. Titan also shows evidence of "cryovolcanic" eruptions of slushy ice onto the surface.

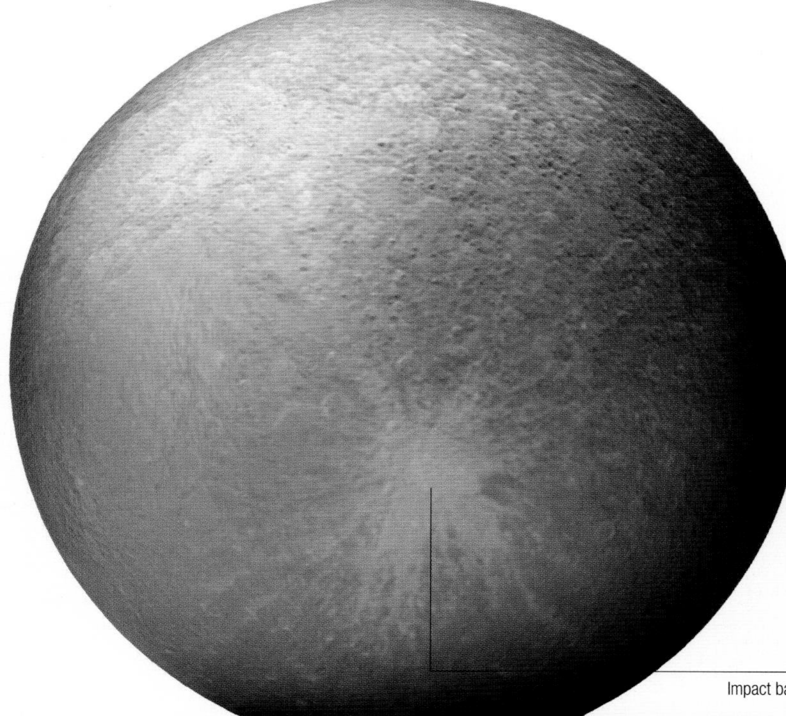

Impact basin

△ **Rhea**
Rhea is the second largest Saturnian moon, but it is a great deal smaller than our Moon. It is a ball of ice and rock that has compressed under its own gravity to create an unusually dense form of ice. Rhea's heavily cratered surface, which includes two large impact basins, suggests it has been geologically inactive for billions of years.

Engelier Crater

△ **Iapetus**
The outermost of Saturn's major moons has a curious appearance, with a dark leading hemisphere and a much brighter trailing one. The dark pattern may be caused by deposits of carbon dust from Saturn's Phoebe ring. The sooty dust absorbs extra heat from the Sun, causing surface ice to evaporate and making the affected area even darker.

Cliffs, formed by the fracturing of crust
Ithaca Chasma is a 2,000km (1,250mile) long canyon.
Long fractures known as sulci run across the surface of Enceladus.
Herschel Crater

△ **Dione**
This mid-sized icy moon has a heavily cratered surface and contains substantial amounts of denser rock within. Large-scale variations in the frequency of craters on Dione's surface suggest that some areas were smoothed out in the past by the eruption of cryovolcanoes. A network of faults across Dione's trailing hemisphere appears from a distance as bright streaks.

△ **Tethys**
Superficially similar to Dione, Tethys is lower in density, suggesting it consists of almost pure water ice. Although heavily cratered, it seems to have been active more recently than its neighbours and has large, smooth plains formed by cryovolcanic activity. Ithaca Chasma, a canyon-like surface crack, probably formed as Tethys's interior froze and expanded.

Enceladus △
This small moon is pulled in a gravitational tug of war between Saturn and Dione, which causes internal friction and heating. Melted ice erupts through the surface as vapour and water, forming spectacular geysers around the south pole. The fountains of ice are the source of the material in Saturn's faint E ring.

△ **Mimas**
Mimas is one of the smallest bodies in the Solar System to have become spherical through its own gravity. Its pitted surface is dominated by the massive Herschel Crater, which measures 130km (86 miles) wide. The impact that created this crater almost destroyed Mimas.

DESTINATION **LIGEIA MARE**

IN THE FAR NORTH OF SATURN'S LARGEST MOON, TITAN, IS A GLASSY LAKE SO HUGE THAT A PERSON STANDING ON THE SHORE WOULD SEE NO END TO IT. THIS IS LIGEIA MARE, WHICH IS NOT WATER BUT METHANE – A GAS THAT LIQUEFIES IN COLD AS INTENSE AS TITAN'S.

Several seas or large lakes of liquid hydrocarbon chemicals such as ethane and methane have been discovered near Titan's poles. Ligeia Mare is one of the biggest, larger than any of Earth's great freshwater lakes. Radar signals from NASA's Cassini orbiter have penetrated the lake and bounced back from its floor, revealing its depth and suggesting that it is composed of more or less pure methane. The surface is smooth and flat, though seasonal weather changes might stir up disturbances. Ligeia Mare's ragged shoreline is broken by bays and coves. Some areas of the shore flatten out into smooth beaches, or possibly methane mudflats; elsewhere the terrain is rougher and rises into hummocks.

The **amount of methane** in Ligeia Mare is estimated to be **40 times greater** than Earth's global reserves of liquid fuels.

Artist's impression based on Cassini radar and altimeter data

LOCATION

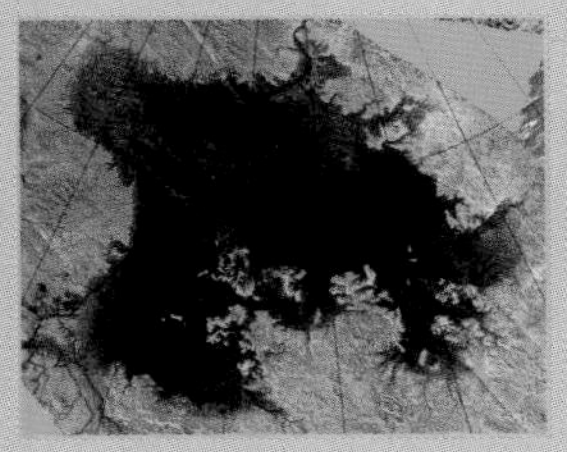

Latitude 80°N; **longitude** 248°W

170M (560FT)
DEPTH OF LIGEIA MARE RECORDED BY RADAR SIGNALS FROM CASSINI ORBITER

LAKE PROFILE

Ligeia Mare is located close to Titan's north pole, along with the majority of the moon's lakes, and covers an area of approximately 126,000km² (48,650 sq miles). The lake has a shoreline of some 2,000km (1,240 miles) and, unlike the few lakes in the south, shows no signs of shrinkage due to evaporation of chemicals. Such differences may be linked to seasonal cycles in the opposing hemispheres.

Cassini radar image of Ligeia Mare. Smooth liquid areas are shown in blue.

Satellite view of Lake Superior (top) in North America to scale with Ligeia Mare.

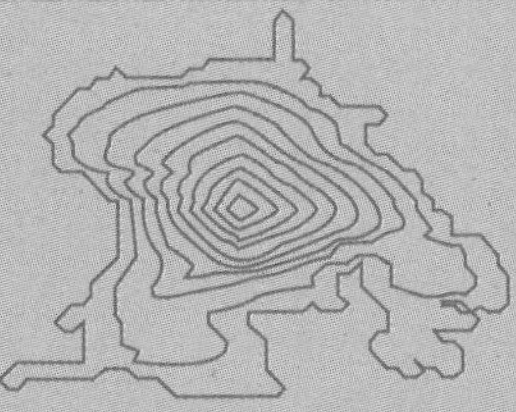

NASA profile of the lake floor showing depth to an estimated maximum of 210m (690ft) in the centre.

TITANIC RIVER

Dramatic evidence of methane rain and liquid run-off on Titan is provided by Cassini images of a 400km (250 mile) river that drains into Ligeia Mare. It is named Vid Flumina after a poisonous river in Norse mythology.

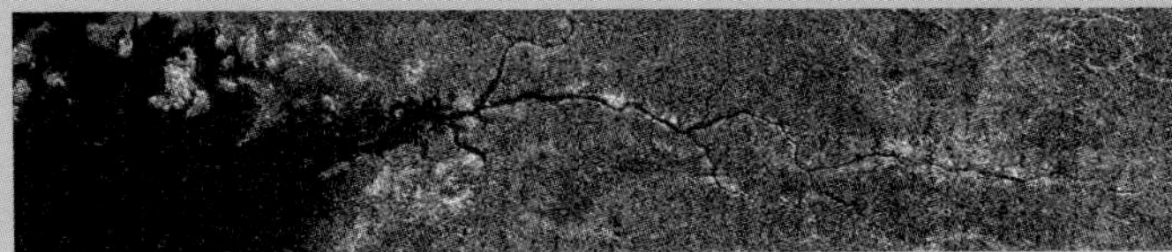

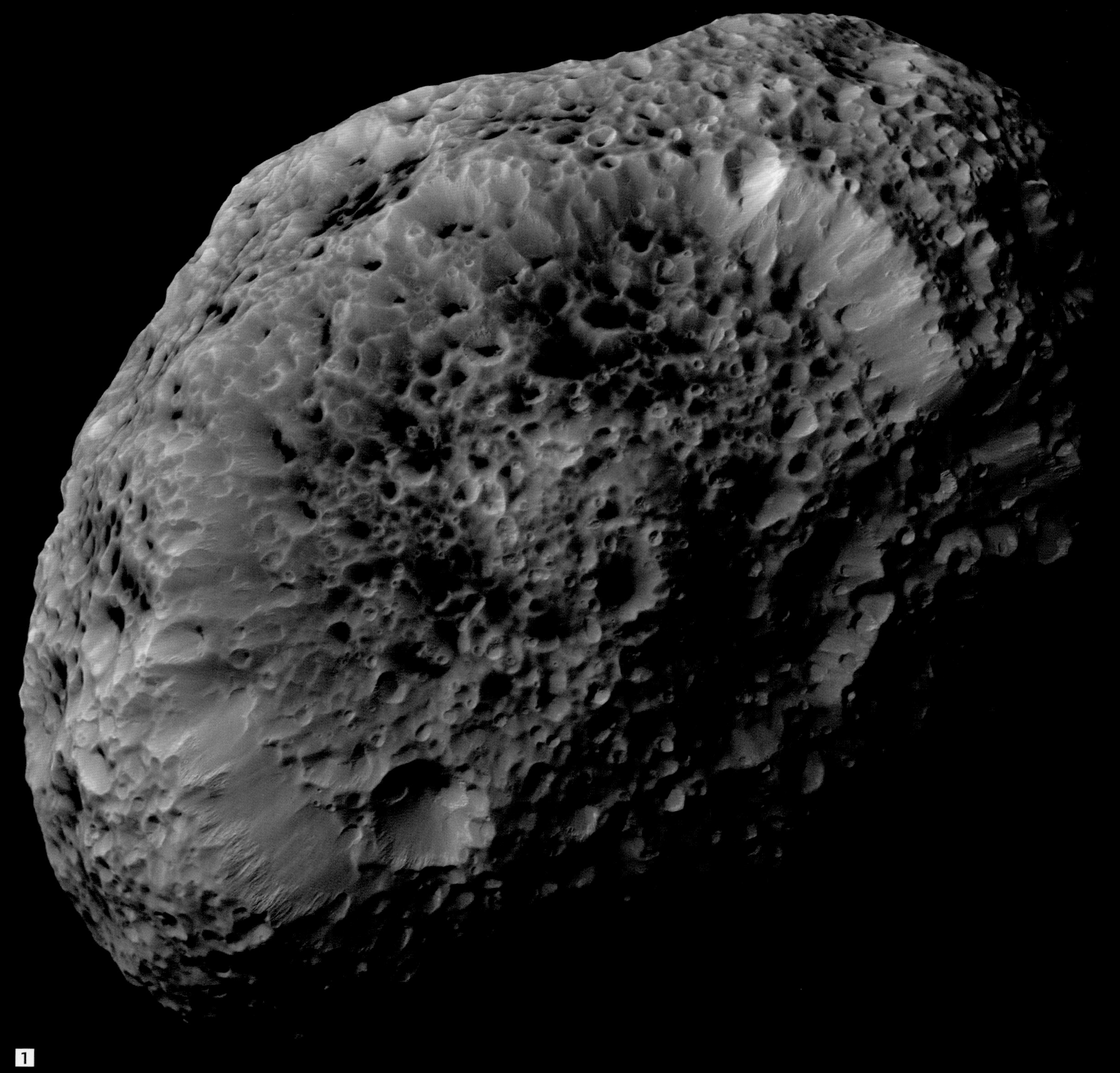
1

CASSINI'S **VIEW**

1 Hyperion
NASA's Cassini spacecraft has captured many spectacular images during its tour of the Saturn system, including this close-up of one of Saturn's oddest moons. Hyperion is not quite large enough for gravity to pull it into a sphere. Its odd shape, chaotic rotation, and sponge-like surface suggest it is a fragment of a larger moon destroyed in a collision.

2 Dione
During a close encounter with Saturn's small, icy moon Dione, Cassini captured this breathtaking view across a sunlit crescent. Deep shadows starkly delineate the rims of impact craters on Dione's meteorite-scarred face. Much of the moon's surface is heavily pitted with such craters, some of the largest exceeding 100km (62 miles) in diameter.

3 Mimas
Dwarfed by its parent, Saturn's innermost major moon Mimas hangs against the backdrop of the planet's northern hemisphere. The dark bands across Saturn's cloudscape are shadows cast by the rings onto the winter hemisphere. The scattering of sunlight through the relatively cloud-free northern sky tints the atmosphere blue.

4 Titan
Magnification diminishes the huge size difference between Saturn and its haze-covered moon Titan in this view. Titan's orbit is in the same plane as the rings of Saturn. The dense A and B rings cast a broad, dark band of shadow onto Saturn's southern hemisphere, with the Cassini Division creating a bright split within it.

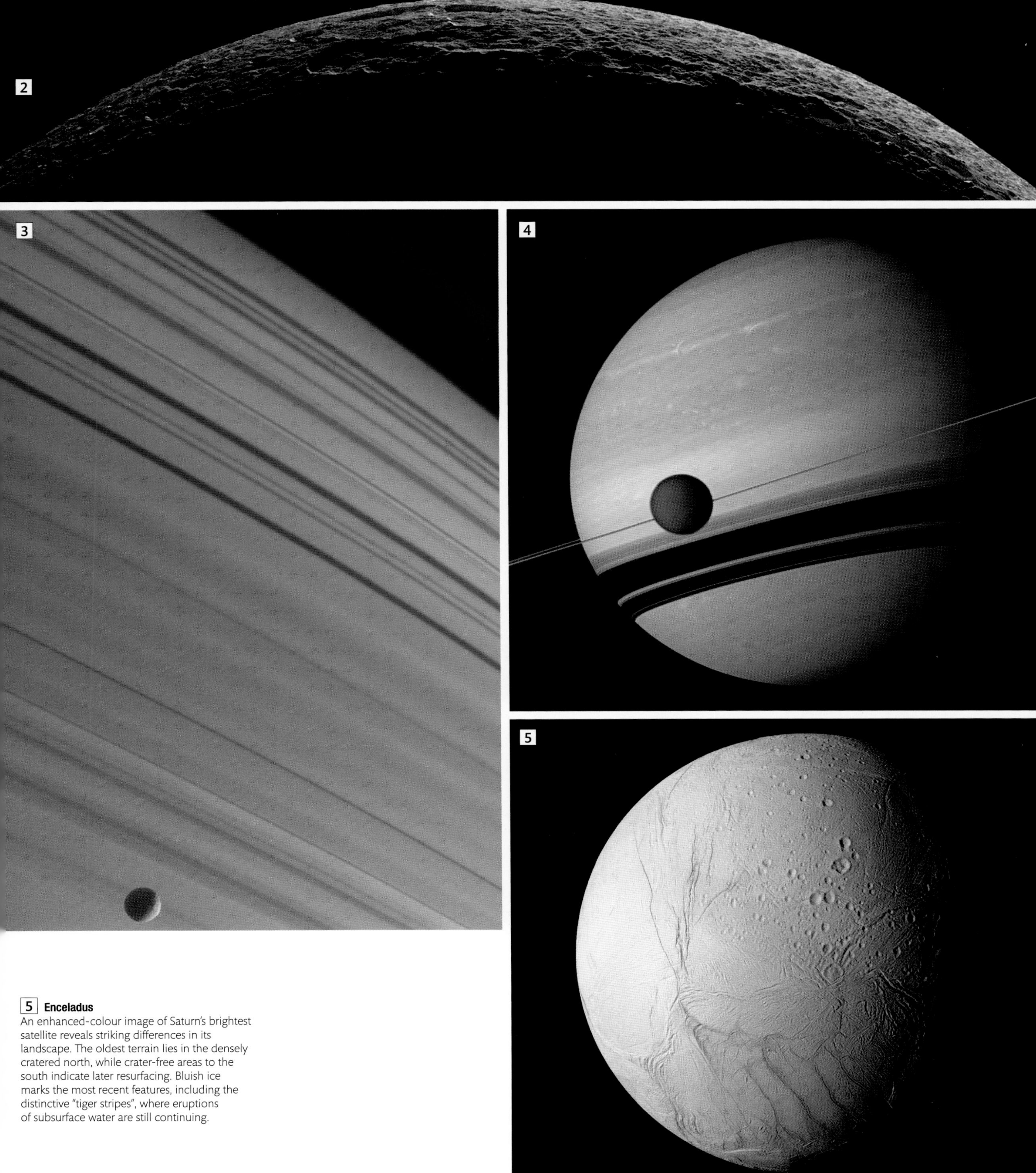
2
3
4
5

5 Enceladus
An enhanced-colour image of Saturn's brightest satellite reveals striking differences in its landscape. The oldest terrain lies in the densely cratered north, while crater-free areas to the south indicate later resurfacing. Bluish ice marks the most recent features, including the distinctive "tiger stripes", where eruptions of subsurface water are still continuing.

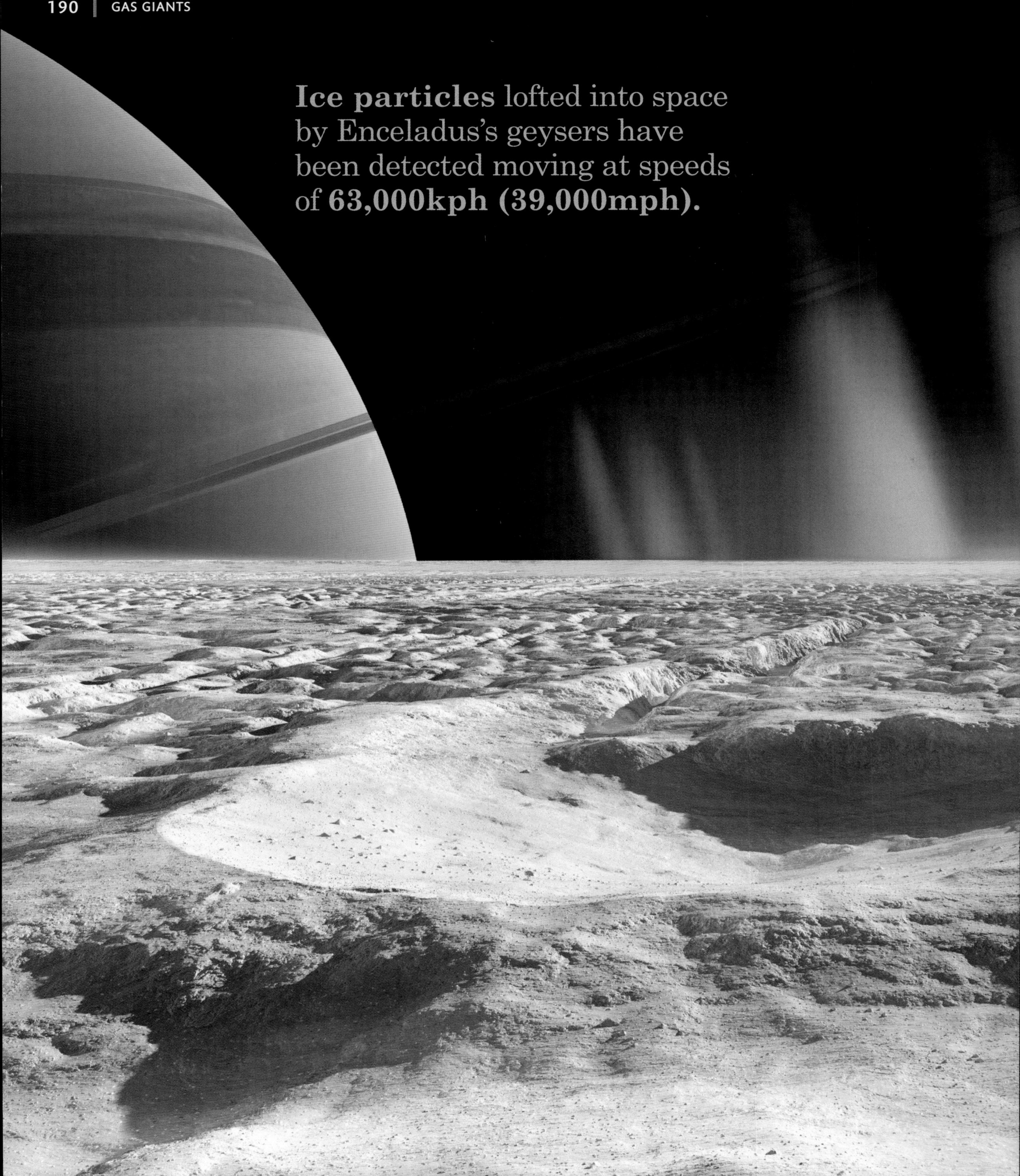

Ice particles lofted into space by Enceladus's geysers have been detected moving at speeds of **63,000kph (39,000mph).**

DESTINATION ENCELADUS

A BRIGHT MOON WITHIN SATURN'S E RING, ENCELADUS IS SO TINY THAT A VISITOR COULD HIKE AROUND ITS EQUATOR IN TWO WEEKS. LOOKING SOUTH, THE TRAVELLER WOULD SEE THE MOON'S VAST ICE GEYSERS SHOOTING ABOVE THE HORIZON.

The thick layer of bright snow that blankets Enceladus ensures that the surface of this tiny satellite remains cold as it reflects light and heat from the distant Sun. However, tidal forces, generated as Enceladus is pulled in different directions by Saturn and outer moons such as Dione, warm the interior enough to generate pockets of subterranean meltwater. Near the south pole, where tidal flexing creates deep fissures known as "tiger stripes", the water erupts to the surface, where it violently boils into the vacuum of space as a mix of vapour and ice crystals.

LOCATION

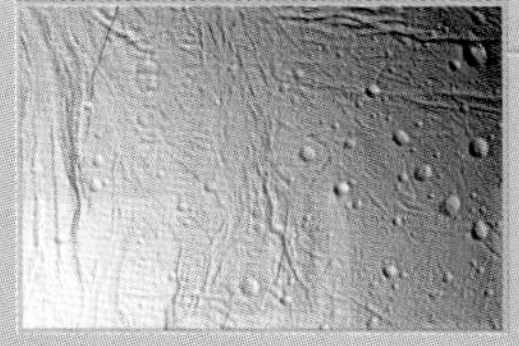

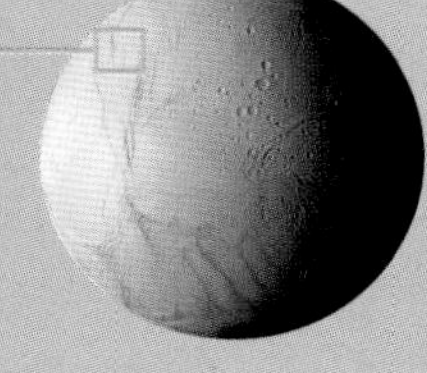

Latitude 4°N; **longitude** 209°W

COLD GEYSERS

Heat generated by tidal forces creates a reservoir of meltwater in Enceladus's interior. Under pressure, this erupts from the surface in jets of water vapour and ice particles.

Water vapour and ice particles
Vent to surface
Pressurized liquid water pocket
Hot rock
Tidal heating

SPECTACULAR PLUMES

This image from NASA's Cassini spacecraft shows icy plumes from Enceladus's geysers streaming high into space. The view is colour enhanced to reveal the density of the plumes more clearly.

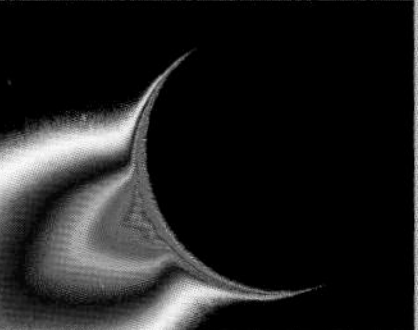

Artist's impression based on Cassini images

LORD OF THE RINGS

BEAUTIFUL SATURN HAS ENCHANTED ASTRONOMERS EVER SINCE THE PLANET'S RINGS WERE FIRST SEEN THROUGH A TELESCOPE. MORE RECENTLY, SPACECRAFT HAVE REVEALED THE PLANET'S MOONS TO BE JUST AS FASCINATING.

Before spacecraft discovered rings around other planets, those around Saturn were thought to be unique. Although first seen in the 17th century, the rings remained a mystery for nearly 250 years before physicist James Clerk Maxwell explained their true nature. While few features on Saturn itself were seen until the mid-19th century, improving telescopes revealed structures and divisions within the rings, as well as a host of orbiting moons. However, it was not until the first interplanetary missions that astronomers began to grasp the complexity of the Saturnian system.

Ptolemy observing Saturn

127

The outermost world
For early astronomers, Saturn has special significance as the slowest of the five known planets. Greek scholar Ptolemy places Saturn on the outermost of the crystal spheres he believes surround Earth, with only a shell of the fixed stars beyond it.

Galileo's interpretation of Saturn's rings

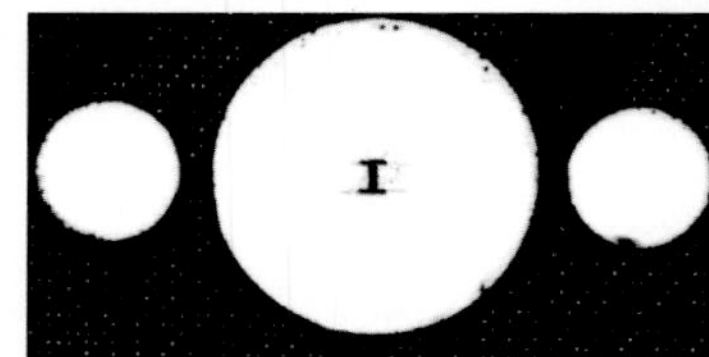

1610

Saturn's strange shape
The crude telescope of Galileo Galilei reveals that Saturn has a strange shape, leading the Italian scientist to suspect it has jug-like "handles" or is orbited by two big moons. Unbeknown to Galileo, he has seen a distorted view of the planet's rings.

Voyager 1 image of Titan

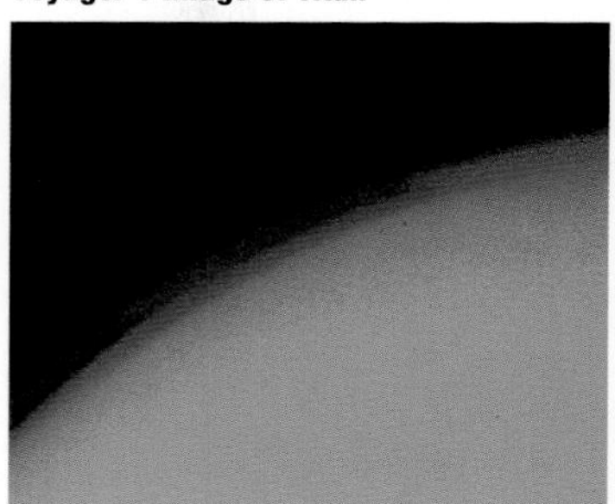

1980

First look at Titan
NASA's Voyager 1 spacecraft reaches Saturn. Its trajectory is revised to take it close to the giant moon Titan, allowing it to send back the first close-up images. Titan's thick atmosphere makes the surface beneath impossible to see.

Fine ring structures

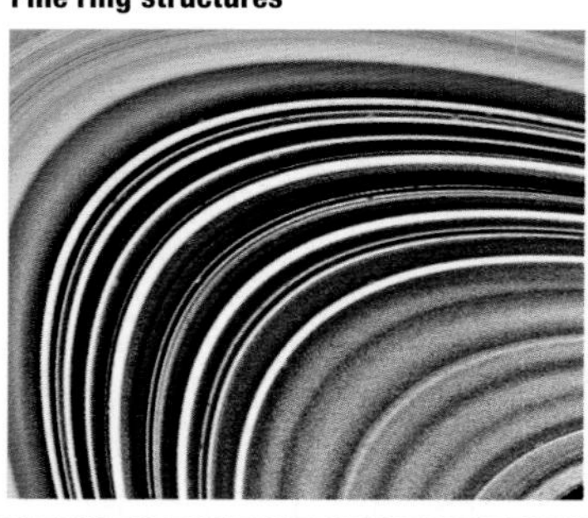

1981

Structure in the rings
Voyager 2 arrives at Saturn eight months after its sibling. Together, the Voyagers image all the major moons and reveal fine details within the rings, including individual ringlets and radial "spokes" of darker material rippling out across the ring system.

Saturn's large outer moon, Phoebe

2004

Phoebe flyby
After a long journey, NASA's Cassini spacecraft arrives and orbits Saturn. During its final approach, Cassini passes close to Phoebe, the mysterious outer moon. It sends back images of a cratered surface that suggests the moon is a captured comet or minor planet.

Cassini image of Titan

2005

Piercing the veil
Cassini's infrared instruments peer through Titan's hazy atmosphere and photograph the surface. The images reveal a world whose features have apparently been smoothed by erosion processes, such as the flow of liquid methane across the landscape.

Ice plumes over Enceladus

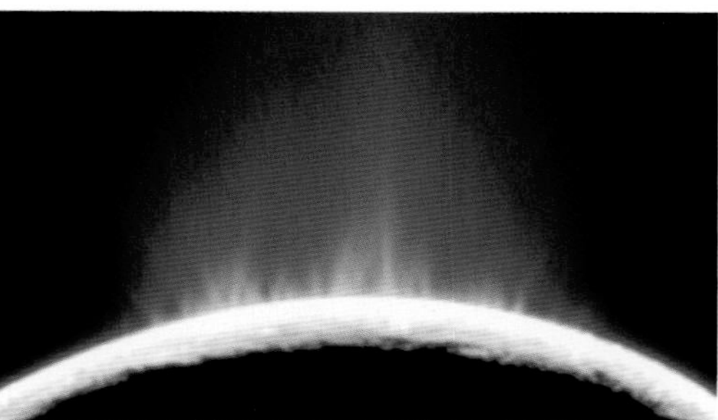

2005

Active Enceladus
During a close encounter with the small, bright moon Enceladus, Cassini sees plumes of icy material erupting hundreds of kilometres into space. Further studies reveal that the active geysers, powered by tidal heating of the moon's interior, emerge from surface faults near the south pole.

A sketch by Huygens showing Saturn's changing appearance

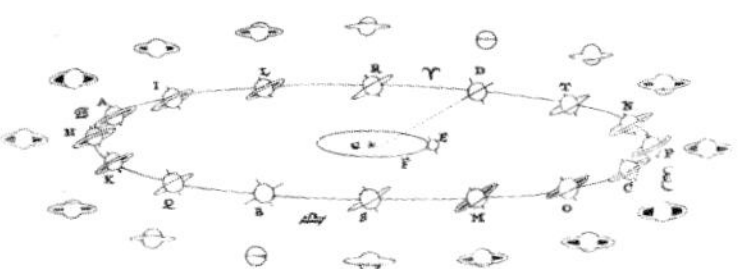

1655

Discovery of the rings
Dutch astronomer and instrument-maker Christiaan Huygens studies Saturn using a powerful telescope of his own design. He concludes that the planet is surrounded by a thin, flat ring. In the same year, Huygens discovers Saturn's largest moon, Titan.

The Paris Observatory

1675

Splitting the rings
At the Paris Observatory, Italian-French astronomer Giovanni Cassini sees a dark circle within the rings – the boundary between the A and B rings, today called the Cassini Division. This is the first hint that the rings have a complex internal structure.

The contrasting hemispheres of Iapetus

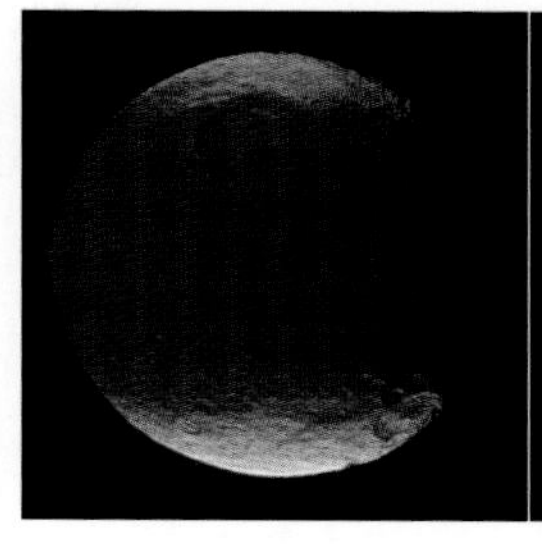

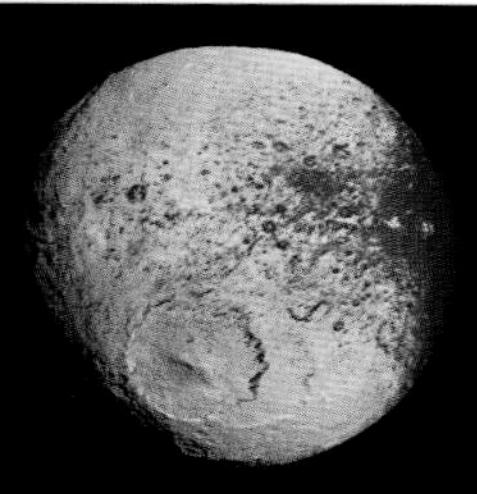

1705

Two-tone moon
Having observed Iapetus on one side of Saturn since 1671, Cassini now detects the moon on the opposite side of the planet, finding that it is much fainter. He correctly concludes that Iapetus has a dark leading hemisphere and a brighter trailing one.

1859

True nature of the rings
James Clerk Maxwell explains the true nature of Saturn's rings for the first time, showing through mathematics that they cannot be solid planes or ringlets, but must instead be made of countless tiny particles following independent, circular orbits.

Will Hay

1933

The Great White Spot
British comic actor and amateur astronomer Will Hay discovers a huge white outburst on Saturn, later confirmed to be a storm similar to spots seen in 1876 and 1903. The Great White Spot is now recognized as Saturn's most prominent recurring weather feature.

Pioneer 11 view of Saturn

1979

Pioneer 11
The first spacecraft to visit Saturn passes the planet at a distance of 21,000km (13,000 miles) and beams back the most detailed images yet of Saturn's rings and atmospheric weather systems. Pioneer 11 also investigates flight paths for the later Voyager missions.

Ontarius Lacus on Titan

2005–2007

Lakes of Titan
Although Cassini's daughter probe, Huygens, lands in a dry equatorial region of Titan in 2005, Cassini's radar later finds lakes around Titan's poles. In 2007, Cassini uses infrared cameras to detect sunlight reflecting from a south polar lake called Ontarius Lacus.

2010

Fine ring structures
Images from Cassini reveal ripples and peaks at the outer edge of the B ring that cast their shadows across the mostly flat plane. These short-lived vertical structures are thought to be caused by the gravitational influence of small moonlets within Saturn's rings.

The 2011 storm eruption

2011

A storm up close
Cassini charts the development of a huge white-spot storm that grows to cover an area more than eight times the size of Earth in Saturn's northern hemisphere. The storm seems to have been driven by warming from the onset of the northern spring.

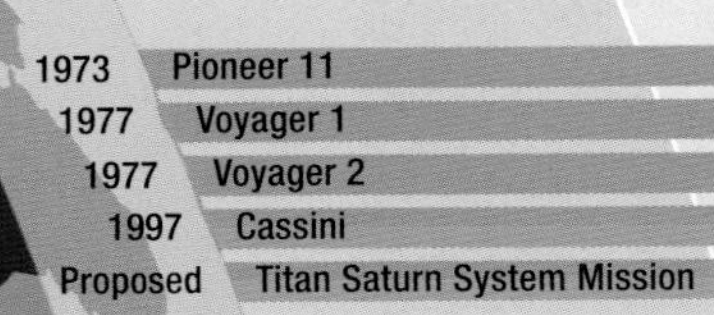

LAUNCH
EARTH ORBIT
JOURNEY TO SATURN
1973 Pioneer 11
1977 Voyager 1
1977 Voyager 2
1997 Cassini
Proposed Titan Saturn System Mission

MISSIONS TO **SATURN**

SATURN AND ITS MOONS HAVE BEEN VISITED BY SEVERAL SPACECRAFT SINCE THE 1970S. THE FIRST MISSIONS WERE FLYBYS, BUT MORE RECENTLY A DECADE-LONG INVESTIGATION WAS UNDERTAKEN BY NASA'S CASSINI ORBITER.

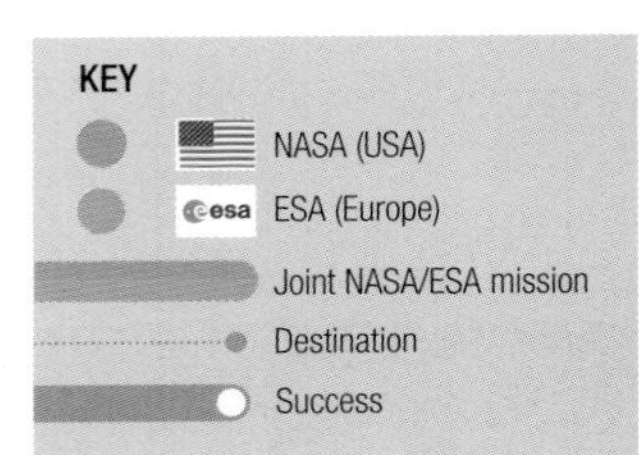

KEY
NASA (USA)
esa
ESA (Europe)
Joint NASA/ESA mission
Destination
Success

Saturn was a key destination for the Pioneer missions that paved the way for the exploration of the outer Solar System. While Pioneer 10 merely flew past Jupiter, Pioneer 11 used a "gravitational slingshot" from the giant planet to propel itself to Saturn in September 1979. The twin Voyager probes arrived in November 1980 and August 1981, and gave the first detailed views of Saturn's intriguing family of moons. Saturn was not revisited until 2004, when Cassini (and its companion, the Huygens Titan probe) became the first craft to orbit the ringed planet.

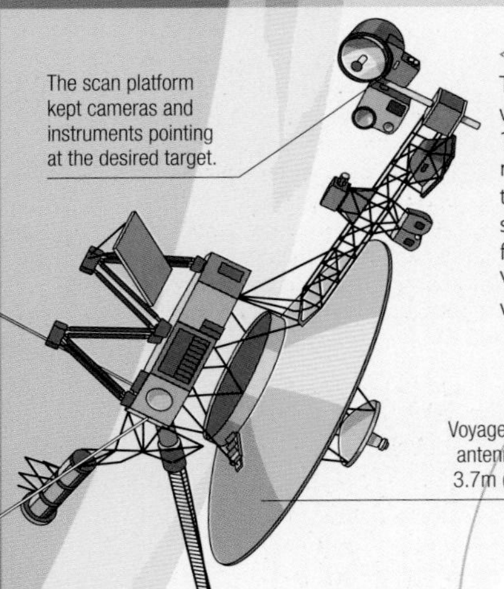

The scan platform kept cameras and instruments pointing at the desired target.
Voyager's high-gain antenna measured 3.7m (12ft) across.
Voyager

◁ Voyager spacecraft
The two identical Voyager spacecraft each weighed around 773kg (1,700lb) and carried 105kg (231lb) of scientific instruments. A large radio dish (high-gain antenna) kept the craft in touch with Earth, while a radioactive power source generated electricity without the need for solar panels. Each mission carried with it a Voyager Golden Record – a gold disc inscribed with information about Earth.

▷ Discoveries
The Voyager flybys confirmed the existence of countless individual ringlets within Saturn's main rings, as well as short-lived structures such as radial spokes. Although Titan's thick atmosphere proved impenetrable, the Voyagers discovered surface features on several of the other moons for the first time, as well as details of Saturn's own weather systems.

Colour-enhanced Voyager 2 image of the rings

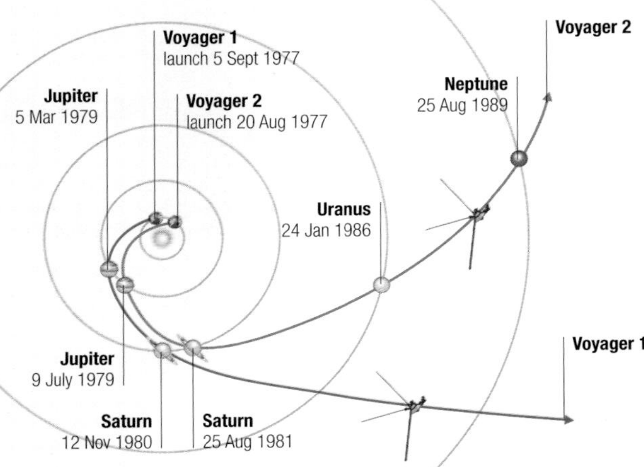

Voyager 1
launch 5 Sept 1977
Voyager 2
launch 20 Aug 1977
Jupiter
5 Mar 1979
Jupiter
9 July 1979
Saturn
12 Nov 1980
Saturn
25 Aug 1981
Uranus
24 Jan 1986
Neptune
25 Aug 1989
Voyager 2
Voyager 1

▷ Mission profile
Voyager 1 travelled considerably faster than Voyager 2, and overtook its sibling on the way to an encounter with Jupiter in 1979. Upon arrival at Saturn, Voyager 1 flew close to Titan before leaving the plane of the Solar System. Voyager 2 moved on to visit Uranus and Neptune.

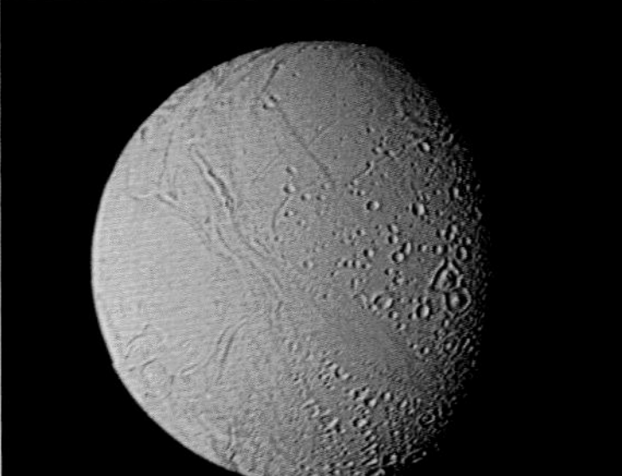
False-colour Voyager 2 view of Enceladus

FLYBY

ORBITER

Saturn's moons **Titan** and **Enceladus** are key targets for **future missions.**

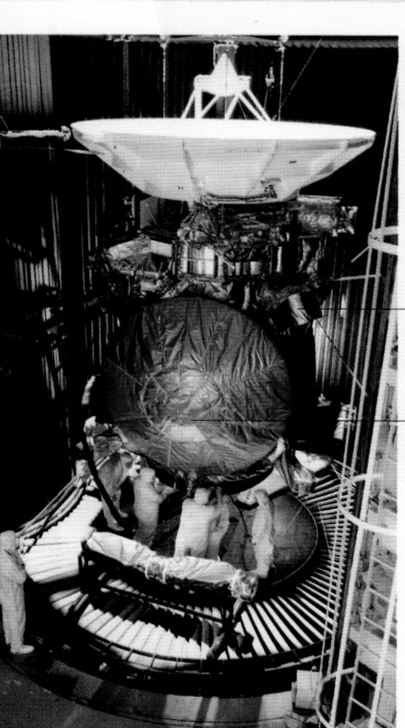

◁ **Cassini**
The enormous Cassini spacecraft is the size of a bus and has a mass of 2,150kg (4,740lb), making it the largest and most complex interplanetary craft sent into space to date. On-board instruments include advanced radar, visible and infrared mapping cameras, magnetometers, and particle analysis tools. Cassini also transported the Huygens Titan probe, adding a further 350kg (770lb) to the overall payload.

Cassini is 6.8m (22ft) tall and contains over 14km (8.7 miles) of cabling.

The Huygens probe was released over Titan in December 2004.

▷ **Launch**
In October 1997, Cassini blasted off from Cape Canaveral, USA, aboard a Titan-IVB/Centaur rocket. Its complex trajectory – including two flybys of Venus, one of Earth, and one of Jupiter, gaining speed with each encounter – meant that Cassini took nearly seven years to reach Saturn.

▽ **Discoveries**
Still in orbit after more than a decade at Saturn, Cassini has revolutionized our ideas about the planet and its satellites. Key breakthroughs include the confirmation of lakes on Titan and the discovery of ice plumes on Enceladus. Cassini has also revealed fine structure within Saturn's rings, and improved our understanding of the planet's complex weather systems.

Dark patches left by disappearing ice on the moon Iapetus

Huygens' view of its landing site on the surface of Titan

URANUS

ENIGMATIC URANUS KEEPS ITS SECRETS HIDDEN UNDER AN ALMOST CLOUDLESS FACE. UNIQUELY, URANUS SPINS ON ITS SIDE AS IT ORBITS THE SUN. ALTHOUGH NOT THE FURTHEST PLANET FROM THE SUN, IT IS THE COLDEST OF ALL.

"A curious nebulous star or perhaps a comet", recorded William Herschel, a German-born British musician and amateur astronomer, on 13 March 1781. In fact, Herschel had discovered a new planet far beyond Saturn and, at a stroke, doubled the size of the known Solar System.

Uranus is a giant world, but one so distant that it is barely visible to the naked eye. Even telescopes reveal little more: a handful of moons, whose orbits indicate that the planet is tipped sideways, and faint evidence of some dark rings. The Voyager 2 spacecraft flew past Uranus in 1986, but the images it returned proved disappointingly featureless, even under close scrutiny.

Over the following decades, as Uranus's orbit brought different parts of its face into the Sun, the planet has emerged from hibernation. Powerful telescopes are now revealing clouds swirling around this aquamarine world.

Data

Equatorial diameter	51,118km (31,763 miles)
Mass (Earth = 1)	14.5
Gravity at equator (Earth = 1)	0.89
Mean distance from Sun (Earth = 1)	19.2
Axial tilt	82.2°
Rotation period (day)	17.2 hours (east to west)
Orbital period (year)	84.3 Earth days
Cloud-top temperature	–197°C (–323°F)
Moons	27

The amount of sunlight **Uranus** receives is only **0.25 per cent** of that reaching **Earth.**

Unlike Saturn's rings of water ice, the rings around Uranus are made of dust and dark, rocky material.

▽ **Northern hemisphere**
Night and day at the poles each last for 42 years. The northern polar region is now coming into sight, brightening as Uranus moves around the Sun; the planet's changing seasons expose the region to more intense sunlight.

▽ **Tilt**
Uranus's axis is tilted at almost a right angle to its orbit, and the planet rotates the opposite way to all the other planets (except Venus). This is probably because Uranus was knocked over by a giant impact soon after the planet's formation.

▽ **Southern hemisphere**
Voyager 2 sped directly towards the south pole of the tipped-up planet, which at the time was midway through its 42-year day. When the images of Uranus were enhanced, this was the brightest region; it is now fading.

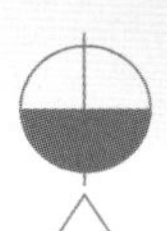

During Uranus's northern summer, the northern atmosphere becomes more active as it warms up.
Clouds of frozen methane appear as white streaks.
Lacking methane clouds, the region round the equator is darker.
Methane clouds are blown around the planet by winds of up to 500kph (300mph).

◁ **Ice giant**
Uranus is a giant planet four times wider than Earth. Its density indicates that Uranus consists mainly of water, ammonia, and methane – substances that are normally frozen at such a vast distance from the Sun.

Methane clouds

Like Neptune, Uranus may have a diamond sea around its core, with diamond hailstones raining into it.

URANUS STRUCTURE

BENEATH AN ATMOSPHERE TINGED BLUE-GREEN BY METHANE LIES A VAST, SLUSHY OCEAN AND, POSSIBLY, A ROCKY CORE. URANUS HAS A LOPSIDED MAGNETIC FIELD THAT MAY BE GENERATED BY A HIDDEN OCEAN OF ELECTRIFIED WATER.

If you were to descend into Uranus's aquamarine atmosphere, you would pass though successive cloud decks, the air becoming steadily thicker until you found yourself in a warm ocean with no distinct surface. This liquid ocean makes up most of the planet.

In the depths of Uranus's hidden ocean, water molecules break down to form a soup of hydrogen and oxygen ions. Currents in this sea of electrically charged particles are thought to generate Uranus's magnetic field, which is lopsided and off-centre. If Earth had such a magnetic field, its poles would be as near to the equator as Cairo in Egypt or Brisbane in Australia.

Unlike the other giant planets, Uranus radiates less heat into space than it receives from the Sun. This may be because it was suddenly cooled by the immense impact that knocked the infant planet on its side.

Most planets **spin like tops** – Uranus rolls on its side.

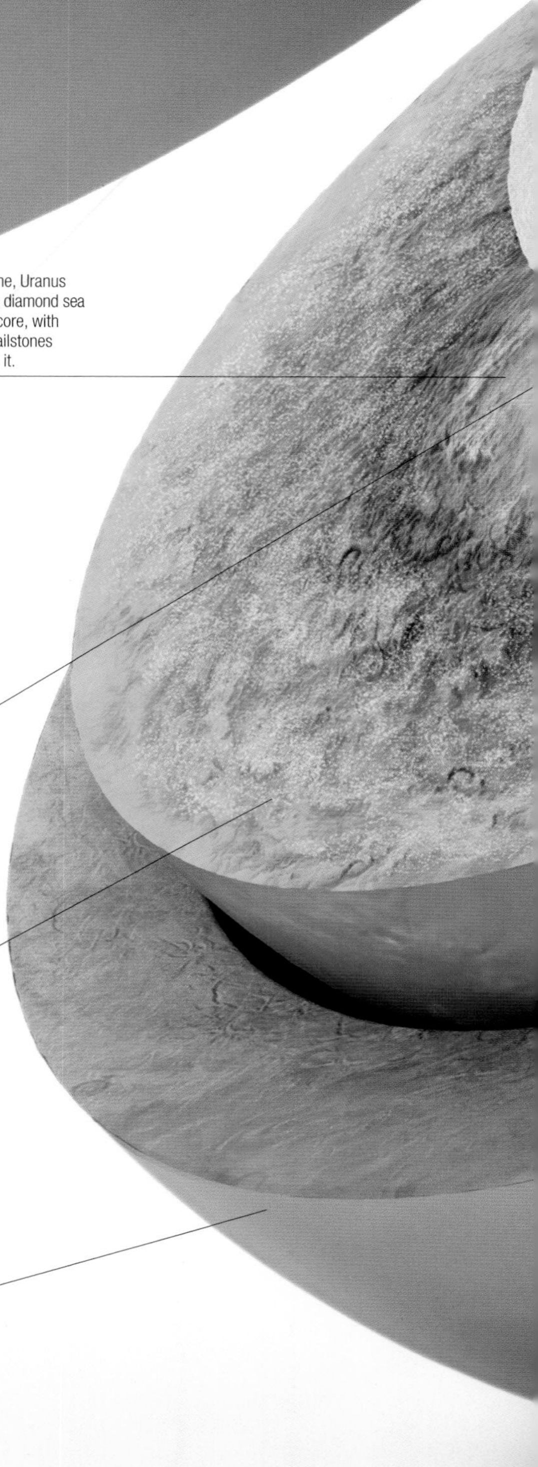

Core
Uranus's core is slightly less massive than planet Earth. A molten mixture of iron and magma, it has a temperature of more than 5,000°C (9,000°F) and is squeezed by pressure 10 million times greater than atmospheric pressure on Earth's surface.

Mantle
Astronomers call Uranus an ice giant because water, ammonia, and methane – the planet's main constituents – are normally frozen this far from the Sun. However, the high temperatures within the planet melt these substances to form a slushy ocean with a depth of 15,000km (9,300 miles).

Atmosphere
The "air" on Uranus is mainly hydrogen and helium. There are layers of cloud at different depths in the atmosphere. Unique among the giant planets, Uranus has a tenuous outer atmosphere that is several times larger than the planet itself.

At the base of the mantle is a layer of superionic water (electrically charged hydrogen and oxygen) that glows yellow.
Clouds of ammonia form in the atmosphere. The deepest clouds consist of frozen water droplets.
Churning fluid within the mantle generates the planet's magnetic field.
The brightest and densest ring, Epsilon, is shepherded by two tiny moons, Cordelia and Ophelia, whose gravity helps maintain its shape.
Uranus has the coldest atmosphere of any planet, with temperatures plunging to −224°C (−371°F) in the troposphere – the densest part of the atmosphere.

◁ **Rings**
Uranus has a set of 13 rings. The first rings were discovered in 1977 when they unexpectedly blocked out the light of a distant star. Other rings were detected by Voyager 2 in 1986 and by the Hubble Space Telescope in 2003–05. All the rings of Uranus are narrow and, unlike Saturn's brilliant rings, as dark as coal.

THE **URANUS** SYSTEM

Moons to scale
Titania and Oberon rank among the Solar System's top ten largest moons, but even all 27 moons combined would be no match for a single major moon of Jupiter, Saturn, or Neptune. Most of Uranus's moons are named after characters in plays by William Shakespeare, and a few from the poetry of Alexander Pope.

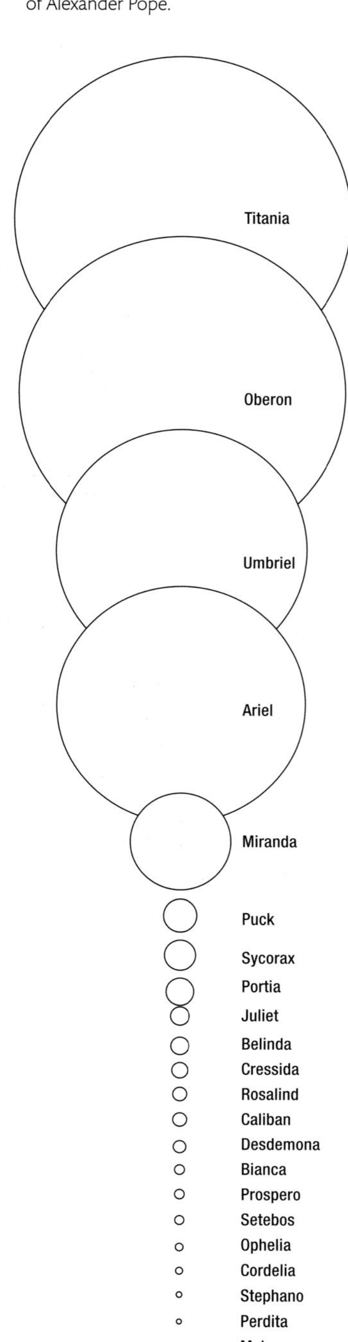

Titania
Oberon
Umbriel
Ariel
Miranda
Puck
Sycorax
Portia
Juliet
Belinda
Cressida
Rosalind
Caliban
Desdemona
Bianca
Prospero
Setebos
Ophelia
Cordelia
Stephano
Perdita
Mab
Francisco
Margaret
Ferdinand
Cupid
Trinculo

ASTRONOMERS DIVIDE URANUS'S 27 MOONS INTO THREE GROUPS: FIVE MAJOR MOONS, 13 SMALL INNER MOONS, AND NINE SMALL OUTER MOONS.

William Herschel discovered Uranus's two largest moons, Titania and Oberon, in 1787 – six years after he had found the planet itself. Another amateur astronomer, the English brewer William Lassell, tracked down Umbriel and Ariel in 1851, and Dutch-American Gerard Kuiper located Miranda in 1948. Astronomers on a flying observatory, based aboard a Lockheed C-141A Starlifter transport plane, detected the narrow rings in 1977.

When Voyager 2 flew past Uranus in 1986, it captured detailed images of the moons and rings that were known at the time. Another 11 moons and two more rings turned up in the Voyager images. Since then, the Hubble Space Telescope and powerful instruments on Earth have identified the remainder of Uranus's moons and rings of which we are now aware.

▷ **Inner moons**
The five largest moons, which orbit directly above the planet's tipped-up equator, were formed from the same spinning disc of gas and ice as Uranus itself. The 13 moons that lie closer to Uranus are in unstable orbits: past collisions have filled this region with rubble that still orbits Uranus, now corralled into narrow rings by the gravity of nearby moons.

Umbriel
The darkest of Uranus's moons, Umbriel is composed mainly of ice, coated in a layer of dark material perhaps made of organic (carbon-rich) compounds.

Oberon
This is the outermost of Uranus's five major moons. It is composed of a mixture of ice and rock, and its dark surface has a reddish tinge. Debris from space has smashed into Oberon, making it the most cratered of all Uranus's moons; one crater's central peak is 11,000m (36,000ft) high – taller than Mount Everest.

Titania
Titania is Uranus's largest moon and the eighth biggest moon in the Solar System. Titania's face is blemished by massive canyons and scarps, which formed when this moon expanded soon after its formation. Titania may have a very tenuous atmosphere of carbon dioxide.

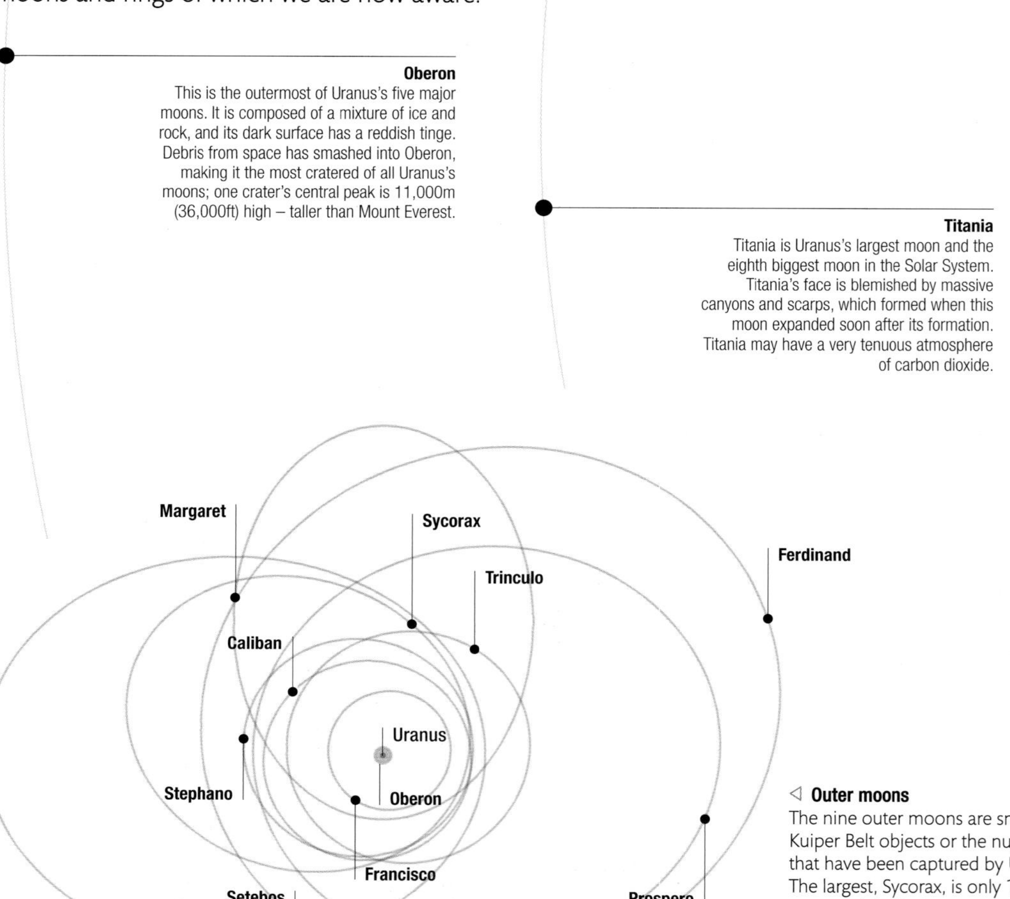

Margaret
Sycorax
Trinculo
Ferdinand
Caliban
Uranus
Stephano
Oberon
Francisco
Setebos
Prospero

◁ **Outer moons**
The nine outer moons are small icy worlds – Kuiper Belt objects or the nuclei of comets – that have been captured by Uranus's gravity. The largest, Sycorax, is only 150km (93 miles) across, while diminutive Trinculo has a diameter of less than 20km (12 miles). These moons pursue crazy orbits, tilted at odd angles and looping in and out; Margaret has the highest eccentricity (least circular orbit) of any moon in the Solar System.

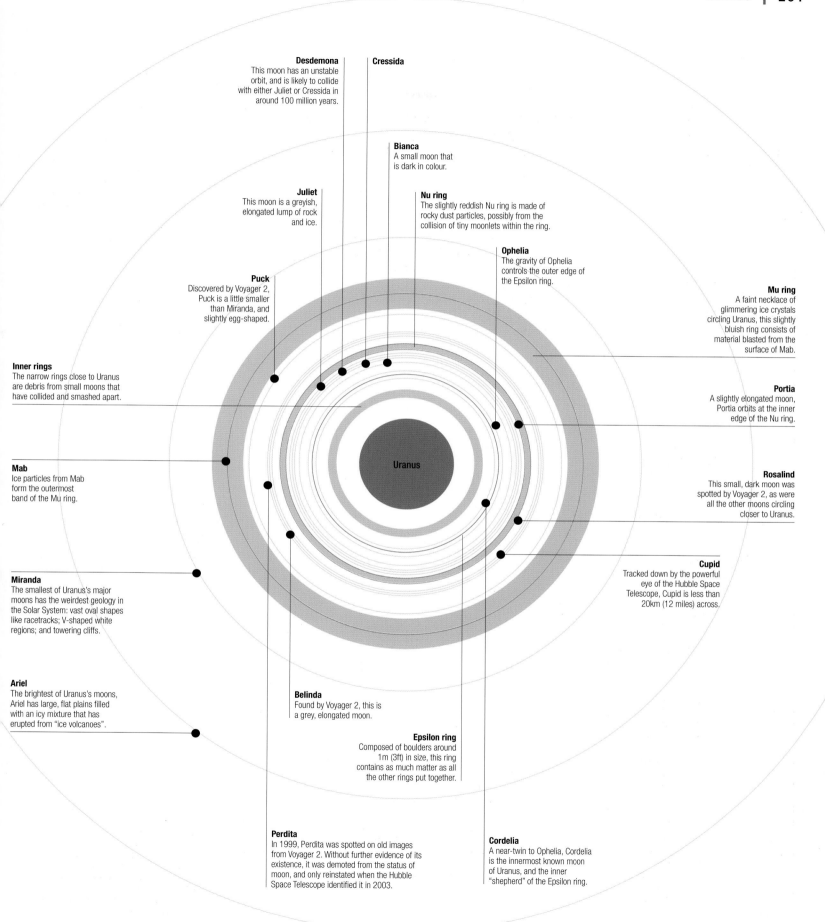

Desdemona
This moon has an unstable orbit, and is likely to collide with either Juliet or Cressida in around 100 million years.

Cressida

Bianca
A small moon that is dark in colour.

Juliet
This moon is a greyish, elongated lump of rock and ice.

Nu ring
The slightly reddish Nu ring is made of rocky dust particles, possibly from the collision of tiny moonlets within the ring.

Ophelia
The gravity of Ophelia controls the outer edge of the Epsilon ring.

Puck
Discovered by Voyager 2, Puck is a little smaller than Miranda, and slightly egg-shaped.

Mu ring
A faint necklace of glimmering ice crystals circling Uranus, this slightly bluish ring consists of material blasted from the surface of Mab.

Inner rings
The narrow rings close to Uranus are debris from small moons that have collided and smashed apart.

Portia
A slightly elongated moon, Portia orbits at the inner edge of the Nu ring.

Mab
Ice particles from Mab form the outermost band of the Mu ring.

Uranus

Rosalind
This small, dark moon was spotted by Voyager 2, as were all the other moons circling closer to Uranus.

Cupid
Tracked down by the powerful eye of the Hubble Space Telescope, Cupid is less than 20km (12 miles) across.

Miranda
The smallest of Uranus's major moons has the weirdest geology in the Solar System: vast oval shapes like racetracks; V-shaped white regions; and towering cliffs.

Ariel
The brightest of Uranus's moons, Ariel has large, flat plains filled with an icy mixture that has erupted from "ice volcanoes".

Belinda
Found by Voyager 2, this is a grey, elongated moon.

Epsilon ring
Composed of boulders around 1m (3ft) in size, this ring contains as much matter as all the other rings put together.

Perdita
In 1999, Perdita was spotted on old images from Voyager 2. Without further evidence of its existence, it was demoted from the status of moon, and only reinstated when the Hubble Space Telescope identified it in 2003.

Cordelia
A near-twin to Ophelia, Cordelia is the innermost known moon of Uranus, and the inner "shepherd" of the Epsilon ring.

DESTINATION
VERONA RUPES

THE TALLEST CLIFF IN THE SOLAR SYSTEM IS FOUND ON ONE OF THE SMALLER MOONS, URANUS'S MIRANDA. NAMED VERONA RUPES, THIS CLIFF IS SO HIGH – AND MIRANDA'S GRAVITY SO LOW – THAT A ROCK WOULD TAKE TEN MINUTES TO FALL FROM TOP TO BASE.

The near-vertical face of Verona Rupes, glistening with water ice like the rest of Miranda's surface, is almost 10km (6 miles) high. It is not clear how such a huge structure was thrown up on so small a moon. The most likely explanation is tectonic activity early in Miranda's evolution. A more sensational theory suggests that Miranda was smashed to pieces in a colossal collision with another body and randomly reassembled itself, creating a scarred and fragmented surface pitted with craters, gouged with canyons, and crisscrossed by huge ridges.

Artist's impression based on NASA images

LOCATION

Latitude –18°S; longitude 348°E

LAND PROFILE

Even the impressive walls of the Grand Canyon, which rise 1.8km (1 mile) from the canyon floor, are dwarfed by Verona Rupes, which is about six times higher.

Elevation (km)
10
5
0
Miranda
Grand Canyon
0
200
300
400
Distance (km)

116 **KM (72 MILES)**
APPROXIMATE LENGTH OF VERONA RUPES RIDGE

FORMATION

Verona Rupes probably formed when a fault cracked Miranda's surface, and blocks of crust rose on one side of the fracture line and dropped on the other. Friction and erosion as the blocks rubbed against one another left grooves called slickensides on the cliff face.

Fault forms
Crust displaced vertically

NEPTUNE

YOU MIGHT EXPECT NEPTUNE TO BE A PLACID WORLD, SINCE IT IS THE MOST DISTANT PLANET FROM THE SUN. IN FACT, NEPTUNE HAS VIOLENT WEATHER SYSTEMS, HEAT WELLING UP FROM ITS INTERIOR, AND A MASSIVE ERUPTING MOON.

Neptune was discovered by deduction. In the 19th century, astronomers realized that Uranus was being pulled by the gravity of an unknown planet. French astronomer Urbain Leverrier calculated its position in 1846 (after a lead from John Couch Adams in England), and astronomers in Berlin found Neptune just where he had predicted, less than a year later.

A near twin to Uranus in size, Neptune is so far from the Sun that you need a telescope to see it at all. The eighth planet probably has the same internal structure as Uranus, along with a set of dark rings. When Voyager 2 passed Neptune in 1989, it showed an atmosphere in turmoil, with the fastest winds in the Solar System. Even Neptune's most prominent feature, the Great Dark Spot, was short-lived.

NEPTUNE DATA

Equatorial diameter	49,528km (30,775 miles)
Mass (Earth = 1)	17.1
Gravity at equator (Earth = 1)	1.1
Mean distance from Sun (Earth = 1)	30.1
Axial tilt	28.3°
Rotation period (day)	16.1 hours
Orbital period (year)	168.4 Earth-years
Moons	14
Cloud-top temperature	–201°C (–330°F)

The near-supersonic winds of **Neptune's dark spots** can exceed **1,200kph (700mph).**

Atmospheric methane absorbs red wavelengths in sunlight, giving the planet its characteristic blue colour.

Neptune is surrounded by a system of thin and sparsely populated rings.

▽ Tilt

Neptune's axis is tilted at a similar angle to Earth's, so like Earth the planet experiences seasons as it moves around the Sun. However, Neptune is so far from the Sun that each of its seasons lasts for more than 40 years.

▽ Northern hemisphere

It's currently winter in Neptune's northern hemisphere, so there is little activity in the region. Voyager 2 flew less than 5,000km (3,000 miles) above the northern hemisphere's cloudtops – the closest of all its planetary encounters.

▽ Southern hemisphere

The southern hemisphere has been bathed in summer sunlight for the past 40 years. As a result, the south pole is the hottest spot on the planet, with temperatures rising to –190°C (–310°F).

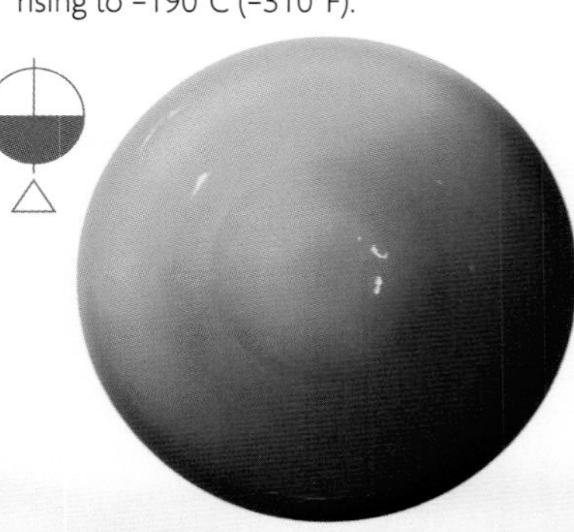

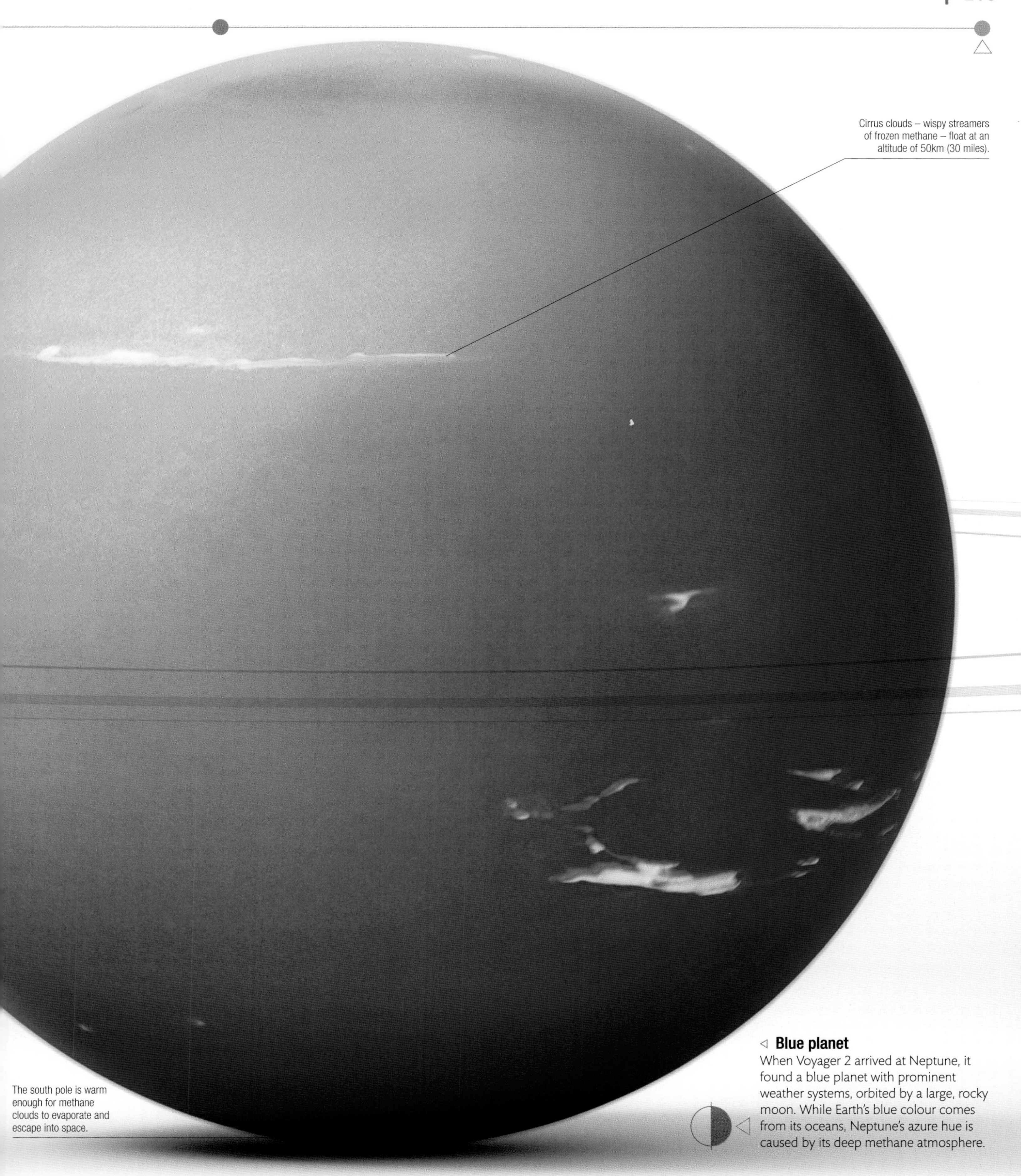

Cirrus clouds – wispy streamers of frozen methane – float at an altitude of 50km (30 miles).

The south pole is warm enough for methane clouds to evaporate and escape into space.

◁ Blue planet

When Voyager 2 arrived at Neptune, it found a blue planet with prominent weather systems, orbited by a large, rocky moon. While Earth's blue colour comes from its oceans, Neptune's azure hue is caused by its deep methane atmosphere.

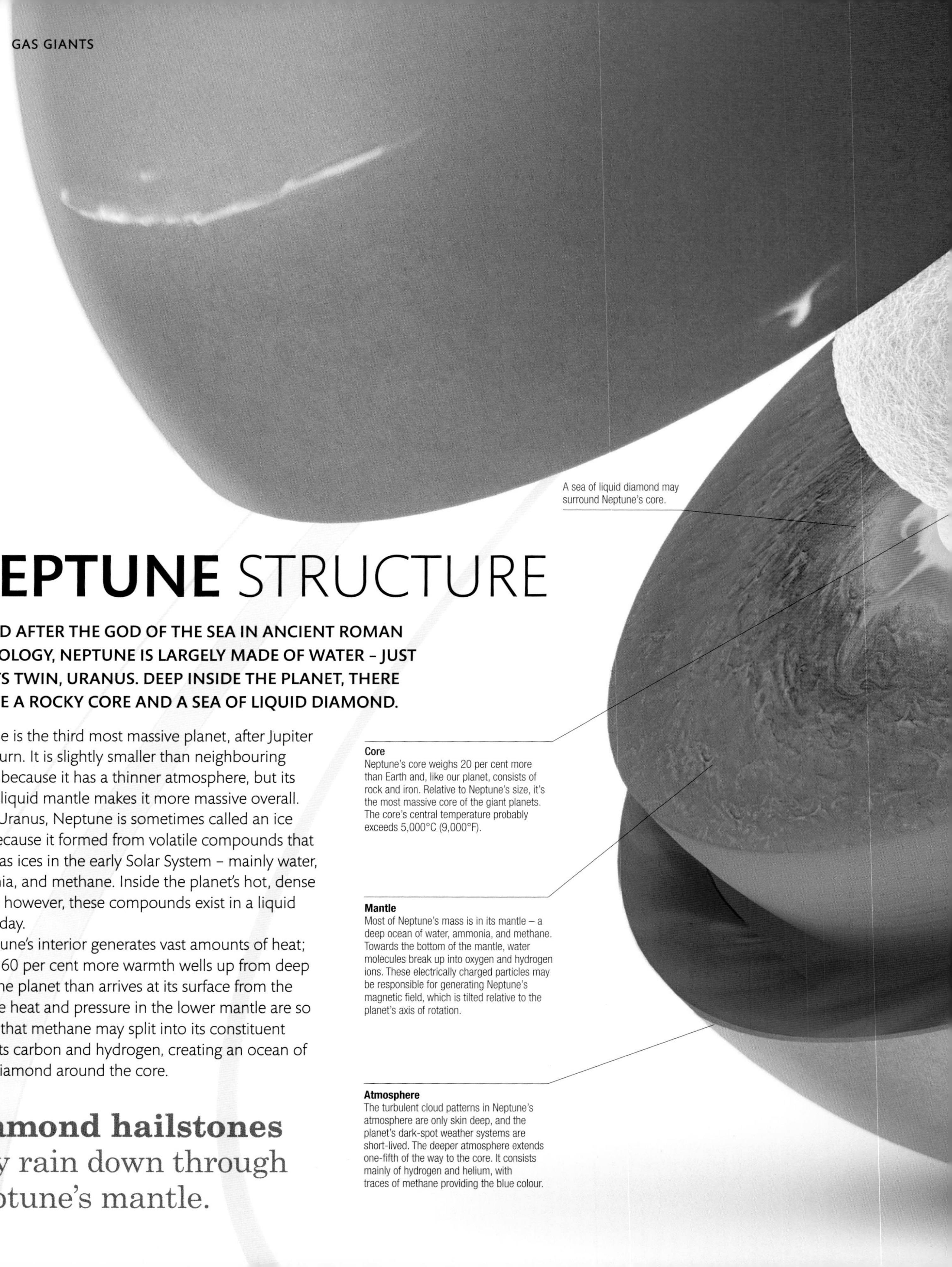

A sea of liquid diamond may surround Neptune's core.

NEPTUNE STRUCTURE

NAMED AFTER THE GOD OF THE SEA IN ANCIENT ROMAN MYTHOLOGY, NEPTUNE IS LARGELY MADE OF WATER – JUST LIKE ITS TWIN, URANUS. DEEP INSIDE THE PLANET, THERE MAY BE A ROCKY CORE AND A SEA OF LIQUID DIAMOND.

Neptune is the third most massive planet, after Jupiter and Saturn. It is slightly smaller than neighbouring Uranus because it has a thinner atmosphere, but its deeper liquid mantle makes it more massive overall.

Like Uranus, Neptune is sometimes called an ice giant because it formed from volatile compounds that existed as ices in the early Solar System – mainly water, ammonia, and methane. Inside the planet's hot, dense interior, however, these compounds exist in a liquid form today.

Neptune's interior generates vast amounts of heat; around 60 per cent more warmth wells up from deep inside the planet than arrives at its surface from the Sun. The heat and pressure in the lower mantle are so intense that methane may split into its constituent elements carbon and hydrogen, creating an ocean of liquid diamond around the core.

Diamond hailstones may rain down through Neptune's mantle.

Core
Neptune's core weighs 20 per cent more than Earth and, like our planet, consists of rock and iron. Relative to Neptune's size, it's the most massive core of the giant planets. The core's central temperature probably exceeds 5,000°C (9,000°F).

Mantle
Most of Neptune's mass is in its mantle – a deep ocean of water, ammonia, and methane. Towards the bottom of the mantle, water molecules break up into oxygen and hydrogen ions. These electrically charged particles may be responsible for generating Neptune's magnetic field, which is tilted relative to the planet's axis of rotation.

Atmosphere
The turbulent cloud patterns in Neptune's atmosphere are only skin deep, and the planet's dark-spot weather systems are short-lived. The deeper atmosphere extends one-fifth of the way to the core. It consists mainly of hydrogen and helium, with traces of methane providing the blue colour.

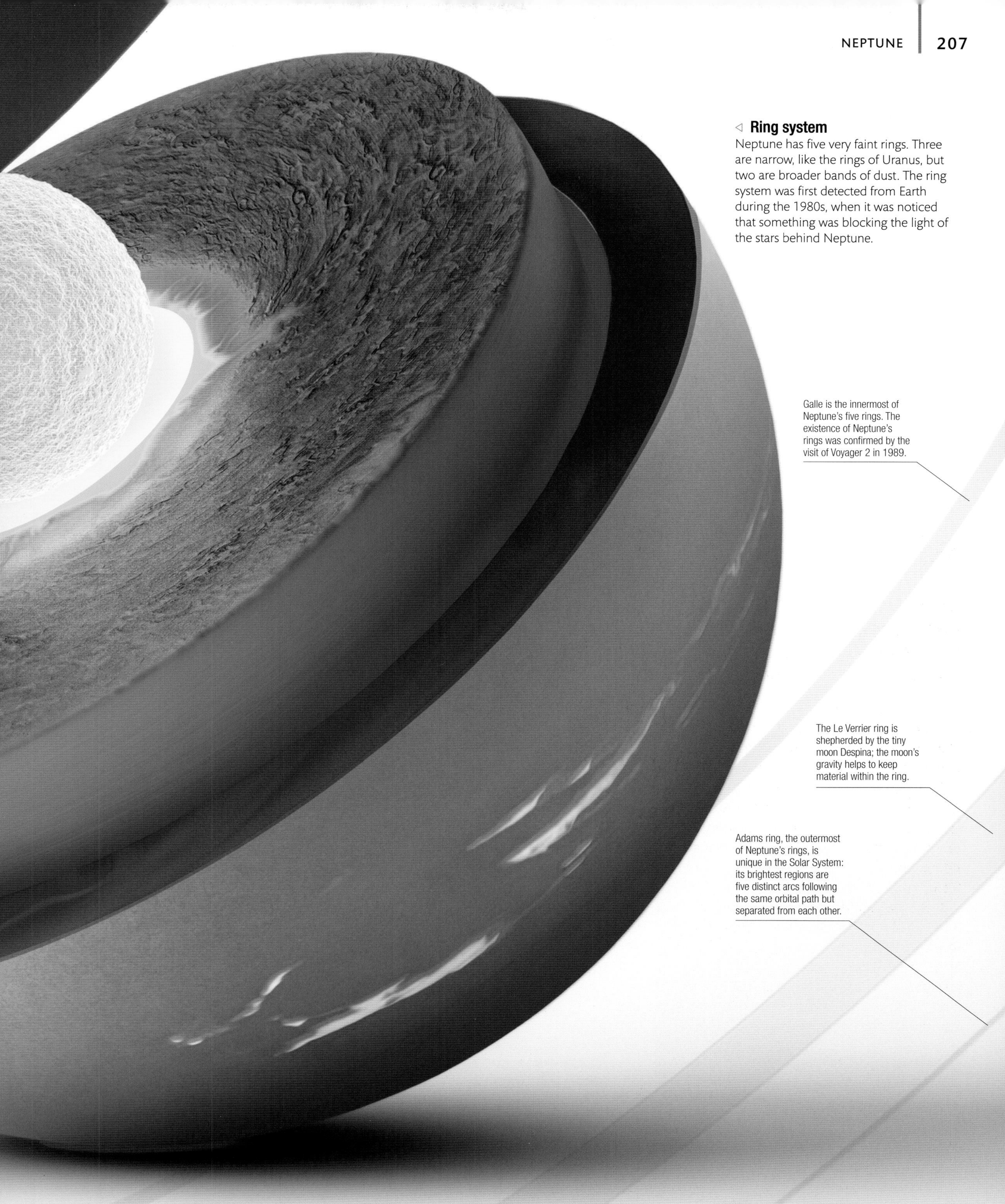
Galle is the innermost of Neptune's five rings. The existence of Neptune's rings was confirmed by the visit of Voyager 2 in 1989.
The Le Verrier ring is shepherded by the tiny moon Despina; the moon's gravity helps to keep material within the ring.
Adams ring, the outermost of Neptune's rings, is unique in the Solar System: its brightest regions are five distinct arcs following the same orbital path but separated from each other.

◁ **Ring system**
Neptune has five very faint rings. Three are narrow, like the rings of Uranus, but two are broader bands of dust. The ring system was first detected from Earth during the 1980s, when it was noticed that something was blocking the light of the stars behind Neptune.

THE **NEPTUNE** SYSTEM

LIKE ALL THE GAS GIANTS IN THE OUTER SOLAR SYSTEM, NEPTUNE IS SURROUNDED BY A FASCINATING, DYNAMIC ENVIRONMENT. HOST TO AT LEAST 14 MOONS, THE PLANET IS ALSO CIRCLED BY A SET OF FIVE VERY THIN RINGS.

The first moon to be identified was mighty Triton – only 17 days after Neptune itself was discovered in 1846. The astronomer who tracked it down was Englishman William Lassell. A fortune amassed as a brewer in the northern town of Bolton enabled Lassell to build giant telescopes and indulge his passion for astronomy.

Over a century passed before Nereid was discovered in 1949; a third moon, Larissa, followed in 1981. The rest of the moons were found more recently, either by the Voyager 2 spacecraft, which flew past Neptune in 1989, or by powerful, ground-based telescopes. The latest addition to the family – as yet unnamed – was spotted by the Hubble Space Telescope in 2013. All currently named moons of Neptune are named after water gods and spirits in Greek mythology.

Moons to scale
Triton dominates Neptune's family of moons, accounting for 99.7 per cent of the total mass of Neptune's entourage. At 2,700km (1,700 miles) wide, it is the Solar System's seventh-largest moon. Unlike Triton, which is spherical, Neptune's other moons are all probably irregular in shape.

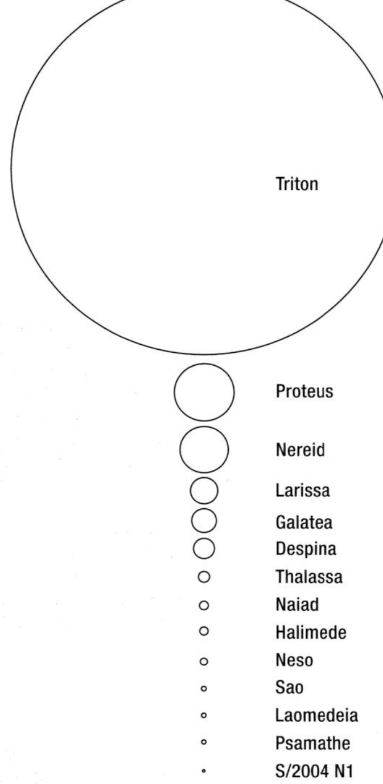
Triton
Proteus
Nereid
Larissa
Galatea
Despina
Thalassa
Naiad
Halimede
Neso
Sao
Laomedeia
Psamathe
S/2004 N1

Triton
This moon is an oddball, orbiting its planet backwards – a characteristic not shared by any other large moon in the Solar System. Like the outer moons, Triton was captured by the planet's gravity. The taming of such a large body wreaked havoc on the Neptune system, sending other moons into strange orbits. Triton's own orbit isn't stable: its future destiny is to crash into Neptune.

Ring arcs

◁ **Rings and arcs**
Neptune is surrounded by five faint rings. Like Jupiter's rings, they consist largely of cosmic dust. The rings are named after astronomers who studied Neptune: Galle, Le Verrier, Lassell, Arago, and Adams. The outermost Adams ring has distinct clumps in it known as arcs, revealed in this image from Voyager 2. Ring particles normally spread out into a uniform circle, but astronomers believe the particles in the Adams ring are being confined by the gravity of Neptune's small moon Galatea, causing clumping.

Neso
Halimede
Triton
Psamathe
Neptune
Nereid
Laomedeia
Sao

△ **Outer moons**
None of Neptune's outer moons has a circular orbit. Instead, they loop around the planet in great ellipses. Some of the orbits are highly inclined, and these orbits vary between prograde (forwards) and retrograde (backwards). All the outer moons, bar Nereid, are comparatively tiny. The majority of these moonlets were probably captured from the icy Kuiper Belt by Neptune's gravity.

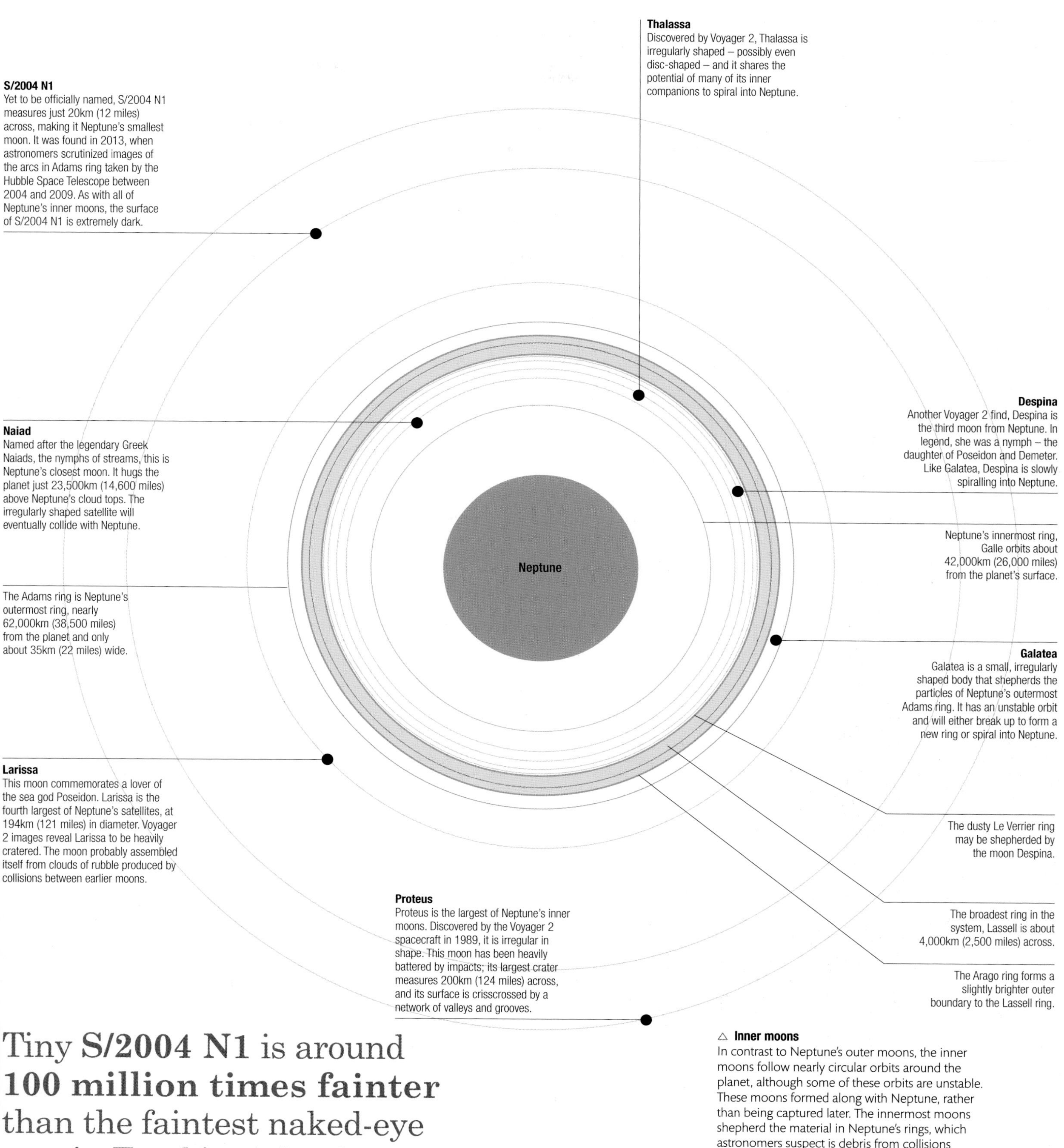
Thalassa
Discovered by Voyager 2, Thalassa is irregularly shaped – possibly even disc-shaped – and it shares the potential of many of its inner companions to spiral into Neptune.
S/2004 N1
Yet to be officially named, S/2004 N1 measures just 20km (12 miles) across, making it Neptune's smallest moon. It was found in 2013, when astronomers scrutinized images of the arcs in Adams ring taken by the Hubble Space Telescope between 2004 and 2009. As with all of Neptune's inner moons, the surface of S/2004 N1 is extremely dark.
Despina
Another Voyager 2 find, Despina is the third moon from Neptune. In legend, she was a nymph – the daughter of Poseidon and Demeter. Like Galatea, Despina is slowly spiralling into Neptune.
Naiad
Named after the legendary Greek Naiads, the nymphs of streams, this is Neptune's closest moon. It hugs the planet just 23,500km (14,600 miles) above Neptune's cloud tops. The irregularly shaped satellite will eventually collide with Neptune.
Neptune's innermost ring, Galle orbits about 42,000km (26,000 miles) from the planet's surface.
Neptune
The Adams ring is Neptune's outermost ring, nearly 62,000km (38,500 miles) from the planet and only about 35km (22 miles) wide.
Galatea
Galatea is a small, irregularly shaped body that shepherds the particles of Neptune's outermost Adams ring. It has an unstable orbit and will either break up to form a new ring or spiral into Neptune.
Larissa
This moon commemorates a lover of the sea god Poseidon. Larissa is the fourth largest of Neptune's satellites, at 194km (121 miles) in diameter. Voyager 2 images reveal Larissa to be heavily cratered. The moon probably assembled itself from clouds of rubble produced by collisions between earlier moons.
The dusty Le Verrier ring may be shepherded by the moon Despina.
Proteus
Proteus is the largest of Neptune's inner moons. Discovered by the Voyager 2 spacecraft in 1989, it is irregular in shape. This moon has been heavily battered by impacts; its largest crater measures 200km (124 miles) across, and its surface is crisscrossed by a network of valleys and grooves.
The broadest ring in the system, Lassell is about 4,000km (2,500 miles) across.
The Arago ring forms a slightly brighter outer boundary to the Lassell ring.

Tiny **S/2004 N1** is around **100 million times fainter** than the faintest naked-eye star in Earth's night sky.

△ **Inner moons**
In contrast to Neptune's outer moons, the inner moons follow nearly circular orbits around the planet, although some of these orbits are unstable. These moons formed along with Neptune, rather than being captured later. The innermost moons shepherd the material in Neptune's rings, which astronomers suspect is debris from collisions between former inner moons.

DESTINATION TRITON

WITH A SURFACE TEMPERATURE OF –235°C (–391°F), NEPTUNE'S MOON TRITON IS ONE OF THE COLDEST PLACES IN THE SOLAR SYSTEM. YET THIS FRIGID WORLD IS VOLCANICALLY ACTIVE.

Triton's "retrograde" orbit – which runs in the opposite direction to the planet's rotation – suggests this moon is probably a captured Kuiper Belt object from the icy outer limits of the Solar System. Images from Voyager 2 reveal the surface to be a jumble of rocky outcrops, ridges, furrows, and occasional craters. All of these tell us that Triton's surface is very young – just a few million years old.

Triton has a tenuous atmosphere of nitrogen and a reddish surface coated in methane and nitrogen ice. But its most famous features are the geysers discovered by Voyager in 1989. They spew out plumes of nitrogen gas mixed with dark dust and can reach heights of 8km (5 miles), before falling back to stain the surface. An eruption can last a whole year.

Triton's shiny surface of **methane ice** and **nitrogen frost** reflects **70 per cent** of the sunlight it receives.

Artist's impression based on images from Voyager 2 spacecraft

LOCATION

Latitude 31°S; longitude 37°E

SOUTH POLAR CAP

Titan is so cold that its air freezes on the ground. The highly reflective south polar cap is made of frozen nitrogen and methane. Cosmic rays striking the methane have created other organic compounds, giving the frost a pinkish hue. The polar cap is also peppered with dark spots and streaks from geysers.

Not imaged
Polar cap

WIND DIRECTION

Voyager images reveal the speed and direction of winds in the south polar region. The winds carry dark material from geysers northeast before it falls back, leaving black streaks. Scientists estimate the southwesterly winds reach speeds of 40kph (25mph).

Deposit
Wind
Deposit
Geyser
Geyser

THE **BLUE PLANETS**

FOR MILLENNIA PEOPLE KNEW ONLY THE INNERMOST FIVE PLANETS, SO IT WAS A GREAT SURPRISE WHEN WILLIAM HERSCHEL STUMBLED UPON URANUS IN 1781 – A DISCOVERY THAT TRIGGERED THE HUNT FOR MORE HIDDEN WORLDS.

The discovery of Uranus and, later, Neptune were all the more surprising because these planets were giants, four times wider than Earth. Ever since, astronomers have continued to scour the skies for new planets. Many smaller worlds have been found, including Pluto, but these are now classed as dwarf planets or Kuiper Belt Objects. Careful study of the orbits of these distant icy bodies may yet reveal another giant lurking in the dark depths of the outer Solar System.

True-colour view of Uranus

False-colour view of Uranus

1612

Galileo spots Neptune
Galileo observes Jupiter's moons and draws Neptune – which lies behind Jupiter in 1612 – but thinks it is a star. Had he checked its motion, Galileo would have found Neptune before Uranus was known – and pre-empted its discovery by over 230 years.

John Flamsteed

1690

Observation of Uranus
The first Astronomer Royal, John Flamsteed, enters Uranus into his star catalogue, naming it 34 Tauri. It is the planet's first recorded observation. Uranus is seen a further 22 times before its discovery, but astronomers dismiss it as a star.

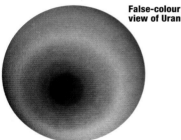

Clyde Tombaugh

1930

Discovery of Pluto
Amateur astronomer Clyde Tombaugh continues the search at Lowell Observatory. In February 1930, he photographs a faint moving object. Tombaugh calculates that it lies beyond Neptune. British schoolgirl Venetia Burney suggests the name Pluto.

1977

Uranus's rings discovered
Astronomers aboard a flying observatory over the Pacific Ocean are amazed as they watch a distant star disappearing behind Uranus. The star dims briefly, five times in all. They deduce that the planet must have a set of dark, very narrow rings that block the star's light.

1986

Voyager 2 visits Uranus
The first close-up images from Voyager 2's trip to Uranus reveal a bland planet with 11 dark rings and ten previously unknown moons. The highlight is the contorted surface of the moon Miranda, with high cliffs and strange, racecourse-shaped markings.

Neptune's Great Dark Spot

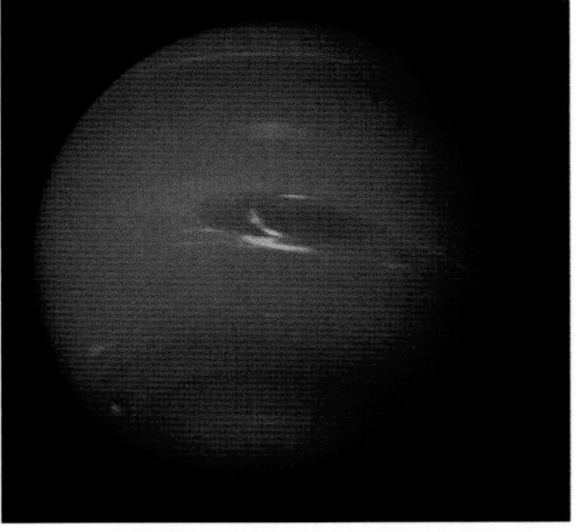

1989

The Great Dark Spot
Voyager 2 reveals Neptune's violent weather, with speeding clouds and a huge weather system, the Great Dark Spot. It confirms Neptune has a set of patchy rings. It also finds geysers erupting from the frozen surface of the planet's giant moon Triton.

1994

The Great Dark Spot disappears
The Hubble Space Telescope views Neptune and discovers that the Great Dark Spot has vanished; it was a transitory weather system unlike Jupiter's 300-year-old Great Red Spot. The next year, Hubble views a large dark spot on the opposite side of Neptune.

Pair of rings around Uranus

2005

Extra rings for Uranus
Long-exposure images from Hubble reveal two faint rings around Uranus, farther out than the known ring system. The outer ring consists of dust ejected from the moon Mab, while the other ring may be the remains of a moon shattered in a collision.

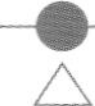

William Herschel

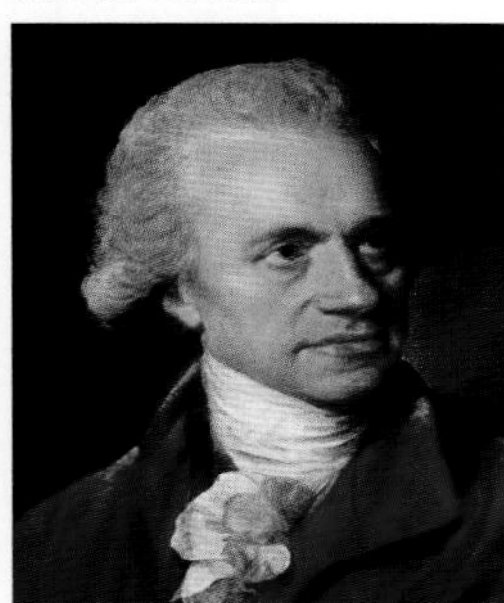

Herschel's telescope

John Couch Adams

1781

Discovery of Uranus

British astronomer and musician William Herschel spots Uranus in his telescope, at first suspecting it is a star or comet. When astronomers calculate its orbit, it becomes clear that Herschel has discovered a new planet. He is the first person ever to do so.

1787

Two moons of Uranus seen

Using a large telescope, Herschel discovers Titania, Oberon, and four spurious moons and rings. Herschel notes their orbits are at "a considerable angle" – a clue to the planet's tilt. For 50 years, no one else has a telescope powerful enough to see them.

1843

Uranus's orbit

Astronomers find Uranus is straying from its orbit, probably pulled by the gravity of an unknown planet. Mathematician John Couch Adams calculates the location of the object responsible, but his work is ignored by Astronomer Royal, George Airy.

Urbain Leverrier

1846

Discovery of Neptune

French astronomer Urbain Leverrier comes up with the same position for the planet as Adams. He sends the prediction to the Berlin Observatory, which has a new star chart for that region of sky. On the first night he looks, Johann Galle sees Neptune.

George III

1850

Naming of Uranus

Herschel had called his new planet Georgium Sidus, "George's Star" (after King George III). This clashed with the other planets' mythological names and was unpopular. Johann Bode suggested Uranus, father of Saturn. In 1850, Britain's Nautical Almanac Office agrees.

Lowell's observatory

1906

Search for Planet X

Astronomers note that Uranus and Neptune seem to feel the tug of another world. Boston businessman Percival Lowell had established an observatory in Arizona, USA, to study the supposed canals of Mars, and here he begins to search for the mystery "Planet X".

Pluto and its moons

Eris and its moon Dysnomia

2006

Pluto is demoted

The International Astronomical Union reclassifies Pluto as a dwarf planet. Astronomers have now discovered more than 1,000 similar icy bodies beyond Neptune. These include Eris, which is about the same size as Pluto.

1

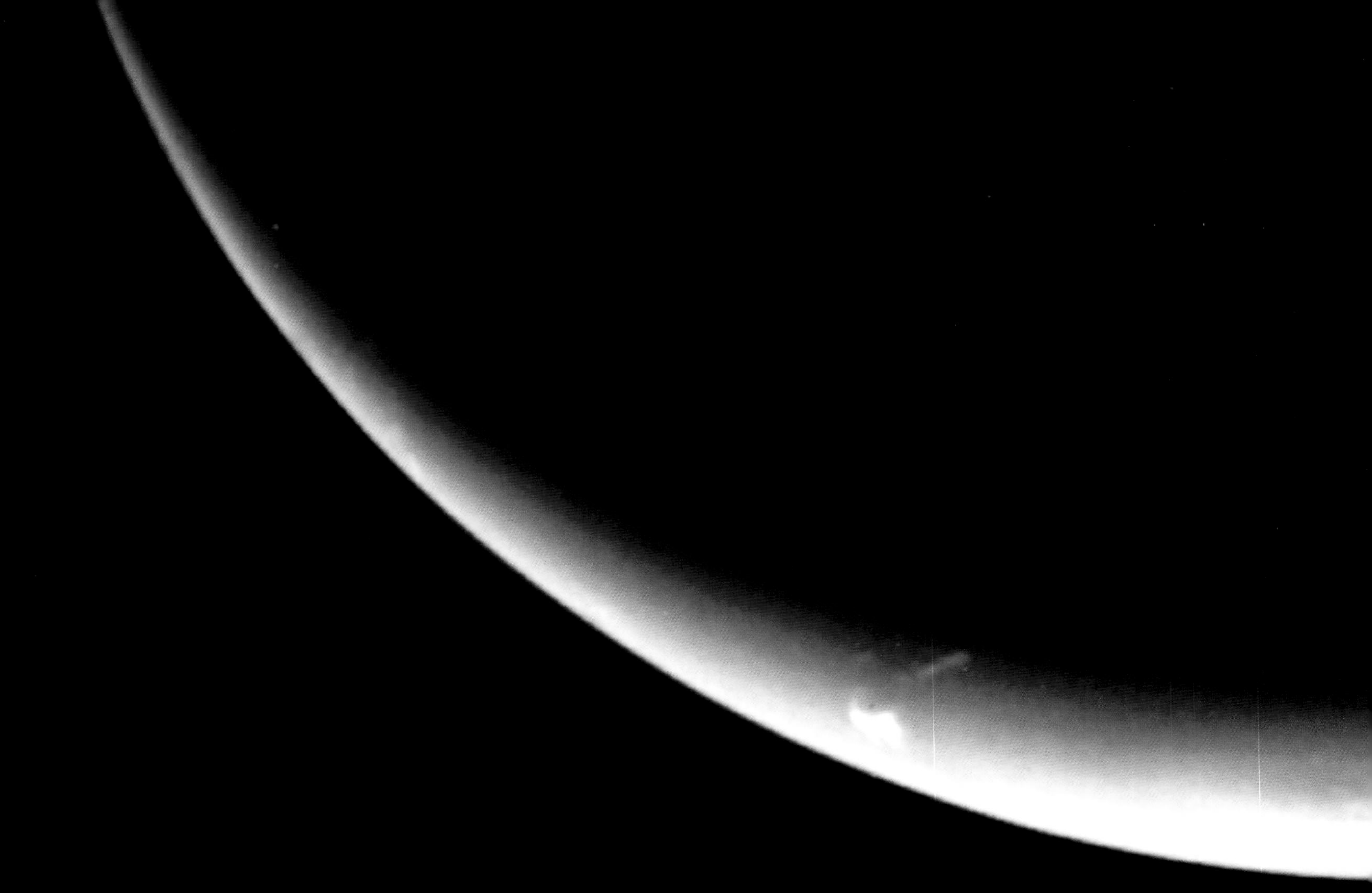

2

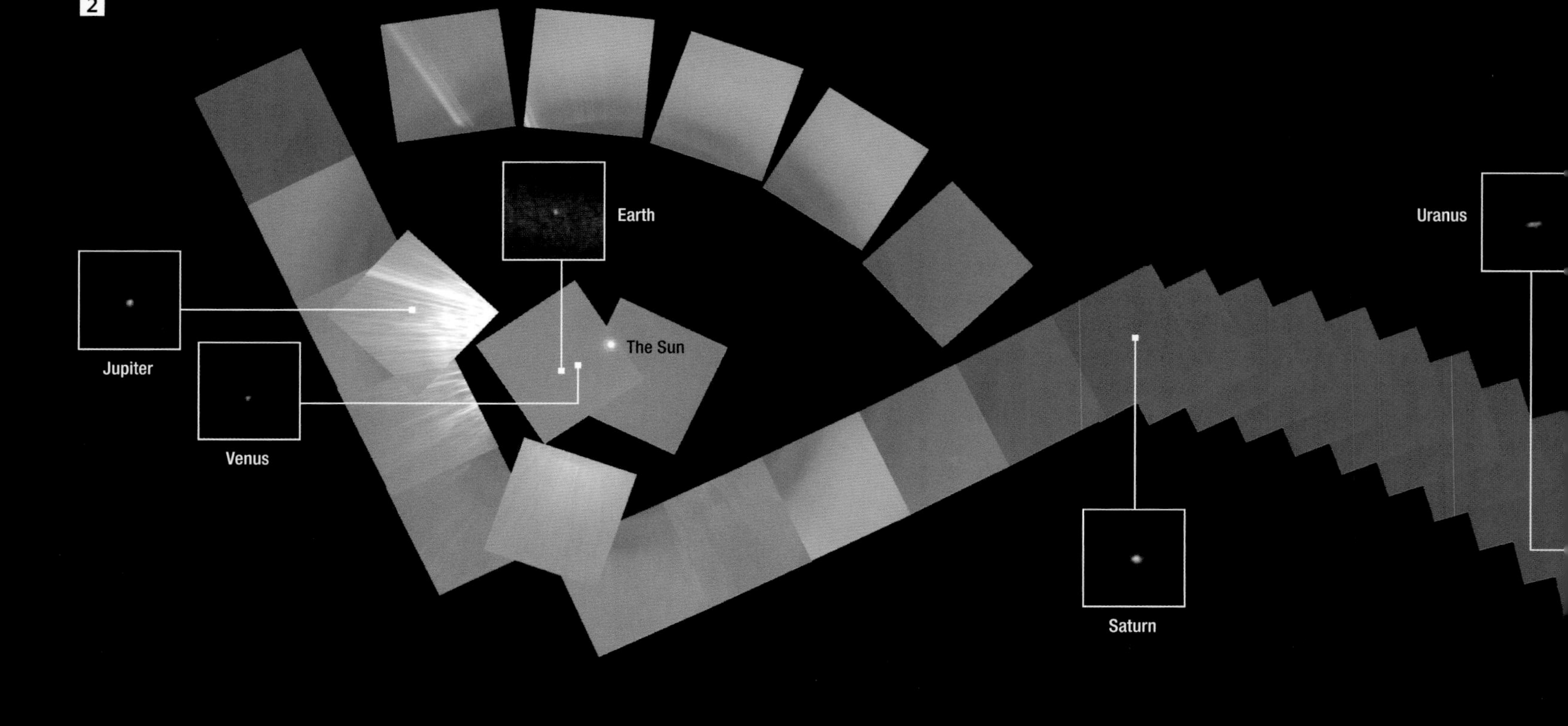

Earth

Uranus

Jupiter

The Sun

Venus

Saturn

Neptune

VOYAGERS' **GRAND TOUR**

1 Goodbye to the planets
This stunning arc of the crescent Neptune was captured by the outward-bound Voyager 2 in 1989 as it departed from its final encounter with a planet. The twin Voyager spacecraft were launched in 1977 to explore the giant planets. Voyager 1 flew past Jupiter and Saturn, but Voyager 2 visited all four gas giants.

2 Looking back
Voyager 1's portrait of the Solar System, captured in 1990 when the spacecraft was 6 billion km (3.7 billion miles) from Earth, was the first-ever image of our planetary system taken from outside. It was also the last image taken by either Voyager. The mosaic comprises 60 wide-angle frames; insets show the planets magnified many times. From Voyager's great distance, Earth was a point of light measuring only 0.12 pixels across.

OUTER **LIMITS**

THE **KUIPER BELT**

A BIG QUESTION AT THE END OF THE 20TH CENTURY WAS WHETHER ANYTHING LAY BEYOND PLUTO. THE EXISTENCE OF A BELT OF ICY OBJECTS WAS PREDICTED BUT NOT CONFIRMED UNTIL THE 1990S WHEN THE FIRST OBJECTS WERE FOUND.

The Kuiper Belt begins about 30 times farther from the Sun than Earth (30AU) and stretches to 50AU. More than 100,000 Kuiper Belt objects (KBOs) larger than around 100km (60 miles) wide are believed to exist in the belt. They formed at the dawn of the Solar System and were thrown into their present eccentric orbits by the gravitational fields of the giant planets. Typical KBOs are classed as cubewanos (pronounced "qb1-0"), which are found throughout the belt. The name comes from 1992 QB1, the first cubewano discovered. KBOs on the far edge of the belt follow eccentric orbits. This region, termed the scattered disc, is the source of short-period comets.

△ **Search**
A typical telescope used to search for KBOs and scattered disc bodies is the Samuel Oschin 1.2m (48in) telescope on Mount Palomar, California, USA. It was used to find the KBO Orcus and the dwarf planet Eris. Two images are made of a region of sky, a week apart. Anything that moves from one image to the next is a Solar System body. The non-moving objects are stars.

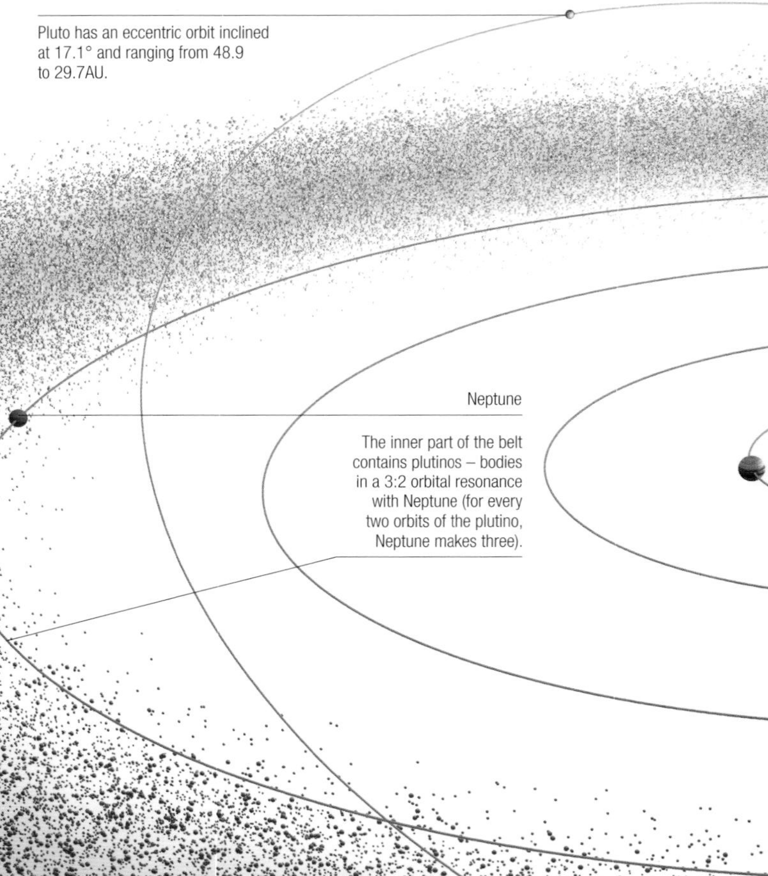
Pluto has an eccentric orbit inclined at 17.1° and ranging from 48.9 to 29.7AU.
The main belt is a flattened disc measuring about 3 billion km (2 billion miles) from edge to edge.
Neptune
The inner part of the belt contains plutinos – bodies in a 3:2 orbital resonance with Neptune (for every two orbits of the plutino, Neptune makes three).

▷ **Ice ring**
We know of more than a thousand KBOs. Made of rock and ice, they are similar in composition to the nuclei of comets, but the larger ones are more dense. Their surfaces, which measure less than –220°C (–364°F) in temperature, are covered with ices including water, carbon dioxide, methane, and ammonia, and are coloured by interactions with cosmic rays. The Kuiper Belt was originally termed the Edgeworth-Kuiper Belt after Kenneth Edgeworth, who predicted its existence in 1943, and Gerard Kuiper, who in 1951 declared it no longer existed.

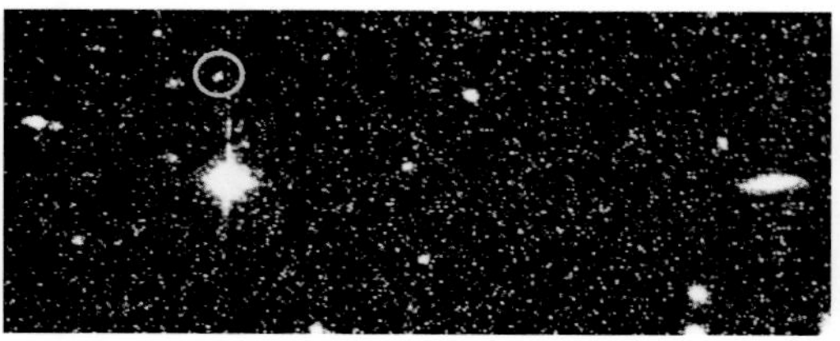

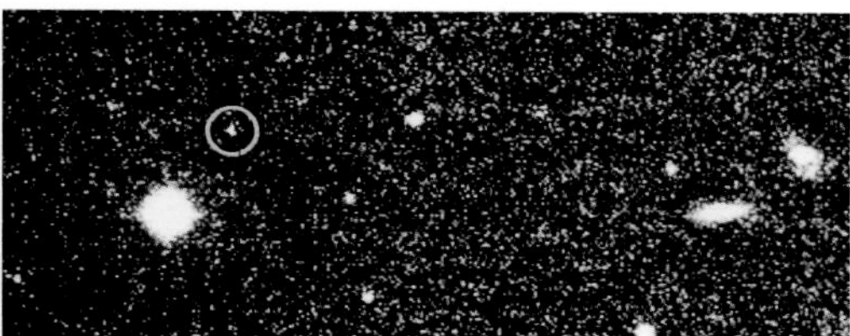

△ **Discovery**
After five years of searching, David Jewitt and Jane Luu discovered the first KBO in August 1992 using the 2.2m (87in) University of Hawaii telescope on Mauna Kea. Named 1992 QB1, it was located about 6 billion km (4 billion miles) from the Sun and was about 100,000 million times fainter than Jupiter. These European Southern Observatory images were taken one month after discovery.

In the centre of the circle is 1992 QB1, imaged on 27 September 1992, four hours after the image at left.

A day later, 1992 QB1 had moved position against the background stars, travelling at a few seconds of arc per hour.

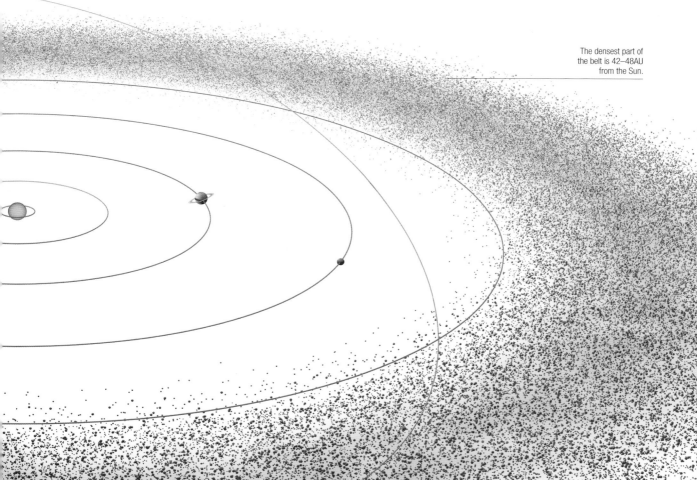

The densest part of the belt is 42–48AU from the Sun.

The outer edge contains scattered disc objects. Their eccentric orbits stretch to about 15 billion billion km (9 billion billion miles) from the Sun.

DWARF PLANETS

LIKE TRUE PLANETS, DWARF PLANETS HAVE ENOUGH MASS TO BECOME SPHERICAL THROUGH THEIR OWN GRAVITY. HOWEVER, THEY LACK THE GRAVITATIONAL FORCE TO SWEEP THEIR ORBITS CLEAR OF OTHER BODIES.

As they form, planets clear their orbits of minor objects, such as asteroids, either by pulling them in and amalgamating with them or by flinging them elsewhere. Dwarf planets cannot do this, though they may have sufficient gravity to capture their own moons.

The definition of a dwarf planet was agreed upon by the International Astronomical Union in 2006. The most famous example is Pluto, which orbits far from the Sun in the freezing Kuiper Belt at the edge of the Solar System. Once referred to as the ninth planet, Pluto was demoted and assigned to the new category along with several similar bodies found in the outer Solar System. Among these are Eris (the largest known dwarf planet), Haumea, and Makemake. The asteroid Ceres, located in the Asteroid Belt between Mars and Jupiter, was also given dwarf planet status in 2006.

Eris
Diameter 2,326km (1,445 miles)

Pluto
Diameter 2,306km (1,433 miles)

Haumea
Diameter 1,960km (1,218 miles)

Makemake
Diameter 1,440km (895 miles)

Quaoar (possible dwarf planet)
Diameter 1,070km (665 miles)

Sedna (possible dwarf planet)
Diameter 995km (618 miles)

Ceres
Diameter 952km (592 miles)

Orcus (possible dwarf planet)
Diameter 917km (570 miles)

Ixion (possible dwarf planet)
Diameter 650km (404 miles)

Earth
Diameter 12,742km (7,917 miles)

Discovering Pluto

US astronomer Clyde Tombaugh discovered Pluto in 1930 while searching for "Planet X" – a hypothetical ninth planet thought to be responsible for irregularities in the orbits of Neptune and Uranus. Pluto was named the ninth planet, though it turned out to have too little mass to exert gravitational pull on the gas giants. Its eccentric and tilted orbit is typical of Kuiper Belt bodies.

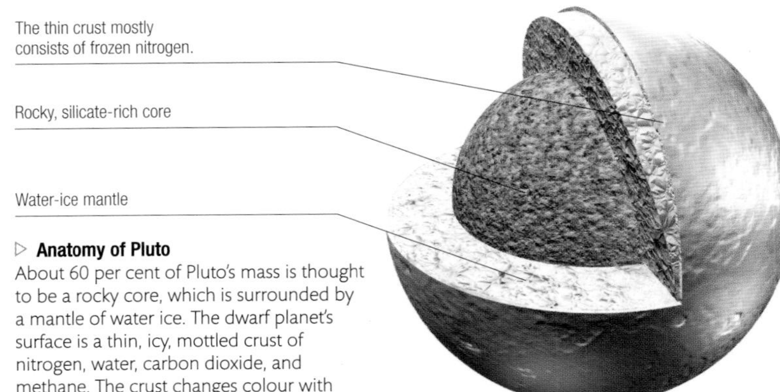
The thin crust mostly consists of frozen nitrogen.
Rocky, silicate-rich core
Water-ice mantle

▷ **Anatomy of Pluto**
About 60 per cent of Pluto's mass is thought to be a rocky core, which is surrounded by a mantle of water ice. The dwarf planet's surface is a thin, icy, mottled crust of nitrogen, water, carbon dioxide, and methane. The crust changes colour with seasonal vaporizing and refreezing of ice.

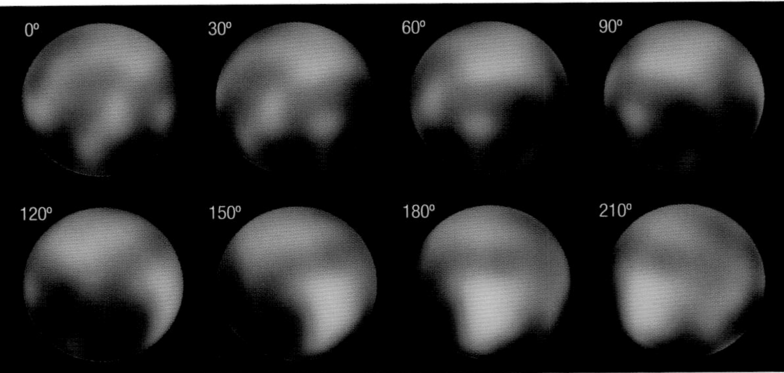
0°
30°
60°
90°
120°
150°
180°
210°

△ **Hubble view of Pluto**
Pluto is so small and distant that sharp images are impossible to obtain. Even the Hubble Space Telescope is unable to resolve details smaller than several hundred kilometres wide. Here we see Pluto in rotation. The dark areas are carbon-rich residues that have formed where ultraviolet radiation and solar wind particles have caused methane to react with carbon dioxide ice.

▽ **New Horizons mission**
In January 2006, NASA launched the New Horizons mission to Pluto. After a nine-year interplanetary journey, the spacecraft is due to fly past Pluto and its various small moons at 11km (6 miles) per second on 14 July 2015. It will obtain detailed coloured images of the dwarf planet's sunlit surface and will use scientific instruments to measure its surface temperature and analyse its atmosphere.

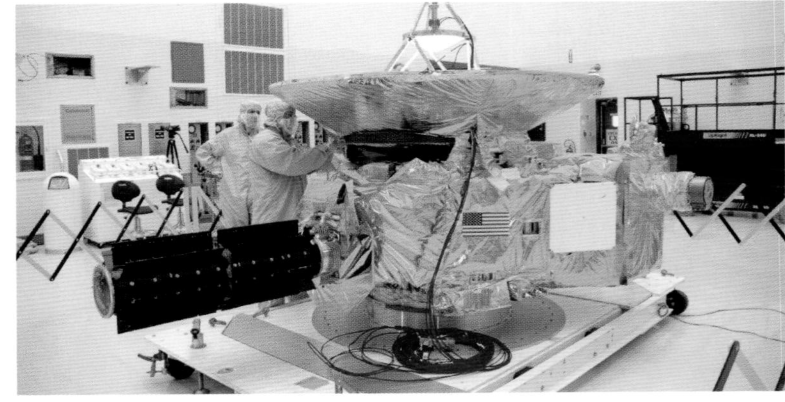

Moons of Pluto

Pluto has five known moons, all with names linked to the underworld in classical mythology. The New Horizons spacecraft is expected to find more. Charon, the largest moon, was discovered in 1978 by American astronomer James Christy and is named after the ferryman of Hades, in Greek mythology. The four smaller moons were discovered in the 21st century using Hubble Space Telescope data. Nix and Hydra are about 100km (60 miles) in diameter, while Styx and Kerberos are a mere 20km (12 miles).

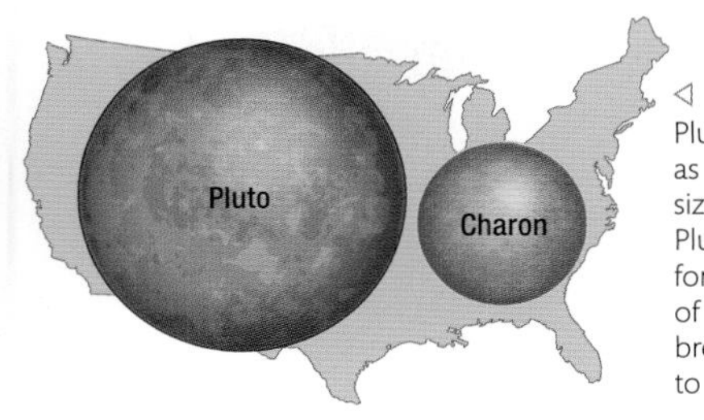
Pluto
Charon

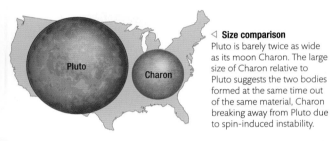

◁ **Size comparison**
Pluto is barely twice as wide as its moon Charon. The large size of Charon relative to Pluto suggests the two bodies formed at the same time out of the same material, Charon breaking away from Pluto due to spin-induced instability.

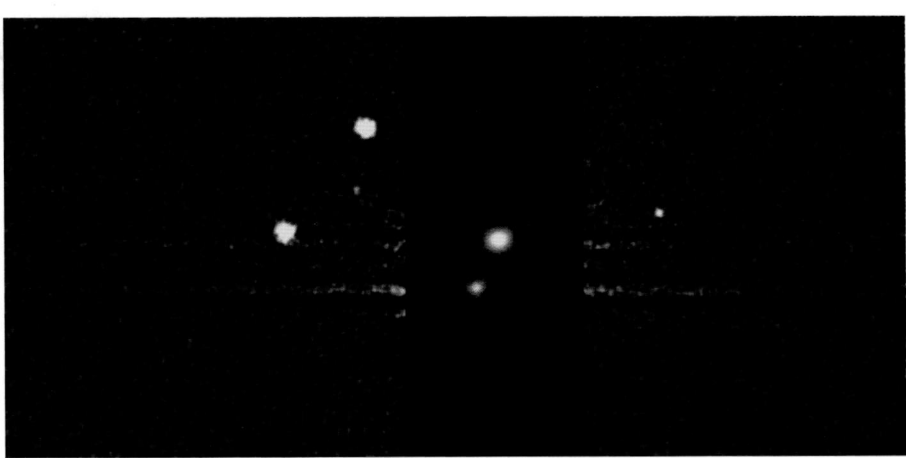

△ **Pluto and moons**
This Hubble image shows Pluto with its five known moons. The brightness of Pluto and Charon (in the dark band) has been reduced to make the other moons visible. From left, the objects are: Hydra, Styx, Nix (top), Charon, Pluto, and Kerberos. All the moons have circular orbits close to Pluto and in the same plane, indicating they are not captured objects. They may have formed after a collision between Pluto and another body.

▽ **Artist's impression**
A visitor standing on the icy surface of Pluto would see a faint, distant Sun, the moon Charon, and traces of the hazy nitrogen-methane atmosphere. The roughness of the surface is caused by cratering by smaller Kuiper Belt bodies, cryovolcanic activity, and seasonal variations in temperature during which upper layers of ice and snow turn to vapour and then refreeze.

COMETS

COMETS ARE MOUNTAIN-SIZED, DIRTY SNOWBALLS THAT FORMED AT THE DAWN OF THE SOLAR SYSTEM. OCCASIONALLY ONE APPROACHES THE SUN, CHANGES RADICALLY IN SIZE AND APPEARANCE, AND BECOMES BRIGHT ENOUGH TO BE SEEN.

An estimated 1,000 billion comets exist in the freezing outer reaches of the Solar System. Unchanged since the planets formed, each is a lump of snow, ice, and rocky dust: a cometary nucleus. These icy bodies are too small to be seen from Earth, but if one ventures into the planetary part of the Solar System, it can develop a spectacular glowing halo and tails, making it bright enough to be detected. Many comets are found using telescopes, often accidentally by asteroid hunters, but many also pass unnoticed. Some revisit us regularly, with return periods ranging from a few years to hundreds. Others are unexpected and may not pass our way again for thousands or millions of years – or ever. Newly discovered comets take the name of the discoverer. The greatest number of discoveries, over 2,500, has been made by the SOHO spacecraft.

Close to the Sun

When a comet gets closer to the Sun than the Asteroid Belt, solar heating causes its nucleus to lose mass. This material forms a coma – a huge cloud of gas and dust around the nucleus – and two tails that continuously disperse into space. Each time the nucleus passes the Sun, a layer of surface material about 1m (3ft) deep is used up in a fresh coma and tails. A comet such as Halley, which orbits the Sun every 76 or so years, will eventually run out of material and vanish.

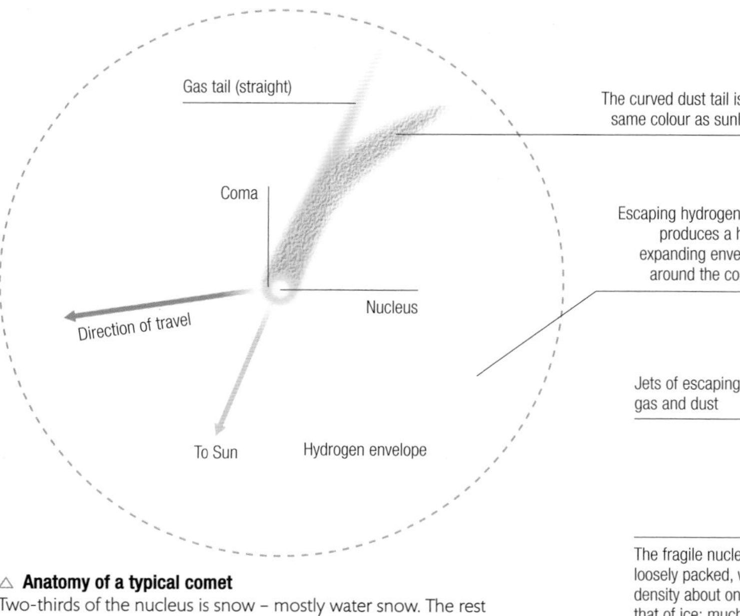
Gas tail (straight)
The curved dust tail is the same colour as sunlight.
Coma
Escaping hydrogen gas produces a huge expanding envelope around the comet.
Nucleus
Direction of travel
To Sun
Hydrogen envelope

△ **Anatomy of a typical comet**
Two-thirds of the nucleus is snow – mostly water snow. The rest consists of small rock particles and dust. Released gas and dust form the coma, which may grow to 100,000km (60,000 miles) wide, and two tails, both of which are pushed back by the solar wind. The gas tail is straight but the dust tail curves back towards the comet's orbital path.

△ **Hale–Bopp**
Bright, naked-eye comets occur at a rate of one per decade. Comet Hale–Bopp, one of the 20th century's brightest comets, was visible to the naked eye in 1996 and 1997. Here, the material in its two tails is being pushed right out of the Solar System. The white dust tail shines as sunlight reflects off its dust particles. The blue ionized gas tail actually emits its own light and is more structured – the paths of the particles within it are determined by magnetic fields in the solar wind.

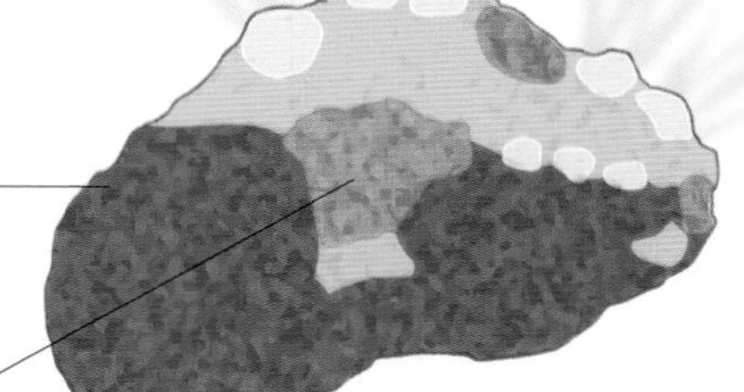

Jets of escaping gas and dust
The fragile nucleus is loosely packed, with a density about one-tenth that of ice; much of the interior is void.
Surface depression
Nucleus of Halley's Comet

◁ **Cometary nucleus**
The nucleus of a comet is irregularly shaped and typically about 1km (0.6 miles) across, with a black, dusty surface. Where the dust is thinnest, the transmission of solar heat causes the snow beneath to change into gas. The gas escapes, taking some of the overlying dust with it and leaving depressions on the surface of the comet.

◁ **Sungrazer**
Some comets fly close enough to the Sun to pass through its outer atmosphere, the solar corona. Others, such as Comet SOHO 6 (left), get so close that they dive into the Sun and are destroyed. Called sungrazers, many such comets are seen by the SOHO spacecraft as it studies the Sun. In this SOHO image, the Sun is blocked out by a disc to reveal the Sun's corona and Comet SOHO 6's final moments (top left).

▷ **Meteor shower**
Larger dust particles do not get pushed into the comet tail but slowly gain on, or fall behind, the cometary nucleus. They eventually form an annulus – a ring of dust around the comet's orbital path. If Earth travels through a comet's annulus, individual dust particles form meteors – shooting stars – as they speed through Earth's atmosphere. The meteors in a shower radiate from a specific spot in the sky.

COMET ORBITS

MOST COMETS EXIST WITHIN THE OORT CLOUD, FAR BEYOND THE PLANETS AND OUR VISION. WE KNOW THEY EXIST BECAUSE OCCASIONALLY ONE OF THESE BODIES IS DIVERTED INTO THE INNER SOLAR SYSTEM AND FORMS A COMA AND TAILS.

Cometary orbits, unlike planetary ones, are highly elliptical (oval), so a comet's distance from the Sun varies greatly over time. Comets that leave the Oort Cloud and travel towards the Sun are classed according to how long one orbit takes. Short-period comets hug the plane of the planets and have periods of less than 20 years. Intermediate-period comets pass close to the Sun every 20–200 years and their orbits have a wide range of inclinations. Long-period comets, which are also randomly inclined, have periods ranging from 200 years to tens of million of years. Some travel so far from the Sun that they may fly halfway to nearby stars.

Cometary orbits are affected by the gravitational fields of the planets. Short-period comets have become trapped in the inner Solar System by Jupiter's gravity, and Jupiter can easily flip a comet from a short orbit back to a longer one. Some long-period comets are ejected from the Solar System altogether and sail off into the galaxy. Others are pulled closer to the Sun, giving astronomers a chance of detecting them.

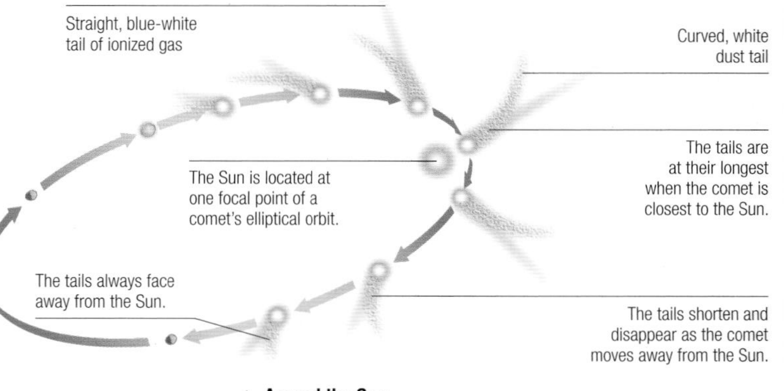

Straight, blue-white tail of ionized gas
Curved, white dust tail
The tails are at their longest when the comet is closest to the Sun.
The Sun is located at one focal point of a comet's elliptical orbit.
The tails always face away from the Sun.
The tails shorten and disappear as the comet moves away from the Sun.

△ **Around the Sun**
Comets follow elliptical orbits – oval-shaped loops around two focal points. They do not travel along these orbits at a constant speed, but accelerate as they move closer to the Sun, then slow down again as they move away from it. Comets are visible from Earth only when they fly close to the Sun, as what we see of them is their tails, which are created when the Sun's heat vaporizes material on the comet's surface, creating a streak of debris.

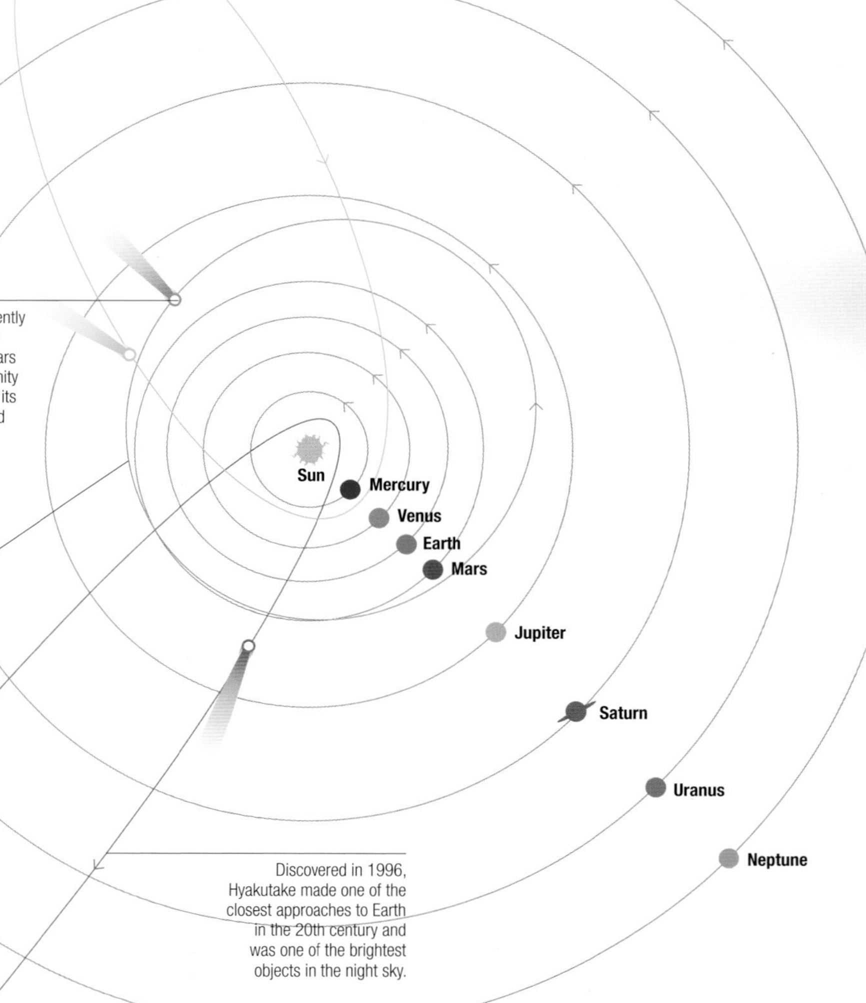

Comet Halley's orbital period varies from 76 to 79.3 years. It was last seen in 1986 and will next appear in 2061.
Comet Tempel 1 currently orbits every 5.5 years within the orbits of Mars and Jupiter; its proximity to Jupiter means that its orbital path and period will change.
Sun
Mercury
Venus
Earth
Mars
Jupiter
Saturn
Uranus
Neptune
Short-period comets have less elliptical orbits and are regular visitors to the inner Solar System.
Long-period comets have extremely elliptical orbits and only rarely make an appearance in the inner Solar System.
Discovered in 1996, Hyakutake made one of the closest approaches to Earth in the 20th century and was one of the brightest objects in the night sky.

▷ **Comets in the inner Solar System**
By the end of 2013, astronomers had detected about 5,000 comets passing through the planetary part of the Solar System. Around 500 are short-period comets, such as Comet Tempel 1. First recorded in 1867, Tempel 1 returned in 1873 and 1879 but then did not reappear until 1967, due to a change in its orbit. Comet Halley is an intermediate-period comet first recorded in 240 BCE and seen 30 times since. The long-period Comet Hyakutake appeared brightly in Earth's sky in 1996. It previously visited the Sun 17,000 years before, but on its 1996 orbit gravitational interaction with the giant planets disturbed its orbit so much that it will not return for 70,000 years.

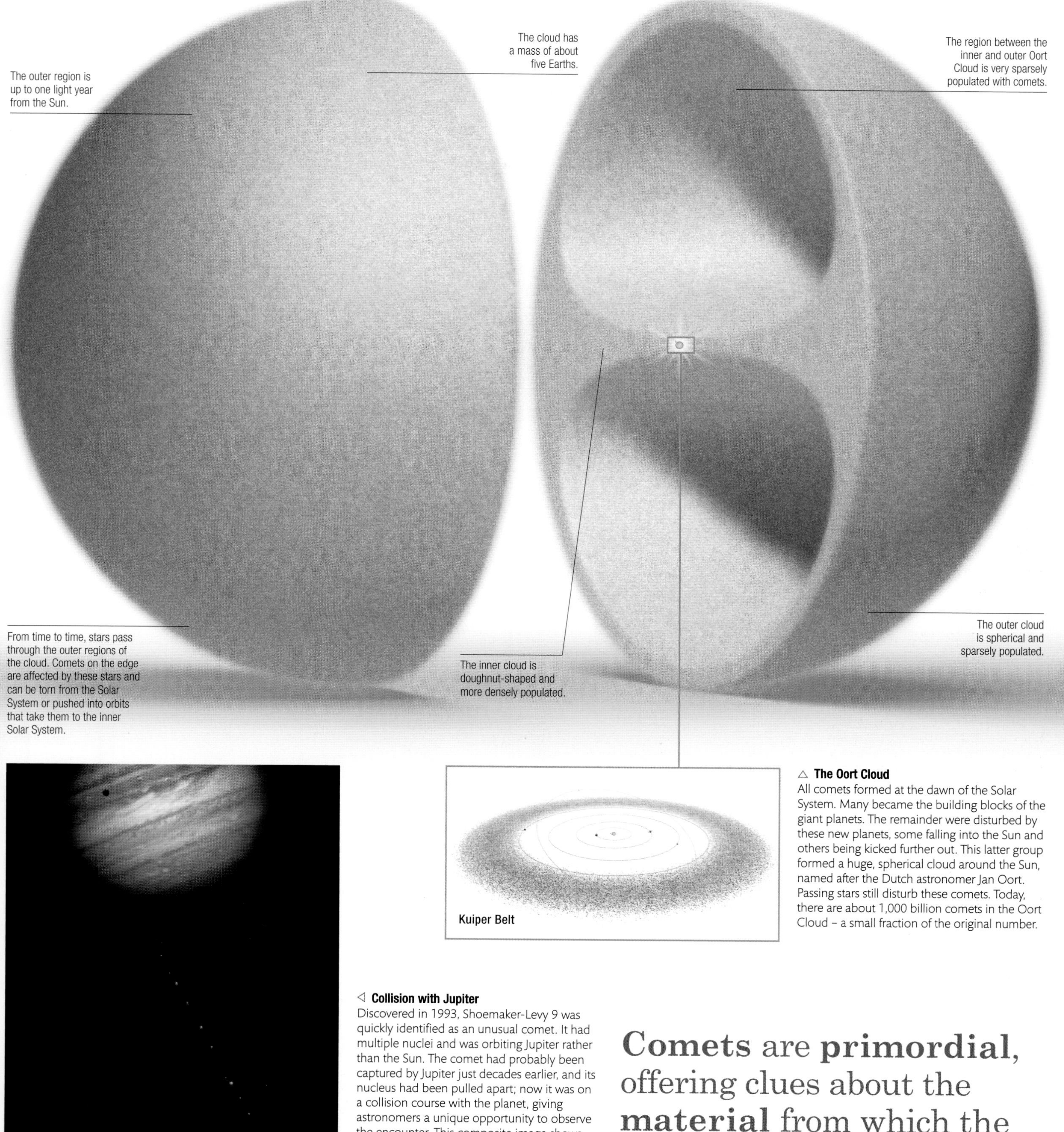
The outer region is up to one light year from the Sun.
The cloud has a mass of about five Earths.
The region between the inner and outer Oort Cloud is very sparsely populated with comets.
From time to time, stars pass through the outer regions of the cloud. Comets on the edge are affected by these stars and can be torn from the Solar System or pushed into orbits that take them to the inner Solar System.
The inner cloud is doughnut-shaped and more densely populated.
The outer cloud is spherical and sparsely populated.
Kuiper Belt

△ **The Oort Cloud**
All comets formed at the dawn of the Solar System. Many became the building blocks of the giant planets. The remainder were disturbed by these new planets, some falling into the Sun and others being kicked further out. This latter group formed a huge, spherical cloud around the Sun, named after the Dutch astronomer Jan Oort. Passing stars still disturb these comets. Today, there are about 1,000 billion comets in the Oort Cloud – a small fraction of the original number.

◁ **Collision with Jupiter**
Discovered in 1993, Shoemaker-Levy 9 was quickly identified as an unusual comet. It had multiple nuclei and was orbiting Jupiter rather than the Sun. The comet had probably been captured by Jupiter just decades earlier, and its nucleus had been pulled apart; now it was on a collision course with the planet, giving astronomers a unique opportunity to observe the encounter. This composite image shows the line of 21 cometary fragments prior to their collision with Jupiter in July 1994.

Comets are **primordial**, offering clues about the **material** from which the **Solar System formed.**

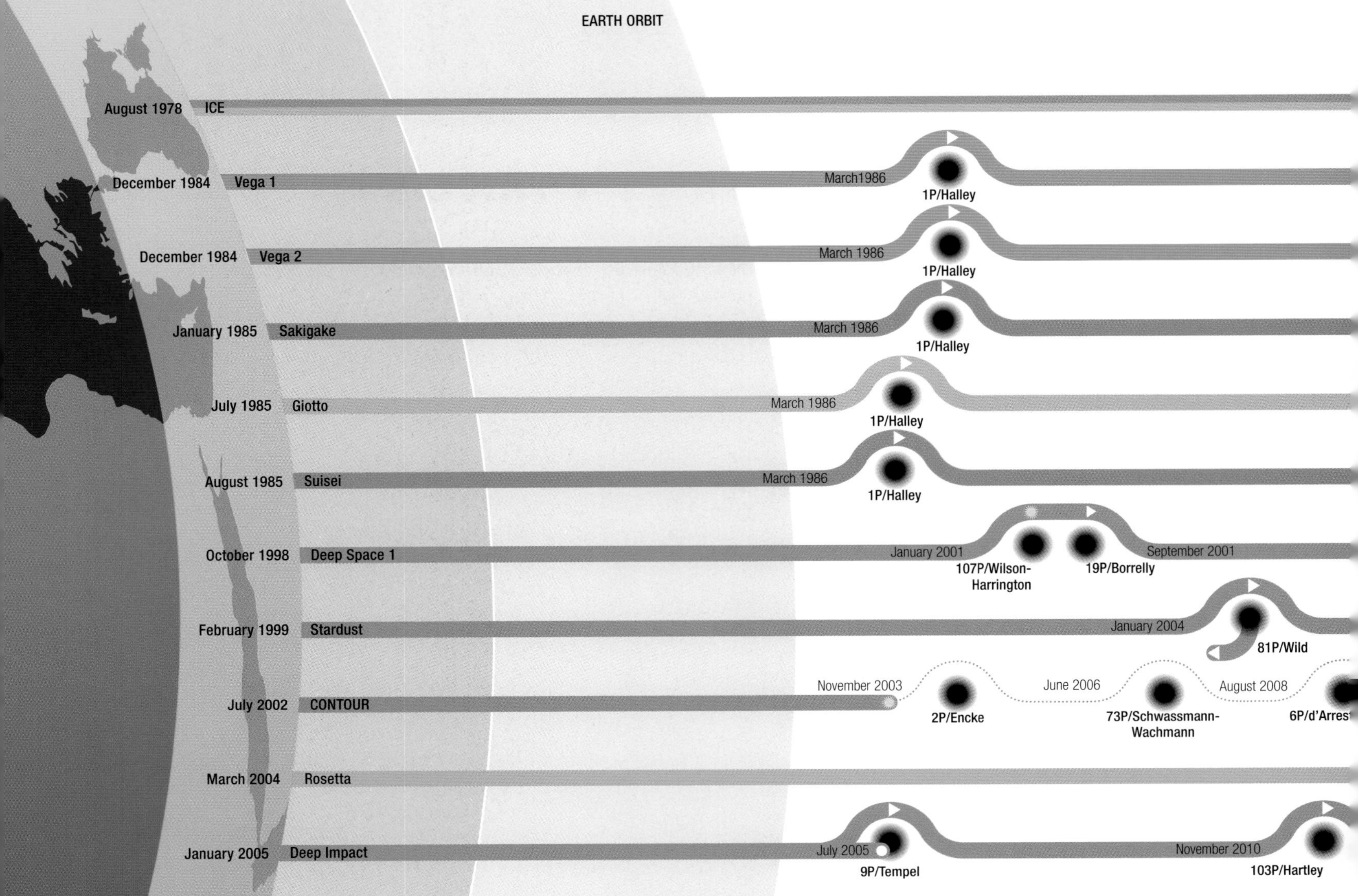

EARTH ORBIT

August 1978 ICE

December 1984 Vega 1 — March1986 — 1P/Halley

December 1984 Vega 2 — March 1986 — 1P/Halley

January 1985 Sakigake — March 1986 — 1P/Halley

July 1985 Giotto — March 1986 — 1P/Halley

August 1985 Suisei — March 1986 — 1P/Halley

October 1998 Deep Space 1 — January 2001 — 107P/Wilson-Harrington — 19P/Borrelly — September 2001

February 1999 Stardust — January 2004 — 81P/Wild

July 2002 CONTOUR — November 2003 — 2P/Encke — June 2006 — 73P/Schwassmann-Wachmann — August 2008 — 6P/d'Arrest

March 2004 Rosetta

January 2005 Deep Impact — July 2005 — 9P/Tempel — November 2010 — 103P/Hartley

KEY

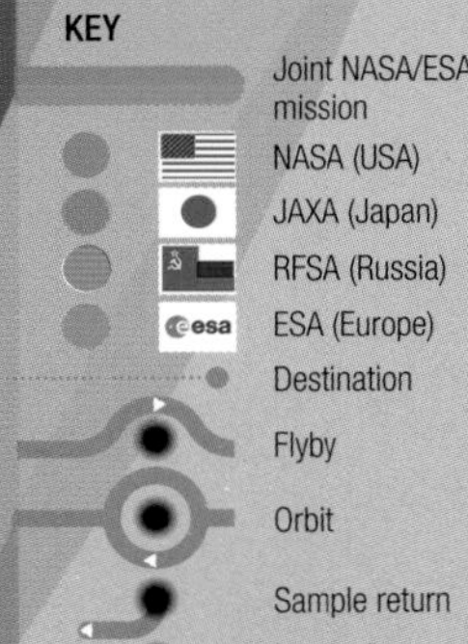
Joint NASA/ESA mission
NASA (USA)
JAXA (Japan)
RFSA (Russia)
ESA (Europe)
Destination
Flyby
Orbit
Sample return
Lander/impactor
Failure

▷ **Giotto**

Prior to 1986, astronomers had no idea what a comet nucleus looked like. Their first view came on 13 March of that year when ESA's Giotto imaged the nucleus of Halley's Comet. It revealed a 15.3km (9.5 mile) long, potato-shaped mass with bright jets of gas and dust erupting from its surface. Hills and valleys could be seen on the nucleus's generally smooth surface. Giotto was inside the comet's coma and only just survived the battering from its dust. Its mission extended, Giotto flew by Comet Grigg-Skjellerup in 1992.

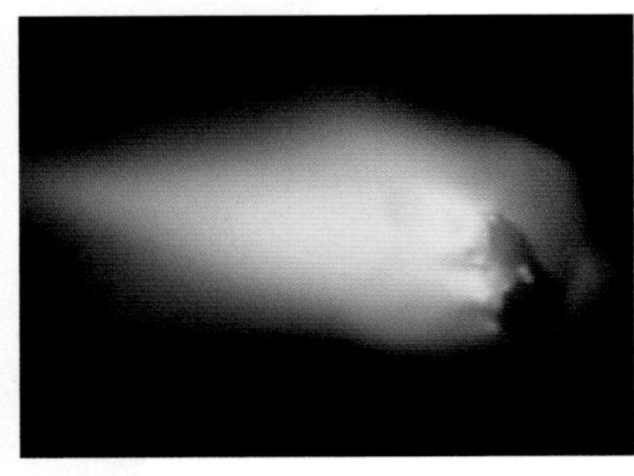

Giotto image of nucleus of Halley's Comet

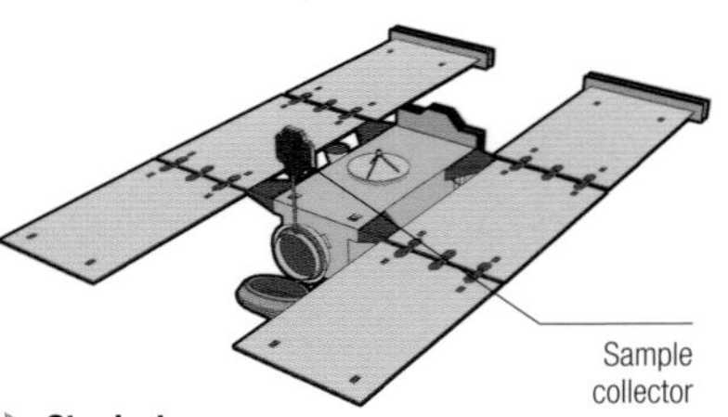
Sample collector

▷ **Stardust**

The first sample of comet material was obtained by NASA's Stardust spacecraft. To capture dust particles from the comet without vaporizing them, Stardust used an incredibly lightweight, porous material known as aerogel, which was mounted on a collecting device shaped like a tennis racket. The collector and its precious cargo separated from Stardust and returned to Earth in January 2006.

September 1985 **21P/Giacobini-Zinner**

July 1992 **26P/Grigg-Skjellerup**

November 1998 **21P/Giaobini-Zinner**

February 2011 **9P/Tempel**

August 2014
67P/Churyumov
-Gerasimenko

MISSIONS TO **COMETS**

IN THE PAST 30 YEARS OUR KNOWLEDGE OF COMETS HAS IMPROVED ENORMOUSLY, THANKS TO A SMALL NUMBER OF SPACECRAFT THAT HAVE SAILED THROUGH THE GLOWING COMAS AROUND COMETS TO VISIT THEIR ICY NUCLEI.

Hidden in the glare of their brilliant comas, and too small to be viewed with telescopes, comet nuclei can be seen clearly only by spacecraft. The first craft to return detailed images of a comet nucleus was Giotto, which launched in 1985 and passed within 600km (375 miles) of Halley's Comet less than a year later. Its images confirmed the theory that comets are made of dirt and snow. More ambitious missions followed, including NASA's Stardust, which scooped a sample of dust from Comet Wild 2 and brought it back to Earth, and ESA's Rosetta – the first craft designed to land on a comet nucleus.

In the **ten-year** journey to its comet target, the Rosetta spacecraft orbited the Sun **five times**.

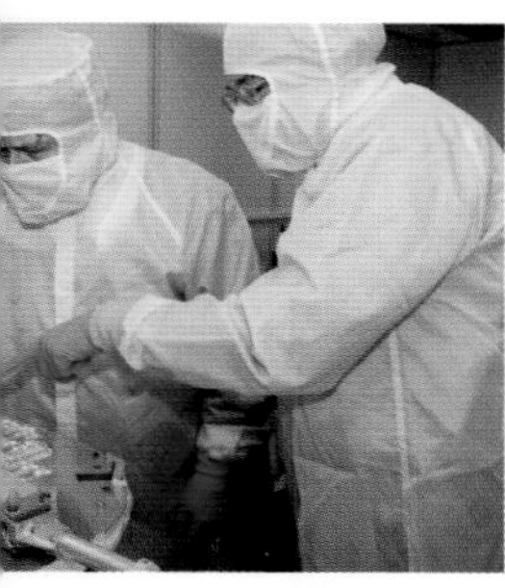
Scientists analysing the Stardust sample

▷ **Deep Impact**
With the aim of studying a comet's interior, Deep Impact fired a self-guided impactor into the nucleus of Comet Tempel 1 in 2005. A cloud of debris obscured the craft's view, but the Stardust craft was redirected to Tempel 1 and later imaged the impact crater. Deep Impact moved off to meet Comet Hartley 2, getting within 700km of its peanut-shaped, 2km (1.2 mile) long nucleus.

Deep Impact image of nucleus of Comet Hartley 2

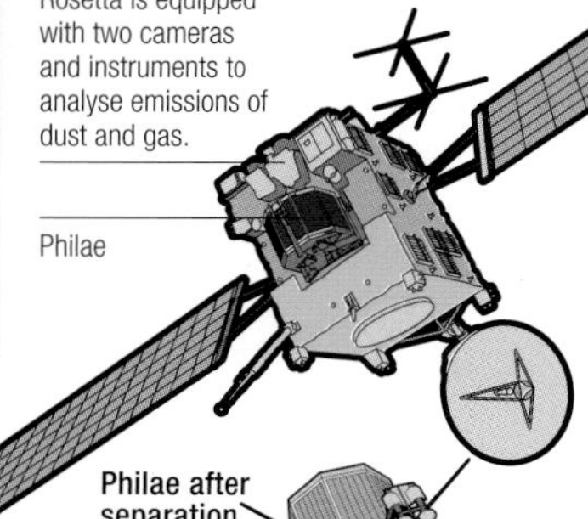
Rosetta is equipped with two cameras and instruments to analyse emissions of dust and gas.
Philae
Philae after separation

◁ **Rosetta**
ESA's Rosetta is the most ambitious comet mission to date. Launched in 2004, Rosetta is designed to orbit the 4km (2.5 mile) wide nucleus of Comet Churyumov-Gerasimenko for more than a year, monitoring the comet as its coma and tails form. Rosetta carries a small lander, Philae, designed to land on the nucleus.

1

COSMIC SNOWBALLS

1 McNaught
In early 2007, McNaught became the brightest comet since 1965, easily visible with the naked eye – even in daylight. Here, McNaught and the Sun are seen setting over the Pacific Ocean. It is not a sight that will be repeated; McNaught is a single-apparition comet that will never return to the inner Solar System.

2 Hyakutake
In March 1996, this comet, named after the Japanese amateur astronomer who discovered it, came within 15 million km (9 million miles) of Earth. In May, ESA's Ulysses spacecraft unexpectedly detected Hyakutake's gas tail 570 million km (355 million miles) from the nucleus – the longest comet tail ever detected. Hyakutake was also the first comet observed to emit X-rays.

3 C/2001 Q4
Discovered in 2001 by NASA's Near-Earth Asteroid Tracking (NEAT) system in Pasadena, California, C/2001 Q4 was first visible in the southern hemisphere. The comet reached full brightness in May 2004, when it was about 48 million km (30 million miles) from Earth. It will not return; the eccentric orbit of this comet will eject it from the Solar System.

4 Hale-Bopp
The most widely observed comet of the 20th century, Hale-Bopp was present in the sky for 18 months, its brightness peaking in April 1997. Hale-Bopp's nucleus is unusually large, at 30–40km (19–25 miles) across. Jupiter's gravity altered the comet's orbital path, reducing its orbital period from around 4,200 years to about 2,500.

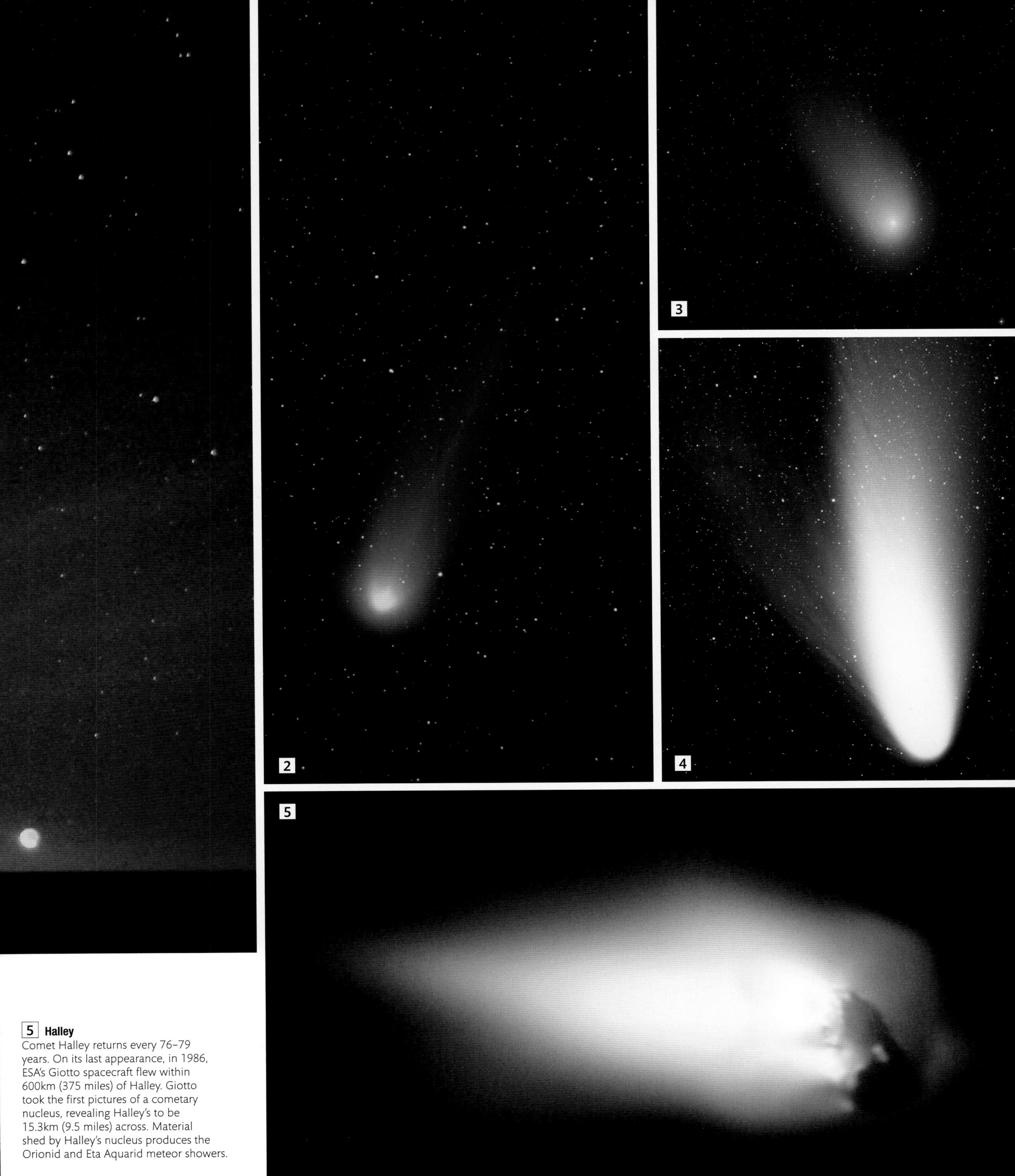

3
2
4
5

5 Halley
Comet Halley returns every 76–79 years. On its last appearance, in 1986, ESA's Giotto spacecraft flew within 600km (375 miles) of Halley. Giotto took the first pictures of a cometary nucleus, revealing Halley's to be 15.3km (9.5 miles) across. Material shed by Halley's nucleus produces the Orionid and Eta Aquarid meteor showers.

PROPHETS OF DOOM

ONCE SEEN AS MYSTERIOUS CELESTIAL APPARITIONS OF ILL-OMEN, COMETS ARE NOW KNOWN TO BE PRIMORDIAL PLANETARY BUILDING BLOCKS LEFT OVER FROM THE FORMATION OF THE SOLAR SYSTEM.

It was only after English astronomer Edmond Halley realized in the 1690s that certain comets are permanent members of our Solar System that astronomers began hunting for comets in the night sky. Cometary masses were found to be insignificant, so the source of the gas and dust in their comas and tails was a mystery. In 1950, American astronomer Fred Whipple proposed that comets have a "dirty-snowball" nucleus that loses mass with each orbit of the Sun. A nucleus was seen for the first time in 1986, and in July 2005 the Deep Impact spacecraft became the first craft to make physical contact with a comet nucleus.

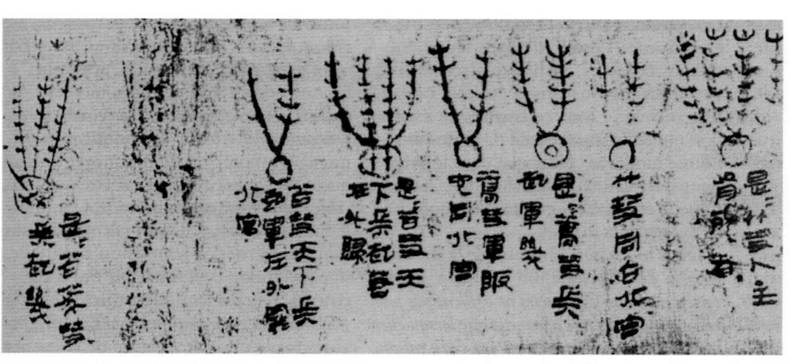

Silk Atlas of Comets

2500 BCE

Earliest observations
Chinese astronomers are convinced that comets are astrologically significant. They monitor the sky for these "broom stars", said to bring bad luck. The 185 BCE *Silk Atlas of Comets* (above), from a tomb in Mawangdui, shows the oldest representations of comets.

5 BCE

The Star of Bethlehem
The biblical star said to have led the Magi to baby Jesus could have been a planet or a comet. For his nativity fresco in the Arena Chapel, Padua, Italian artist Giotto de Bondone bases his Star of Bethlehem on the 1301 apparition of Comet Halley.

Great Comet photograph by Gill

1868

Chemical make-up
English astronomer William Huggins uses spectroscopy to prove that comets contain hydrocarbon compounds. Spectroscopy also shows that curved comet tails contain dust particles, while straight, bluish tails consist of ionized molecules from cometary snow.

1882

Great Comet photographed
Scottish astronomer David Gill takes the first photograph of the Great Comet of 1882, showing background stars through the spectacular tail. American astronomer Edward E. Barnard makes the first cometary discovery by photography – Comet 1892 V.

1900

Formation of tails
Swedish physicist Svante Arrhenius proposes that solar radiation pressure pushes cometary dust into the tail. Fifty years later astronomers realize the gas tail takes shape as magnetic field lines in the solar wind become draped around this tail, sometimes disconnecting part of it.

Jan Oort

Nucleus of Comet Halley

1932

Oort Cloud
Estonian astrophysicist Ernst Öpik suggests that long-period comets come from a huge comet cloud surrounding the Solar System – now known as the Oort Cloud after Dutch astronomer Jan Oort.

1950

Comet nucleus
American astronomer Fred Whipple suggests that the heart of a comet is a "dirty-snowball" nucleus, just a few kilometres across, made of water ice, snow, and dust. An image of a comet nucleus is later taken in 1986, when the Giotto spacecraft visits Comet Halley.

1979

Comets and life
British astronomers Chandra Wickramasinghe and Fred Hoyle suggest that life arrived on Earth via comets, but others disagree. However, comets often collide with planets: in 1994, astronomers watch Comet Shoemaker-Levy 9 impacting with Jupiter's atmosphere.

ISTI MIRANT

Bayeux Tapestry

1066 CE

Battle of Hastings

Comets are believed to foretell doom, disease, death, and disaster. Comet Halley is in the sky six months before the death of England's King Harold at the Battle of Hastings. In this scene from the Bayeux Tapestry, soldiers point at the bad omen.

1531

Comet tails

In *Astronomicum Caesareum*, the German astronomer Petrus Apianus shows that comet tails always point away from the Sun. They grow longer as a comet approaches the Sun, then die away as the comet travels out to the colder reaches of the Solar System.

Edmond Halley

1680

Comet orbits

English mathematical genius Isaac Newton is the first to calculate a comet's path. Edmond Halley later calculates more cometary orbits, realizing that a comet he saw in 1682 had been seen before. Halley's Comet returns about every 76 years.

1755

Origin and mass

Prussian philosopher Immanuel Kant suggests that comets are remnants of the planetary formation process. Lexell's Comet gets to within 2.3 million km (1.4 million miles) of Earth in 1770. Its mass is calculated as less than 0.02 of Earth's.

Caroline Herschel

1786

Caroline Herschel

British astronomer Caroline Herschel becomes the first woman to discover a comet, using a special telescope made by her astronomer brother William Herschel. Comet Herschel-Rigollet, discovered in 1788, is named after her.

1833 Leonid meteor shower

1866

Comets and meteors

The Italian astronomer Giovanni Schiaparelli realizes that comets and meteoroid streams are related. As a comet decays, dust slowly spreads around its orbit, forming a meteoroid stream. If Earth intersects this stream, we get a meteor storm, such as the Leonids.

Impactor strikes Comet Tempel 1

2005

Deep Impact mission

A 370kg (815lb) impactor from NASA's Deep Impact spacecraft is launched at Comet Tempel 1 and strikes the nucleus. In February 2011, the comet is visited by the Stardust spacecraft, which takes images of the 150m (500ft) wide crater formed by the impactor.

ESA's Rosetta team celebrate the spacecraft's reawakening

2014

Rosetta reawakening

After 31 months in hibernation mode, the ESA's Rosetta spacecraft, launched in 2004 on a trip to Comet Churyumov-Gerasimenko, is successfully reawakened. Rosetta is set to orbit Churyumov-Gerasimenko for 17 months as the comet journeys around the Sun.

WORLDS BEYOND

The Milky Way galaxy, seen here arching over Cape Palliser in New Zealand, may be home to hundreds of billions of planets, but most are impossible to see. The first extrasolar planets beyond the Solar System were detected in 1992, since when over 2,000 have been found. Usually invisible to even the most powerful telescopes, they reveal their presence by pulling on their parent star, making it wobble, or by causing a tiny diminution in the star's light as they pass in front. Since large exoplanets close to stars are easiest to detect, most discovered to date are "hot Jupiters" – gas giants that orbit their star in just a few days, typically on a wild, elliptical path. Nevertheless, astronomers have begun to capture faint but tantalizing images of exoplanets, and just a few appear to have water in their atmospheres, making them possible habitats for life. The search is now on for Earth's twin – a small, rocky world similar to our own.

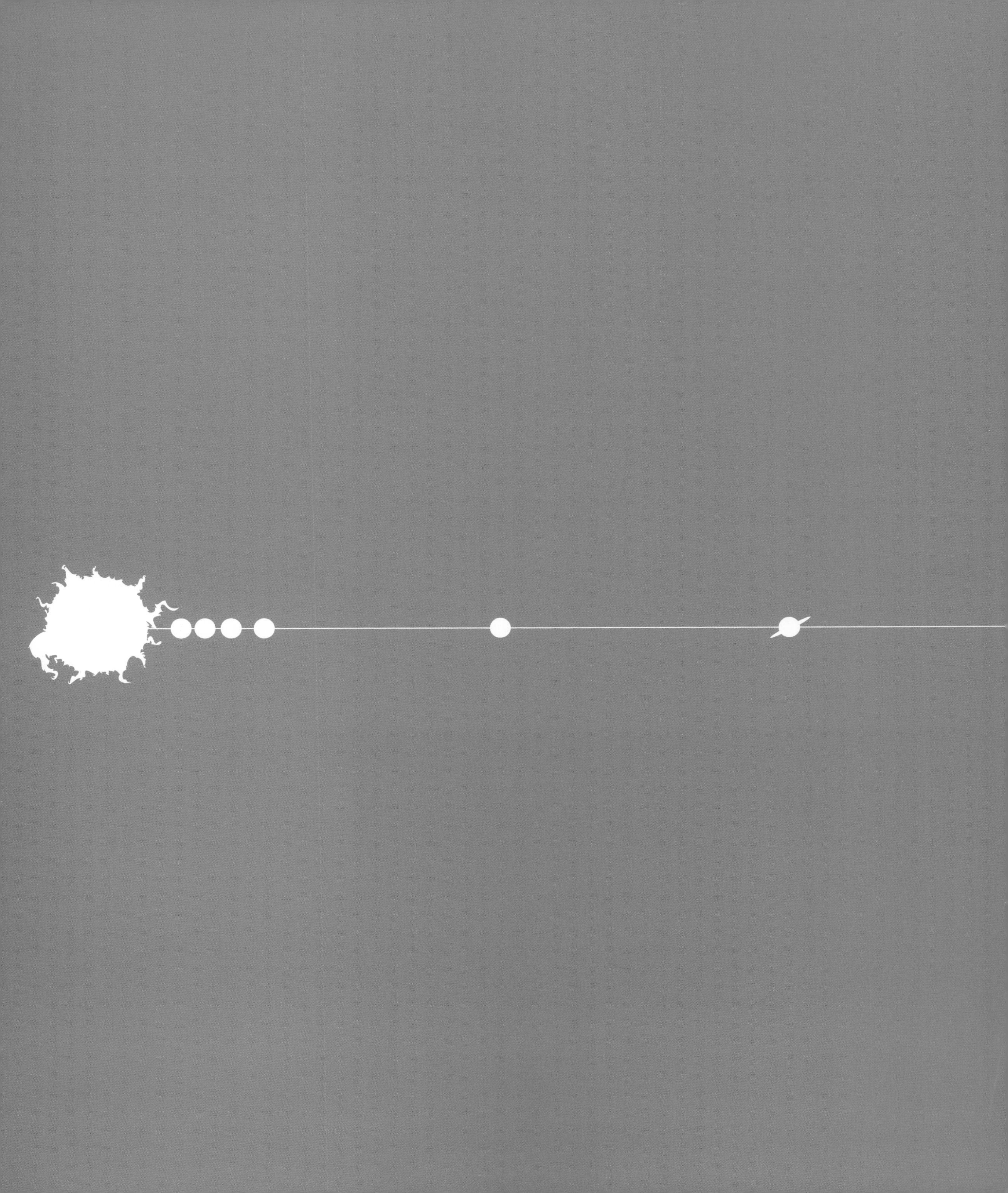